CONTEMPORARY ACTION THEORY

VOLUME 1:

INDIVIDUAL ACTION

SYNTHESE LIBRARY

STUDIES IN EPISTEMOLOGY,

LOGIC, METHODOLOGY, AND PHILOSOPHY OF SCIENCE

VOLUME 266

CONTEMPORARY ACTION THEORY

VOLUME 1:

INDIVIDUAL ACTION

Edited by

GHITA HOLMSTRÖM-HINTIKKA
Boston University and *University of Helsinki*

and

RAIMO TUOMELA
Academy of Finland

Springer-Science+Business Media, B.V.

A C.I.P. Catalogue record for this book is available from the Library of Congress.

Printed on acid-free paper

ISBN 978-90-481-4914-8 ISBN 978-94-017-0439-7 (eBook)
DOI 10.1007/978-94-017-0439-7

Originally published by Kluwer Academic Publishers in 1997.
Softcover reprint of the hardcover 1st edition 1997

PREFACE

A couple of decades ago one could speak of a boom in the field of philosophy of action, but in recent years this field has seemingly been leading a more quiet life. Nevertheless, important developments have taken place not only in the traditional philosophical and logical problems of action but also in the computational aspects of action as well as in the new field of the theory of social (especially multi-agent) action. To mention an example from outside philosophy, in artificial intelligence problems of coordination and cooperation have recently acquired enormous importance and have led to much interesting new theoretical work as well as to practical applications.

Contemporary Action Theory is a two-volume work which attempts a comprehensive assessment of the current state of the art by leading researchers. We believe that such an assessment is warranted in view of the most recent developments in action theory – especially as no other similar current work is available. The two volumes of *Contemporary Action Theory* are entitled *Individual Action* (Vol. I) and *Social Action* (Vol. II). Although there is some overlap between the fields covered by the two volumes, the first basically concerns the logic and philosophy of single-agent actions while all the papers in the second one are concerned with social action. Volume I covers standard questions in the philosophy of single-agent action, while Volume II is concerned with the social aspects of human action, especially with multi-agent action. Volume II contains papers not only by philosophers but also by researchers working in artificial intelligence (or in closely related fields). The anthology was not intended to cover contemporary action theory systematically, but in fact it ends up doing almost that. Thus practically all central questions dealt with by traditional philosophy and theory of action are discussed in the papers included here.

This project has been a genuinely joint one, and the order in which the authors are listed has only alphabetical significance. Our project would not have been possible without invaluable support by the Academy of Finland which facilitated not only Tuomela's contribution to the months-long editing process, especially to that of volume 2, but also the practicalities of the process including the translation of G.H. von Wright's paper and the preparation of the index.

We are grateful to all our contributors for sharing with us the insight of their ongoing research. We also extend our thanks to Mrs. Auli Kaipainen. Her work was supported by Kluwer Academic Publishers, to whom we are grateful for accepting our volumes to the series Synthese Library. Without her excellent

G. Holmström-Hintikka and R. Tuomela (eds.), Contemporary Action Theory, v–vi.

copy-editing this material and carrying out the other secretarial responsibilities, this work would not have been possible. Our thanks are also due to Mr. Pekka Mäkelä for assistance in preparation of this anthology.

March 1997

GHITA HOLMSTRÖM-HINTIKKA
Boston University and
University of Helsinki

RAIMO TUOMELA
Academy of Finland

TABLE OF CONTENTS

VOLUME I: INDIVIDUAL ACTION

INTRODUCTION

Human action never ceases to fascinate human beings and the human mind. Ordinary people as well as specialists in fields as diverse as philosophers, psychologists, lawyers and theologians all take deep interest in the explanation and understanding of actions. A layperson might simply want to understand why someone did what she did. But so do lawyers and psychiatrists also – although for different reasons and with certain purposes in mind. In the contemporary philosophical literature on action theory beginning in the fifties serious developments have taken place in this particular area. Influential in this regard has been Georg Henrik von Wright whose *Explanation and Understanding* (1971) has caused a flow of discussions and brought about numerous articles. Significantly enough his paper in this very volume is entitled "Explanation and Understanding in Action". He is also subject to a comparison with Collingwood in Rex Martin's paper "von Wright and Collingwood on Causation and the Explanation of Human Action". What are actions? How can we understand actions? What causes people's actions? A causal explanation is not easy to come up with, nor is it usually a matter of one single explanation. "Metaphysical Foundations of Action Explanation" by Ausonio Marras and "Reasons as Causes *for* Action" by George Wilson are good examples of the subtleties we are dealing with even in the most basic matters, the causes for our actions.

Other aspects of the explanation of human action are dealt with in the various writings on action logic, in particular the logic of individual action. In this regard several famous logicians have forcefully developed far-going theories on single-agent action. Be it enough here to mention only a few representatives. Among others, Nuel Belnap, Brian Chellas, Stig Kanger, Ingmar Pörn, Krister Segerberg, Georg Henrik von Wright and Lennart Åqvist have all in a major way contributed to the development of this subarea of action theory. In his paper "On States, Actions, Omissions and Norms" Risto Hilpinen helps us to understand some of the developments in action logic and also to put these things into perspective with regard to other modalities, in particular to deontic concepts. One instantiation of the Fenno-Scandian tradition (Kanger – Lindahl – Pörn) mentioned by Hilpinen is Ghita Holmström-Hintikka's further developments of her action theory based on the tripartition of agent causation. The basic elements, including actions are conditions (states of affairs) as they are in Kanger's theory.

Activity, passivity, competence, practical reason, all these concepts touch upon central features in human action, features which have a bearing on

G. Holmström-Hintikka and R. Tuomela (eds.), Contemporary Action Theory. Vol. I, ix – xvii.

people's health and well-being as well as to their social and legal behaviour. All these matters are discussed in the logic group of papers appearing below.

When behaviour is being evaluated, praise and blame will depend, not only on results accomplished or not accomplished, but also on the intentions behind the actions. This topic can be dealt with from a theoretical point of view as by Robert Audi or from a "practical" causal point of view as by Myles Brand.

Freedom of Action and Freedom of the Will are classical and yet always inspiring topics. It seems as if there is always something new and interesting to be said. These two topics support the still more specialized topics on mental action and the Causal Theory of Action versus the Agent Causation Theory, not to mention cognitive trying.

A SHORT PRESENTATION OF THE PAPERS IN VOLUME I

1. An important type of explanations of action makes reference to reasons, says Georg Henrik von Wright in "Explanation and Understanding of Actions". The author of the paper calls them "understanding explanations." Often there are several reasons for one and the same action – and possibly also reasons against performing it. The fact that something is a reason for an action does not necessarily mean that the action is performed *for that reason*. One must, in other words, distinguish between the *existence* and the *efficacy* of reasons for actions. This raises the question of the *veracity* of a suggested explanation when the action is correctly identified and the reasons for its performance are known.

The author defends a thesis that the efficacious reasons for an action are those in the light of which we understand the action. The "tie" between the action and the (efficacious) reason(s) is thus created by the act of understanding. When there is disagreement between the self-understanding of the agent and an outside observer, the latter may sometimes succeed in "converting" the former to a new understanding of his motives. The nature of such "conversions" is discussed in the paper, and it is maintained that neither the agent nor the outsider can claim an exclusive right to authority in the question which is the correct explanation. The "criterion of truth" of the explanation is *consensus* in the understanding of the action. It cannot be taken for granted that such agreement of opinion can in all cases be attained even "in principle."

2. In "von Wright and Collingwood on Causation and the Explanation of Human Action" Rex Martin makes comparisons between the two philosophers. Section one of this paper is concerned with setting out the views of Collingwood and von Wright on the explanation of action. Here a single main model or schema for the explanation of actions is identified (that is, for explanations of actions by reference to reasons – to certain thoughts and motivations of the agent). This model provides the root of both von Wright's notion of practical inference and Collingwood's idea of re-enactment. In this first section the

author turns as well to a critique of their two theories, by taking up and contrasting the role of understanding or intelligibility, often called *Verstehen*, in each of their accounts. In the second section two alternative claims are considered, looking first at von Wright's contention that the schema is not itself a causal principle and, hence, that those thoughts of agents which figure in proper action explanations are not causes of those actions. This is contrasted to Collingwood's claim that such thoughts are, indeed, causes of action.

3. Ausonio Marras observes in "Metaphysical Foundations of Action Explanation" that disagreement abounds with respect to the question of *how to account* for the causal powers of reasons. How *can* reasons be causes, how can beliefs, desires, etc. be causally efficacious in the production of behaviour so as to be explanatory of it in a causally relevant sense? The problem, essentially, is to provide a metaphysical underpinning for the possibility of *mental causation* so as to account for the *explanatory* role of reasons.

The supervenience and metaphysical dependence of mental on physical properties grounds the causal relevance of mental properties and explains their suitability for featuring in genuinely causal laws. The author suggests how this idea of metaphysical dependence might in turn be explained, in accordance with a broadly functionalist and (non-reductive) physicalist approach to the mental, in terms of the notions of physical realization and implementation. He also explains how psychological laws, while genuinely causal in that they are implemented by physical mechanisms, are nonetheless irreducible to the physical laws governing those mechanisms. This accounts both for the (albeit dependent) causal status of psychological laws and for their indispensibility for explanations of intentional action. This account of how reason explanations can be causal explanations departs radically from the Davidsonian 'anomalist' account inasmuch as it strives to bring psychology within the domain of the *natural* sciences while preserving its integrity as a *special* science. This account is one way of vindicating the chief motivating force behind naturalistically inspired forms of non-reductive physicalism in philosophy of mind: a belief in the *metaphysical dependence* of the mental on the physical, coupled with a belief in the *methodological autonomy* of the science of mind.

4. George Wilson in his paper "Reasons as Causes *for* Action" raises the question whether reasons are rational causes. In most summary accounts of the theory of action, a section is devoted to "The Reasons vs. Causes Debate." Thus advertised, the topic will sound to the neophyte as if it were constituted by some mighty conceptual struggle, with well-defined forces lining up on either side. I have come to believe, says Wilson, that the long term disadvantages, in the present case, are weightier. We give the impression that our understanding of the nature of the problems is relatively sharp and that nothing is left but a matter of working out details that will point toward a satisfactory

solution. He is less confident that our questions have been well-drawn in the reasons vs. causes debate. In this essay, he explains some of the more significant doubts he feels about recent discussions of the subject and indicates some of the areas that are likely to require extensive clarification if substantial progress is to be achieved.

5. In his paper "On States, Actions, Omissions and Norms" Risto Hilpinen analyzes actions as world-state transitions or as relations between world-states. This model fits actions which can be said to lead to a certain result and characterized by means of their results, and it explains the temporal and situational indeterminacy of actions. According to this conception of actions, we have to distinguish action descriptions from 'ordinary' propositions which are interpreted as sets of situations; the latter include agency statements, that is, sentences which state that a certain result (a fact, a state of affairs) is due to the actions of a certain agent.

The distinction between action descriptions and propositions underlies the traditional distinction between two kinds of *ought* (or two kinds of ought-statements), viz. the ought-to-be and the ought-to-do (between *Seinsollen* and *Tunsollen*). An ought-to-do statement is a normative statement to the effect that a certain action is required (or obligatory), permitted or forbidden in a certain situation, whereas ought-to-be statements say that a certain state of affairs ought or ought not to obtain in a given situation.

If actions are represented as binary relations between world-states or as transitions from one world-state to another, a simple semantics of directives (ought-to-do sentences) can be obtained by applying the basic ideas of the standard semantics of deontic logic to such transitions or ordered pairs of possible worlds (world-states). Instead of dividing world-states into deontically perfect (ideal) worlds and deontically imperfect (unacceptable) worlds, we divide the movements from one world-state to another into legal (or acceptable) transitions and illegal (unacceptable) transitions (Czelakowski 1997).

What is the relationship between the two kinds of ought? The normative status of an action may be considered from a consequentialist viewpoint in the light of the interests and objectives of an agent or of a norm-authority, and the normative status of a state of affairs may be considered deontologically on the basis of the actions which led to it or could have led to it.

6. In "Actions in Action" Ghita Holmström-Hintikka deals with second-order actions. She observes that three kinds of agent causation can be identified: *mere causation*, for the agent, x, a particular means, m, suffices to make sure that a result, r, obtains, $C(x,m,r)$; *instrumental action*, the agent sees to it, by a particular means, that a particular result obtains, $E(x,m,r)$; *purposive action*, the agent sees to it that a result obtains for a particular purpose, $A(x,r,p)$. Mere causation, which is not considered an action, takes place for instance when a

person walks in the street and moves sand on his shoes. This happens non-purposively. Here *m*, *p*, *r*, are, like the causation descriptions, considered conditions which are realized when the result obtains – as opposed to propositions.

Instrumental and purposive actions are proper actions; they are performed for one purpose or other. The concept of *goal-directed will* constitutes the fourth basic concept in the theory; the agent wills that *p* aiming that *q*, $W(x,p,q)$. As the logic for these first-order, one-agent concepts has been developed in earlier works, this paper concentrates on developing it further into a treatment of second-order agent causations with one and the same or separate agents.

A central part in this paper is devoted to the discussion of 'influence' which here for the first time becomes defined in terms of a second-order action with separate agents: *x* influences *y* with respect to $\varphi(y)$ iff *x* sees to it that $\varphi(y)$, i.e.,

$$\text{(DfI)} \qquad I(x,y,\varphi(y)) =_{\text{df}} E(x,\varphi(y))$$

where $\varphi(y)$ stands for one of the four basic concepts with *y* as the agent.

Can computers see to it on purpose that some person sees to it that a particular result obtains? Can a computer have aims? These and similar questions are also discussed in this paper.

7. In his paper "Passive Action" Alfred Mele demonstrates by means of an example how passive action is to be conceived of. Peter opted for the devious strategy of lying still on the sled without grasping the handles or making any voluntary motions. He was prepared to take control of the sled should disaster threaten: the rogues might have placed a log in the path of the speeding sled. But, as it happened, he had no need to intervene and simply allowed the sled to take its course.

If it is correctly held that Peter intentionally sleds, or slides, or travels down the hill, we have here a case of what might provocatively be termed "passive action." In a well known paper, "The Problem of Action" (1988, essay 6), Harry Frankfurt appeals to action of this kind in an attempt to undermine causal theories of action. Mele argues that passive action does not constitute a special problem for a relatively standard causal theory of action.

8. In "On Ability, Opportunity and Competence: An Inquiry into People's Possibility for Action" Lennart Nordenfelt raises important questions. What does it mean to say that a man is able to perform an action? Is it true, as the standard philosophical analysis of ability indicates, that this man is in a state which is such that he would perform the action if he were to try? Is the counterfactual conditional the proper form for the analysis of the notion of ability?

In this paper such a contention is seriously questioned and it is instead argued that there are various versions or layers of ability which are logically weaker than the counterfactual conditional suggests. At one level of analysis this is common knowledge. There is a traditional distinction between a person's internal possibility for action, his or her ability, and the person's external possibility for action, his or her opportunity. It is only when the person has both ability and opportunity, it is generally claimed, that all grounds are present for the counterfactual conditional to hold true. The purpose in this paper, however, is to question also this statement. It is in particular argued that competence and skill are species of ability which do not fulfil the traditional conditions. During the course of this argument the traditional distinction between ability and opportunity are investigated and the author points to the logical interdependence between these notions.

The discussion is focused upon ability in the context of intentional human action, but several of the observations can be shown to be valid for other notions of capability and power as well. The notion of ability which is under scrutiny could then be formally characterized in the following way: A is able to perform φ (where A is a human agent and φ is an intentional action) if, and only if, A would do φ if A were to try to do φ.

9. In "Actions and Inconsistency" Douglas Walton deals with the closure problem of practical reasoning. The problem in this paper is to specify when a knowledge-based goal-directed inference leading to an action (or a recommendation for a course of action to be taken) may be said to be structurally correct (or closed), parallel to the sense in which a deductive argument is said to be valid (deductively closed).

Solving this problem will require a formalization of practical reasoning in the end, to be carried out in the way that the analysis of the problematic case developed in the article will indicate. However, this article will merely pose and sharpen the problem, making certain questions to be asked more precise. By solving the philosophical and practical problem of closure, the way is opened to developing a formalization of practical resolving as a distinctive type of reasoning that can be evaluated as normatively binding on a rational agent.

A structure of practical reasoning is presented, and it is argued that the job of evaluating cases of arguments based on a criticism of inconsistency of actions, or "not practising what you preach", is best accomplished by applying this structure. In general, the task addressed by the article is one of evaluating the argumentation reconstructed from the text of discourse given in a particular case, and then using this evidence to judge whether the given argument meets the standards of practical rationality or not, as defined by the structures that should be used to judge such cases. Thus the goal of this article is seen to be one of applied logic, or as evaluating argument, as "correct" or "incorrect", as opposed to being a psychological inquiry into the agent's actual intentions.

10. Robert Audi's paper "Intending and Its Place in the Theory of Action" is aimed at contributing to our understanding of intending in two ways: first, it will reinforce and clarify his original account of intending by bringing the account to bear on a number of important problems central for intending in particular and the theory of the will in general; secondly, it will reply to a number of objections to the account that have emerged or re-emerged in the past several years. The topic of intending is important in both the literature of action theory and, more generally, that of ethics and the law.

11. Myles Brand in his contribution "Intention and Intentional Action" remarks that an adequate theory of human action will explain, among other things, how external events and the agent's recent psychological history initiates bodily activity, which, in turn, affects changes in the world. If we take the initiating event to be an intending and the resultant activity to be an intentional action, then any adequate action theory will explain the relationship between intending and acting intentionally. This paper aims at partially specifying this relationship. An attractive approach is to identify the content of an immediate intention with the ensuing intentional action; in which case, a person intentionally *A*ed only if he had a present-directed intention to *A*. This approach, which Michael Bratman has labelled 'The Simple View', connects the initiating mental event and the action in a simple and straightforward manner. He correctly argues against it, says Brand.

Being clear why the Simple View is not acceptable requires an understanding of the nature of intending. In the second part of the paper, a brief stretch of intending is provided; and armed with it, an account of the central feature of the relationship between intentional action and intention is developed.

12. Hugh J. McCann in his contribution "On When the Will is Free" turns to Peter van Inwagen who has defended the view that will is at best seldom free, because in the great majority of cases only one available alternative has significant motivational backing, and without a positive reason to perform an action one is unable to do it. The author argues that such cases must be exceedingly rare, and so pose no significant danger to libertarian views. Moreover, there is reason to think that even where an agent's motives line up entirely on the side of just one alternative, he may still choose differently, although it would not be rational to do so.

13. In "When Is an Action Free?" Gottfried Seebass writes that there are good reasons not to give up the traditional concept of *strong accountability*. This implies that actions can be traced back to a number of relevant mental events which include wants and volitions. Also it can reasonably be assumed that strong, no less than weak accountability depends on a certain condition of *freedom*. Traditionally, *freedom of action*, FA, or more specifically *conditional*

freedom of action, CFA, have been considered the adequate conceptual tool for giving an explication of a certain condition of *freedom* by the majority of both philosophical as well as theological thinkers. Moreover, it has been thought that FA and CFA are sufficient theoretical tools to dispose of the traditional problem of "freewill and determination". This is a mistake in principle.

The theoretical background for the dismissal of the free will problem is a tacit reliance on the fallacious Augustinian proof that the will is free *per se*. However, it is more than doubtful that there will ever be found a cogent theoretical substitute for it. Once this is realized one becomes free to make a fresh start and to specify the condition of freedom required for strong accountability, independent of the conceptual bonds of FA, CFA and Augustinianism. Hume should be taken seriously, says Seebass. The Humean conception is incomplete without a specification of the notion of *"spontaneity"*. This notion should be explicated thoroughly, systematically and without tacit evasions to Augustinianism. Having done this, however, one may well find that Hume's "liberty of spontaneity" is *liberty* of spontaneity only because it *is*, or *entails*, "liberty of indifference".

14. John Bishop in "Naturalising Mental Action" makes the observation that the naturalising of personal agency by means of a Causal Theory of Action (CTA) faces the problem of accommodating mental actions, since it seems clear that – even if mental actions are not implicated in the causal antecedents of *every* action – they do feature in the aetiology of significantly free actions. Recent criticisms of CTA by J.R. Cameron and Fred Dretske, it is argued, do no more than highlight this problem. It is argued that the problem can be solved: a CTA can accommodate mental actions, provided it is acceptable to posit certain general higher-order intentions as constitutive of rationality.

15. David-Hillel Ruben points out in his paper "Doing Without Happenings: Three Theories of Action" that there seems to be a distinction of some sort between my actions on the one hand, like my bending my finger and my raising my arm, and mere 'passive' events that occur to my body on the other, like my finger's bending and my arm's rising. My finger can bend without my bending it; my arm can rise without me raising it.

There are two current theories about action which attempt to illuminate what action is by identifying every token action with an event token of some kind: the Causal Theory of Action (the CTA); and the Agent Causalist Theory (the ACT). How can some events be actions, which, if anything is, are active? That is the question both theories must answer: How can activity 'emerge' from, or supervene on, the passivity of events? This is called 'the problem of passivity'. The two theories of action, the Causal Theory of Action and the Agent Causalist Theory, are rejected, by rejecting an assumption that both share and which explains at least in part where they both go wrong. Ruben's theory leaves action unreduced, as a basic type of item in one's metaphysics of the world. Perhaps such a simple position should not be called a 'third theory' of action, he writes, and to that extent the title may be misleading but it definitely presents an important alternative to the CTA and ACT.

16. In his paper "Cognitive Trying" Frederick Adams develops a cognitive theory of trying. He defends the view that what makes something an attempt is its being nested in the appropriate constellation of other cognitive states and its causing appropriate mental states (mental trying) or bodily movements (bodily trying). The view is teleological in that the causing of these appropriate states must be for the right reason. The paper also defends the view that what makes something the attempt to do *A* (rather than *B*) is that it is initiated, sustained and guided by the intention to do *A* (rather than *B*). Finally, the paper applies the theory to some interesting general questions surrounding the activity of trying and to some specific arguments in recent philosophical literature by Bratman, Ludwig, and Mele.

Ghita Holmström-Hintikka
Boston University and
University of Helsinki

REFERENCES

Czelakowski, Janusz (1997), "Action and Deontology" in Sten Lindström and Eva Ejerhed (eds.), *Logic, Action and Cognition*. Dordrecht and Boston, Kluwer Academic Publishers.
Frankfurt, Harry (1988), *The Importance of What We Care About*. Cambridge, Cambridge University Press.
von Wright, G.H. (1971), *Explanation and Understanding*. Ithaca, NY, Cornell University Press.

GEORG HENRIK VON WRIGHT

EXPLANATION AND UNDERSTANDING OF ACTIONS

This lecture was given at the Universities of Graz, Innsbruck, and Salzburg in November 1984. It was originally published in *Conceptus* vol. **19**, Number 47 (1985), pp. 3–19, under the title "Probleme des Erklärens und Verstehens von Handlungen." This particular piece has been included among the papers published by von Wright in his recent book *Normen, Werte, und Handlungen* (Frankfurt am Main: Suhrkamp, 1994), at pp. 141–165. In the version published in *Conceptus*, the text of the lecture proper was preceded by a two-paragraph abstract (or "Summary"), in German and in English; that summary is not found in the Suhrkamp edition. The summary, in English, has been retained (in slightly revised form) in the present translation. The lecture *per se* begins on p. 4 of the *Conceptus* issue. The translation from the German is by James Gilkeson. It has been prepared for publication by Rex Martin (with thanks to Tim Tessin for providing an improved version of one paragraph and to Georg Henrik von Wright for suggesting certain corrections and for other helpful comments). For convenience, the *Conceptus* page numbers are included in this translation, in brackets. All the numbered notes in this translation are the translator's, as are all bracketed items in the text.

SUMMARY

An important type of explanations of action makes reference to reasons. The author of the paper calls them "understanding explanations." Often there are several reasons for one and the same action – and possibly also reasons against performing it. The fact that something is a reason for an action does not necessarily mean that the action is performed *for that reason*. One must, in other words, distinguish between the *existence* and the *efficacy* of reasons for actions. This raises the question of the *veracity* of a suggested explanation when the action is correctly identified and the reasons for its performance are known.

The author defends a thesis that the efficacious reasons for an action are those in the light of which we understand the action. The "tie" between the action and the (efficacious) reason(s) is thus created by the act of understanding. When there is disagreement between the self-understanding of the agent and an outside observer, the latter may sometimes succeed in "converting" the former to a new understanding of his motives. The nature of such "conversions" is discussed in the paper, and it is maintained that neither the agent nor the outsider can claim an exclusive right to authority in the question which is the correct explanation. The "criterion of truth" of the explanation is *consensus* in the understanding of the action. It cannot be taken for granted that such agreement of opinion can in all cases be attained even "in principle."

G. Holmström-Hintikka and R. Tuomela (eds.), Contemporary Action Theory. Vol. I, 1–20.

1. Explaining an action means answering the question, "Why was this action carried out?" The same applies to the question of why an action is *not* carried out. Generally, the illustration given can be related to a variety of types of explanations of action. For reasons which will soon become clear, I shall limit this discussion to a single type of explanation which I call understanding explanations [*verstehende Erklärungen,* see Summary]. In explanations of this type, actions are explained or understood under the assumption that they have arisen out of a particular reason or out of a particular motive.

Before we go further, we should, however, briefly mention two additional types of explanations. One of these might be termed "medical." In this type of explanation, an action (or, alternatively, the *non*-performance of an action) is traced back to an illness or impediment of the agent; specifically, to an inability which is perhaps caused by a physical defect[1] or disturbance in bodily functions. Explanations of the second sort I call, in turn, "sociological." These explanations generally refer not to the performance or non-performance of individual actions, but rather to categories or types of actions which the agent either is or is not capable of carrying out. The type of explanation states, for example, that persons in certain economic circumstances, or because of a lack of [sufficient] schooling, or due to their membership in a particular social class or affiliation with a particular religious belief, are [as a result] incapable of performing a particular kind of act – or, conversely, are [because of those preconditions] compelled to perform a particular kind of act.

Both of the above types of explanations for actions are, in a certain sense, what tend to be called "scientific" explanations. They are often connected to a particular "depiction" or "theory" of humanity and society. Their purpose might be to heal a person from an illness, or to correct some insufficiency in that person, or to deliver a critique of some injustice or crookedness in the status quo. This type of explanation has what might be called an "emancipatory" function.

Understanding explanations, on the other hand, differ from these. If they have a purpose outside of that of merely understanding, then it is the purpose of evaluation. The answer to the question as to whether an action ought to be praised or condemned is decidedly dependent upon the reasons for which the agent acted, the motives and frame of mind in which the agent acted. In order to judge the action, we must first understand the action.

In order to accept an *understanding explanation* as complete, there are three conditions which must be met. First, we must know *what* the agent has done. Second, we must determine the reasons[2] which were present to the agent when he performed this particular action. Thirdly, out of all the reasons which present themselves, we must determine from which of the reasons the agent *actually* acted. None of these three conditions is unproblematic. The action, the reasons and the connection between action and reason(s) create a unit, the components of which cannot be clearly distinguished from one another as concepts. In the following, I hope to demonstrate the meaning of this as well as the problems to which this can lead. [p. 4/p. 5]

2. What does it mean when we say that something is a reason for an action? One might say that the reason for the performance (or non-performance) of an action is something to which the performance (or non-performance) of that action is an appropriate[3] reaction, or correct response or "answer." Some examples of this: An answer is an appropriate (adequate) reaction or response to a question; the performance of a service is an appropriate (adequate) reaction to a request; applying the brakes in one's car is an appropriate (adequate) reaction to a street light turning red; the fulfillment of a promise is an appropriate (adequate) reaction to making a promise. One who makes a promise has a reason for doing something. Whether or not he actually *does* what he has a reason to do is another question; it can also be that he has reasons for not doing it; or perhaps he does it, but not specifically for the reason that by doing it he will fulfill a promise which was made.

In these examples, the reason is either something which the agent experiences external to himself, or something which he has himself done and which "demand" actions of him (for example, the carrying out of something which he has promised). Reasons of this kind would be *external* reasons. A second kind of reason is that which I would call *internal (or inner)*. There reasons are not encountered external to the agent, but rather they "spring up" from within the agent. For example, I can do something in order to avoid something which is repugnant to me, or in order to escape some danger by which I am threatened. I believe or even know that my action fulfills that purpose. Or I do something in order to obtain something I have had my eye on, or to attain something which I had set as a goal. In this case, my belief or knowledge is that my action is purposeful, which in conjunction with my will to accomplish something, constitutes a reason for my action.

It is easy to see that reasons of this second, internal, type have two components. The first might be called cognitive, while the second might be called volitional [*volitiv*], or voluntary: it is my intention or my will to accomplish something; it is my view (which may be correct or incorrect) that a particular action is useful or even necessary for reaching an intended goal.

What I call *Grund* in German would mean "reason" or "ground" in English. The first English word, "reason," indicates the human capability to act rationally. In German, as well, this connotation can be made explicit in the compound word *Vernunftsgrund*[4]. The reasons for an action are often referred to as *Ursachen* (in English "causes"). In order to differentiate between such "reasons" and "causes" of events in nature, it can be useful to refer to the reasons for actions as rational reasons (*Vernunftsgründe*), as opposed to the *causal* reasons or grounds behind natural events.

A second frequently used term is 'motive.' The German word for a motive for an action is *Beweggrund*[5]. This term is often used interchangeably with reason '*Vernunftsgrund*' [rational reason]. Seeing that some differences can be noted in the usage of these words, we want to pose the question: "What is the difference between a reason [*Vernunftsgrund*] and a motive [*Beweggrund*] for an action?"

Let's say I obey an order. The order was a reason for me to act. One might also say that the order was the "motive" for my action, but (at least in my ears), that does not quite ring true, it does not seem completely natural. Let's say, however, that I comply with the order because I fear the wrath of the one giving the order, should I not comply. [p. 5 ends/p. 6 begins in the midst of this sentence] In that case, it would not be unnatural to say that the motive for my action was the fear of my commander. How might one more clearly describe the difference between reasons and motives?

In the previous situation, we have two reasons for my action. One of them is external: I received an order. The other reason is internal: I do not wish to have the wrath of my commander visited upon me, and thus, I know that it is advisable to do as I am told. Two things are of note here: one, the internal reason is based on the [existence of the] external reason; two, the external reason might not be effective if it were not for the internal reason.

The motive has to do with the internal reason, although it cannot be identified with that reason. The motive which moved me [to act] was, as I stated, fear of the anger of the commander. This motive can also not be equated with the *volitional* [italics added] components of the internal reasons for my actions; that is, with my intention to not incur the anger of the commander. One would be more likely to see the motive (the commander's anger) as the cause [*Ursache*] for this component of the reasons for my action. If I were not afraid of the commander's anger, I would also not have had the specific motive of not wanting to incur his anger. Hence, the internal reason for following the order would not have existed.

The relation between the motive for my action and the volitional components of the internal reason requires one further observation. My intention (my striving, my will), to avoid the anger of the commander are *expressions* of my fear; these expressions, along with other, similar reactions are what "constitute" my fear. It would not be pertinent to say that these expressions are "caused" by my fear. If one were to say that the motive is the "cause" for one's will, then one is using the term "cause" in a way which can be philosophically misleading. Motives do not "move" [something] in the same sense that, for example, a shove moves a body.

Fear and rage, love and hate, attraction and repulsion and other so-called passions of the soul are typical motives for actions. Usually, they have an object: *something which* is feared, hated or loved, something which is striven *for* or of which one is afraid. Under certain circumstances (for example, when that object is either present or readily attainable), these passions express themselves in the form of an intention to do something which seems fitting or purposeful from the standpoint of the agent and his relation to the object. In other words, under such circumstances there arises an internal reason for the agent to either carry out, or not carry out, a particular action.

In and of themselves, passions are conceptually distinct from human rationality and reason. Sometimes we even call them, depending on their objects or their strength, "irrational" or "blind" [both words are quoted in the original, in English]. Hate can make a person just as blind as love. A "blind" passion can, however, be the motive for a perfectly rational action; namely, when it is expressed in the volitional component of the reason[ing] for an action [*Handlungsgrund*], the cognitive component of which is a well-grounded belief in the purposefulness of a particular action as it relates to the object of that passion. An example would be a cleverly and cold-bloodedly planned murder.

In what follows, I will, however, no longer make a sharp distinction between the motive [p. 6/p. 7] and rational reason [*Vernunftsgrund*] of an action. Instead, I will call the entire body of motives and reasons, both internal and external, the motivational background [*Motivationshintergrund*] of an action.

3. Sometimes, an action has only one single reason. If such an action is carried out, the explanation for it is usually not very interesting. Let us assume, however, that an action is *not* carried out, although an obvious reason for such an action is present. This already makes the situation somewhat more interesting. Perhaps, in addition to the reason, there was also a "counter-reason," a reason for *not* carrying out the action. And perhaps the reason against the carrying out of the action, this "counter-reason," was stronger (i.e. more compelling and consequential) than the reason for carrying it out.

When an action has both a reason for and a reason against its being carried out, the motivational background should be termed *complex*. The complexity of motivation can also be represented in the fact that there are numerous reasons, both for and against carrying out the action. Complexity of motivation is increased by the fact that these reason may vary in strength; some may be stronger – that is to say, of more consequence – than others. When there are several reasons, both for and against an action, the agent is required, so to speak, to "weigh" the "sum" of the reasons for the action against the "sum" of those reasons against the action in an attempt to arrive at a "final score" (at an "action-resultant").

The complexity of the motivational background for human actions has long been well known to psychologists. As far as I can see, however, philosophers

– at least those operating in the analytical tradition of the "Philosophy of Action" – have generally ignored this point of view in their discussion of the problematic aspects of the explanation of actions. This amounts to a one-sided treatment [of the explanation for actions], which must be rectified. [If this is done], many things will then appear in a new light.

Let us turn to the following example: A person promises to do something; as a result he has an external reason to carry out a particular action. At the same time, he has been promised a reward if he will carry out the action. The prospect of receiving the reward is pleasurable to him; as a result he also has an internal reason to fulfill his promise. But now, let us say that the action which he has promised to carry out is morally questionable, or even criminal. He is aware of this fact and, thus, has an external reason to *not* carry out the action. The agent must now weigh the reasons for and against the action against one another. He has made a promise and one ought to keep promises. He has the prospect of receiving a reward if he carries out the action and this prospect is pleasurable to him. However, what he has promised to do is wrong; such promises are not always seen as binding.

Now let us say that our agent keeps his promise. How then is his action to be understood or explained? Is he such an "uncompromising moralist" that he believes that promises which one makes are to be carried out without exception? Or is he quite the opposite: morally so insensitive and depraved that the only thing which influenced him was the prospect of receiving a reward for carrying out his harmful act. Or are all of these reasons, at least in part, responsible for "fueling" his action? How should this be decided? [p. 7/p. 8]

Strong reasons are also called "good" reasons for doing something, while weak reasons are called "bad" reasons. The words "good" and "bad" can, however, also be used to pass moral judgment on the reasons for an action. But here, we will not take the [strictly] moral evaluation of the reasons into consideration.

4. Appropriate reactions/responses to orders, questions, promises, rules and regulations of all kinds can also be called *institutionalized* behaviors, seeing that they always occur in the context of life lived in human community. The reasons for behaviors of this kind are what I have called external reasons.

An external reason for an action might exist without the conscious knowledge of the agent. For example, let us say that a person is given an order. In order for that order to be a reason for that person to act, he must first have heard, or otherwise taken note of the communication [of the order]; secondly, he must have sufficient command of the language of symbols in which the order is communicated; thirdly, he must comprehend the "meaning" of orders – that is, he must understand that orders are to be carried out, regardless of whether or not he wants to do it. It is only when these three conditions are met that an order becomes a reason for an action – that is to say, it is only when these three conditions are met that the order becomes relevant as an explanation for the action. The same applies to other external reasons as well. They must be *taken in*[6] and *understood* by the agent in order to make up part of the motivational background of the agent. It can by no means be taken for granted that these conditions are always fulfilled. A foreigner travelling along the street of one of our cities might not comprehend the "meaning" of a traffic signal; accordingly, the signal does not "motivate" his behavior. In such cases, we sometimes find fault with the person for his ignorance and say, "He ought to have been better instructed [about our ways here]."

It is different with internal reasons for action. They cannot be present in an "objective" sense without belonging to the motivational background of an agent. It may, however, not be concluded that the agent acted according to these internal reasons, or that he necessarily followed them in any other way, or that the existence of these internal reasons is even clearly conscious. The motivations behind his action might be, as we say, "unconscious," yet effectual.

Let us assume that I am invited to lunch at the home of a family. I decline the invitation and give as my reason the fact that I have accepted another invitation at the same time. The reason which I give is external – it has to do with our rules of good conduct. Using the reason, I "excuse" myself for declining the invitation. But is it certain that the reason I have given is the "real" reason for declining the invitation? It could be that a meal with *X* would be unspeakably boring; [maybe] I am very shy and I do not like to be in the company of many people at the same time. It could also be that *Z* is invited to the meal as well, and that is a person whom I would rather not see (in fact, I am even afraid of an encounter with this person).

All of these latter circumstances give me more or less strong (or good) internal reasons for declining the invitation. When I am asked, however, why I am declining, the only reason I give is the other invitation which I had accepted. Perhaps I had not even thought of all the above mentioned other reasons at the moment that I declined, for the very reason that I had a good "excuse." It might be that it never even occurred to me that I might encounter *Z* at *X*'s house. And provided that this is *actually* the case – that is, if this possibility [p. 8/p. 9] did not make up part of the motivational background of my behavior – then my attitude toward *Z* is completely irrelevant for the explanation of my action. But can one be sure of just how things stand? Suppose someone says, "But he knows good and well that *Z* is often a guest at *X*'s house. He has to have known that he might encounter *Z* there. And seeing that he has good reasons for not wanting to meet up with *Z*, that [and not what he used as an excuse] was his [real] reason for declining the invitation. Who knows?

I shall return to cases of this sort, but now I want to call attention to the following: First, it is not always clear which reasons for and which against a particular behavior belong to the agent's [real] motivational background. Secondly, reasons which without doubt are based in reality – for example, that I am shy and I do not feel well in the company of unfamiliar persons – do not necessarily influence my actual behavior. In other words, one must differentiate between *existing* reasons and *effectual* reasons.[7] An existing reason which is however not an effectual reason, but which is presented as a reason by the agent, is what one calls a pretense [or a pretext: *Vorwand*]. Only effectual reasons for and against an action belong to a correct explanation for an action.

When a motivation is complex, it is always possible that an action is co-determined by several reasons. An exhaustive explanation must necessarily name them all. Thus, it is obviously not possible to say that the action was carried out for a particular reason; there was not one single reason, but rather several, for the action. It could, however, be the case that one single reason (or a combination of a number of reasons) would have sufficed to bring about the action. If that is the case, this action was what one calls *over-determined*[8]. This concept of over-determination is well-known to psychologists and psychoanalysts.

5. Before we switch to the question of how an action is connected to its reasons, we must first say a few things about how a particular action and particular reasons for the action are ascribed to a person. We see a person moving his arms and hands. In one hand, he is holding a key and, in the other, a lock which is fastened to the door of a cabinet. What is this person doing? Or, to use the terminology of modern philosophers, under which description is his behavior (his bodily movement) intentional? There are numerous possibilities. One is that he is about to open the cabinet door. Another is that he is testing whether the lock can be opened – we are assuming here that the mechanism is complicated. A third possibility is that he is trying to determine whether the key fits the lock – he has several keys on his key chain and forgets sometimes which key belongs to which lock. In the first case, the person's intentions are carried out only when the cabinet door opens. In both of the other cases, he carries out his intention, regardless of whether or not the cabinet door opens.

A description of "mere/naked" behavior – that is, of the bodily movement connected with a particular action – is never sufficient to definitively characterize the deed (that which actually took place). It is important to comprehend this. In order to say what the agent has done, we must know what it was that he *intended* or *meant* or *wanted* in the carrying out of his action. This is something which he supposedly knows himself, and so, the simplest "method" of finding this out would be to ask him. If we are unable [p. 9/p. 10] to do this, or if we mistrust his answer, then we must [either] look to the evidence of further observations concerning his actions – for example, that he takes something out of the open cabinet – or remember things he might have said or done before he began his activities with the cabinet – for example, that he was looking for something that could perhaps be found in the cabinet.

In order to identify a behavior as an act[9] usually also means pointing to a possible reason (or several possible reasons) for such an act. If the man in our example wanted to get something out of the cabinet, then he had a reason for doing as he did with the lock and key. What he then did was in order to open the cabinet door and not, for example, in order to check to see whether a certain key fit the lock. As we can see, identifying a given behavior as an act is, at the same time, a kind of rudimentary explanation of the act. We ascribe reasons to the agent for carrying out this particular act, but by what right do we do that? Usually, we do it because of other acts we have seen performed by the same agent or because of acts which we ascribe to him for other reasons. As we can see, both of these factors – the ascribing of an act to a person and the ascribing of particular reasons for just such an act – qualify each other mutually.

6. Let us now turn our attention to the second task, namely that of ascribing to a person reasons for a particular act. How does one determine that a person has understood an order, or believes that an action is instrumental for reaching a goal, or wishes to obtain something, or to avoid something else? As I have already said, one relies for the most part on what that person himself says he understands, believes, strives for or wishes to avoid. But this particular avenue is not always open to us. It could be, for example, that we do not trust what the other person says. We might say something like, "It is impossible that this person truly believes that he will achieve his goal with that action; apparently he has something else in mind to have acted in that way." In order to uncover the reasons we must rely upon other criteria than the verbal. In order to gain clarity about the motivations of this person, we might, for example, look to his earlier behavior, insofar as that is known to us. Or we might wait and watch how this person behaves himself after the action.

The presence of a reason for an action [*Handlungsgrund*] can not be identified with conditions that [may have] held sway at one particular point in time or with events that arise. It is, so to speak, a "global" fact of indefinite temporal duration that a reason for an action exists. Facts of this sort are ultimately ascribed to logical individuals of the kind we call *persons* by virtue of their verbal and other physical/bodily behavior.

The behavior, on the basis of which we ascribe reasons to a person for a particular action, is neither necessary nor sufficient to guarantee that these reasons actually exist. But neither is it merely a symptom or sign of something whose presence might be determined with "absolute certainty" on the basis of any "defining characteristics" other than this behavior. Accordingly, I have chosen to refer to the ways of behaving [*Verhaltensweisen*] which we are examining as *criteria* of the reasons for the action. This usage of the term 'criterion' [*'Kriterium'*] is familiar from Wittgenstein's later philosophy and has been discussed widely. There is no need for us here to go further into the whole question of "external criteria" [*äusseren Kriterien*] for "internal states" [*innere Zustände*]. [The split between pages 10/11 occurs in the midst of this last sentence.]

We have reached a critical point in the philosophy of psychological concepts, among them, concepts pertaining to action. There is a tendency to think that so-called inner or mental or intra-psychic conditions and processes could be "equated" or even "identified" with physical conditions and processes of the central nervous system. These processes of the nervous system would then give us criteria which would ultimately decide whether a corresponding mental condition actually exists.

The idea of a "correspondence" between mental and neural conditions is unclear; we do indeed know something about the actual context in which the two interact, but what we know is not much. Let us suppose that a person carries out a particular act for a particular reason, and let us also suppose that certain processes in his nervous system were simultaneously in effect, such that the bodily movements [*Körperbewegungen*] with which he carries out his actions are caused and guided by those processes in his nervous system. Then it would be completely unproblematic to say that the "manifest" effect of the motive upon the agent is identical with the effect which the processes in that person's nervous system have upon his bodily movements. This is because the "activating effect" [*"aktivierende Einwirkung"*] of the motive consists of certain impulses (innervations) from the nervous system of the agent which set his bodily members in motion, or more precisely, cause certain muscles in his body to relax and contract.

In order for it to be more than a mere triviality, this assertion of the identity of mental and neural events must be brought into such sharp focus that one can describe them exactly; then one must pose a testable hypothesis which states that if the same neural events repeat themselves, then the agent will carry out a particular action for a particular reason. Let us suppose that we have posed just such a hypothesis, tested it, and found that it proved itself. That would mean that we could look upon certain determinable neural facts as sure signs or symptoms that a persons will do something for a particular reason. It would not mean that the neural facts are identical with the motive [*Beweggrund*] for the action.

Moreover, the criteria for the existence of motives are the same as before; namely, the statements of the agent about his actions, his earlier and, perhaps also his later behavior, his upbringing and early experiences, etc. But let us suppose a case in which we cannot rely upon these criteria to such a degree that we can say with absolute certainty that the agent actually acted out of a specific motive or reason. Further, let us also suppose that we know with certainty that certain pertinent neural events have taken place [pertaining, that is, to the agent's actions][10]. In such a case, it would be thinkable to say that these neural events were of decisive importance. We might say, "The agent apparently acted for such and such a reason, although this is not evidenced by any of the usual criteria; we conclude this because the condition of the agent's nervous system matches that of persons who act for that reason." Such a case is thinkable, though in our experience exceedingly rare. In such a case, one would in fact make use of neural conditions and processes as *criteria* for determining the presence of a particular reason for an action. Facts pertaining to the condition of the agent's nervous system would not, however, of themselves necessarily suffice for a decision; their weight would depend upon the degree to which they agree with other criteria for the same [type of] circumstances. [The split between pages 11/12 occurs in the midst of this sentence.] It is just as implausible to equate or identify a particular reason or motive of an agent with events taking place in the agent's nervous system as it is to equate or identify it with other features of his external behavior.

7. In an explanation for actions of the kind which I have termed "understanding," one sees the commission or the omission of an action in the light of its reasons, thus seeing the action against the background of its motivation. This assumes that the action has been correctly identified and that the reasons given actually exist. As we have seen, these prerequisites are not trivial, but are more often than not problematic. If we assume here, however, that no such difficulties remain, then the question arises: What is it that will guarantee the correctness (or truth) of a given understanding explanation for an action?

To begin with, there is a purely "formal" answer which can be given to this question: The explanation is correct if the reasons indicated in the explanation were not only *present* but also *effectual [wirksam]* in such a manner that one can say: "He committed (or omitted) this action *for* these reasons (or because he had these reasons, or by virtue of these reasons)." Our question as to the accuracy (or, alternatively, the truth) of the explanation is then identical with the question: "How can one know whether an existing reason is also an efficacious one, which therefore actually influenced the action?"

I will now answer this new form of our original question as follows: Efficacious reasons are precisely those in whose light we understand the action. In other words, I submit that the *understanding explanation* for an action presents no basis for [determining] truth (no criterion for [determining] accuracy) beyond the *connection* [italics added] formed in the act of understanding between the action and its reasons. If we were to exaggerate, we might say that an *understanding explanation* for an action is neither true nor false; it lies outside the categories of truth and falsehood. Such an assertion may appear challenging. Can it be defended at all? If so, how?

One reservation that arises immediately is that we have opened the door for subjective opinions. Surely not all explanations for actions are equally good. Even if one does not bring questions of truth or falsehood into the picture, surely one can distinguish whether one has understood or misunderstood an action – that is, between a better or a worse understanding of an action (in the light of present reasons). What other possible reason for such differentiations could there be except "objectively" existing truths which pertain to the *connection* between the action and its reasons/motives, and not merely the action and the reasons as such [that is, *without* the connection between them]?

As a reminder of the complexity of these questions, remember what it means to *misunderstand* an action. Frequently (if not always), this means that one either does not correctly identify the action, interpreting, for example, a random arm movement (i.e. one without intention) as a signal, or ascribes to the agent reasons or motives which he did not have at all. In this case, the misunderstanding applies to the action and the reasons and not the *connection* between them. But this type of misunderstanding is not the subject of our present discussion. [p. 12/p. 13]

8. Understanding something assumes not only the presence of an object, but also that of a subject (someone who understands). When there is a general agreement as to how something is to be understood, one sometimes uses impersonal forms of expression such as, "Nowadays, it is understood that ..." or "It is self-evident that ... (i.e. it is universally understood and accepted that ...)," but normally a subject must be named.

So now, if understanding means explaining an action in the light of its reasons, the question arises, *whose* understanding are we talking about? Here, we can distinguish between two different possibilities: the one is: how the agent himself understands his action; the other is, how an outsider understands the action of the agent. In the first case, we speak of the self-understanding of a person; in the second case, we should speak of the understanding of an external party.

It is obvious that the self-understanding of an agent plays a key role in the correct explanation of an action. Normally, the agent knows *what* he has done – that is to say, he knows in what way his behavior has been intentional. He likewise also knows what his reasons were for and against carrying out the act and which reasons actually moved him to carry out the act. If we as outsiders wish to know *why* he acted as he did, the simplest way to find out is to ask him.

But why do we even want to know this at all? In the large majority of cases this question does not even come up – not even for the agent. If he (for some reason) had reflected on his actions, or if someone had asked him (for some reason), he could have given an immediate answer which no one would have reason to doubt. Implicit here is, admittedly, an agreement of opinions, and, as already has been intimated, this consensual agreement [*Konsens*] guarantees the truth of the explanation, should one be necessary.

Only under certain relatively rare circumstances does an action require any explanation at all. These are circumstances about which we cannot assume automatically that a consensus exists – for example, when an outsider wonders *why* the agent acted *as he did*. The first thing to examine is whether the agent even did that which we assume he did. Perhaps we have not correctly identified the action (i.e. the agent has not done what we thought he did). But let us assume here that we have identified the action correctly. The next question is: Why did he not omit this action instead? Let us assume that we can imagine that there were consequential reasons against committing the act. We ask the agent and he gives us a reason which we did not know about. It may be that that is the end of it – that is to say that between the agent and the outsider a consensus has been reached. But perhaps this is not the case – that is to say, the answer given did not satisfy the outsider; the situation makes him "suspicious." Can it really be that the reason given by the agent was the one which moved him to act as he did? Or is he hiding something from us?

Let us reconsider the example in which a person had promised to carry out a questionable act for which he also expected to receive a reward. We know that he made the promise and that he was aware of the prospect of a reward. Did he not then know that what he promised was something reprehensible? Yes, he says he was aware of that, "but a promise [p. 13/p. 14] is a promise." [He says further that] the prospect of a reward had nothing to do with the act. We are, however, not sure about that. How should we go about reaching a decision about this?

Maybe the case is quite clear: the agent is clearly lying about his motives. He knows very well that he kept his promise for selfish reasons and not because he had given a promise. If that is the case, then there is no contradiction between that which is self-evident to him on the one hand, and the explanation which the outsider is inclined to believe, on the other hand. They both implicitly share the same opinion; there is only a seeming lack of consensus.

But the situation can also be more complicated: Perhaps the agent is lying, not only to the outsider, but to himself as well; such things happen. He kept his promise for selfish reasons, but does not wish to admit it – not even to himself. Maybe he has misunderstood his own behavior and believes quite sincerely that he only did what he did because of the promise he made and not because of the reward he stood to reap for carrying out the act (although he was aware of it).

By what right, though, could the outsider assert that he knew the motives of the agent better than the agent himself? Perhaps he will cite knowledge, based on earlier experience, of the agent's character. He might say something like, "I have known him for ages and I know that he would only keep a promise if it served his own purposes. The moral duty to keep one's promises means nothing to him." This outsider sees this particular case, the deed which has been done, against the broad background of facts from the life of the agent. His explanation agrees more with that which we know about the agent than with the explanation we hear from the agent; besides that, the explanation of the outsider is more compatible with the agent's doings and his character.

The outsider's explanation gains in its power to convince if it is coupled with predictions. "Just you watch! Next time he makes a promise, he will not keep it unless it is to his advantage." This prognosis does not always prove itself true, but if it should often show itself to be true, it also indirectly supports the explanation posed by the outsider vis à vis the explanation given by the agent.

9. If the explanation of the outsider contradicts that of the agent, one thing that can happen is that the outsider admits – on the basis of additional discussion and in the light of new evidence or experience – that he was wrong [*im Unrecht*]. He had misunderstood the agent and his motives and perhaps asks to be excused. Such cases may be plentiful, but in general, they are of neither philosophical nor psychological interest.

The interesting cases in which conflict arises are those in which the outsider insists on his point of view and attempts to "convert" [*"bekehren"*] the agent to a new understanding of the situation. The outsider may say that, though the "mouth" of the agent says that he acted for reason *X*, his "heart" knows that he acted for reason *Y*. Maybe it will be possible to move him to confess the truth with his "mouth." [p. 14/p. 15]

In the background of this kind of reasoning is the notion of the acting subject (agent) as the highest authority regarding his own case: only the acting subject can directly see the truth of the matter. The outsider's evidence is always only indirect and external. For that reason, an agreement with the self-understanding of the agent (sometimes after it has been altered) is the decisive criterion for the correctness of any explanation of his actions.

What kinds of argument could the outsider use in his attempt to convert the agent? Merely persuading him would not be just. If the outsider were to succeed at this – it might merely mean that he had managed to "brainwash" the agent – how much would the agent's own understanding be worth as a basis for proof? Even in the cases when that understanding was not totally worthless [as evidence], we would still not be able unreservedly to assign to it the status of "highest authority" in the matter.

The rational arguments which the outsider might be able to rest his case upon would generally be the same ones that he would use in creating the basis for his own explanation – different from that of the agent – of the agent's action. He might, for example, attempt to move the agent to see his behavior in a broader "autobiographical" perspective. He might point to certain universally known events in the past, which the agent will not want or be able to deny. He would bring to the agent's attention the image he (the agent) has created in the eyes of others and ask him to reflect on that image, and what that image is based on, an image which the agent himself has created. Further, he might ask the agent to pay a closer attention to his future behavior and the motives for it.

There is an unclear boundary between reasonable argument and persuasion, between brainwashing and founded conviction. For this reason, we are justified in asking whether the status of "highest authority" can be assigned to the agent's understanding of himself in questions of truth when that understanding has been the product of such a conversion. Does not the opinion of the outsider carry as much, or even more, weight than the agent's own understanding?

Let us assume that a "conversion" has taken place. The agent says something like, "I admit that I did not keep my promise for the reason that I felt a moral obligation to keep it, but rather because I was expecting to enjoy a [personal] advantage for keeping it." Or, to return to the example of the invitation, he says, "The reason why I did not accept the invitation at *X*'s house was because I was uncomfortable with the possibility of running into *Z* while there; the meeting with *Y* could easily have been postponed to another time and using that as the reason for not coming to *X*'s house was only a [convenient] excuse." Further, let us assume that we do not doubt the sincerity of the agent's admissions; moreover, we rely on them.

At this point a philosophically significant question arises: How do we correctly *describe* what has happened? Ought we to say that the agent *now* sees the truth about himself? This truth was, so to speak, always present, only hidden behind the veil of the agent's self-deception. When the veil was torn asunder, then even the agent saw the truth which the outsider already believed to have seen – of course, without being absolutely sure of what he believed – until the agent confirmed the accuracy of his impression. Or should we say instead that the agent now sees his behavior in a *new* way, his self-awareness [p. 15/p. 16] having changed, and he came to a new understanding [*Verständnis*] of his past actions? In other words, the question is one of whether we should say that the connection between the action and its (real [*wirklich*]) reasons were always there and were only later discovered, *or* should we say that a new connection has been made.

I would like to call the reader's attention to the plethora of images and metaphors filling this talk about the truth. The truth was there, it could "be seen," but "in his heart" it was "veiled." When the agent was "converted," it was "revealed" to the agent, who is now able to recognize his "true self."

We are now entering into an area which could be called the "epistemology of psychoanalysis." A psychoanalyst might say that the super-ego of the agent indeed recognized the connection between motive and action from the outset, but that only by means of the psychoanalytical process could that knowledge be lifted out of the depths of the subconscious to the surface of consciousness, in order to be revealed to the ego which had repressed the knowledge. It is seductive to make use of such metaphors as the psychoanalytical metaphor of "layers or strata of consciousness," or the religious image of "conversion." These metaphors virtually force themselves on us; they are *good* images (metaphors) and, as such, they are "philosophically innocent." However, the danger is that they lead us into a *conceptual* mythology and mystification. The intention then is to build a theory of how the unconscious functions and how the various layers of the self (super-ego, ego and id) work together. Here is where the work of the philosopher begins. His job is to "de-mystify" these concepts and that means to describe findings in such a manner that one's thinking is no longer misled. This is, admittedly, a difficult task.

To understand in what respect it can be misleading to speak of the truth of an explanation for an action, we need to ask the following question: *What* was it that at first was "hidden" from the agent, which he later came to "see"? Answer: The connection between his action and the reason (or reasons), why he performed the action. But it is this connection (or bridge) which does not exist until the agent builds it in his understanding. This could also be called a "bridge of one's understanding" [*Selbstverstehens*], which must first be erected by the agent. Assuming that the agent is not engaging in an obvious lie, this connection, which he now "admits to," was not yet there when he performed the act. There was nothing to be seen "behind the veil." The object of his insight *came into being* the moment the veil was pierced.

As we have said, we assume here that the agent was not lying as he gavc his first explanation of his action, an explanation which the outsider found suspect and which the agent later retracted. If he was not lying, then he was sincere. But how can he have been sincere if he later admitted that his first explanation did not "hold water" [*nicht stichhaltig*]. If we choose to not see his "conversion" as the result of brainwashing, then we would therefore have to say that he could not have been entirely sincere. His new insight, after all, was not forced upon him, but rather it [supposedly] represents a genuine realization of what his earlier motives had been. Therefore, this genuine realization must have somehow been "in him" all along. He was, so to speak, half honest and half dishonest. How should such a circumstance be understood [p. 16/p. 17], or described?

Let us return again to the example of the promise. If we explain the action by saying that the agent expected to be rewarded for his deed, then this expectation must also have existed at the same time that the action was carried out. Otherwise we would not be able to state truthfully that the agent indeed had (also) this reason, in addition to others, for carrying out this action, regardless of its questionable character. He had to have known – perhaps based on earlier experience – that he could expect some reward or return of the favor from the one to whom he made his promise. It can be that he did not have this in mind at the moment of carrying out the action. Perhaps he had a "bad conscience" as he moved to carry out his reprehensible act; perhaps he had pushed the thought of a reward completely into the background, while [at the same time] convincing himself that he had to do the deed because of the *promise* he had made (and one ought to keep one's promises). This is more or less how such a description might sound in a case in which the agent is half sincere and half insincere in reflections upon his own actions. This description tells us in which sense we would be justified in asserting that the connection between the action and selfish motive existed from the very beginning, and not just after the agent's having had the insight about its existence.

For this reason, I say that in the case of what we are calling a "conversion," the agent connects his actions with their motivational background *in a new way* in his self-understanding [*Selbstverständnis*]. He understands himself and his action in a different way – not because new facts have come to his attention, but because he assembles already present facts into a new image. If we say that this new image is "more true" or that it bears a greater similarity to reality than the old one, that merely means that it better matches a more comprehensive assortment of facts concerning his life and character – facts in whose light the external judge of these events had [already] seen the action of the agent.

After all of this, what should we say about the position stated earlier that the agent himself is the highest authority when it comes to judging his own motives? I believe that we must concede that there is no compelling support for this position, once we have seen and admitted that the effect of a "conversion" does not lie in the agent's having discovered something about himself, but rather in the fact that there is now agreement in the evaluation, or explanation, of his actions.

This notion of the highest authority of the subject in such matters has a basis in experience which can, however, easily be misunderstood. As we have already said, the agent normally knows better than any outsider what he has done and what the reasons were for his doings. For that reason, the outsider who doubts or disapproves of the agent's explanations is generally dependent on information which only the agent is in a position to provide. The outsider must enter into a communicative speaking relationship with the agent. This is a necessary aspect of the process which I refer to as "conversion." This aspect is, however, not comprehensive. As anyone who "knows people" is aware, a person can disclose what is in him in ways other than verbal. What he does can contradict what he says. Clearly, the agent possesses the "key" to the meaning of his action. But it is also not necessarily the case that he is the most adept at using that key. It is perhaps the outsider who can use those keys [p. 17/p. 18] more skillfully to open the door to the soul's secret chamber; but not with absolute certainty. Neither the subject himself nor the outside observer can show compelling philosophical reasons to legitimize an exclusive claim to the highest authority in the explanation of actions.

10. To conclude, let us look into a case in which no consensus is reached. Both the agent and the outsider insist on their respective explanations of the action. Neither of them allows himself to be won over to the standpoint of the other. Does this mean that the case must remain undecided?

It is important to pay attention to what the word "undecided" means here. It means that no consensus is reached – *not* that already existing facts cannot be discovered. For this reason, one must ask which conditions must be fulfilled before one can say that there is an "agreement." This concept also has no *clear-cut* borders. Normally, it is enough that some [people] affirm a position and that no one contests that position. Is *one* divergent opinion sufficient to destroy the consensus? Not necessarily. To some "divergent opinions" we do not give much significance. We may have good reasons to push them aside and label them "eccentric," "notoriously unreliable," "not to be taken seriously," or even "insane." But could one really put aside the voice of the acting subject in such a manner as this? If we have denounced the myth of the highest authority of the subject, then it would seem that one can answer this question in the affirmative, at least in some extreme cases.

One such case would be when we determine that the agent is lying about his motives and actually shares our opinion regarding the correct explanation of his actions. Then there is only a seeming lack of consensus. But this case is, for that reason, of little interest.

Of greater interest are those cases in which we see the character of the agent as being so morally corrupt and perverse, or see his judgment as being weak and confused to such a degree that we judge his "explanations" of his own actions as being without value. We see him as incapable of giving an honest account of himself and therefore deny him the right to be the judge in his own case. Consensus regarding his behavior now depends exclusively on the opinions of outsiders. It is also very possible that all those who know about the matter and have taken a position regarding it have the same opinion as to the [correct] explanation [of the agent's actions]. The matter is seen herewith as decided, and this without the "input" of the agent.

There is no denying that such decisions are sometimes made. But there is something tragic about them. It is humiliating when an outsider judges himself to be the highest authority in matters concerning my inner life, while disregarding my own opinion in the matter. Such authority can be abused – for example, in order to force conformity of opinions. In the worst cases, this can lead to the grossest injustices in the treatment of a person. It would be in order – in this ominous year of 1984 – to bear these dangers in mind.

How much easier it would be to take a position in matters such as these if we could hold fast to the notion of an objective truth – a truth existing independent of how one [p. 18/p. 19] attempts to explain the motivations for his actions. It is characteristic of those who misuse their authority in order to repress a subject's opinions regarding himself to justify their abuse of authority by saying that they are acting in the name of a "higher" or "more scientific" truth – a truth which is to be forced upon the miscreant. It is also a part of the same picture, however, that those who resist such [misuse of] power and defend their own opinion, seek strength and comfort in the thought of an "inner" truth which is accessible to them alone. The insight that there is no such unqualified truth, either without or within, is the weapon with which we must fight against both the self-glorification of exaggerated subjectivity and the claims of a false objectivity.

Academy of Finland

Translated from the German by James Gilkeson

NOTES

1 Von Wright describes this kind of defect as "*körperlich (oder somatisch)*," both of which designations refer to the body: *Körper*=soma=body.

2 The word used here is *Gründe*: reasons. In the previous paragraph, the word was followed by "the motives and frame of mind in which the agent acted," and one suspects that this is the intention here as well, the context being the same.

3 The word used here is *adäquat*, which, like its cognate in English, implies that that which is done fulfills requirements, is sufficient, etc. I have inferred that such a response is also appropriate, meaning that it bears a significant congruency with that which is being responded to.

4 Literally, "rational reason."

5 Literally, "moving reason," as in, "It was for this reason that I was moved to act as I did."

6 The word used here is *aufgefasst*, which means that something has been consciously perceived, taken in, taken note of.

7 Beginning at 'between' the German reads: *zwischen **vorliegenden** (bestehenden, existierenden) und **wirksamen** Gründen* . . . .

8 The German words used are *überbestimmt* and *überdeterminiert*, which both translate directly and naively to "over-determined," which suggests that more than one sufficient reason exists for an action.

[9] Here, we have the same word, *Handlung*, which has been used all along and has generally been translated as "action." In all cases, whether I use "act" or "action," I am referring to a deed carried out by a person (here, for reasons), as opposed to "actions" which refer to movements which happen without there necessarily being persons (or reasons) behind them, such as mechanical actions (or reflex actions).

[10] ... *betreffende neurale Geschehnisse* ... literally, neural events regarding ..., or neural events with reference to ... but translated here as *pertinent* neural events. The idea I am reading into von Wright's words is that we are not taking all neural events into consideration, but rather specific ones which are relevant to the agent's action.

REX MARTIN

VON WRIGHT AND COLLINGWOOD ON CAUSATION AND THE EXPLANATION OF HUMAN ACTION

In my judgment R.G. Collingwood and Georg Henrik von Wright have done some of the most interesting and creative work, in our time, on the theory of action explanation and of causation. The present paper sets out to explore and contrast their main contributions in these areas.[1]

SECTION 1: ACTION EXPLANATIONS AS 'UNDERSTANDING' EXPLANATIONS

One of the standard kinds of explanation is that in which an action of an agent is accounted for by reference to certain thoughts and motivations that the agent has. Characteristically, such an explanation would go something like this: the agent does *A*, the deed performed, *because* (1) the agent is in a particular situation, in which he or she is motivated to act; (2) one of the courses of action the agent might take is the action *A*, (3) the agent has a purpose or end in view, (4) to resolve the situation by accomplishing such-and-so thing, and (5) doing *A* is judged by the agent to be a means to, or part of accomplishing, this purpose. We can call this schema the fundamental or basic schema for the explanation of actions done for a reason.

More complex schemas could, of course, be generated out of the basic one. We could do so by adding further details at one of the focal points – the agent's situation *cum* motivation, the agent's relevant purpose, or the deed performed – or along one of the lines of their connection. The point of any such attempt to move beyond the basic schema is to identify a set of conditions contextually sufficient to *explain*, upon reflection, the performance of a typical individual action, where that action is said to be "done for a reason." We can take some such schema, in a suitably amplified version, as the standard one for the purposes of this paper.[2]

An explanation of an individual action (in the account I am giving) is, then, an exemplification of the schema just developed. Such an explanation is afforded by substituting, under each condition of the schema, statements of fact that satisfy – in one way or another – the terms of that condition. Every such explanation breaks down, then, into two main parts: (a) the formal part as given in the schema itself and (b) a material one, represented by the statements of fact that satisfy the schema in a given case.

I want, now, to indicate a second dimension to this account, the dimension of understanding (or *Verstehen*). In his more recent writings, von Wright has

G. Holmström-Hintikka and R. Tuomela (eds.), Contemporary Action Theory. Vol. I, 21–43.

attempted to give *Verstehen* a constitutive role in his account of intentionalist explanations. This particular line of development reaches its fullest statement in his idea of an "understanding explanation."[3]

In this more recent work, von Wright has, in effect, bifurcated intentionalist explanations into two main kinds (or sub-schemas, if you will). One sub-schema follows, roughly, the means/end analysis he originally seemed to lean to (in his book). Here the sense – the only important sense – in which we *understand* a person's action is that, once we have the agent's actual *beliefs* in hand, then we can "see" or interpret (even if we had not been able to beforehand) the agent's action as a means to some particular end or goal.

In defense of this view von Wright has said, "[I]f we come to the conclusion that *he* really *believes* that he must do *A* in order to achieve *B* and that *B* is what he is after, then we also understand why he did *A*."[4] For, clearly, there is a sense in which we understand the agent's action in such a case; we understand it as a means to *B*. That is how we see it – as serving in that role. Accordingly, we can be said to understand why the agent did *A* (namely, to achieve *B*). Or, to put the point differently, we can explain the agent's doing *A* by referring to *B* (and to the agent's means/end belief).

However, the sense in which we *understand* a person's action in the *other* sub-schema von Wright had in mind is quite different from this. Here the agent's particular situation *cum* motivation is envisioned as a sort of "external impulse" or "demand" to which various possible alternative courses of action (including the action actually performed) are responses. But one does not understand these various courses of action by reference to the agent's *belief* that some (or one) of them would be responses to demands. Rather the onlooker or investigator here more or less directly "sees" or interprets these courses of action as responses – and does so without any intermediary agent's belief as an element (or necessary element) in the resultant interpretation.[5]

Von Wright appears to think that, of these two distinctive types of understanding, the response approach is the basic one.[6] It gets closer to how most actions happen, how they get started or come about in the first place. For not only particular deeds performed but also goals themselves (that is, the end states that are envisioned, in a specific goal or purpose, as something to be brought about or established) are typically responses to given situational demands.

Now, let us quickly complete the picture here. We will have a full "understanding explanation," then, when we go back to the first of von Wright's sub-schemas and pick up a crucial detail. Here the investigator identifies and relies on the agent's *belief* that the particular action performed was in fact a means to the end in view and interpolates that belief into the explanatory account, thereby filling the remaining gap in it.

At this point it would prove useful to turn to Collingwood. A convenient way, indeed perhaps the best way, of understanding Collingwood's idea of the explanation of action is to regard it as building on the very same schema we used in the case of von Wright. Here Collingwood laid special stress on judgments of intelligibility or plausibility.

If we were to put the matter in the way Collingwood put it, we would say that these judgments of intelligible connection allow us, once we have in mind a particular situational motivation and a particular purpose of the agent, to *re-enact* the agent's action. For we can see, with these points in mind and in the light of available evidence, that *one* of the courses of action – the deed actually performed – makes sense in the situation envisioned and its being done is plausible. Thus, we can successfully get to the deed performed, by citing thoughts and beliefs that the agent had, and in that sense re-enact it (in imagination).

For Collingwood, then, what must underwrite the claim that a given action *A* is a response to a demand is the intelligibility of that action in that role; likewise, what must underwrite the similar claim that a given action *A* is a means to an end, to a purpose or end in view of the agent, is the intelligibility of that action in *that* particular role. Thus, what underwrites these interpretative claims, in his view, is the *same* sort of thing in each case. There is no bifurcation here at all.

A fully successful (or fully satisfactory) intentionalist explanation of an individual action, in this Collingwoodian conception, is a special sort of exemplification of the standard schema mentioned earlier (and sketched out in note 2). Here the factual filler which provides the stuff of any given intentionalist explanation should not only instantiate one or another of the conditions of the schema (in an instantiation well supported by available evidence) but should do so in an intelligible or plausible way. This is provided for when three main points in the schema – that is, the agent's situation *cum* motivation, the agent's relevant purpose, and the deed performed – are satisfied by facts which are themselves *intelligibly* connected in the specific relationships they have with one another as, respectively, (a) a plausible thing to do in a particular situation, (b) a situationally responsive end in view, (c) an individual action that serves understandably as a means to that end (or as part of accomplishing it).[7]

Thus, to give an example: Caesar was faced with a lot of trouble from the British tribes (for they were engaged in raids and were causing unsettlement in the Gaulish world) and he wanted to put an end to this trouble, in order to facilitate his conquest of Gaul, so he invaded Britain to carry out an expedition against the tribes, hoping thereby to pacify them. The points identified here are connected with each other in the ways just prescribed. The end in view (the goal of pacifying Britain) is connected with Caesar's original motivating perception of the situation (as a troublesome unsettlement in the Gaulish world, stemming from the British incursions) in that it represents a responsive way of resolving that particular situation. And the action (Caesar's invasion) is an understandable means to the end in view, or part of accomplishing it. Finally, invading Britain is a plausible thing to do in view of the British incursions, a main feature of the unsettlement which Caesar hoped to quell.

In making coherence or intelligibility the central issue – as Collingwood has here, in the relations cited in points (a), (b), and (c) above – one is saying something over and beyond what the agent thinks (believes or intends) in the matter and, thus, over and beyond what the evidence might support as to the truth about agent beliefs and so on. For one is saying – to cite one possible case – not so much that the agent's action (e.g., Caesar's invasion) was *intended* to be part of, or a way of accomplishing, the agent's particular end but that it was intelligible to us, and presumably to any other serious inquirer, in that role. And the same could be said for the other intelligibility relations cited above.

A useful parallel might be noted here. An attempt at explanation which used false statements might count as schematically sound, but it would be clearly unsatisfactory or inadequate as an explanation. By the same token, we would have an explanation of sorts (where the relevant conditions were factually filled) even if the facts cited were *not* intelligibly connected in the specific relationships they have with one another along the various lines cited in (a), (b), and (c) above. Imagine here an action that does *not* serve *understandably* as a means to such-and-so end (or as part of accomplishing it).[8] Such an explanation would only be schematically sound; it would not be fully adequate or satisfying. For it would fall below a certain standard for "understanding explanations," that are given by having intelligible connections at all the appropriate points.

Now, let us consider in greater detail the case where the called-for "fit" or "coherence" was not present. For example, we might look at the explanation offered by an ancient Aztec priest for their practice of human sacrifice: the explanation that such ritual slaughter helped slow the decline of the universe and thus kept the present age (or eon) in existence. This, I surmise, is a case where deed and reason do not match up, where their conjunction in a means/end relationship, for example, seems at least to us "crazy, unintelligible, irrational."[9]

Clearly, von Wright allows for such cases. I mean cases where no consensus may exist, between agents and investigators, as to why the agent did the act in question; more particularly, cases where agents and investigators differed, not on the facts of the matter, but on whether certain facts, juxtaposed in certain specific relationships, are plausible or even intelligible in those relationships.[10]

As best I can make out, von Wright proposes to resolve these interesting non-consensus cases by turning to the idea that what we are after (in an explanation) is the *efficacious* reason,[11] the reason that *actually* makes the action occur.

Several things are involved, I think, in this emphasis on efficacious reasons. (i) That reason, whatever it might be, that was actually efficacious in the *performance* of an action is always to be chosen for purposes of explaining the action. (ii) Von Wright thinks efficacy can be modelled in two distinct ways (in accordance with his two sub-schemas). (a) In the one case, the efficacious reason is the agent's *belief* that a certain action is a way to accomplish such-and-so end; the belief here is efficacious, for, given the belief, the agent will do that thing to achieve the end intended. (b) In the other case, we try to have in view (on the basis of evidence) the agent's overall motivational background: the set of existing reasons for or against a given action. That reason (or balance of reasons) that *actually* moved the agent to perform the action is here the efficacious one. (iii) In any event, it is the agent's actual way of seeing or comprehending (*verstehen*) the action, and the reasons for it, that counts. For only this understanding allows "entry into the subjectivity involved with the act of understanding"[12] and hence, through *that* particular understanding (and only through that one), with the efficacious reason for the agent's deed. (iv) Thus, in the end, von Wright's account (especially in the sub-schema concerned with means/end beliefs) is tied to the perspective of agent's understanding. (v) Agent's understanding, as here characterized, is not the same as what the agent *reports*. For the agent can be lying or mistaken or even merely insufficiently self-conscious. The point, rather, is that to find the efficacious reason, the agent and the investigator always take one and the same perspective: they look to the agent's relevant means/end beliefs, in the one sub-schema; they look to the agent's existing motivational background, in the other. (vi) Von Wright's principal rationale for taking up this particular perspective is that it allows us more or less successfully to duplicate, at certain crucial points, the features of what might be called the standpoint of agency – of performative understanding.

But how does one know that the reason selected as efficacious is the one that *actually* figured in the agent's deed? Von Wright's answer here involves two claims. The first is that we use evidence of a certain sort: consideration is given to what the agent has said and done in the past (or has recently said and done, more or less at the time of acting), and consideration can be given to relevant things the agent says or does in the future. It is on the basis of evidence of this sort that one selects, from the agent's existing motivational background, that one reason which actually moved the agent in the case at hand. To this von Wright adds, as a way of achieving explanatory closure, the agent's relevant means/end belief (as attested to by evidence, of course).

But again one asks, how do we know *this*: how do we know that *this* is the reason that moved the agent? that *this* belief brought about the action in question? We come, then, to von Wright's second claim. There is, he says, no further fact that one can adduce to answer these questions. Rather, if the data used has been assembled as completely and carefully as possible on a basis of considering extensive relevant evidence and if, in so assembling, one can then achieve a continuity between deed and thought, a coherence or fit between them (of the sorts identified in the two sub-schemas), that is all there is to it. It is simply that we do *understand* the deed as done from these reasons. And this understanding (with the firm evidential base on which it rests kept in full view) is what warrants the claim that the agent actually acted for these reasons.[13]

It is not so much that efficacy claims are *true* (for this suggests some pre-existing matter of fact that we could find, a real connection out there somewhere) but, rather, that they are warranted – by understanding. Here it is not the case that understanding is itself certified for use by its attachment to efficacy (where efficacy is a matter that can be independently established – by neurology, for example). Rather, it is the very opposite: here claims to efficacy are themselves warranted, in von Wright's view, by the sheer fact of understanding (as spelled out in his two sub-schemas) – and the base of evidence on which it rests.[14] This is the only support these claims have, or can have.

We have no guarantee, in understanding so conceived, that investigator and agent will always agree in given cases on the reasons for deeds (and this brings us back to the non-consensus case from which we started). Most often they will agree, however, and that is an end on it.

But sometimes they will not. Here another party attempts to overrule the agent's own account: the onlooker says, "No, you didn't act for the reason you profess but for another; you acted for *this* reason, as the evidence of your overall behavior suggests." Perhaps an impasse results. The one can then try to "convert" the other, at the time or later on (even in the history books), but this may not avail.[15]

The point is, neither the agent nor the investigator is the court of last appeal, or the highest authority; neither has nor can have a uniquely privileged and infallible access to the truth, to *the* correct understanding. Rather, in the end, we must rely simply on understanding (and the firm evidential base on which it rests); rely, that is, on an understanding of the sort that is *typically* but not always shared between agents and investigators, as the warrant for efficacy claims.

These remarks do not solve the problem of non-consensus; they simply locate the problem, indicating how it might be resolved. They tell us where to look – to the agent's existing motivational background and stock of means/end beliefs – and they suggest the sort of resolution we seek.

At this point I think we have arrived at that which principally serves to separate the views von Wright and Collingwood have taken on understanding. Von Wright is concerned with efficacious reasons; and because he is, he is committed to the perspective of agent's understanding – to the perspective of the agent's existing motivational background and relevant means/end belief(s). If challenged, he would likely say: but it is the way the agent *actually* understands things, the agent's efficacious reason (as exhibited, for example, in the agent's means/end belief), that brings about the deed.

Collingwood, on the other hand, was more concerned with explanatory reasons; and, because he was, he was committed to the view that the reasons used in an explanation must be intelligible to the investigators (to those who are in the explanatory mode, as givers or as receivers of explanations).[16] Explanations that do not exhibit intelligible connections in this regard (that are not re-enactible by investigators) are not satisfactory as explanations of action.

If challenged, Collingwood or, rather, the defender of Collingwood might say something like the following: performing an action and explaining it are two different things. A person can perform an action even where intelligibility of connection fails, for crazy people do act; and actions can be done that *we* do not understand (by people in another culture, say). What we cannot do, however, is have a *satisfactory* explanation of action where intelligibility of connection fails for the explainers. For where re-enactibility is not exhibited or not present, an explanation is simply not intelligible. Though it may be an explanation of sorts (in fulfilling the terms of the schema, say) it nonetheless falls below a certain standard. For a proper explanation of an action should yield intelligibility. We want explanations which are satisfactory by *that* standard.

One main difference between von Wright's position and Collingwood's, then, is the perspective each takes up. In von Wright's case (certainly in the means/end sub-schema, and in the other sub-schema as well), it is the perspective of the agent and the efficacious reason for the agent's action. In Collingwood's, it is the perspective of persons in an explanatory mode. Significantly, Collingwood described such persons as engaged in re-enactment. For *re-enactment* (note the name) is something *investigators* attempt to achieve; it is something they achieve when they use intelligibly connected reasons in an effective way, so as to afford plausibility in an explanation.

Neither perspective here identified is *the* correct one (just as neither is wrong); they are compatible, in fact. It would be well if they could be brought together more completely, then.

It may prove, though, that the various strategies we employ do not readily lead to an consensus between agents and investigators. What then? The situation is not irretrievable on the basis Collingwood has provided.[17] But it may well be irretrievable on the one von Wright provided – that is, if we insist, as he has done, on the primacy of efficacious reasons, as determined from the agent's perspective, in non-consensus cases.

My assessment of the main differences between Collingwood and von Wright can now be summarized briefly. First, von Wright bifurcated the notion of understanding, Collingwood (by contrast) attempted to give a unified account. Second, Collingwood's account of understanding was different from von Wright's (most clearly so from the account where von Wright emphasized the agent's means/end *belief* as the key to *one* of his two kinds of understanding). Collingwood would, I think, regard von Wright's emphasis here as simply inappropriate – in that using the agent's means/end *belief* might not yield intelligibility to anyone (not even to the agent, upon reflection). Finally, the perspective each occupied was different: in von Wright's case it is the perspective of the agent and the efficacious reason for the agent's performance of an action, as seen from that perspective; in Collingwood's, it is the perspective of persons in an explanatory mode who are thereby using re-enactible (that is, intelligibly connected) reasons.

These differences are crucial, especially the latter two. And we have or may have good reasons to prefer Collingwood's stance on both these points. Thus, the first difference (the unified versus the bifurcated account) could be resolved as well, along the lines Collingwood has suggested.

Von Wright's bifurcation of ways of understanding is really quite arbitrary, in my judgment. It is simply not necessary to think that the means/end relationship is always and necessarily mediated by a belief of the agent. That relationship can be established in exactly the same way as was a response to a demand: we can straightforwardly see or interpret a given action as a means to an end, without the mediation of an agent's means/end belief.

The problem runs deeper than this, though. The problem is that von Wright's account of understanding, as modeled in the two sub-schemas, is bivalent. Thus, each of his senses of 'understanding' can work against the other and (in so doing) can threaten to take over the domain that the other sense ostensibly controls. It might be the case, for example, that the kind of intelligibility identified with the "response" sub-schema could become completely dominant, thereby suppressing the emphasis found in the *other* sub-schema on certain beliefs of the agent, while at the same time undermining reliance on the sort of understanding such beliefs can yield. Conversely, the other or means/end belief schema might come to predominate totally, thus requiring reliance on mediating beliefs at other specific points as well (for example, such beliefs as the more or less self-conscious one, on the part of the agent, that a certain end in view is a suitable response to a given situational "demand"). And that change would underwrite a wholesale deployment of the notion of understanding characteristic of the means/end belief schema and, with it, the abandonment of the kind of intelligibility identified in the "response" sub-schema. The point is that the approach in each of these sub-schemas is equally eligible in von Wright's account, so the tension I have described can never be tamped down completely. The bifurcation von Wright suggests, then, is both arbitrary and unstable. But this particular tension, I have already noted, is not present in

Collingwood's account and would not be a problem there.

What I want to show next is that one can map the notion of causation (that is, of contributory causation in the special case of a singular event) onto the account of explanation given in the present section. At least, we can do so with one plausible analysis of causation, as developed by Morton White and Donald Davidson.

SECTION 2: AN ANALYSIS OF CONTRIBUTORY CAUSATION

In this analysis of causation there are two leading ideas: (1) that of a sound explanatory argument in which (2) the elements named as part of the explanation are *necessary* for that set of factors to be sufficient to account for the occurrence of some particular event or action or state of affairs (which is then said to be explained). Explanatory elements that pass this test – in being necessary parts of a given sound explanatory argument – can be designated contributory causes of that particular event (or action or state of affairs) which they explain. Let me emphasize, in passing, that this two-part analysis of contributory causation (in the case of a particular event or deed) is intended only as a partial explication of that particular notion of causation.[18]

The idea of a sound explanatory argument is basic in this analysis. By a 'sound argument' here I mean a valid argument with *true* premises, premises that are contextually sufficient to account (explanatorily) for the occurrence of *e*.

In this regard, then, logical entailments are sufficient (that is, sufficient for the conclusion to be drawn that some event or action or state of affairs *e* has occurred,), as are "deductive, nomological arguments" based on strict general laws. (The well-known phrase is, of course, Hempel's.)

The *instantiation* model of explanation discussed in section 1 (where a very general schema or formula for the explanation of a particular singular action is said to be exemplified by a specific set of matters of fact) has this same trait in common with both the above models: that the set of instantiating matters of fact are sufficient for the conclusion (here "the action *e* is done") to be drawn.

Even statistical arguments are not ruled out, as regards sufficiency. That is, they may not be ruled out if they are, so to speak, fully explanatory, as they might well be at the quantum level or where some notion of randomness was operating as essential.

Thus, a number of eligible possibilities present themselves under the heading of sufficiency. But, as I said earlier, the idea that bears the weight, in the end, is that of an *explanatory* argument; hence the controlling idea is going to be *explanatory* sufficiency. Can we use that particular idea to tighten the analysis and to further restrict these possibilities?

To focus attention we ask, then: What is a sound *explanatory* argument? At this point, in order to indicate the drift of things, I will provide just one (necessary) condition for what is to count as an explanatory argument. Here I rely on the simple claim that we *cannot* explain *p* by *p* (that is, by an explicit or syntactic redundance). If this is so, it is also the case, then, that we cannot explain that the agent "does *A*" by a set of conditions which themselves imply or logically entail "does *A*" (on the basis, for example, of the *meaning* of one or more of the conditions in the presence of the other conditions).[19] And here we have a convincing reason – I would think a conclusive one – for thinking that the relationship between initial conditions and the event to be explained (or "conclusion") in an explanatory argument must be such that it is *logically* possible that when the conjunct set of initial conditions is true, the statement "does *A*" *could* be false.[20]

Interestingly, both von Wright and Collingwood (each for his own reasons) can plausibly be taken as holding that there is such a relationship of logical *independence*, in the standard schema, between the set of initial conditions and the action *A*. Or, in a somewhat different language, each can be taken as holding that the connection of these elements is contingent, synthetic, or Humean, and not analytic.[21]

So, the beginnings of a plausible case have been made for saying that the schema developed in the first section fits the pattern of sound explanatory arguments required (according to the analysis developed so far in the present section) for attributions of contributory causation in the case of particular actions.[22]

Thus, if we had a particular sound explanatory argument in hand, then we could say of *any* one of the singular matters of fact cited as explanatory (say, Caesar's disposition to curb hostile incursions by the British tribes) that it was an initial condition in an argument with "Caesar invades Britain" as its conclusion. This would license our saying, then, on the analysis developed in this section, that Caesar's disposition as described was a *contributory cause* of Caesar's invasion of Britain.

One distinct virtue of this analysis is that it does not require (or imply) the existence of a *law* as the first premise and ground of each and every "sound explanatory argument" and, hence, of every causal attribution. Indeed, talk of causation does not imply the presence of general laws – either directly (as Hempel and von Wright seem to think) or indirectly (as White and, perhaps, Davidson seem to think). There is no implication from causation to such laws whatsoever – at least in the present analysis.[23]

This conclusion and the one reached earlier about Humean connection are crucial to the setting of my overall argument. For, first, if the relation of elements in the standard schema – as between the set of initial conditions and the action performed (*A*) – were not one of logical independence, then there could not possibly be a causal relation between them. And, second, if the analysis of causation developed in this paper actually did imply the existence of a law (or, more generally, if all talk of causation did imply the existence of a law, in some form), then it could not apply to the crucial case of action explanations we are here contemplating. For like von Wright I am convinced that the practical inference (PI) schema is not disconfirmable in principle and, hence, is *not* a general law. Thus, so long as we stay with the PI account of action explanations I have been using (as in section 1), any commitment to the claim that causation necessarily involves general laws would in and of itself prohibit our talking of the instantiating elements in such explanations as *causes* of the action. For the PI schema, I repeat, is not a general law and hence (were such a commitment ever admitted) could not be a causal principle either. This, in my view, is the hinge point on which the issue turns. Clearly, then, *both* the key conclusions I have identified are necessary in order to sustain my claim that the thought-factors of agents can be causes of their deeds.

Interestingly, Collingwood (unlike von Wright) did not appear to think that talk of reasons (in the form of thoughts and motivations of an agent) as causes of actions was out of place. Thus, the position I have sketched (and that I have myself come to rather belatedly, I must confess) is one that Collingwood held all along.

In his book on metaphysics, Collingwood identified three senses of the word 'cause'; two of these will concern us here. Sense I, he says, is typical of history: "here that which is 'caused' is the free and deliberate act of a conscious and responsible agent and 'causing' him to do it means affording him a motive for doing it."[24]

Sense II, in contrast, is typical of what Collingwood called "the practical sciences of nature" (e.g., engineering or medicine): "here that which is 'caused' is an event in nature, and its 'cause' is an event or state of things by producing or preventing which we can produce or prevent that whose cause it is said to be." The leading idea here is that of a means/end relationship: the means is typically an action; the end, then, is some natural event or state of affairs which, directly or indirectly, is brought about or suppressed (as the case may be) by that action.[25]

A brief comment on the first of Collingwood's two main senses is in order. Collingwood allowed for what might be called two-agent causes under his sense I.

These two-agent causes (e.g., a "solicitor's letter [which] causes a man to pay a debt" or Iago's promptings to Othello) introduce an interesting wrinkle into the analysis. For they do not precisely conform to the standard case, under sense I, where an agent's action is said to be caused by certain factors *internal* to the agent's thought (situational motivation and relevant purpose, in particular). Here, instead, person two's *deed* is said to be a cause of person one's action. Thus, we have a connected or iterated sequence of actions, where the action that resulted from the *first* agent's thoughts and motivation (say, Iago's) helps set the stage by configuring the situation in which the *second* agent stands and, ultimately, acts – and acts with a certain definite result (say, Othello's killing of his wife).[26]

Further and, perhaps, more interesting these two-agent (or, if you will, second-agent) cases of causation are very like those which Collingwood developed under his *second* sense of causation. They have crucial features in common: in each, an act of an agent is said to produce or prevent a deed or an event or a datable state of affairs on the part of another agent or another thing. In fact, if we did not restrict sense II to causes of "events in nature," then there would appear to be no real difference between sense II causes and second-agent causes (under Collingwood's first sense).[27]

Now, initially, Collingwood had grouped simple practical inferences and iterated practical inferences together. Something else, then, must be involved here than merely the putative *senses* of 'cause' that he invoked.

I would suggest that Collingwood initially grouped simple practical inferences and iterated practical inferences together *because* they rely on one and the same model of explanation (and do so exclusively). These things belong together for *this* reason, and not because they exhibit the same sense of 'cause' (for they probably do not, at least not in Collingwood's account of these senses and if we take the means/end relationship as the core of his second sense).

Thus, we might accept Collingwood's initial grouping here but not his ostensible reason for it. To get to a plausible reason for that grouping we would have to shift from what he explicitly alleged was its basis (as given in the notion of certain definite senses of the term 'cause') to something else that he probably had foremost in view (that they had in common a single more or less uniform model of explanation).

By that same criterion, then, actions which are a means to some effect *e*, where *e* is an event in *nature* should be separated out. For instance, the causal model for the destruction of Hiroshima would build on a practical inference explanation for the *dropping* of the bomb, but the bomb's subsequently exploding and the ensuing devastation of the city would have to be explained in a wholly different way (presumably by reference to laws of nature). Unlike simple or iterated practical inferences, such explanation patterns rely on the conjunction of two distinct explanatory models. And one of these models (the one that involves a focal use of natural laws) is radically different from the model of re-enactible practical inferences.[28]

Others, though, such as William Dray, have tended to stick with Collingwood's apparent informing idea (the idea of putatively different senses of 'cause') and have tended to emphasize his *second* or means/end sense of causation (and have done so almost exclusively, while largely ignoring his crucial first sense, on which the second is built). Thus, they have advocated the view that for Collingwood causes are manipulable changes, changes brought about through human intervention that are, in turn, the means to certain effects.[29]

I do not think this focus on manipulable changes, effected by human agents, will work as an explication even of causes in Collingwood's sense II. For Collingwood does allow *some* cases (under this sense) in which the causal action is not a *human* action (is not a case of human agency). Thus, he says (as an example of a sense II cause) that "the cause of malaria is the bite of a mosquito."[30]

In any event, this particular sense of causation (so-called sense II) cannot be taken as basic, contrary to what Dray suggests, for it depends on the notion of an action (a human action). And actions, for Collingwood, have sense I causes (as captured in the notion of re-enactible practical inferences). Even if we allowed that some of these actions are actually the results of two-agent causes we would still need the notion (or would need to allow for the notion) that sometimes the initiating agent (e.g., Iago) in a two-step sequence of actions acted without themselves being caused so to act by yet another initiating agent, further up the line, so to speak. In other words, some actions are explainable as simple practical inferences and some of these, in turn, can be means to which some *e* (either an event in nature or some other agent's action) is an end. And where this is so, sense *two* causes can't be regarded as basic for they rely on actions not themselves caused along sense II lines.[31]

In any event, even if we focussed on two-agent causes, it is unlikely we would want to assimilate the first agent's action to a manipulable "handle" by which that agent brings about or prevents the occurrence of an action (with further effects) performed by some second agent. Certainly, Collingwood would be reluctant to take such a reductive view: to regard all second-agent actions, in a wholesale way, as simply manipulated effects of first-agent actions. What he might say of events in nature he would certainly not be willing to say, typically, of human actions.

For on Collingwood's view human beings thinkingly respond to their situations. They can moderate their motivations within the same sort of situation and are capable of engendering a variety of ends in view and even actions performed with respect to a given situation. They can often find different ways to act in achieving their ends. People generally are not the passive objects of someone else's manipulations.

It should be noted, finally (and here we turn to a direct consideration of sense I causes), that the thoughts of agents, in terms of which we explain their actions, are not themselves typically described as manipulable interventions by those selfsame agents. For that which is thought – the content of those thoughts – is not the performance of an action (with some intended end in view) nor the direct result of such an action. To think otherwise is to plunge into an infinite regress and into a deep error, confusing the beliefs and motivations of agents in a wholesale way with intentional actions they perform or with the results of those actions.

We must allow, of course, for cases of what might be called "thinking to some purpose" (as I am doing now in writing this essay) and even for cases of auto-suggestion and self-help motivational rehearsals by agents. These are special cases, but not the general rule. For it is not logically possible that *all* the thoughts of agents could be understood on the model of such self-initiated manipulable interventions.

For a variety of reasons, then, I do not believe that the notion of *manipulability* through human action should be singled out as the root idea; it is too narrow a notion to play this role and is, in any event, but a special case of the more general idea that Collingwood emphasized in discussing contributory causes of particular events or actions or states of affairs. I mean the idea of intervening changes.

It is this notion, then, that I take to lie at the core of a Collingwoodian conception of singular causation. It is a notion that would cover the two main senses and the two main explanatory models we have identified in Collingwood's discussion. It is what these types of causation have in common and what they focus on.[32]

Collingwood's view, that such causes are changes which intervene in a situation, can be contrasted to von Wright's understanding of the matter. For von Wright, unlike Collingwood, does emphasize *manipulable* changes, changes that can be effected (perhaps can only be effected) through *human* intervention.

Von Wright begins from the same point as Collingwood, in supposing that causes are intervening changes. But after that von Wright veers off in a different direction of his own.

He reasons as follows here. Change of some sort intervenes (or is imagined as intervening) in a situation. If the expected occurrence of some event *e* was prevented by that intervention, say by removing some factor *c*, we can say that *c* was necessary (under the test of omission) for a given set of conditions to be sufficient for *e*. Or, if we add *c* and then *e* did occur (when without the addition of *c*, it would not have), then we can say that *c* was necessary (under the test of introduction) for a given set of conditions to be sufficient for *e*.[33]

In von Wright's view these tests, of introduction and omission (as just described), are crucial tests for identifying causes. They are tests *we* can perform. He concludes then, from the important role played by such tests (and their character as performable), that the idea of intervention *through human action* is part of the *concept* of causation.[34]

But, clearly, this is not so. For the concept of a cause can be stated (as was done in the partial analysis summarized at the beginning of the present section) without reference, explicit or implicit, to such manipulable interventions.

Moreover, many of the crucial interventions – as indicated in the tests for *establishing* causal claims – need not be conceived as actions or as possible actions.[35] They can as readily be played out in imagination or in a simulation; they need not involve real performances by real agents in the world.

Indeed, in order to allow for talk of contributory causes in nature – where human action has not intervened, or *could* not intervene – we need to be clear that the tests (under which the causal determinations are to be established) must not reduce to saying that we, or some other human being, can actually bring about or omit the change that, in turn, produces or prevents some event or state of affairs.

I have argued, in sum, that an interventionist account of causation, as both von Wright and Collingwood have developed it, does not imply intervention (that is, intervening changes) through human action. For Collingwood, in contrast to von Wright, while holding to an interventionist account of causation (thus occupying ground they had in common), did not think that such accounts implied that causal interventions were necessarily performances or manipulable interventions by human agents.

And Collingwood, again unlike von Wright, did not think talk of causes implied the existence of laws. Thus, he was quite willing to describe the thoughts and motivations of human agents as contributory causes of the particular deeds they did, and he was quite willing to describe re-enactible practical inference explanations as themselves causal.[36]

Thus, Collingwood (given these differences) could go on to explore an issue that von Wright could not even allow to be considered. Collingwood could explore the sense in which thoughts – reasons – of agents could be contributory causes of their actions.

Let me suggest very briefly how such an exploration might go. Here, thoughts could count (or be allowed to count) as contributory causes of actions insofar as they exemplify relevant terms of the schema (as credibly supported by the available evidence). But they are explanatory of actions (in accordance with the standards set by re-enactment) only if, in addition, these thoughts and other elements, in certain designated relations they have to one another, are intelligibly connected. When this criterion of intelligible connection is satisfied, we can refer to such thoughts as reasons for the action. Accordingly, the very thoughts here designated reasons for action (as satisfying the criterion of intelligible connection) can also be designated contributory *causes* of action (as intelligibly connected instantiations of something – the schema – which is itself a causal principle).

Von Wright's work, like Collingwood's, is not particularly easy to grasp in the areas we have been examining, the areas of understanding (or intelligibility) in action explanations and of causation. I have, accordingly, sought to locate the thought of each on these matters more precisely by putting it in close relation to that of the other. Letting their ideas play against one another, in this way, should make the views of each of them clearer to us.[37]

Department of Philosophy, University of Kansas and
Department of Politics, University of Wales Swansea

NOTES

[1] So far as von Wright is concerned, the paper concentrates on certain themes first raised in his important book *Explanation and Understanding*. Ithaca, NY: Cornell University Press, 1971 [hereafter: EU]. In particular, I want to examine one fairly recent development in his thinking on these themes: the idea of what he calls "understanding explanations" ('verstehende Erklärungen'), an idea developed in two papers in 1985 and further developed in a paper in 1989. (The papers cited here are G.H. von Wright, "Sulla Verità Delle 'Spiegazioni' Comprendenti" ["On the Truth of 'Understanding' Explanations"], pp. 127–135 in F. Bianco. Editor. *Dilthey e il Pensiero del Novecento* [*Dilthey and the Thought of the Nineteenth Century*]. Milan: F. Angeli, 1985 [hereafter: D]; "Probleme des Erklärens und Verstehens von Handlungen" [Problems in the Explanation and Understanding of Actions], *Conceptus* 19 (1985), 3–19 [hereafter: C]; "Das Verstehen von Handlungen – Disputation mit Georg Meggle" ["The Understanding of Actions ..."] in *Rechtstheorie* 20 (1989), 3–37 [hereafter: R], at pp. 7–8, 12–17, 24–30, 35–37.)

It is the last named of these papers that I will emphasize in my account of "understanding explanations." I should add that the term 'understanding explanation' is also used in von Wright's "Of Human Freedom," pp. 107–170 in S.M. McMurrin. Editor. *The Tanner Lectures in Human Values* vol. VI. Cambridge: Cambridge University Press; Salt Lake City, UT: University of Utah Press, 1985 [hereafter: TL], at p. 136. (And for discussion see esp. part I, sects. 7–16, pp. 128–147.) TL (shortened, with all but sect. 8 of those sections omitted) and C and R are reprinted (in German) in von Wright's recent book *Normen, Werte und Handlungen* [*Norms, Values and Actions*]. Frankfurt am Main: Suhrkamp, 1994, in sect. III, pp. 141–255.

[2] Thus, the resultant schema I have in view might read as follows: The agent did *A* (the deed performed) *because* (1) the agent perceived that he or she was in a certain situation and was disposed to act toward it in some definite way; (2) there were a number of alternative courses of action (designated *A*, *B*, *C*, *D*, and so on) open to the agent who had the situational motivation described in (1); (3) the agent did want to achieve or accomplish such-and-so end, which (4) the agent believed would satisfy his or her initial situational motivation; (5) the agent believed that doing *A* was, in the circumstances already described, a means to accomplishing the stated purpose in (3) or a part of achieving it; (6) there was no action other than *A*, which action was believed or seen by the agent to be a means to the goal, that the agent preferred or even regarded as about equal; (7) the agent had no other purpose which overrode that of accomplishing such-and-so; (8) the action to be taken was timely and, when the time was ripe, the agent had not forgotten the relevant purpose, overlooked the time, or what have you, and (9) the agent knew how to do *A*, was (generically) able to do it, and physically able to do it in the situation as given and, at the timely moment, had the opportunity, and so on.

This schema, as will become clear as we proceed, draws upon both von Wright and Collingwood.

[3] There are intimations of what von Wright later came to call "understanding explanations" in his pre-1985 writings, most especially in "The Explanation and Understanding of Action," *Revue Internationale de Philosophie* 135 (1981), 127–142 (reprinted in von Wright, *Practical Reason. Philosophical Papers*, vol. 1. Oxford: B. Blackwell, 1983 [hereafter: PR]). See sects. 14–16 esp.

[4] I quote from a letter he sent me, dated 29 August 1990 [hereafter: L1990]. See also C, p. 5; R, pp. 14–15.

[5] The idea of the agent's situation *cum* motivation as a "demand" or "challenge" to which an agent then responds by acting is developed most fully in C; see sects. 2–4. Much the same ground is covered in von Wright's article "An Essay on Door-Knocking," *Rechtstheorie* 19 (1988), 275–288 [hereafter: Door-K], at pp. 275–277, 280–283, 286–287 in particular; see also R, pp. 15–17, 24, and TL, p. 129.

For the point about simply understanding or "seeing," see Door-K, p. 277; R, pp. 25–26.

[6] See R, p. 17.

[7] I am here summarizing what I take to be Collingwood's account of understanding or intelligibility in action explanations. I have based my view of Collingwood here, principally, on what he says in his book *The Idea of History* (T. M. Knox [ed.]. New York, New York: Oxford University Press, 1956; originally published Oxford: Oxford University Press, 1946 [hereafter: IH]), in part V, chs. 1–5.

[8] Consider, for example, a peasant who, having inflicted a knife wound (accidentally) on his own leg, proceeds to clean the knife meticulously while leaving the wound itself totally unattended. Here the facts, as described, are not intelligibly related to one another in the relationship of means (cleaning the knife)/end (getting the wound to heal) – even though we could affirm that they apparently stand in that relationship (on the basis, for example, of what the agent reports). For discussion, see my book *Historical Explanation*. Ithaca, NY: Cornell University Press, 1977 [hereafter: HE], at pp. 88–89.

Another example, of failure of intelligible connection, is offered in the next paragraph of the present paper.

[9] The quoted phrase is found in L1990, p. 2.

[10] Von Wright makes precisely such a point in the paragraph that continues from R, p. 35 onto p. 36. See also D, p. 133, and C, p. 10.

[11] R, p. 25. See also C, pp. 9, 12, and TL, pp. 135, 137.

[12] R, pp. 29–30. See also D, p. 134.

[13] For the main argument here see C, sect. 7. Von Wright describes his account of understanding explanations (in R, p. 24, D, p. 135, and elsewhere) as a coherence theory of understanding (*Kohärenztheorie des Verstehens*). What he particularly had in mind, I surmise, is that there is a "fit" or "matching," a coherence, if you will, between deed and reason (R, p. 25). Thus, he says (using this time the notion of a "consensus in the understanding" to describe a coherence of agreed-upon facts): "The 'subjectivity of understanding' does not make the explanations arbitrary. Every attempted explanation ought to respect the *facts* of the case: that there existed such and such reasons for, and perhaps also against, the action and that an action which matches the proposed description actually took place. But when these facts are established, agreed upon, there is no further fact in addition to the consensus in the understanding which establishes that the action took place for *that* reason and not for that other one. *Finis*" (in a letter to me of 30 July 1993 [hereafter: L1993], pp. 1–2).

[14] Thus, "That which links an action with one or more reasons [*Gründen*] is simply the fact that we *see* or *understand* [*verstehen*] the action as having arisen from these reasons. We see the action 'in the light of' particular reasons – and it is in this [fact of] seeing or understanding that the 'effectiveness' [or 'efficacy'] of these reasons lies" (R, pp. 25–26). See also D, p. 130; C, p. 12.

And again: "[T]he position was taken in the moment of recognition [from context: in the moment of the actor's acknowledgment of it], and it is not until this moment that the connection of reason and action is created" (R, p. 29). See also R, p. 27; D, pp. 132, 134; C, pp. 12, 16; TL, 143–144.

"What I am saying amounts to this: The effectiveness/ efficacy of these reasons or motives [*Beweggründe*] cannot be separated from the recognition and acknowledgment of them in the process of taking a *comprehending position* [*verstehende Stellungnahme*]. The truth of an explanation of action is created together with and is identical to the position taken to the reasons for acting. This position is not 'complete' or 'closed' [*'fertig'*] until it is recognized [that is, until this sort of recognition has occurred]" (R, p. 29). See also D, pp. 132–134; C, pp. 18–19; TL, p. 137.

But von Wright notes, "I'm afraid many would consider my position much too 'subjectivist' when it makes *understanding* itself the criterion of truth of explanations" (L1990, p. 2). See also D, p. 130; C, p. 12; R, p. 26; TL, p. 137.

In a subsequent letter to me (L1993) von Wright returned to the same theme with the following observation: "There is an aspect of my idea about 'understanding explanations' ... which to me seems crucial – though probably very hard to digest for most explanation theorists. It is this: One cannot separate the *truth* of the explanation from the very *act of understanding* itself. The 'efficacious' reasons for an action are those in the light of which the action is understood or explained." See also C, p. 12; TL, p. 143.

15 Von Wright regards such cases of disagreement as possible ones, but not as typical: "Usually the agent himself relates his action to the same reason for doing it as most outside observers of his conduct. But sometimes there is a disagreement – and neither the agent nor the observer can be 'converted' to see (understand, explain) the action in the same way. Sometimes the observers are unanimous and the agent is 'judged,' praised or blamed, sentenced or acquitted on the basis of their understanding of him" (L1993, p. 1). See also D, pp. 133–134; C, sects. 8–10; R, pp. 28–29; TL, pp. 134, 139–141.

16 By intelligible I mean, of course, what I said in the paragraph in the text to which note superscript 7 is appended.

17 What we would need, to supplement Collingwood's theory, though, is a further theory of how actions (in other times or other cultures) might be understood (or, better, come to be understood) even in non-consensus cases. See here my paper, "The Problem of Other Cultures and Other Periods in Action Explanations," *Philosophy of the Social Sciences* 21 (1991), 345–366 [hereafter: POC]. (The Aztec example is discussed there, at some length.)

Investigators, in Collingwood's view, are trying to provide an internal understanding, one that tracks and is ultimately faithful to the agent's own thoughts. Sometimes, though, the agent's thoughts may have to be redescribed (perhaps extensively so) to achieve re-enactibilty. And often, even then, investigators may need to learn to think in new ways in order to track the thoughts of agents. But in no case does the investigator desert the perspective of investigator. To try to "become" the agent would be pointless, for then one would simply be acting (and not even trying to explain). Nor does the investigator attempt to "duplicate" the agent's thought; for if the agent's thought is already explanatorily opaque (as, by hypothesis, it is here, as in the Aztec or the knife/wound example), then reproducing it accurately will not result in something intelligible to the investigator, something the investigator can re-enact. In the end, the thought of the agent and that of the investigator are separate and may even be distinctive; what a successful re-enactment can achieve, in those cases that remain irreducibly disparate, is a "fusion of horizons" (in Gadamer's phrase). For discussion see POC, pp. 362–363 and n. 8 on p. 365.

My point here, then, is that Collingwood's theory is open to the resolution I have just been describing, but von Wright's really is not (as I now go on to suggest, in the text).

18 Let me put the two central ideas in this partial explication more formally now, as follows:

> A statement of the form "some event or thought or state of affairs *c* is a contributory cause of an event or state of affairs *e*" is true if and only if (1) there *exists* a sound explanatory argument containing "C" as a premise and "E" as its conclusion and (2) *c* (the thing named in "C" as having happened, obtained, or held good) is, among the particular set of facts named in the premise set, *necessary* for the set to be a sufficient condition for the occurrence of *e* (i.e., the particular thing named in "E" as having happened, obtained, or held good). ...

My formulation, based on White's, differs from his in two main particulars. I speak of a "sound explanatory argument," he of an "explanatory deductive argument." His analysis of singular contributory causation is roughly equivalent to (1), with the change just noted, but does not include (2).

It should be noted, then, that (for rather technical reasons) the partial explication of contributory causation (if it were confined *simply* to point [1]) would not prove adequate. For that restricted account would not allow us to discriminate mere antecedent conditions or other seemingly irrelevant conditions from proper contributory causes. So we need to add another element to the analysis (that is, point [2] above) to deal with this problem.

I am indebted to Keith Coleman, John Skorupski, and Bob Hale for helping me refine my account in this section. For a discussion of some of the additional steps required to round out such an analysis, see sects. 3.7 and 3.8 of my paper in *Pragmatik*, mentioned in note 37.

[19] For one example of the argument I am criticizing see Alan Donagan, *The Later Philosophy of Collingwood*. 2d ed. Chicago: University of Chicago, 1985, p. 185. And for a more extended version of the criticism itself, see HE, ch. 9, as cited in note 20.

[20] Von Wright describes the crucial relationship here (that of logical independence) as the relationship of "Humean connection" (after David Hume). Humean connection exists between the statement of the set of initial conditions (v) and the statement of the thing to be explained (w) when v and w are logically independent of one another – that is, when *all* of the following combinations hold as *logical possibilities*: (i) v and w, (ii) not-v and w, (iii) not-v and not-w, and crucially (iv) v and not-w. (See EU, p. 93 – also pp. 18, 44, 97, 139, and 195 n. 13 and n. 18.)

For my main argument that the formula for practical inference exhibits humean connection, see my book HE, ch. 9, esp. pp. 164–180; also p. 197.

[21] Von Wright says, "[I] think it a mistake – of which I myself and others have been guilty – to understand the intentionalist view to mean that there is a relation of logical *entailment* between the premisses and the conclusion of a practical argument" ("Determinism and the Study of Man," 1976 [reprinted in PR, at p. 41; see also PR, pp. 42, 43–45; D, p. 130]).

Now, as is well known, Collingwood distinguishes the "inside" of an action from its "outside" and then goes on to assert the "unity" of these two sides; and he says that when we understand *what* happened we also understand *why* it happened. But neither of these claims should be taken as suggesting that there is an "internal" or analytic connection – a "unity" of logical entailment – between the thoughts of an agent and the deeds they are said to bring about. For the passages in question, see IH, pp. 213–214. And for discussion, see HE, chs. 2 and 3.

Rather, Collingwood's view, I would suggest, is that something like the schema is an absolute presupposition of action explanations (in the domain of contemporary history, social science, legal reasoning, etc.). As an absolute presupposition, the schema per se can be neither true nor false; hence, it cannot exhibit "a relation of logical *entailment* between the premisses and the conclusion of a practical argument" (to use von Wright's phrase), for that would make it a logical truth (and hence a true statement).

It is nonetheless a *meaningful* statement-like formulation, and one that can be changed or revised over time. Perhaps the best way to represent these two distinct Collingwoodian claims is to say that the schema per se is a synthetic formulation, which in and of itself lacks truth value. And that which such a presupposition formulates, if I may put it so, is some sort of objective pattern or structure in our way of knowing. Behind the formulation, assuming it to be accurate, then, is simply a particular mode or aspect of scientific practice, as it existed at a given time in history.

The only sense in which such a formulation could be true, then, is that it is *descriptively* true of this particular practice. And, again, its essentially 'synthetic' status is here exhibited.

For discussion of Collingwood's interesting views here, see my papers: "Collingwood's Doctrine of Absolute Presuppositions and the Possibility of Historical Knowledge," in L. Pompa and W.H. Dray (eds.), *Substance and Form in History: A Collection of Essays in Philosophy of History*. Edinburgh, Scotland: Edinburgh University Press, 1981, pp. 89–106, in sects. 1 and 2, and "Collingwood's Claim that Metaphysics is a Historical Discipline," *Monist* 72.4 (October 1989), 489–525, in sect. 1.

22 Let me add, in passing, that the practical inference schema (as stated in n. 2) is incomplete. (Note the "and so on" with which it ends.) Nonetheless, the schema seems sufficiently complete for practical inferences to meet the requirement in our analysis that – arguably – some sound explanatory argument *exists* for them. The schema is intended, ultimately, as a principle of reasoning; its function is to indicate the main sorts of considerations that are brought into play in all such intentionalist explanations.

23 Reasons for thinking that an analysis of the sort offered by White does not *imply* the existence of a general law of any sort are set forth in HE, ch. 9, esp. pp. 159–163 (on the so-called indirect argument). The arguments for saying that the "if ... then ..." formula for practical inference is not itself a general law are found in HE, ch. 10, esp. pp. 186–200; see also pp. 180–184.

Now, von Wright does not hold to White's idea of "existential regularism," so far as I know, but like White he does subscribe to the idea that the presence of a general law is implied (indeed, for von Wright, *directly* implied) in all strict talk of causes. (See, for example, von Wright, EU, 15–16, 97–98, n. 4 on p. 193; "Determinism and the Study of Man," 1976, in PR, 40, 44; "Explanation and Understanding of Action," 1981, in PR, 53, 62.) Accordingly, the argument against White here would constitute an argument against von Wright on this point as well.

24 Collingwood's discussion of causation is found in R. G. Collingwood, *An Essay on Metaphysics* (Oxford: Oxford University Press, 1940), Part IIIC, pp. 285–343. This part of *Metaphysics* is based on Collingwood's article, "On the So-Called Idea of Causation," *Proceedings of the Aristotelian Society* n.s. 38 (1937–38): 85–112 [hereafter: PAS]. These two versions are quite similar but not identical.

The quotation defining sense I is from Collingwood, *Metaphysics* [hereafter: *Met.*], p. 285; for discussion, see also pp. 286, 290–295, 316, 320. The important discussion of *causa quod* (what I earlier called a situational motivation) and *causa ut* (what I earlier called a relevant purpose or end in view) is found in *Met.*, 292–293.

Note also Collingwood's remark about causation in IH, at pp. 214–215:

> When a historian asks "Why did Brutus stab Caesar?" he means "what did Brutus think, which made him decide to stab Caesar?" The cause of the event, for him, means the thought in the mind of the person by whose agency the event came about ... .

Finally, the idea of sufficient conditions as complex and the idea of a contributory cause as being necessary for any such complex to be sufficient, ideas which I have used in my reconstruction of a general sense of 'cause,' can be found in Collingwood's account. See, for example, *Met.*, 301, 313–314. Note also that Collingwood says of *causa quod* and *causa ut*, "Neither of these could be a cause if the other were absent" (*Met.*, 292).

25 The quotation defining sense II is from *Met.*, 285; see also PAS, 89. In this latter citation, the explicit definition doesn't mention "events in nature," a point I will turn to later. Of course, the context makes clear (in both *Met.* and PAS) that Collingwood is talking about events in nature; for discussion, see *Met.*, 286–287, 296–312, 316. The phrase "practical sciences of nature" is from *Met.*, 286 (italicized in original). The point about means/end can be found in *Met.*, 308–309, esp. 311, and PAS, 86, 94, 96.

In sum, there are three senses of 'cause' in Collingwood's analysis (the first two of which we've now briefly canvassed):

1. thought-factors (beliefs and motivations of the agent) as contributory causes of action
2. means/end (typically: actions [means]/events in nature [ends])

3. events in nature which happen "independently of human will" (*Met.*, 287) as contributory causes of other such events (and, for more general discussion, see *Met.*, pp. 313–327)

The third type of cause will not be discussed in the present paper. That is, it will not be discussed (except incidentally) beyond a brief comment or two in this paragraph of the present note. Collingwood's main objection to causes of the third type is that one can make no sense in saying, just one on one (and without further ado), that some set of initial conditions is *sufficient* to the production of some *particular* event, and no sense in saying that those particular initial conditions are each necessary to that sufficiency. Collingwood's argument, which depends on Hume's, is fundamentally sound (though it is confused, in that he puts 'necessary' where I have put 'sufficient'). However, his argument in no way rules out talk of events in nature, which happen "independently of human will," as contributory causes of other such events. It is merely that to do so we'd need the idea of laws of nature which could mediate the connection between some such set of initial conditions, on the one hand, and the effect they produce, on the other (see *Met.*, p. 327).

26 The quoted example is from *Met.*, 290. Two-agent (or second-agent) causes are explicitly mentioned by Collingwood under sense I (see *Met.*, 293) and, indeed, seem often to be the type he emphasizes in his discussion of that sense (see *Met.*, 290, 309, 325). For the claim that Collingwood would call an action like Iago's a cause of Desdemona's death, even though Othello actually did the killing, see *Met.*, pp. 293–294.

27 Collingwood did not himself make such a restriction (to "events in nature") in his *explicit* definition of sense II causes in PAS, 89.

28 Georg Henrik von Wright has carefully outlined the difference between sequenced actions (where one is said to cause the other), on the one hand, and means(actions)/ends (events in nature), on the other. He does so by distinguishing 'quasi-causal' explanations (see EU, pp. 85–86, 137, 139–143, 153–155; also pp. 135–138) from what he calls 'quasi-teleological' ones (see EU, pp. 59–60, 80–85, 153, and esp. 156 and 160). The crucial difference is that the latter explanations, though they *look* teleological, actually require causal natural laws for completion (hence the name 'quasi-teleological'); and the former, though *causal* in appearance, can be completed using iterated practical inference explanations (hence the name 'quasi-causal').

In the text, the Iago example is quasi-causal (in von Wright's sense) and the Hiroshima one is quasi-teleological.

29 William Dray, for example, interprets Collingwood as holding that the things denominated causes are always, in some sense, manipulable "handles" by which *we* (presumably human beings) can bring about or prevent the occurrence of some other thing, typically an event in nature. (See Dray, *Laws and Explanation in History* [Oxford: Oxford University Press, 1957], ch. 4, pp. 92–97, esp. pp. 95–97.)

30 See *Met.*, 299. Some of the other examples could be given a similar construction, with a bit of prodding. Of course, in conformity with the analysis of causation I have been developing, all these causal statements would be written as statements of singular contributory causation.

31 See here *Met.*, p. 321, where Collingwood treats so-called sense I causes as a "foundation."

32 In short, I am suggesting here that there is a single conception of cause (that is, a single conception of contributory cause in the special case of a singular event or action) that lies beneath the senses Collingwood explicitly identified. I am suggesting, moreover, that this conception can figure in both the explanatory models I have identified: it can figure in practical inferences (either simple or iterated) and in means (action)/end (event in nature) explanations.

33 See EU, 56.

34 See, in particular, von Wright, *Causality and Determinism*. New York: Columbia University Press, 1974, pp. 48, 50, 57 [hereafter: C&D] and EU, 36. Others have advocated the view of causes as manipulable changes, as human interventions, besides von Wright. For example, Douglas Gasking ("Causation and Recipes." *Mind* 64 [1955], 479–487) has put the view forward as part

of the concept of causation. And Collingwood can be interpreted this way (with his sense II causes).

But by far the most interesting and most successful attempt to develop such a conception of causation is provided by von Wright himself. (See here EU, chap. 2, esp. pp. 36, 38–39, 61–66, 70, n. 29 on p. 187, n. 40 on pp. 189–190; and C&D, esp. pp. 50–53, 57–60, 86–87, 120.) The latter book, in particular, applies this conception in a comprehensive way to *natural* causes. A detailed working out of this extension of the conception of causes-as-interventions to such cases, or any systematic criticism of von Wright's project on this point, is well beyond the scope of the present paper.

For von Wright's discussion of the two tests (of introduction and of omission), see also C&D, pp. 87–88.

[35] As J.L. Mackie indicated in his review of C&D, in *Journal of Philosophy* 73 (1976), 213–218, at 216.

[36] Collingwood, as I have already pointed out in note 24, was in no wise averse to treating thoughts (motivation, beliefs) as causes of actions. To this should be added the etymological point he makes about *aitia* and *causa*, respectively the Greek and Latin terms for 'cause' (see *Met.*, 291; also p. 289).

[37] In the present paper I have drawn on earlier writings of my own: on (a) "Collingwood on Reasons, Causes, and the Explanation of Action," *International Studies in Philosophy* 33.3 (1991), pp. 47–62, on (b) "On G. H. von Wright's Theory of Practical Inference," *Archiv für Rechts- und Sozialphilosophie* (ARSP) Beiheft 51 (1993), pp. 185–197, and on (c) "Collingwood and von Wright on 'Verstehen', Causation and the Explanation of Human Action," *Collingwood Studies* 1 (1994), 143–162. There is, of course, some overlap in content between the present paper and these other three.

Further citations to von Wright's writings and supporting arguments to points made in the present paper can be found in my article, "G. H. von Wright on Explanation and Understanding: An Appraisal," *History and Theory* 29 (1990), pp. 205–233. For further discussion of causation, in particular, see my paper "Causation and Intentionalist Explanations in History," in H. Stachowiak (ed.), *Pragmatische Tendenzen in der Wissenschaftstheorie* (Pragmatic Tendencies in Scientific Theory). *Pragmatik* Vol. 5. Hamburg, Germany: F. Meiner Verlag, 1995, pp. 370–402. That paper provides (in sect. 2) citations to the writings of Morton White and Donald Davidson, upon which my own account of causation is largely based. And the brief exploration mentioned at the very end of the present paper is recounted in greater detail in sect. 4 of that paper.

I want to thank audiences in Germany, England, Canada, and Wales for their comments on earlier versions of the present paper. And for providing me with serviceable translations from German and Italian texts, I want to thank James Gilkeson and Mirella Vaglio respectively.

REFERENCES

Bianco, F. (ed.) (1985), *Dilthey e il Pensiero del Novecento* [*Dilthey and the Thought of the Nineteenth Century*]. Milan, F. Angeli.

Collingwood, R.G. (1937–38), "On the So-Called Idea of Causation," *Proceedings of the Aristotelian Society* n.s. **38**, 85–112 (cited as PAS).

Collingwood, R.G. (1940), *An Essay on Metaphysics*. Oxford, Oxford University Press (cited as *Met.*).

Collingwood, R.G. (1956), *The Idea of History*, T.M. Knox (ed.). New York, Oxford University Press; first publ. in 1946 (cited as IH).

Donagan, A.H. (1985), *The Later Philosophy of R.G. Collingwood*, 2nd ed. Chicago, University of Chicago Press.

Dray, W.H. (1957), *Laws and Explanation in History*. Oxford, Oxford University Press.
Gasking, D. (1955), "Causation and Recipes," *Mind* **64**, 479–487.
Mackie, J.L. (1976), review of von Wright (1974) in *Journal of Philosophy* **73**, 213–218.
Martin, R. (1977). *Historical Explanation*. Ithaca, NY, Cornell University Press (cited as HE).
Martin, R. (1981), "Collingwood's Doctrine of Absolute Presuppositions and the Possibility of Historical Knowledge," in L. Pompa and W.H. Dray (1981), pp. 89–106.
Martin, R. (1989), "Collingwood's Claim that Metaphysics is a Historical Discipline," *Monist* **72**, 489–525.
Martin, R. (1990), "G.H. von Wright on Explanation and Understanding: An Appraisal," *History and Theory* **29**, 205–233.
Martin, R. (1991a), "Collingwood on Reasons, Causes, and the Explanation of Action," *International Studies in Philosophy* **33**, 47–62.
Martin, R. (1991b), "The Problem of Other Cultures and Other Periods in Action Explanations," *Philosophy of the Social Sciences* **21**, 345–366 (cited as POC).
Martin, R. (1993), "On G.H. von Wright's Theory of Practical Inference," *Archiv für Rechts- und Sozialphilosophie* Beiheft **51**, 185–197.
Martin, R. (1994), "Collingwood and von Wright on 'Verstehen', Causation and the Explanation of Human Action," *Collingwood Studies* **1**, 143–162.
Martin, R. (1995), "Causation and Intentionalist Explanations in History" in H. Stachowiak (1995), pp. 370–402.
McMurrin, S.M. (ed.) (1985), *The Tanner Lectures in Human Values*, vol. VI. Cambridge, Cambridge University Press.
Pompa L. and W.H. Dray (eds.) (1981), *Substance and Form in History: A Collection of Essays in Philosophy of History*. Edinburgh, Edinburgh University Press.
Stachowiak, H. (ed.) (1995), *Pragmatische Tendenzen in der Wissenschaftstheorie* (Pragmatic Tendencies in Scientific Theory), *Pragmatik* Vol. 5. Hamburg, Germany: Meiner Verlag.
von Wright, G.H. (1971), *Explanation and Understanding*. Ithaca, NY, Cornell University Press (cited as EU).
von Wright, G.H. (1974), *Causality and Determinism*. New York, Columbia University Press (cited as C&D).
von Wright, G.H. (1981), "The Explanation and Understanding of Action," *Revue Internationale de Philosophie* **135**, 127–142.
von Wright, G.H. (1983), *Practical Reason, Philosophical Papers*, vol. 1. Oxford, Blackwell.
von Wright, G.H. (1985a), "Probleme des Erklärens und Verstehens von Handlungen" [Problems in the Explanation and Understanding of Actions], *Conceptus* **19**, 3–19 (cited as C; note this essay is published, in English translation, in the present volume).
von Wright, G.H. (1985b), "Sulla Verità Delle 'Spiegazioni' Comprendenti" ["On the Truth of 'Understanding' Explanations"] in Bianco (1985), pp. 127–135 (cited as D).
von Wright, G.H. (1985c), "Of Human Freedom" in McMurrin (1985), pp. 107–170 (cited as TL).
von Wright, G.H. (1988), "An Essay on Door-Knocking," *Rechtstheorie* **19**, 275–288 (cited as Door-K).
von Wright, G.H. (1989), "Das Verstehen von Handlungen – Disputation mit Georg Meggle" ["The Understanding of Actions ..."], *Rechtstheorie* **20**, 3–37 (cited as R).
von Wright, G.H. (1994), *Normen, Werte und Handlungen* [*Norms, Values and Actions*]. Frankfurt am Main, Suhrkamp.

AUSONIO MARRAS

METAPHYSICAL FOUNDATIONS OF ACTION EXPLANATION

INTRODUCTION

As is widely recognized, the publication of Donald Davidson's "Actions, Reasons, and Causes" in 1963 marked the revival of the causal theory of action and action explanation – a theory which, in one guise or another, has gained wide, albeit not universal, acceptance.[1] According to the causal theory, an intentional action – an action that is performed *for* a reason (however trivial the reason) – is one that is *caused* by that reason; and to explain an action by citing the reasons for which it is performed is to give a *causal explanation* of the action. Whether the reasons that rationalize and cause the action can be fully accounted for in terms of the agent's prevailing beliefs and desires, or whether other intentional states (such as occurring or sustaining intentions or volitions) must be posited, is still a matter of controversy among various authors;[2] but the basic claim that there exists both a *conceptual* and a *causal* link between reasons and the actions they rationalize – i.e., that an action's reasons *are* its causes – is indeed widely accepted.

Disagreement abounds, however, with respect to the question of *how to account* for the causal powers of reasons. How *can* reasons be causes, how can beliefs, desires, etc. be causally efficacious in the production of behaviour so as to be explanatory of it in a causally relevant sense? The problem, essentially, is to provide a metaphysical underpinning for the possibility of *mental causation* so as to account for the *explanatory* role of reasons. It is the problem of articulating and defending a set of metaphysical and epistemological assumptions about the nature of causation and causal explanation and about the place of mind in the causal structure of the world, on the basis of which we can vindicate our commitment to a causal interpretation of action explanation.

Deplorably, there are some who view this type of concern as altogether unmotivated. Such "worries" about the possibility of mental causation have been regarded by Tyler Burge, for example, as "symptomatic of a mistaken set of philosophical priorities" (Burge 1993, 97): they reportedly result from lending too much weight to a materialist metaphysics, and if only sufficient attention were given to *actual explanatory practices*, the problem of mental causation would, as Lynn Baker has recently put it, just "melt away" (Baker 1993, 93).

I find this sort of deflationary stance somewhat puzzling. First, it is not at all clear that ordinary explanatory practices unambiguously reveal, or entitle us to assume, that "intentional mental events are often causes, and that psychological

G. Holmström-Hintikka and R. Tuomela (eds.), Contemporary Action Theory. Vol. I, 45–64.

explanation is often a form of causal explanation" (Burge 1993, 118). To just assume this is to beg the question not only against those 'eliminativists' who question the probity of our ordinary ('folk psychological') explanatory practices, but also, and more importantly, against those teleologists who are perfectly happy with our explanatory practices but nonetheless reject the thesis that reasons can be causes, or that intentional explanation is a species of causal explanation.[3] (Davidson, recall, had to *argue* against an orthodoxy of 'ordinary language' non-causalists.)

Second, even granting that no *epistemic warrant* is needed for the *truth* of the claim that reasons (beliefs, desires, etc.) are causes beyond what reflection on ordinary explanatory practices can provide, it does not follow that the problem of mental causation just "melts away". To suppose this is to misunderstand the philosophical nature of the problem. The point is well put by Jaegwon Kim:

> The problem of mental causation is primarily a theoretical metaphysical problem. It is the problem of showing *how* mental causation is possible, not *whether* it is possible. In raising the *how* question, we are assuming that the *whether* question has already been affirmatively answered. (Kim 1995, 128)

In raising the mental causation problem one need not question the probity of our explanatory practices, or the belief that "intentional mental events are often causes, and that psychological explanation is often a form of causal explanation" (Burge 1993, 118). This much was clear from Davidson's own account of psychological explanation in his (1963) paper. There he appealed to our intuitions about a variety of explanatory contexts to defend the thesis that reasons *must* be causes if they are to explain, and not merely justify, an action. But he did not stop there: in the same paper he thought it important to refute philosophical arguments, popular among the Ryleans and neo-Wittgensteinians (who were highly respectful of ordinary explanatory practices), meant to demonstrate that reasons *could not* be causes; and those arguments heavily depended on metaphysical and epistemological assumptions about the nature of causal and conceptual relations, induction, laws, and the like. Further, Davidson also thought it important, in later papers (particularly in "Mental Events", 1970), to actually provide a positive account of *how* reasons can be causes – how mental events can causally interact with other events. He did so by proposing his doctrine of 'anomalous monism' – a doctrine steeped in metaphysical and epistemological assumptions. Though the account was, I believe, ultimately unsatisfactory, the present point is that *some* metaphysical account of how reasons can be causes was rightfully perceived to be needed in order to provide *philosophical* legitimacy to our appeal to reasons in our explanations of behaviour. Davidson was no more "worried" than Burge or Baker that the mental might really turn out to be inefficacious, or that epiphenomenalism might really be true, or that psychological explanations might after all not be causal; his "worry", or theoretical concern, was rather how to *reconcile* the possibility of mental causation and intentional causal explanation with *other* widely accepted (though surely defeasible) metaphysical and epistemological commitments which seemed, at least *prima facie*, to conflict with that possibility. In this sense the problem of mental causation is as theoretically real as the Kantian problem about the possibility of scientific knowledge; and, at least in the context of the Davidsonian problematic, it is integral with the problem of providing a philosophical theory of action explanation.

DOES MENTALITY DO CAUSAL WORK?

Let us assume, then, that a philosophical theory of action explanation depends in part on certain underlying metaphysical and epistemological assumptions (if only because it depends in part on an underlying theory of human action); and let us briefly review how the problem of mental causation arises in the context of Davidson's account of action explanation. As mentioned, a successful explanation of an intentional action must, according to Davidson, satisfy the following two condition: 1) it must cite the prevailing beliefs and desires of the agent in light of which the action appears reasonable; 2) such rationalizing beliefs and desires must in fact have caused the action (and done so 'in the right way'[4]). An explanation that meets these conditions will be at once a rationalizing explanation (in virtue of citing the reasons for the action) and a causal explanation (in virtue of citing its cause).

Two questions immediately arise: *how* can reasons be causes, and under what conditions does *citing the cause* of an action constitute a *causal explanation* of it?

As mentioned, Davidson's account of how reasons can be causes was in terms of his anomalous monism, a form of 'non-reductive materialism' encompassing two theses: (a) *token-physicalism* – each mental event is token-identical to some physical event (where an event for Davidson is a structureless, concrete, spatio-temporal particular[5]); (b) *non-reductionism* – mental properties, being 'anomalous', are not reducible to physical properties. Given token physicalism alone, the efficacy of mental *events* (and thus of reasons) follows directly: mental events are causally efficacious because they *are* physical events, and the latter are causally efficacious *par excellence*.[6]

However, the fact that reasons are causes does not by itself warrant the thesis that reason explanations are causal explanations – even when reasons cause the action 'in the right way' (that is, without being involved in 'wayward' causal chains). For, given Davidson's understanding of the causal relation as an *extensional* relation between events and the explanatory relation as a *non-extensional* relation between events 'under a description', citing the cause of an event may fail to provide an explanation of it. A singular causal statement may be *true* without being *explanatory*.[7] To be explanatory the statement must identify the cause and the effect in terms of their 'causally relevant' properties, and these, on the traditional nomological conception of causation and causal explanation, are *law-instantiating* ('nomic') properties. As Fred Dretske puts the point,

A causal explanation of an event is ... more than a specification, under some description or other, of the event's cause. An explanation requires, in addition..., some indication of which of the properties of the cause, by being law instantiating properties, underlie the cause's efficacy in producing the effect (1989, 1).[8]

So here is the problem for Davidson's account of action explanation: In order to be a causal one, the explanation must represent the cause under a law-instantiating description, and thus, given Davidson's principle of the anomalism of the mental (PAM)[9], under a physical description; but under a physical description, the cause does not rationalize the action: only under an intentional, mental description does the cause rationalize the action. On the other hand, citing the cause under an intentional, rationalizing description fails to display the cause under a law-instantiating description, there being, according to (PAM), no psychological, law-instantiating descriptions. Thus, a *reason* explanation, as such, fails to be a genuine *causal* explanation. Rationalizing properties and causally relevant, nomic properties seem to pull in opposite directions; and while they can both be instantiated by one and the same event – e.g. by the event that causes the action, however described – they do not thereby serve equivalent explanatory functions. So beliefs and desires can indeed cause behaviour, but, given Davidson's commitment to (PAM), it is altogether unclear how such beliefs and desires can possibly cause what they do *in virtue of* their mental properties rather than in virtue of their physical properties alone.[10] And unless we have reasons to suppose that a mental event causes what it does in virtue of its mental properties – that is, because of the *kind* of mental event it is (in particular, because of the *content* it has), then we have no reason to suppose that citing the event in terms of its mental properties is at all relevant to explaining what it causes.

Recall Ernest Sosa's and Dretske's well know analogies: a loud gunshot causes a death, but not because it was loud; and the soprano's singing caused the glass to break, but not because of what the words meant.[11] How can it be then, on Davidson's account, that the mental properties of my desire for water are any more relevant to explaining my drinking than the loudness of a loud gunshot is to the death of the victim, or the meaningfulness of sounds is to their breaking the glass? Lacking an answer to this question, many of Davidson's critics have charged that anomalous monism amounts to a form of *property epiphenomenalism*: mental properties 'make no difference' to what mental events cause, and are thus causally irrelevant.[12] As Kim has put it, "under Davidson's anomalous monism, mentality does no causal work" (1989b, 35).

Given then that only those properties of a cause that are nomically connected to certain properties of the effect are responsible for determining what was caused, whatever it is in virtue of which mental events cause what they do, it can't be their mental properties, for these, according to Davidson, are not nomic. How then can the singular causal statements in terms of which Davidson wishes to cast action explanations – statements of the form '*S* did *A* because of such and such beliefs and desires' – be genuinely explanatory, that is, explanatory in a *causal* sense of 'because'?[13]

MENTAL CAUSATION IS NO PROBLEM. DAVIDSONIAN PERSPECTIVES

We have seen, then, a clear way in which the problem of mental causation arises. It arises in the context of a philosophical theory of action explanation, given certain philosophical assumptions about causation and causal explanation, and a commitment to a principle – the 'anomaly' principle (PAM) – which forbids extending those assumptions to the psychological domain. It would be philosophically irresponsible to simply reject those assumptions, or that principle, in the name of our explanatory practices whose probity vouches for the reality of mental causation, without replacing them with some *other* set of assumptions and commitments in the light of which the problem of mental causation is no longer a problem.

There are other ways in which the mental causation problem can be seen to arise. 1) Given an 'externalist' conception of *intentional content*, according to which the content (and thus the type-identity) of a mental state is partly determined by external, ecological, or historical factors,[14] how can the content of a mental state play a role in what the state causes, since intentional content so-conceived does not reduce to, or supervene on, the *intrinsic* properties of the mental state, which alone seem to be responsible for the state's causal powers? (cf. Dretske 1990). 2) Given the 'causal closure' of the physical domain ('every physical event has sufficient physical cause and a sufficient physical explanation'), and given the principle of *explanatory exclusion* ('there can only be one complete and independent causal explanation of any given event'; cf. Kim 1990b), how can a piece of behaviour – a physical event caused by a reason (and thus by a physical event, given token-physicalism) – have *both* a complete and independent explanation in terms of the physical (neural) properties of its cause, *and* a complete and independent explanation in terms of the mental properties of its cause?

I believe there are a variety of arguably plausible proposals in the literature for dealing with the 'externalist' version of the mental causation problem.[15] I also believe, as I propose to explain in due course, that the explanatory exclusion problem does not arise if certain epistemic and pragmatic conditions on explanation are heeded. For the moment, I shall return to the 'Davidsonian' version of the problem and consider the implications of what would seem the obvious way of dealing with it, namely, denying the anomalism of the mental (PAM).

A number of philosophers (and Davidson himself recently) have pointed out that (PAM) does not deny the existence of psychological laws but only the existence of *strict* psychological laws.[16] By a strict law Davidson means, roughly, an empirical generalization that is not only 'lawlike' (counterfactual supporting and confirmed by its instances) but also "as deterministic as nature can be found to be, and free from caveats and *ceteris paribus* clauses" (1970, 219). A generalization can meet this condition, he goes on to say, "only if it draws its concepts from a comprehensive closed theory" (ibid.); and since only a "developed physics" can aim to be a comprehensive closed theory, he concludes that a strict law is "something one can only hope to find in a developed physics" (1993, 8). The only laws to be found outside of basic physics are thus non-strict; yet surely no one would deny that these are genuine, counterfactual supporting laws suitable for causal explanations.[17] In being confined to non-strict laws intentional psychology is thus no worse off than any of the other so-called special sciences.

I think it is highly doubtful, however, that the kinds of psychological generalizations that are compatible with Davidson's anomalism and whose existence Davidson seems willing to acknowledge, can legitimaly be regarded as *empirical, covering laws* comparable to those of the other special sciences and capable of playing a serious explanatory role. Surely Davidson's defense of (PAM) in terms of the, 'normativity', 'autonomy', and 'integrity' of the psychological domain, and the distinctly 'interpretationist' methodology he advocates for thought ascriptions and reason explanations, strongly suggest that, in his view, the generalizations of intentional psychology are not to be regarded as empirical, covering laws at all.[18] And the thrust of his (1976) critique of Hempel's covering law account of psychological explanation was precisely that psychological generalizations are not only "very low grade"[19] but hardly have any empirical content: what sets them apart from genuine empirical laws, he has always insisted, is the normative character of mental concepts resulting from the assumption of rationality that governs their domain of application – an assumption that "may lack empirical import ... [in that it] suggests no empirical law that can be used in reason explanations generally" (1976, 267–268).[20]

IS THE CAUSAL RELEVANCE OF MENTAL PROPERTIES SECURED?

Suppose we give up the attempt to reconcile (PAM) with the existence of genuine, albeit non-strict, psychological laws. Can we then simply deny (PAM) and ground the causal relevance of mental properties and of reason explanations on the existence of non-strict psychological laws? I think the answer to this question is ultimately 'Yes', but an account of its plausibility is much more complex than is generally realized.

Consider, for example, Lepore and Loewer's (1987) proposal that mental properties are causally relevant (roughly) in the following sense of causal relevance:

> Where *c* causes *e* and where *c* is *F* and *e* is *G*, *c*'s being *F* is causally relevant to *e*'s being *G* just in case the following counterfactual holds:
>
> $-Fc > -Ge$ (i.e., if *c* had not been *F*, *e* would not have been *G*),
>
> and the counterfactual is supported by a (nonstrict) law to the effect that (*ceteris paribus*) *F*s cause *G*s.

On this proposal, my desire for water can be said to have been causally relevant to my drinking because the event which caused my drinking would not have caused my drinking had it not been a desire for water. On the assumption that there are (nonstrict) psychological laws able to support counterfactuals like the one just mentioned, the causal relevance of mental properties and of reason explanations in terms of those properties is thereby secured.

However, certain important questions are begged, or simply not addressed, by this type of proposal. First, the assumption that there *are* non-strict psychological laws is an assumption in need of justification. There are many who, like Davidson, are inclined to view the generalizations of intentional ('folk') psychology as no more than a priori principles of rationality with no empirical import at all. (More on this later.) Second, even if there are non-strict psychological laws able to support counterfactuals like the above, what reasons are there to believe that they are genuinely *causal* laws and not mere laws of *covariance* – e.g., nomological generalizations relating the effects of some independent common cause, or reflecting some sort of 'pre-established harmony'? Third, even if these objections are met, the fact remains that as long as we acknowledge a nomological principle of causation of the sort invoked by Davidson in his argument for anomalous monism,[21] we have to acknowledge that *c* causes *e* only if there are *physical* properties of *c* and *e* that are related by strict physical laws. Given the existence of such physical laws, *c* would have caused *e* as long as the relevant physical properties were present, irrespective of what *other* properties *c* might have had. So just as in Dretske's example the meaningful sounds would have shattered the glass irrespective of what meaning they had, as long as they occurred at the right pitch and amplitude, so too the physical event in my brain that was in fact a desire for a drink would have caused my drinking, irrespective of its being that desire, as long as it had the right sort of physical (neural) properties. So even if my desiring and my drinking instantiate a non-strict psychological law, this fact would be irrelevant to explaining my behaviour if my behaviour would have occurred just the same if its cause did *not* exemplify any psychological properties, as long as it did exemplify the relevant physical (neural) properties. Any causal explanation of an event by subsumption of it under a non-strict psychological law would, it seems, be *preempted*, or 'screened off', by an explanation of it that appealed to strict physical laws.[22]

The only way I know to block this third type of objection is to posit a relation of *supervenience* of mental on physical properties strong enough to rule out any nomologically possible world in which the mental cause of one's behaviour might retain its physical properties without also retaining its mental properties. A relation of supervenience equivalent to Kim's (1984a) 'strong' supervenience would be adequate for this purpose:

(S) Necessarily, for any event x and for any mental property M_i, if x has M_i then there is some physical property P_i which x also has and which is such that, necessarily, any event y which has P_i also has M_i.[23]

According to (S), 'supervenience conditionals' of the form $P_i y \rightarrow M_i y$ hold *across* possible worlds, so if the property of desiring a drink (strongly) supervenes on a certain physical property of my desire, then there is no counterfactual situation in which the physical event that was in fact my desire could have failed to be that desire while remaining that kind of physical event, and so the Sosa–Dretske type of objection is blocked.[24] The mental properties of a cause are not 'screened off' by its nomic physical properties if the former supervene on the latter, so the appeal to non-strict laws in an account of the causal relevance of mental properties and reason explanations may still hold promise.

Let me stress that this appeal to supervenience merely enables us to block a certain type of epiphenomenalist objection, by preventing the mental properties of a cause from being screened off by its physical properties as causally irrelevant. So supervenience on physical properties provides at best a *necessary* condition for the relevance of mental properties. Furthermore, as Kim (1990a) has pointed out, definitions of supervenience like (S) merely specify a *functional* relation of (non-symmetric) *covariance* of mental with physical properties, and surely a mere correlation, even if nomological, cannot guarantee the *causal* and *explanatory* relevance of mental properties as distinct from their merely *predictive* relevance. Dretske (1990, 9) puts the point incisively: "Pre-established harmony allows one to say that Harold will do *A when* he thinks *T*; ... one may even say that he *wouldn't* have done *A unless* he believed *T*. It will not, however, support the claim that he did *A because* he thought *T*." Surely the kind of covariance specified by (S) is consistent with a mere epiphenomenal role of mental properties: it guarantees a *counterfactual* dependence of behavioural on mental properties, but such counterfactual dependence does not amount to *causal* dependence.[25]

Nonetheless, if psychophysical supervenience is true, the appeal to non-strict psychological laws may, as remarked, still hold promise for an account of mental causation. For if there are psychological laws *and* the mental properties that figure in these laws are not screened off by the nomic physical properties on which they supervene, then can we not simply ground the causal relevance of mental properties in their aptness to occur in non-strict psychological laws and in the counterfactuals supported by such laws?

I think this proposal is fundamentally sound as long as we have reason to believe that the intentional generalizations of commonsense psychology have the status of genuine (albeit non-strict) *empirical* and (furthermore) *causal* laws. The mere fact that the intentional generalizations to which we (implicitly) appeal in our ordinary explanatory practices have the general *form* of a law (that is, the fact that they have the form of universally quantified conditionals) does not guarantee that they are indeed empirical, causal laws. Consider, for example, Kim's formulation of the so-called Desire-Belief-Action Principle:

(DBA) If a person desires that p, and believes that doing A will secure p, then *ceteris paribus* he will do A. (Kim 1984b, 311)

There is a real issue, as Kim points out, "whether (DBA) is a contingent empirical law about belief, desire, and action, or whether it is an a priori truth grounded wholly in a conceptual relationship among the three interdependent notions of belief, desire, and action" (ibid.). Davidson, for example, would regard (DBA) as an a priori truth[26]; and Kim explicitly denies (DBA) *descriptive* status altogether and regards it as a "*normative* or *regulative* rule," that is, as a "normative principle that tells us the conditions under which a given action is rationalizable as an appropriate thing to do" (1984b, 314). Patently, under such interpretations of (DBA), subsumption of intentional behaviour under psychological "laws" of that form will not yield *causal* explanations of people's behaviour in terms of their beliefs and desires. And even if, *contra* Kim and Davidson, we regard generalizations of the (DBA) form as genuine *empirical* laws – perhaps on the basis of reliable regularities in the way people's behaviour follows upon their beliefs and desires – the epiphenomenalist concern would still remain as to whether the regularities in question are genuinely causal rather than a mere manifestation of some sort of "pre-established harmony" (as Dretske would put it), or the effects of some independent common cause.

PSYCHOPHYSICAL DEPENDENCE

I believe the most promising strategy for vindicating the empirical and causal status of psychological laws is to develop a metaphysically robust conception of *psychophysical dependence* – one that goes beyond the merely functional conception of nomological covariance expressed by standard definitions of supervenience. What I think is needed, ultimately, is an explication of the core idea implicit in the widely held physicalist principle that all facts and properties – and thus all *mental* facts and properties – *depend on*, or *are determined by*, physical facts and properties. A metaphysical account of this (asymmetrical) relation of dependence or determination would explain why a nomological covariance obtains between supervening and subvening properties, and how the causal powers of the subvening properties might determine the causal powers of the supervening ones. An account of the latter, in the particular psychophysical case, would provide an understanding of how psychological laws in which mental properties figure might 'inherit' the causal status of the physical laws in which the subvening physical properties figure. The ensuing account of mental causation would be schematically representable by the diagram in figure 1.

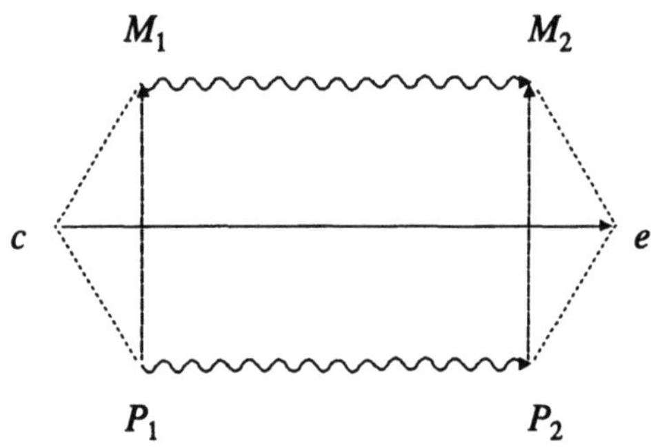

Fig. 1. c and e are individual events – cause and effect respectively; the solid arrow joining them is the causal relation. M_1 and P_1 are, respectively, the mental and the physical property exemplified by c, and M_2 and P_2 are, respectively, the mental (action-theoretic) and the physical (bodily) property exemplified by e. The dotted lines stand for the exemplification relation; the segmented arrows stand for the supervenience/dependence relation; the wavy lines stand for the law relation (whether 'strict' or 'non-strict').

How is the idea of metaphysical dependence to be captured? The following remarks, I think, gesture in the right direction:

1) In accordance with a functionalist approach to the mental and a hierarchical conception of 'levels of description', construe (intentional) mental properties as higher level functional properties defined in terms of their typical functional role in the system in which they are instantiated.[27] States instantiating these properties are typically construed as *dispositions*, where the attribution of a disposition (in a realist sense of 'disposition' to be contrasted with the purely

'iffy' sense of Rylean behaviourism), is the attribution of a *causal* state, i.e., a state which, under appropriate conditions, is causally responsible for certain patterns of behaviour. These patterns are (in principle) specifiable by a corresponding set of *ceteris paribus* generalizations, i.e. the non-strict laws of intentional psychology applicable to each state.[28]

2) Suppose that any functional property *F* is such that, if it can be instantiated at all, it is also *realizable*, where to say that *F* is realizable is to say that there is some lower-level system of entities that is able to play the causal role definitive of *F*. To suppose this is to suppose that there exists an underlying state responsible for the manifestation of the disposition associated with *F*.

3) Suppose further, as seems reasonable, that functional properties are not merely realizable, but also (and perhaps *only*) *physically* realizable: that is, for each functional property *F* there is a system of physical, and ultimately microphysical, entities that is able to play the causal role definitive of *F*, as a nomological consequence of the kinds of physical entities they are and the way they are arranged.[29] This is to say that the state underlying the disposition associated with *F* is ultimately a microphysical state. As is often remarked, a system's disposition is realized in its microstructure.

4) Let us call the underlying physical structure, or the system of physical entities realizing a functional property *F*, a *physical mechanism* (one of possibly many alternative ones) that *implements* the generalizations implied by the attribution of the functional property and the disposition associated with that property. The physical (neurological, ultimately microphysical) mechanisms realizing mental/functional properties will be the ones that implement the 'laws' of intentional psychology. A *functional* specification of such mechanisms is of course the task of *cognitive science*; a specification of the intentional, psychological laws they implement is the task of intentional psychology.

If these remarks are at all in the right direction, then we have the beginning of a story to the effect that the causal powers of supervening mental properties are determined by, and depend on, the causal powers of the subvening physical properties. Since these physical properties are properties of the physical mechanisms that implement the psychological laws in which the supervening mental properties figure, we can begin to understand how psychological laws 'inherit' the causal status of the physical laws satisfied by the entities over which the implementing mechanisms are defined.

POSSIBLE OBJECTIONS AND RESPONSES

The strategy here adumbrated, even assuming that the key ideas underlying it can be adequately fleshed out, is likely to give rise to the following objections.

i) It might be objected that the proposed account robs mental properties of any causal powers of their own, for these would be *pre-empted* by the causal powers of the physical properties of the implementing mechanisms on which they depend. However, I find this type of objection somewhat bizarre.[30] To ascribe causal powers to something is *typically* (save perhaps at the level of *basic* physics) to posit the existence of a physical mechanism *through which* its causal powers may be discharged. When scientists conjectured that smoking caused cancer, and looked for an underlying physical mechanism to bear out their conjecture, it would be bizarre to object, once they found it, that the existence of such mechanism shows that it's not really *smoking* that causes cancer, but only the physical properties of the underlying mechanism. For smoking to cause cancer *is* for it to do so through some physical mechanism. Similarly, for beliefs and desires to cause behaviour *is* for them to do so through the subvening physical properties of the mechanisms implementing belief-desire-behaviour connections.

ii) A related objection might be that the dependent, higher-level status of mental properties deprives psychological laws of any genuine causal status of their own, for they are true only because certain physical laws applying to the relevant mental-property instances are true. But why should we suppose that the dependent status of psychological laws make them any less causal? Causal laws relate event types whose instances are cause-effect pairs, and psychological laws do this no less than physical laws do, even though they do it *because* mental properties are ontologically dependent on physical properties. Nor does their being higher level laws give them a mere *instrumental* status, as Dretske (1989) seems to suggest; putting the point in terms of Jerry Fodor's 'pre-established harmony' between the syntax and semantics of mental representations, he remarks: "It may be useful to couch generalizations in semantic terms, but that is a methodological expedient; semantics is merely a device for generalizing over causally relevant formal properties" (Dretske 1989, 2). But *all* causal laws (including those framed at the *syntactic* level) generalize over the causal facts that make them true; psychological laws merely do it at a higher level of abstraction. Why suppose that generalizing at higher levels implies abandoning a realist stance?

iii) It might further be objected that the existence of physical laws applying to the underlying physical mechanisms renders psychological laws and explanations strictly *superfluous*. Any given causal transaction involving a mental event can, after all, be directly explained by subsuming the event under physical laws (in virtue of the event's physical properties); so is it not redundant to seek an explanation of the same event by subsuming it under psychological laws, whose causal status, furthermore, is at best *derivative*? Worse yet, wouldn't a duality of explanations for a single event – one physical, one psychological – be incompatible with Kim's (1989a, 1990b) 'principle of explanatory exclusion', according to which no event can have more than one complete and independent explanation? I think not.

First, while the dependence of mental on physical properties confers causal status on psychological laws, it does not entail the *reducibility* of mental to physical properties, or of psychological to physical laws (Marras 1993a, 1993b).[31] The supervenience relation preserves a distinction between levels of description and supports the possibility of the multiple realization of mental properties; consequently psychological and physical laws may, and in general *will*, differ in scope and generality, in the sense that *any given* psychological law and *any given* physical law subsuming, on a given occasion, one and the same causal transaction, will in general subsume *nonequivalent classes* of causal transactions. That is, the *range* of behavioural consequences determined by any given mental property differs, in general, from the range of behavioural consequences determined by any of its subvening physical properties, or by any finitely enumerable set of such properties. Mental and physical properties thus partition the *same* causal domain in *different ways*.[32]

Second, explanatory contexts, as generally recognized, are *nonextensional* and *context-dependent*. As previously noted, the causal relation is extensional, holding between events no matter how type-identified, whereas the explanatory relation is non-extensional, holding only between events *as of a type*, i.e., insofar as they exemplify this or that property. What displays the proper form of a singular explanation statement is not '*c* explains *e*' (where *c* and *e* are unstructured Davidsonian events), but '*c's being F* (or *c qua F*) explains *e's being G* (or *c qua G*)'. The explanatory relation thus holds between *facts*, and facts implicate *properties* or event *types*; to explain why a certain event occurred at *t* is to explain why a certain *type* of event occurred at *t*. And once we see this we can also see why explanation is context and interest relative. For, as just noted, in asking why *this* event occurred, one must be asking why an event of *this type* occurred on *this* occasion, and what type one has in mind is surely a context and interest relative matter, depending as it does on *what* about the event to be explained one finds interesting or perplexing, or on which properties of the event one seeks to display as law-instantiating.

Because of the non-extensionality and context dependence of explanation, it is unsurprising that the same event may lend itself to alternative explanations, depending on how it is type-identified, which in turn depends on the context of inquiry. Does this conflict with Kim's previously mentioned 'principle of explanatory exclusion'? It depends on how the principle is understood. Consider the following formulation: "No event can be given more than one complete and independent explanation" (Kim 1989a, 79). If by 'event' is meant a structureless, Davidsonian event, then the principle is surely false, for the same event, as just noted, can be type-identified in more than one way, and thus explained in more than one way. But a more careful formulation of the principle says that no *explanandum* can have more than one complete and independent explanation (cf. Kim 1990b, 41). An *explanandum* just *is* an event *under a description*, that is, an event type-identified in a specific way (or, equivalently in this context, an event in Kim's favorite sense: a structured event individuated by its constitutive property; cf. Kim 1976). Like Kim, I think the principle, so interpreted is indeed true; but under this interpretation there is no reason to suppose that physical explanations exclude reason explanations, for the two kinds of explanations, being directed to distinct *explananda*, are not competing for the same explanatory job.[33]

But would a reason explanation of an event (an action) be a *complete* and *independent* explanation if mental properties *depend* on subvening physical properties for their causal powers? If the answer is 'No', though there is no contravention of the exclusion principle, it might be supposed that reason explanations are nonetheless of an inferior, dependent sort. But I think the answer should be 'Yes', for the acknowledged kind of dependence is an *ontological* dependence, not a *methodological* dependence. The methodological independence of reason explanations from physical explanations derives from the fact that psychological and physical laws have, as previously noted, different *types* of events in their range and will thus in general subsume non-equivalent classes of causal events.

SUMMARY

Unless other sorts of objections, more powerful than the above, are forthcoming, I see no reason why the strategy I am proposing for accounting for the causal relevance of mental properties, should not be regarded as worth pursuing. On this proposal, the supervenience and metaphysical dependence of mental on physical properties grounds the causal relevance of mental properties and explains their suitability for featuring in genuinely causal laws. I have tried to suggest how this idea of metaphysical dependence might in turn be explained, in accordance with a broadly functionalist and (non-reductive) physicalist approach to mentality, in terms of the notions of physical realization and implementation. I have also tried to explain how psychological laws, while genuinely causal as a result of their being implemented by physical mechanisms, are nonetheless irreducible to the physical laws governing those mechanisms: being higher-level laws, psychological laws generalize over, or abstract from, the (non-finitely enumerable set of) physical mechanisms that make them true. This, if true, accounts both for the (albeit dependent) causal status of psychological laws and for their indispensibility for explanations of intentional action. This account of how reason explanations can be causal explanations departs radically from the Davidsonian 'anomalist' account inasmuch as it strives to bring psychology within the domain of the *natural* sciences while preserving its integrity as a *special* science. If workable, this account is one way of vindicating what I take to be the chief motivating force behind naturalistically inspired forms of non-reductive physicalism in philosophy of mind: a belief in the *metaphysical dependence* of the mental on the physical, coupled with a belief in the *methodological autonomy* of the science of mind.[34]

The University of Western Ontario

NOTES

[1] Notable non-causal theorists: Stoutland (1985), Wilson (1989).

[2] See, e.g. Bratman (1987) for an account of the 'structuring' role of intentions. A similar 'directing' and 'controlling' role is ascribed to intentions ('intendings') by Tuomela (1977). Davidson no longer holds, as he did in (1963), that 'intention' is contextually definable in terms of beliefs and desires; see Davidson (1978).

[3] Not to mention Daniel Dennett, who, while perfectly happy with intentional explanations of human action, thinks that they at most amount to 'becausal' explanations in a very loose sense of 'because' that does not beg the question whether reasons are causes. And in fact he argues that they are not (at least not in a 'realist' sense). Nor must one forget the heated debate, in the late 19th century, between the 'mechanists' and the 'hermeneuticists' on the nature of explanation in the 'human sciences' – a debate revived by Carl Hempel and William Dray in this century.

[4] Recall the problem of 'wayward causal chains'; Davidson (1973, 79).

[5] See Davidson (1969).

[6] In view of Baker's and Burge's previously voiced concerns, it is important to realize that Davidson did not propose anomalous monism in order to establish the *truth* of the thesis that reasons can be causes. Rather, he *assumed* the truth of that thesis as an uncontroversial principle. Recall the argument for anomalous monism: given that (P1) some mental events interact causally with physical events, and given that (P2) any causal relation between events must be backed by strict laws, and given, further, that (P3) there can be no strict psychophysical laws (the only strict laws being basic physical laws), it follows that any singular causal relation involving a mental event must be backed by physical laws; hence the mental event must have a physical description; hence it must be a physical event. Obviously, if we use this argument to establish token-physicalism we cannot use token-physicalism to establish that reasons can be causes, for the first premise of the argument assumes just that. The argument, instead, is to be viewed as a sort of 'transcendental deduction' of the thesis that reasons can be causes: granted that some mental events interact with physical events, *how is that possible*, given the constraints imposed by (P2) and (P3)? Answer: it is possible for mental events to interact with physical events if and only if they have law-instantiating physical descriptions, and thus only if they are themselves physical events. Patently, token-physicalism would have to be independently plausible to provide support for psychophysical interactionism.

[7] To use a Davidsonian example: 'The event cited on p. 5 of yesterday's *Times* caused the collapse of the building' (cf. Davidson 1963, 17). This statement may be *true* but surely not *explanatory*.

[8] Strictly speaking, it is not necessary that in order for a singular causal statement to be explanatory, the property by which the cause is identified should be directly 'law-instantiating', in the sense of its actually figuring in a law of nature. It suffices that it bears some appropriate relation to background laws so that the cause and effect, though not, as described, directly subsumable under a law, are nonetheless *backed* by laws. This seems to be what Davidson has in mind in the following passage: "We explain a broken window by saying that a brick broke it; what explanatory power the remark has derives from the fact that we may first expand the account of the cause to embrace an event, the movement of the brick, and we can then summon up evidence

for the existence of a law connecting such events as motions of medium-sized rigid objects and the breaking of windows" (Davidson 1971, 52–53). (I am grateful to R. D. Murray for bringing this point to my attention.)

[9] I.e., (P3) in note 6.

[10] It won't do to protest, as Davidson has recently done (1993, 13), that given an extensionalist view of the causal relation as holding between individual events *however* described, it "makes no literal sense" to suppose that events should cause what they do "in virtue of" this or that property, or, *qua F* or *qua G*. For to suppose that an event *c*, *qua F* causes and event *e*, *qua G*, is, Davidson alleges, to turn the causal relation either into a four-place relation between *c*, *F*, *e*, and *G*, or else into a non-extensional binary relation holding between the *fact* of *c's being F* and the *fact* of *e's being G* – and to do the latter would be to confuse *causation* with *causal explanation*, which explains events under descriptions, that is, as events of this or that *kind*. But, as Kim (1993) and McLaughlin (1993) have rightly insisted, the use of the 'in virtue of' or '*qua*' locution has no such implications. To say that *c* causes *e* in virtue of certain of its properties is to say *both* that *c* causes *e*, *and* that those properties of *c* "played a role" in *c*'s causing *e*. This claim does not deny the extensionality of the causal relation and does not confuse causation with causal explanation: it merely stresses the fact that merely citing the correct cause of an event (an action) is not sufficient as a causal explanation of the effect unless the cause is identified in terms of its causally relevant properties, and these, presumably, are the ones that figure in causal laws. Once this point is clear, there is no harm in interpreting the 'causing-in-virtue-of' (or 'causing *qua*') locution as expressing a complex, multi-term relation – a *qua*-causation relation, or 'quausation', as Horgan (1989) has dubbed it. A theory of *qua*-causation is developed in Tuomela (forthcoming).

[11] See, respectively, Sosa (1984, 277), and Dretske (1989, 1–2).

[12] See, e.g., Honderich (1982), Sosa (1984), Stoutland (1985), Kim (1989b), Antony (1994). It is a matter of controversy whether anomalous monism *entails* property epiphenomenalism, or whether it is merely *consistent* with it (see Marras 1997 for discussion of this point). Anomalous monism cannot of course be charged with *event* epiphenomenalism (the view that mental events do not cause anything). The distinction between event and property epiphenomenalism corresponds to Brian McLaughlin's (1989) distinction between *token* and *type* epiphenomenalism.

[13] It might be protested that this criticism of Davidson depends on our accepting the traditional nomological (covering law) account of causal explanation – an account that many have rejected. My reply is as follows. First, all that needs to be accepted is the assumption that subsumption under laws is least a *partial* condition on causal explanation; many other conditions may apply. Second, Davidson certainly accepts this condition with respect to causal explanation in all the natural (empirical) sciences, so he owes us some good reasons for holding *both* that explanation in psychology is a species of *causal* explanation *and* that, nonetheless, it is not a species of *nomological* (subsumptive) explanation. Why should the *meaning* of 'causal explanation' change as we change domains?

[14] See, e.g., Putnam (1975), Burge (1979).

[15] One way is to insist, against current sentiment to the contrary, that there is some defensible 'internalist' notion of content – 'narrow content' (Fodor 1987), or 'psychological content' (Loar 1988) – as a kind of content that does supervene on the intrinsic physical properties of mental states. Another way is to dispense with narrow content and *either* broaden the physical supervenience-base of content so that it may reach out to some causally relevant portion of the external environment (perhaps defining supervenience over restricted spatio-temporal 'regions' of nomologically possible worlds; cf. Horgan 1993), *or* impose 'accessibility constraints' on possible worlds so that, as a matter of nomological (though not of conceptual) necessity, 'Twin-Earth' cases do not arise (Fodor 1994). On any of these accounts, content co-varies with causal powers, so its causal relevance is not ruled out.

[16] See, e.g., Lepore and Loewer (1987), Fodor (1989), McLaughlin (1989), Davidson (1993).

[17] As David Lewis (1975, 180–191) has shown, non-strict, *ceteris paribus* generalizations, can still be strong enough to support counterfactual conditionals linking the antecedent and the consequent of the generalization, as long as the antecedent is counterfactually independent of the conditions specified by the *ceteris paribus* clause.

[18] For a detailed critique of Davidson's arguments for (PAM), see Lycan (1981).

[19] "if we were to guess at the frequency with which people perform actions for which they have reasons ... I think it would be vanishingly small" (Davidson 1976, 264).

[20] See also Antony (1994) for a very forceful defense of the claim that Davidson's account of the anomalism of the mental rules out the possibility of any genuine empirical psychological laws, whether strict or non-strict. For Davidson, as she convincingly argues, "the generalizations of folk psychology are all instances of the constitutive principles of rationality, and so they are, in effect, analytic" (p. 246).

[21] See (P2) in note 6 above. To question (P2), as e.g. McLaughlin (1993) and Sosa (1993) recently have, is, I think, implausible. For on the assumption that only the laws of basic physics can be strict, (P2) amounts to the principle that any causal relation between events must be backed by physical laws (which of course does not exclude that some causal relations are *also* backed by non-physical laws). To question this principle is to question the physicalist conception of the universe as a closed system at its most basic level – a conception that even a 'minimal' (non-reductive) physicalist ought to embrace. For a critique of Sosa's objections to (P2) see Marras (1997).

[22] Let us say that a property F of c is screened off by a property F' of c, relative to a property G of an effect e of c, if the counterfactual '$(F'c \& \neg Fc) > Ge$' holds non-vacuously (cf. Lepore & Loewer 1987, 304). Unlike Lepore and Loewer, I regard this 'screening' condition as a sufficient condition of causal *ir*relevance; see Marras (1994) for further discussion.

[23] The modal operators range over nomologically possible worlds. Depending on one's preferred way of accounting for the supervenience of *content* properties on physical properties (see note 15), one may wish to impose some 'non-local' conditions on the physical supervenience base – e.g. broaden it to include some external, environment-involving physical properties.

[24] Obviously, there is no supervenience relation between the loudness of a gunshot and its 'lethal' physical properties, or between the meaningfulness of sounds and their pitch and amplitude.

[25] This shows the futility of any attempt to ground the causal relevance of mental properties merely in their aptness to occur in true counterfactuals linking mental and behavioural properties, as e.g. Baker (1993, 93) tries to do.

[26] See esp. Davidson (1974, 236ff, and 1976, 267). See also note 20 above.

[27] By 'higher *level*' property I don't mean 'higher *order*' property, if higher order properties are taken to be properties *of properties* (i.e., higher *type* properties in Russell's sense). A higher level functional property is a property of *individuals* (or *systems* of individuals): it is the property of possessing some (lower level) property that plays a certain functional role. The important point is that while possessing a higher level property requires possessing a lower level property, the higher level property is not to be *identified* with any (non-disjunctive) lower level property.

[28] It is worth noting that Davidson himself construes mental states as dispositions whose attribution "implies" the generalizations of intentional psychology: "The laws implicit in reason explanations are simply the generalizations implied by the attribution of dispositions" (Davidson 1976, 265). Though non-strict, such generalizations are surely non-accidental, if the regularities they express result from the manifestation of dispositions.

[29] This requirement of physical realizability is of course a standard feature of functionalist accounts of the mental; see, e.g., Melnyk (1995). I do not endorse Melnyk's view, however, that the resulting kind of 'realization physicalism' "violates the spirit of non-reductionism" (p. 373).

[30] A similar type of objection has been voiced, for example, by Brian Loar (1992, 249): "If [mental properties] are to be counted as real they must presumably be capable of making a real

difference. ... [But] if they are supervenient on the physical properties that completely account for behavior but they are not identical with such properties, in what sense do they make a difference?" The same sort of epiphenomenalist concern has been expressed by Kim with respect to his own account of 'supervenient causation' (see e.g., Kim 1984b, 1993). Of course, on my account the psychophysical relation is not *merely* a (covariance) relation of supervenience but a metaphysical relation of dependence. Notice that Kim's account of supervenient causation does not even rule out *event* epiphenomenalism, since on *his* 'property exemplification' account of events mental events are *not* token-identical to physical events (Kim 1976).

[31] My arguments, in the papers just cited, are directed against Kim's (1984a) well known thesis, endorsed by Bacon (1986) and others, that strong supervenience entails the possibility of reducing the supervenient to the subvenient (in the standard sense of reduction via biconditional bridge laws), in virtue of entailing the nomological coextention of each supervenient property with a subvenient *disjunctive* property.

[32] See Marras (1994) for an elaboration of this point. Tuomela (forthcoming) holds a similar view, though he gives a first level account of mental properties.

[33] Kim (1990) considers the 'two explananda' strategy as a way of solving the exclusion problem, but argues that it is "fundamentally dualistic, if it is to work" (p. 48). However, he formulates his objection exclusively in the context of the Dretskean distinction between *action* and *bodily movement* ('motor output') – a distinction that for Dretske holds not only at the *type* level but also at the *token* level. Since for Dretske a token of a movement type *M* is never identifiable with a token of an action type *S→M* (the *process* whereby a neural/intentional state of the agent causes a bodily movement), Kim is quite right in arguing that unless tokens of *S→M* are *nonphysical* (and if they are we are stuck with Cartesian dualism), they must have physical explanations even if they have intentional ones, and the exclusion problem arises all over again. This objection, however, does not apply to the two-explananda approach recommended here, for on our (Davidsonian) conception of actions and events, *one and the same* event can be a token of both an *action* type and a *movement* type. As a token of the former type it is (exclusively) a psychological explanandum, as a token of the latter type it is (exclusively) a physical explanandum, and the principle of exclusion is not contravened. Nor is there any threat of Cartesian dualism, since the only dualism involved here is at the level of *types*.

[34] I am grateful to Raimo Tuomela and Scott Walden for their comments on a draft of this paper. This research was supported by the Social Sciences and Humanities Research Council of Canada.

REFERENCES

Antony, Louise (1994), "The Inadequacy of Anomalous Monism as a Realist Theory of Mind" in Gerhard Preyer *et al.*, *Language, Mind and Epistemology: On Donald Davidson's Philosophy*. Dordrecht, Kluwer Academic Publishers, pp. 223–253.

Bacon, John (1986), "Supervenience, Necessary Coextensions, and Reducibility'" *Philosophical Studies* **49**, 163–176.

Baker, Lynn (1993), "Metaphysics and Mental Causation" in Heil and Mele (1993), pp. 75–95.

Bratman, Michael (1987), *Intentions, Plans, and Practical Reason*. Cambridge, Harvard U.P.

Burge, Tyler (1979), "Individualism and the Mental," *Midwest Studies in Philosophy* **4**, 73–121.

Burge, Tyler (1993), "Mind-Body Causation and Explanatory Practice" in Heil and Mele (1993), pp. 97–120.

Davidson, Donald (1963), "Actions, Reasons and Causes" in Davidson (1980), pp. 3–19.

Davidson, Donald (1969), "The Individuation of Events" in Davidson (1980), pp. 163–180.

Davidson, Donald (1970), "Mental Events" in Davidson (1980), pp. 207–225.

Davidson, Donald (1973), "Freedom to Act" in Davidson (1980), pp. 63–81.

Davidson, Donald (1974), "Psychology as Philosophy" in Davidson (1980), pp. 229–244.

Davidson, Donald (1976), "Hempel on Explaining Action" in Davidson (1980), pp. 261–275.
Davidson, Donald (1978), "Intending" in Davidson (1980), pp. 83–102.
Davidson, Donald (1971), "Agency" in Davidson (1980), pp. 43–61.
Davidson, Donald (1980), *Essays on Actions and Events*. Oxford, Clarendon Press.
Davidson, Donald (1993), "Thinking Causes" in Heil and Mele (1993), pp. 3–17.
Dretske, Fred (1989), "Reasons and Causes," *Philosophical Perspectives* 3, 1–15.
Dretske, Fred (1990), "Does Meaning Matter?" in E. Villanueva (ed.), *Information, Semantics, and Epistemology*. Oxford, Oxford University Press.
Fodor, Jerry (1989), "Making Mind Matter More," *Philosophical Topics* **17**, 59–79.
Fodor, Jerry (1994), *The Elm and the Expert*. Cambridge, Mass., MIT Press.
Heil, John and Alfred Mele (eds.) (1993), *Mental Causation*. Oxford, Clarendon Press.
Honderich, Ted (1982), "The Argument for Anomalous Monism," *Analysis* **42**, 59–64.
Horgan, Terence (1989), "Mental Quausation," *Philosophical Perspectives* **3**, 47–76.
Horgan, Terence (1993), "From Supervenience to Superdupervenience: Meeting the Demands of a Material World," *Mind* **102**, 555–586.
Kim, J. (1976), "Events as Property Exemplifications" in M. Brand and D. Walton (eds.), *Action Theory*. Dordrecht, D. Reidel, pp. 159–177.
Kim, Jaegwon (1984a), "Concepts of Supervenience," *Philosophy and Phenomenological Research* **45**, 153–176.
Kim, Jaegwon (1984b), "Self-Understanding and Rationalizing Explanations," *Philosophia Naturalis* **21**, 309–320.
Kim, Jaegwon (1989a), "Mechanism, Purpose, and Explanatory Exclusion," *Philosophical Perspectives* **3**, 77–108.
Kim, Jaegwon (1989b), "The Myth of Nonreductive Materialism," *Proceedings and Addresses of the American Philosophical Association* **63**, 3, 31–47.
Kim, Jaegwon (1990a), "Supervenience as a Philosophical Concept," *Metaphilosophy* **21**, 1–27.
Kim, Jaegwon (1990b), "Explanatory Exclusion and the Problem of Mental Causation" in E. Villanueva (ed.), *Information, Semantics, and Epistemology*. Oxford, Blackwell, pp. 36–56.
Kim, Jaegwon (1993), "Can Supervenience and Non-Strict Laws Save Anomalous Monism?" in Heil and Mele (1993), pp. 19–26.
Kim, Jaegwon (1995), "Mental Causation: What? Me Worry?," *Philosophical Issues* **6**, 123–151.
Lepore, Ernest and Barry Loewer (1987), "Mind Matters," *Journal of Philosophy* **84**, 630–642.
Lepore, Ernest and Brian McLaughlin (eds.) (1985), *Actions and Events: Perspectives on the Philosophy of Donald Davidson*. Oxford, Blackwell.
Lewis, David (1975), "Causation," in E. Sosa (ed.), *Causation and Conditionals*. Oxford, Blackwell, pp. 180–191.
Loar, Brian (1988), "Social Content and Psychological Content" in R.H. Grimm and D. Merrill, (eds.), *Contents of Thought*. Tucson, Arizona, University of Arizona Press, pp. 99–110.
Loar, Brian (1992), "Elimination versus Non-Reductive Physicalism" in David Charles and Kathleen Lennon (eds.), *Reduction, Explanation, and Realism*. Oxford, Clarendon Press, pp. 239–263.
Lycan, W.G. (1981), "Psychological Laws," *Philosophical Topics* **12**, 9–38.
Marras, Ausonio (1993a), "Psychophysical Supervenience and Nonreductive Materialism," *Synthese* **95**, 275–304.
Marras, Ausonio (1993b), "Supervenience and Reductionism: an Odd Couple," *Philosophical Quarterly* **43**, 215–222.
Marras, Ausonio (1994), "Nonreductive Materialism and Mental Causation," *Canadian Journal of Philosophy* **24**, 465–494.
Marras, Ausonio (1997), "The Debate on Mental Causation: Davidson and his Critics," *Dialogue* **36**, 1.

McLaughlin, Brian (1989), "Type Epiphenomenalism, Type Dualism, and the Causal Primacy of the Physical," *Philosophical Perspectives* **3**, 109–135.
McLaughlin, Brian (1993), "On Davidson's Response to the Charge of Epiphenomenalism" in Heil and Mele (1993), pp. 27–40.
Melden, A.I. (1961), *Free Action*. London, Routledge and Kegan Paul.
Melnyk, Andrew (1995), *Philosophy of Science* **62**, 370–88.
Putnam, Hilary (1975), "The Meaning of 'Meaning'" in *Mind, Language and Reality*, Cambridge, Mass., MIT Press, pp. 215–271.
Sosa, Ernest (1984), "Body-Mind Interaction and Supervenient Causation," *Midwest Studies in Philosophy* **84**, 630–642.
Sosa, Ernest (1993), "Davidson's Thinking Causes" in Heil and Mele (1993), pp. 41–50.
Stoutland, Frederick (1985), "Davidson on Intentional Behavior" in Lepore and McLaughlin (1985).
Tuomela, Raimo (forthcoming 1996 or 1977), *Human Action and Its Explanation*. Dordrecht and Boston, D. Reidel.
Tuomela, Raimo (forthcoming), "A Defense of Mental Causation," *Philosophical Studies*.
Wilson, George (1989), *The Intentionality of Human Action*. Stanford, Stanford U.P.

GEORGE WILSON

REASONS AS CAUSES *FOR* ACTION

In most summary accounts of the theory of action, a section is devoted to "The Reasons vs. Causes Debate." Thus advertised, the topic will sound to the neophyte as if it were constituted by some mighty conceptual struggle, with well-defined forces lining up on either side, a philosophical analogue to "The Frazier vs. Ali Fight" or "The 1955 World Series." Of course, there are initial advantages to structuring the issues of the field under vivid headings, but I have come to believe that the long term disadvantages, in the present case, are weightier. We give the impression that our understanding of the nature of the problems is relatively sharp and that nothing is left but a matter of working out details that will point toward a satisfactory solution. The more I contemplate the reasons vs. causes debate, the less confident I am that our questions have been well-drawn. In this essay, I will explain some of the more significant doubts I feel about recent discussions of the subject (including my own)[1] and will indicate some of the areas that are likely to require extensive clarification if substantial progress is to be achieved. In most instances, I will have space only to sketch the pertinent concerns and to adumbrate the perspective on them that I favor.

I. REASONS *ARE* RATIONAL CAUSES

There are hard problems, right from the outset, about how the contending forces should formulate their respective positions. It is wrong to argue vaguely about whether or not reasons are, in some sense or other, causes of action. Of course they are *in some sense*. I take it to be a platitude that if an agent has acted on a certain pro-attitude and instrumental belief, then the pro-attitude and belief *caused* her so to act. This platitude should be accepted on all sides because, by itself, it tells us nothing about what is properly in dispute. Notice that if an agent has a reason for *F*ing,[2] then the relevant pro-attitude and belief *give her cause for Fing*, and if the cause she had for *F*ing was the reason for which she acted, then, by the very same token, that reason gives a *cause for which* she acted. This trivial point is sufficient to yield a deflationary reading of the platitude. It may well be that, in the platitude, the sense in which the agent is said to have been caused by her reason to perform her action amounts to nothing more than this: her reason was a cause *for which* the action was performed. The platitude, on this deflationary reading, helps us not at all,

G. Holmström-Hintikka and R. Tuomela (eds.), Contemporary Action Theory. Vol. I, 65–82.

because, as I will argue later, a chief problem we face in this domain is to explicate our concept of 'a reason (cause) for which the agent acts.'

The causalist will reply that he plainly does not have such a teleologically tainted concept of 'cause' in mind. He holds that reasons are among the *efficient* (or *Humean* or *producing* or *triggering*) causes of the action, and the anti-causalist is supposed to deny this. But, what are these and similar qualifications supposed to add? Certainly I grant that there is a strong intuition that the concept of 'cause' appealed to in the deflationary version of the platitude (call it the concept of a 'rationalizing cause') is somehow quite different from the familiar concept of 'cause and effect' which applies in purely physical domains. Still, in our current state of understanding of causation, the import of the restriction to efficient causes remains seriously unclear. There is simply too much disagreement among philosophers of causality about what the privileged concept does or does not involve.

Suppose that an event *E* causes an object *o* to *G*. There is widespread agreement that *E* is an efficient cause of *o*'s *G*ing only if i) *E*, under a suitable description, contributes to an explanation of *why o G*'ed, and ii) *o*'s *G*ing was counterfactually dependent on *E*. In addition, there is substantial agreement that iii) the pair of events, *E* and *o*'s *G*ing, are subsumed under a general law of nature. However, rationalizing causes certainly satisfy i), and I will argue in section III that they satisfy condition ii) as well despite the fact that the intuitive basis of the dependence seems notably different from what we normally expect when efficient causality is supposed to be at work. The situation concerning condition iii) is the hardest to assess. First, it is still an open question whether even efficient causality universally satisfies condition iii), and, second, there is no consensus about how 'subsumption under law' is to be analyzed and none about the kinds and character of the laws that are permitted to do the 'subsuming.' If 'subsumption under law' is construed weakly enough and the class of available laws of nature is suitably liberal, then it is not obvious that rationalizing causes will not also meet condition iii). For example, if the principles of decision theory are *laws*, it is not obvious that they have the character of *causal laws*, and yet most instances of decision making and consequent action will be subsumed by one or another of these. Further, even if rationalizing causes are not covered by any law, this does not uncontroversially disqualify them from being instances of efficient causality. As indicated above, I share the impression that there are at least two different concepts of 'cause' to be distinguished here, but the impression is murky, and the task of setting out the distinction is fraught with difficulty. When we argue about whether reasons are *efficient* causes of action, I am afraid that the qualification is little more than a gesture towards a conceptual division that we hope to make, and the thesis about which both sides are thought to differ does not have the determinate content we imagine.

Unfortunately then, the prospects for a significant breakthrough in 'the reasons vs. causes debate' are not bright unless and until we have considerably sharpened our overall theory of causation. Although I regard this as a fundamental worry about how the deeper issues are to be defined, I will not here attempt to contribute to the requisite investigation. In the remainder of the essay, I will acquiesce in the usual, but inadequate, framework, but I do so with deep misgivings.

However, to return to my initial observation, the anti-causalist does not deny that reasons are, in some sense, causes. When this has been misunderstood or forgotten, it is easy to pillory anti-causalism as a position that flies outrageously in the face of common sense and common explanatory practice. The platitude, stated above, should be cheerfully affirmed by the various parties to the debate. It is the content of the platitude that divides them.

In the next section, I will begin by outlining one plausible way in which the core question of 'the reasons vs. causes debate' can be construed.[3] Understood along these lines, it appears as though there *is* a tolerably sharp opposition between the causalist and his opponent. This outline will serve as the basis for refining the relevant claims in the disagreement and for explicating some additional puzzles about how these topics should be conceived.

II. CAUSALIST ACCOUNTS OF REASON EXPLANATIONS

The most straightforward version of 'causalism' in the theory of action is the thesis that the components of a primary reason for acting (and associated intentions) are causes or causal conditions of the actions they explain. But, for some purposes at least, it is useful to investigate a related thesis concerning the *content* of reason explanations of action, i.e., the view that

> Reason explanations of actions in terms of an agent's pro-attitudes and associated instrumental beliefs (specified as the agent's reasons for acting) entail or presuppose that the attitudes mentioned in the explanation are cited as causes or causal conditions of the action.

Hereafter, I will refer to this thesis as "minimal causalism," for reasons that will become clearer as we go along. Obviously, there is an intimate connection between minimal causalism and the more straightforward causalist claim stated just before.

In a crucial intervention, Donald Davidson's classic essay, "Actions, Reasons, and Causes," presented a forceful argument in favor of minimal causalism.[4] That argument, in at least one possible version, goes as follows. Suppose that an agent has, at a certain time, a *reason R for F*ing, and that, having that reason he goes on to perform an act of *F*ing. Still, it does not follow from these suppositions that his reason *R* for *F*ing was, in fact, a *reason* *why* he performed his act. There may have been no reason why he *F*'ed at the time in question, or he may have acted because of some reason other than *R*. Moreover, we can add a range of further facts about the agent's circumstances and condition, and it still will not follow that *R* was a reason why he acted. If we are to understand what makes a given reason for acting into a reason why the agent acted, we have to suppose that there is some *explanatory connection* between the psychological states involved in the primary reason, on the one hand, and the behavior that constituted the act of *F*ing on the other. Davidson points out that efficient causation is one such explanatory connection, an essential and ubiquitous one. And, he urges, there simply is no coherent alternative to causation that could serve to ground the explanatory 'force' of the reason explanations that we give. Hence, we cannot make sense of the content of explanations of actions that offer a reason why the agent acted without supposing that the cited psychological attitudes are mentioned there as causes or causal conditions of the act. Hence, minimal causalism is true.

Despite its widespread influence, it has seemed to me and to others that Davidson's argument does not work.[5] In fact, the argument appears to beg the question against the position I take Elizabeth Anscombe to be holding in her monograph, *Intention*.[6] In particular, there does seem to be an alternative to causation which can serve as the explanatory connection that Davidson rightly sought. In genuine reason explanations, when a reason *R* explains why the agent *F*'ed, *R* is presented, more specifically, as a *reason for which* the agent *F*'ed, and this narrower notion was to be understood, as its wording suggests, in teleological terms, i.e., *R* gives the *purpose or goal with which* the agent acted. Stated in a somewhat different way, the alternative proposal is that the following is an explanatory connection and one that plausibly figures in our reason explanations: the behavior that constituted the agent's act of *F*ing *was directed by the agent at* satisfying or promoting the satisfaction of the specified desire, and, moreover, it was directed at that objective by implementing the partial plan expressed in the associated instrumental belief. One way to explain *why* an activity or item of behavior was performed is to mention the function, purpose, or goal that the particular activity had for the organism at the time. Reason explanations, it seems, could be like that. We mention the desires and/or instrumental beliefs so as to indicate the goals or ends *of the particular action* for the agent as he acted – the goals or ends at which that action was directed by its agent. Thus, the thesis, in the first instance, is that this teleological connection between attitudes and action represents a genuine alternative to causation as the grounding for reason explanations of action.

Nevertheless, it is natural enough to hold that the teleological connection just specified can not really be an alternative to efficient causation at all. It is tempting to respond to the proposed alternative by contending that it is a conceptual truth that an agent's behavior was directed at satisfying his desire to

F only if the agent's desire caused the agent to have it as his goal to *F*, and his having that goal (considered as an inner state of the agent) caused the pertinent behavior.[7] The correctness of such a claim would obviously sink the would-be reply to Davidson from the beginning by rendering it circular in the dialectical context. However, it is a central part of what I will call "the teleological alternative" to maintain that such a 'circularity charge' is false. It is crucial for the defense of this alternative to reject the notion that the teleological connection that I have indicated can be reduced conceptually to a complex etiological relation between behavior, on the one hand, and a suitable succession of causally connected attitudes, on the other. We will return to this topic shortly.

A different but related thesis concerns the status of the concept of 'intention' in relation to reason explanations. In another work, I have defended the view that a certain concept of 'behavior *intended* by the agent to *F*' is essentially identical with the concept of 'behavior sentiently directed at the goal of *F*ing.' Thus, this concept of 'intention in action' is *itself* an explanatory connection which links behavior with a reason for *F*ing.[8] Again, this is my interpretation of a crucial theme in Anscombe's book. If we focus specifically on intentional action, then the circularity charge, stated above, will assume the following form: It is a conceptual truth that an agent intends his behavior *b* to satisfy his desire to *F* only if the agent's desire to *F* caused the agent to intend to *F*, and his having that intention caused the behavior *b*.

In assessing the truth or falsity of this form of the circularity charge it is important to keep in mind the rather special character of ascriptions of intention in action. Locutions of the form

The agent intended [his behavior] *b* to *F*

(and variant constructions) are ambiguous in a well-known way. It is a familiar fact that the form of words

The agent believes that he is *G* [or: that he *G*'s]

has at least two salient and notable readings. The form can be used, in merely *de re* ascriptions of belief, to say that the agent believes *of himself* that he is *G* [or: that he *G*'s]. However, the same form of words is more likely to be employed in a *de se* ascription of belief, i.e., to say that the agent believes that *he himself* is *G* [or: that he himself *G*'s]. In my opinion, the *de se* ascription implies the *de re* ascription, but the former semantically conveys something more besides. It tells us that the agent believes, in a characteristic first-person kind of way, about himself, that he is *G* [or: that he *G*'s]. Something similar holds, I believe, when we are dealing with genuine ascriptions of intention in action. Ascriptions of intentions of the type set out above *can* be used simply to ascribe to the agent a mere present directed intention which is about his own behavior. But, I maintain that they may also be used – in fact, are customarily used – to make a stronger claim. They say that the agent intends of his behavior that it is to *F and* that, in so intending, he bears *the characteristic first-person kind of relation* to his own behavior. What does that mean? The only short answer I know to give is the one mentioned before: his behavior is sentiently directed by him at *F*ing. This distinction deserves to be emphasized because, if it gets lost, the claim that intention in action, so conceived, is itself an explanatory connection is drastically obscured.[9]

It will be useful in what follows to separate out more distinctly two kinds of causalist reduction claims that can be at issue in these disputes, the second stronger than the first. Most philosophers who are convinced that the teleological alternative is circular subscribe, I suspect, to both of the reduction claims in question. The first is a causalist account of the concept of 'intention in action.' Or, in the terminology that Davidson tends to favor, this is a causalist account of the concept of "behavior which is 'intentional under a description'."[10] As an adequate first approximation, such an account will assert that

> The agent intends [his behavior] *b* to *F* just in case, at the time that he performs *b*, the agent intends to *F*, and his having that intention causes, in the right way, the behavior *b*.

We can allow that further conditions may be added to the right hand side of the bi-conditional and that more elaborate specification of the specific content of the intention may be developed. Proponents of this reduction claim differ about the possibility of giving a positive account of what it is for the causation to occur 'in the right way.'[11] Many authors, including myself, have criticized this causalist account. It is often pointed out that a deviant or oddball causal chain between the present directed intention to *F* and the behavior *b* raise potential difficulties for this prospective analysis.

However, in this discussion, I will focus more extensively upon the viability of a causalist account of reason explanations of action. Such an account presupposes a causalist account of intention in action but it incorporates more besides. A schematic statement of the position I have in mind is given by Davidson. He says,

> The second obscurity concerns the causal relation between the reasons an agent has for acting and his intention. The answer is that the reasons cause the intention 'in the right way.' ... This leaves the question what the relation between the intention and the action is. In some cases there is no relation because the intention is not acted on. If the intention exists first, and is followed by the action, the intention, along with further events (like noticing that the time has come), causes the action 'in the right way.' If the action is initiated at the moment that the intention comes into existence, then the initiation of the action and the coming into existence of the intention are both caused by the reasons, but the intention remains a causal factor in the development of the action.[12]

Even more schematically, a causalist account of reason explanations of action can be presented as having the following format. Let *R* consist of the agent's desire to *G* and his belief that by *F*ing he will [or: might] *G*. Then

> *R* is a reason for which the agent *F*'ed at *t* just in case the agent's desire to *G* and his associated instrumental belief are causal factors, operating *in the right way*, of his coming to have a present directed intention (at *t*) to *F*, and his having that present directed intention causes him, again *in the right way*, to initiate and/or continue the act of *F*ing he performed at *t*.

As before, one can contemplate a range of elaborations that this schematic account might take. In particular, there are, once again, a variety of views about how much or how little can be said about the concept of 'causing in the right way' in relation to each of its occurrences above. We can be content, for our purposes here, to leave these matters open. In the remainder of the essay, I will chiefly examine the project of constructing an adequate causalist account of reason explanations of action, and the relations of such an account to minimal causalism.

III. ON THE CAUSALIST ACCOUNT OF REASON EXPLANATIONS

In giving a reason explanation of why an agent *F*'ed in terms of the agent's reason *R*, it is not simply that *R* is a reason *why* the agent *F*'ed. Standardly, as noted in the previous section, *R* is mentioned in the explanation as identifying a reason *for which* the agent acted. It is this more specific feature of the explaining reason that crucially defines the type of 'why-explanation' that is being offered. Intuitively, *R* is a reason for which the agent acted just because it somehow contains the goal or purpose *for which* the agent did what he did. Hence, the following more specific question becomes critical: what conditions must be satisfied if an agent's reason for *F*ing is to come to be, in the circumstances of action, a reason *for which* the agent *F*'ed? Presumably, a fully worked out version of a causalist account of reason explanations purports to offer an answer to this question. In my opinion, the prospects of gaining a satisfactory answer from such an account are dim.

First, it is well-known that a range of putative counterexamples to the causalist account of intention in action can be extended to yield putative counterexamples to the causalist account of reason explanations. Suppose that the agent performs certain movements which are caused by the agent's present directed intention to *F*. But, suppose also that the causation here is of such a 'wayward' nature that the resulting movements are involuntary and wholly unintended by the agent. However, purely by happenstance, those movements could constitute an instance of the agent's *F*ing (unintentional *F*ing, of course.) And yet, we can further imagine that the agent's reason for *F*ing gave rise to the present-directed intention to *F* in whatever is deemed to be 'the right way.' Given these assumptions, all that can prevent such a case from being a counterexample to the causalist account of reason explanations is the supposed fact that the intention did not cause the behavior *in the right way*. However, that crucial qualification has remained difficult to clarify in an effective, non-question-begging fashion.[13]

Even if potential counterexamples of this type are waived, the causalist account of reason explanations confronts serious difficulties from different quarters. In the two examples that follow, the agent *F*'s intentionally, and it is granted, for the sake of argument, that the conditions in the causalist account of intention in action have all been satisfied. It is also built into the examples that the more familiar and plausible conditions in causalist accounts of reason explanations are also fulfilled. Nevertheless, as we will see, the reasons for *F*ing in these cases are not among the reasons for which the agent *F*'ed.

Case A. Norbert has broken off from his mistress and has promised his wife not to get in contact with her again. But Norbert is conflicted: he wants very much to call his mistress, but, given his promise to his wife, he also wants strongly not to call. Sitting alone in the den with the phone across the room, he realizes that he can call the mistress simply by walking over to the phone. The temptation in these circumstances is great, and gradually, without actually making any definite decision, he comes to have an intention to phone his mistress. And yet, recognizing that this weak and unworthy intention has, so to speak, formed within him, he guiltily deplores the fact. And, he decides to try to prevent himself from continuing to so intend. This, he thinks, he might accomplish if he were to call his psychiatrist. Her good sense and advice could possibly help him change his set of mind. So, he decides to call the psychiatrist, and, pursuing that aim, he walks to the phone. Here Norbert has wanted to call his mistress, and he believes that he can promote his end by walking to the phone. This reason for walking to the phone – call it 'reason *R*' – is (for the causalist) among the causes of his intending to call his mistress. Nevertheless, *R* also figures, somewhat more indirectly, in his forming the intention to call his psychiatrist. Finally, *both* of these intentions are among the causes (according to the causalist) of his present directed or proximal intention to walk to the phone, and the latter intention 'guides' his behavior 'non-deviantly' as he walks across the room. Therefore, reason *R* meets all of the conditions associated with most causalist accounts of reason explanations, but, *R* is not the reason for which Norbert acted in this case.

Case B. Nancy intends to fly to Boston tonight, and her reasons for doing so pertain entirely to certain business obligations she has. She can choose either flight 1, which takes off quite soon, or flight 2, which leaves a couple of hours later. Up to a certain point in time, she has made no decision about this. But then she recalls that she had the thought of getting a copy of *Newsweek* at the airport newsstand. When this occurs to her, she does not have strong feelings about buying the magazine, but she would like to read the new issue. However, the newsstand is at some considerable distance from her present location in the airport, and, if she goes back to the stand, it is probable that she will miss flight 1. Thus, for a short period, she ponders whether she should take the imminent flight 1 or return to get *Newsweek* and take flight 2 instead. At this juncture, it suddenly strikes her that either of the flights is bound to have a copy of the *Newsweek* on board. Since, other things being equal, she prefers the earlier flight, and she now realizes she will be able to get *Newsweek* on flight 1, she decides to proceed on to that flight. That is, having cleared up the question about whether or not to get the magazine by deciding to get a copy on the plane, she proceeds immediately to flight 1 and leaves for Boston on it.

It is important to the example that Nancy's forming the intention to get herself a copy of *Newsweek* by leaving for Boston on flight 1 does seem to be *a cause or causal condition* of her intention to depart for Boston on flight 1. For, if she had not been able to settle the issue about how and where she would get the magazine (if at all) by deciding to get one on board flight 1, then, we are supposing, her fussing about the matter would have preoccupied her long enough that she would have missed flight 1 and would have been forced to take flight 2 instead. Therefore, Nancy's desire to get a copy of *Newsweek*, combined with her belief that by heading for Boston on flight 1 she would get a copy, constitute (at least in Davidson's sense) a 'primary reason' for her to head for Boston on flight 1. Moreover, this reason plays a causal role in her arriving at her intention to depart when she does, i.e., in time for flight 1, and this present-directed (or: 'proximal') intention presumably guides her actions as she hurries for the plane. Nevertheless, the reason in question is not among the reasons for which she left for Boston, and, central to the present argument, it is not even among the reasons for which she left for Boston on flight 1. She left on that earlier flight simply because it was more convenient to do so and because nothing now stood in the way of suiting her convenience. She knew, of course, that she would also get a copy of *Newsweek* by leaving for Boston on flight 2, and she had no preference between the two ways of getting the magazine.

At the heart of the trouble these examples pose for the causalist account of reason explanations is the fact that it is not the case that the agent performed the relevant type of action *for the purpose of* satisfying the highlighted desire [or: *in order to* satisfy that desire.] Nancy did not leave Boston on flight 1 for the purpose of getting a copy of *Newsweek*, and Norbert did not walk to the phone in order to call his mistress. On the face of the matter, the causalist account fails to capture this central explanatory connection, and it is not obvious how it might be improved to do so.

The challenge that these examples present to the causalist is striking. We have here a kind of counterpart to Davidson's original challenge. In both situations, there are reasons for *F*ing that the agent has, and those reasons are among the reasons that help to explain *why*, in a broad sense, the agent performs his or her act of *F*ing. But, although these are among the reasons why he/she acted, they are not among the reasons *for which* he/she acted. So, the new challenge is to specify the 'something more' that is needed if a reason for acting which contributes to an explanation of why the agent acted is, more specifically, a reason for which the agent acted. A suitable causal connection, by itself, seems to do nothing to specify this 'something more.' I have granted, at least for the sake of argument, that a clear causal track runs between the relevant reasons to the relevant actions. It is true that, in each case, the problematic reason for acting figures in the agent's practical reasoning in a somewhat unusual way, but there is nothing deviant about the kinds of causation that lie along the tracks. The reasons are 'deviant' in these examples because the constituent desire does not represent a goal or end for which the agent goes on to perform the specified act-type, despite the apparent satisfaction of causalist conditions.

It is surely a critical task for any overall theory of reason explanations of action to clarify for us the notion of 'a reason for which the agent acted.' It is a distinctive feature of ordinary reason explanations that they identify, explicitly or by implication, reasons for which the explained action was performed. Causalism's apparent inability to meet this challenge seems to me to be the major objection to it, although the large number of degrees of freedom available within a causalist approach guarantees that no range of putative counterexamples will settle the issue conclusively.

Intuitively, the *contents* of a pro-attitude and associated instrumental belief, cited in an explanation that gives an agent's reasons for acting, are somehow relevant to the force of the explanation given. Causalist accounts of reason explanations inform us that the particular *states* of having the pro-attitude and having the belief, etc., are explanatorily relevant, as efficient causes, to the action. But, the intuitive relevance of the contents of those states has proved highly resistant to elucidation within a causalist framework. It is sometimes thought that if there were strict laws that connect the designated attitude types with associated types of action, then a possible solution to the problem might be constructed. But, I agree with Davidson that no such laws exist. And, in any case, even if they did, it is hard to see how the featuring of contents in purely causal laws would do anything at all to explicate the central fact that those contents often give us the goals or purposes for which the agent acted. Many philosophers seem to think that a causalist account of reason explanations *must* be right, no matter what the short term difficulties might seem to be. I believe that they have misjudged the systematic character of the problems that causalism faces and have underestimated the attractions of the teleological alternative.

IV. MINIMAL CAUSALISM AGAIN

Minimal causalism, it will be recalled, is the view that reason explanation of action cite the components of the reason as efficient causes of the action. Suppose then, as I am prepared to do, that it is possible in principle for there to be a 'complete' causal explanation of the behavior that constitutes action, an explanation which is given in purely neurophysiological terms. Suppose further, as I am also prepared to do, that Jaegwon Kim's principle of explanatory exclusion, applied to 'independent' causal explanations of the same phenomenon, is correct.[14] Under these suppositions, *if* minimal causalism is true, then we are forced with a basic choice. Either a) we admit that the neurophysiological explanations exclude or void the objective truth of common sense reason explanations; or b) we deny that reason explanations of action are causal explanations which are 'independent' of the counterpart neurophysiological explanations of those same actions, i.e., we maintain that the psychological causes are reducible to or strongly supervenient upon the neurophysiological; or c) we accept the position that particular pro-attitudes, beliefs, and, intentions (or their realizations) are strictly identical with appropriate neurophysiological states and processes. Probably the most popular option has been to hold a general token-identity thesis combined with some (possibly, weak) version of the supervenience of common sense psychology upon neurophysiology.[15] Discussion, from the vast literature on this general subject, has shown that choices a), b), and c) all face formidable, although not necessarily insurmountable, objections. It is, therefore, an attraction of the teleological alternative that it opens up a different perspective on the possible place of reasons in a world of (efficient) causes. It does so by rejecting the idea that reason explanations even purport to stand in competition with the causal explanations of neurophysiology.

Consider, in this connection, a different kind of case in which teleological explanations are also at work: the explanation of biological processes and activities in terms of the needs it is their function or purpose to satisfy. It is a striking and suggestive fact that one can explain why, e.g., Smith's blood coagulated on a certain occasion by noting that, in the circumstances, the body had a need to be protected from germs in the vicinity. Because of the wound, a need arose for the body to be protected from neighboring germs, and the coagulation of the blood had the function of satisfying that particular need. Moreover, in giving such a 'function' explanation of the blood's coagulation, nothing whatsoever seems to be implied about the nature of the causes of that coagulation. That there were such causes is unquestionable, but what those are is a task for the chemistry of the blood to uncover. The need for protection from the germs occurred because of the infliction of the wound, and the need itself is not plausibly included as one of those causes. Similarly, there are relatively simple cases of the goal directed activities of simple organisms about which the same observations can be made.[16] Hence, it is an ambition that broadly motivates the teleological alternative in action theory to propose that reason explanations may, in a like manner, explain why the agent performed her action by naming the goals and purposes of that action for the agent. For easily understood reasons, those goals and purposes are frequently identified in terms of the agent's desires and instrumental beliefs. Finally, it seems that these explanations, rightly understood, might also imply nothing about the efficient causes of the behavior. Naturally, it is not to be doubted that actions have causes: it is just that reason explanations might not aim at telling us what they are.

However, it also should be observed that there are explanations of goal directed biological activity in which appeals to the needs of the system play a double explanatory role. Consider the case of homeostatically controlled activities in which instances of the activity type are elicited by the occurrence of intermittent needs for, say, the presence, at certain levels, of some kind of substance in the system. Here it does seem right to say that the need for the substance (the absence of the needed substance) causes the particular activity and that the activity has the function of satisfying the need (providing the needed substance.) But now, this raises a pair of fundamental questions: Why couldn't a similar situation obtain in connection with reason explanations of action? And, why couldn't it be a part of our ordinary conception of the matter that this is so? The state of desiring to *F* could be a cause of the relevant behavior, and it could be the goal or purpose of the behavior to satisfy the object of the desire. Following Abraham Roth, I will call this "the composite view."[17]

At this juncture, we are confronted by a delicate issue which is easily overlooked. Let it be stipulated that explanations that give a reason for which the agent acted involve the teleological connection I have described, and, let it be assumed, in addition, that the causalist account of reason explanations is mistaken, i.e., the teleological connection is not conceptually reducible to a sequence of appropriate causal ties between specified kinds of desires, beliefs, and intentions, on the one hand, and actions, on the other. Nevertheless, it remains the case that the teleological connection is an *alternative* to the requisite mode of causal connection only in the sense that they are irreducibly distinct relations and contribute to the force of explanations in different ways. None of the stipulated theses, singly or together, rule out the possibility that reason explanations of action mention the relevant desires and instrumental beliefs *both* as causes of the constituent behavior *and* as indicating that the behavior is directed at the desired goal in accordance with the believed-in plan. In other words, the 'alternatives' may not be *mutually exclusive*.

In the course of the reasons vs. causes debate, it has not, on the whole, been clear what, if any, alternatives to causalism, exist. In the absence of a relatively definite non-causalist proposal, the present issue is difficult to frame perspicuously. On the other hand, once a reasonable proposal is on stage – the teleological alternative, for example –, then it emerges forcefully that the resulting non-causalism might not itself be incompatible with minimal causalism.

Historically, this composite view would split the difference between a position like Anscombe's in *Intention* and the position that Davidson and many others have endorsed, Or, to put the thought in a grander style, the composite view would achieve a higher synthesis of the erstwhile competing theories. One might argue, from this vantage point, that the whole reasons vs. causes has rested upon a mistake. Each side has focused exclusively and wrongly on one component of the pair of explanatory connections that together ground correct reason explanations. One side asserts that causation is the true basis of these explanations, and the other side insists that intention in action is the explanatory basis. Is it not possible and even plausible that both components are required for the full philosophical story to be told?

I now believe that the composite view deserves to be taken seriously. Having affirmed this point, I will add that I remain unconvinced that there are grounds for embracing minimal causalism, even if it is incorporated in the composite view. As far as I can make out, the composite view is minimally coherent, but that is all. Certainly, Davidson's original argument does not support it, since the teleological alternative suffices to provide a coherent account of the force of the "because" in reason explanations. Moreover, other considerations that are sometimes adduced in favor of minimal causalism are likewise unpersuasive.

For example, Jennifer Hornsby, commenting on Davidson's argument, summarizes two further lines of thought that are or might be put forward in support of his argument's conclusion.

> Not that 'because' is everywhere a causal notion. Where action explanation is concerned, there may be more to say to ensure that causation has been at work when the explanatory claim can be made. But this is supported when it has been seen (a) that the 'because' goes alongside other, recognizably causal idioms ('His belief *led* him to...'; 'Her desire *moved* her to...'; 'Her reason was *operative*'); (b) that the explanations rely on a network of empirical interdependencies, recorded in counterfactuals ('If she had not wanted___, but had still believed that___, then...').[18]

I have, in effect, already commented upon the first suggestion that Hornsby makes in this passage. It is not merely that we use "recognizably causal idioms" like the ones she mentions, but, as I acknowledged in section I, we speak directly about reasons *causing* an agent to act. However, I argued in that section that this 'causal' discourse is ambiguous in a manner that often leaves it uncertain what kind of causality is at stake. Unsurprisingly, I would say the same about the constructions she cites here.

The second of Hornsby's considerations cuts deeper and is, I suspect, much more influential. It is true that when a reason explanation of a particular action is correct, there is a counterfactual dependence between the explaining psychological states and the action they explain. If the agent had not had the desire in question, or, if she had not had the associated instrumental belief, then she would not have performed the action that she did. The causalist, of course, is eager to maintain that the existence of such a dependence can only be explained in a natural way by the assumption that the attitudes and behavior are linked as efficient causes to effects. The issues in this domain are complex, and I will have to be brief in sketching a response. First, acceptance of the causalist interpretation of the counterfactuals is hardly mandatory. There are, after all, several forms of counterfactual dependence that are not grounded in causality. For example, in my book, I discussed a class of cases in which a metal strut has been loaded with a weight that exceeds a certain critical limit.[19] Given these circumstances, the strut will behave in a characteristic manner (wobble around bizarrely) until it settles into one or the other of the positions that constitute a state of equilibrium for the loaded system. Here the character of the wobbling behavior depends in part, but crucially, on what the equilibrium positions for the total system (strut + weight) are. That is, if the equilibrium positions for the total system had been appropriately different, then the behavior of that system as it settled into a state of equilibrium would have been different as well. At the level of physical law, the counterfactual dependence of the strut's behavior upon the equilibrium positions of the strut is engendered by the conformity of this type of simple system to the Law of Least Work.[20]

And yet, the states of equilibrium or the fact that the system had just these states of equilibrium are not among the causes of the wobbling. On the other hand, there *is* a complicated causal history of the system's erratic behavior, a history that involves the evolving interplay of forces which operate within the weighted strut. But, this is a causal history that we are normally in a poor position to describe in any substantial detail, and, in actual practice, we base our predictions and explanations of strut behavior on our knowledge of what behavior is to be expected as the system undergoes its lawful transition from initial weighting into equilibrium. No doubt the general facts that underlie our 'higher order' explanations of transition behavior must *supervene*, in some relatively weak sense, upon the facts contained in the fine-grained causal history, but I believe that it is clear that there is no question here of an *analysis* or *reduction* of the 'equilibria' explanations to causal explanations in terms of the system-internal forces that produce the wobbling. In fact, it is my view that reason explanations of action are probably related to the neurophysiological causation of action in a related manner. But, for the present, the loaded strut example suffices to remind us that not all cases of counterfactual dependence are based on a causal relation between the dependent terms.

Second, I believe that the teleological alternative already has the resources to explain why the pertinent counterfactual dependencies obtain without assuming that the causalist's account of them is needed. There is a distinctly non-causalist story to be told. Suppose that Jones has, in a normal fashion, acted upon her desire to *F*, and let *b* be the behavior that constituted her act of *F*ing. So, we are inclined to judge that Jones would not have performed *b* had she not, at the time, wanted to *F*. Stated most succinctly, my view is that the counterfactual holds in virtue of the fact that Jones's desire to *F* (and not some other pro-attitude she concurrently held) was the one that was *decisive* for Jones in her 'choice in action' to perform *b*. But this succinctness is bound to be misunderstood, so let me expand the thought a bit.

It is a fundamental fact that normal, unakratic agents, who are not otherwise obstructed, perform the behavior which they expect to bring about results that seem to them sufficiently worth acting for. What is more, this is not merely a contingent generalization about rational agents, since it is precisely the role or function of an agent's practical judgements that some potential upshot is worth acting for to provide *targets* for the agent's ensuing courses of activity. These judgements promote an object of desire to the status of a favored objective which the agent's behavior is to aim at, and, in the normal course of things, the agent will reasonably do just that. In light of this, consider Jones again. If she had not wanted to *F* as she did, then she would have had no reason which seemed to her worth acting on for performing a *b*-type action, and, exercising her normal capacity not to act in a way for which she had no reason or no reason which she deemed action-worthy, she simply would have refrained from performing *b*. Therefore, we need not postulate that the counterfactual dependency arises because Jones's psychological states have been among the producing causes of her bodily movements. Rather these connections rest upon the compelling reasonableness of acting upon one's own judgement about what, in the context of choice, it is best for one to do. Since doing some *F*ing is sufficiently attractive to Jones, she chooses, as she acts, to perform *b*. This need not mean that her attraction to an *F*-type action completed a set of conditions sufficient to cause *b*. It is a part of our intuitive conception of the matter that, at the time of acting, *it was in Jones's power* whether or not her desire to *F* would cause her to perform an act of *F*ing, i.e., would be a cause for which she acted. If that intuition is sustained, then the 'causality' upon which the counterfactual dependence is based does not sound like an exemplary instance of *efficient* causation, as it is normally conceived.

I realize, of course, that this rather bald response is bound to be controversial. Many will have the suspicion that the crucial causal relations must somehow be smuggled beneath the surface of the tale I have told. I do not know how to dispel those suspicions, and many longstanding disputes (about the fundamental nature of agency, say) will rage again. Worse yet, these disputes will remain intractable as long as the general questions about the concept or concepts of 'causation' sketched in the first section of this paper have not been answered. Nevertheless, it seems to me that there is defensible position concerning the status of the counterfactuals in question that does not rest on minimal causalism. Too often it is taken for granted that the anti-causalist has nothing plausible to say about this issue, but that impression is simply wrong.

Where then, after all this, do we wind up on the question of the acceptability of minimal causalism? I have just explained why I cannot discern any compelling considerations in its favor, and I want to emphasize that point. I continue to reject the idea that the teleological alternative either implies or somehow presupposes minimal causalism. However, it now seems to me to be implausible that there are considerations in virtue of which minimal causalism can be refuted, and I have also agreed that the conjunction of the two positions ('the composite view') may well be coherent. But, in my judgement, coherence is its only virtue. There appear to be no grounds for *adding* minimal causalism to the teleological perspective I have drawn, because the causalist component would have no philosophical work to do. Further, if minimal causalism is adopted, then we thereby foreclose the somewhat radical response to the problem of explanatory exclusion (with reference to actions) that I outlined at the beginning of this section. We will be forced once again to confront the issue of how it is that complete neurophysiological explanations of action will not threaten to exclude our common sense reason explanations of the same phenomena. Giving up the radical but reconcilitory option seems to me to be a substantial price to pay, but many philosophers will be more sanguine about the other choices.

How then might the debate over minimal causalism proceed from this point? One possibility is that the question of the truth or falsity of that thesis will turn out to be undecidable. If this should be so, however, the undecidability may be a matter of relatively little philosophical importance. That is, the question *is* of small importance if I am right that minimal causalism brings with it no solutions to substantive philosophical questions about reason explanations that are superior to the solutions already provided by the teleological alternative. In any case, no matter how these issues sort out in the end, I am confident about the following assessment. What *is* important is the nature of the teleological connection, its irreducibility to causalist accounts, and the centrality of its role in reason explanations.[21]

Johns Hopkins University

NOTES

[1] The work of mine in question is *The Intentionality of Human Action*, Revised and Enlarged Edition.

[2] Here and throughout "*F*" and "*G*" are used as dummy variables that stand in for predicates, specifically either verb or adjective phrases. As indicated instance by instance, the instatiating

phrases may be featured in one tense or another, and the verb phrases may sometimes occur in a nominalized form.

3 The framework I will be outlining derives, by and large, from Wilson (1989).

4 Donald Davidson (1980, 3–20).

5 For example, see Stoutland (1976, 286–325) and (1985, 44–59). Also see Sehon (1994, 63–72).

6 Anscombe (1963).

7 Because it has not been usual to address the contention that 'the teleogical connection' is a relevant *alternative* to efficient causation, it is not easy to find an explicit endorsement of this kind of circularity charge. However, it seems implicit in many discussions that teleological explanations are themselves causal explanations, distinctive primarily because of the 'teleological' character of some of the causal factors that they cite. This point will be clarified as the discussion proceeds, and some relevant citations will be given. For such a broadly causalist approach to teleology, see, for example, Woodfield (1976). Also, I will discuss later in the paper the important fact that there may be grounds for accepting minimal causalism that do not depend upon acceptance of views that sustain the charge of circularity. I am concerned here with those philosophers who believe that Davidson's challenge can not be met along the suggested lines *because* they hold that the teleological connection is itself to be construed, as specified, in causal terms. Raimo Tuomela pointed out to me the need for this clarification.

8 For much more on this claim, see Wilson (1989, chapters 7 through 10).

9 I discussed this particular point in Wilson (1989, 121–122). The point is missed in the example of roof climbing behavior that Alfred E. Mele gives in (1992, 249). Mele's character Norm merely has a *de re* intention, concerning his behavior, that it satisfy a certain desire, and Mele observes correctly that the having of that intention is not sufficient for the desire to explain Norm's activity. But, it is not my position that such a fact suffices to yield an explanatory relation between the agent's pro-attitude and his action. Further, this aspect of my conception of intention in action and the fact that I identify intention in action with sentient guidance of behavior marks an important difference between my views and the kindred position in Ginet (1990, especially chapter 6).

10 For instance, Davidson says in (1980b, 48), "To describe an action as one that had a certain purpose or intended outcome is to describe it as an effect...". It is clear, in context, that he means that the action is thereby described as an effect of the having of the purpose or of the intention.

11 Davidson, I believe, accepts this account although he despairs of going on to give an informative account of 'causing in the right way.' See his famous concession to that effect in (1980, 79). Perhaps we will not think of the causalist account as being, in a full sense, 'reductive' if that concession is agreed to. But other causalist authors have insisted on the need to go to provide a positive account of the concept of 'causing in the right way,' notably Bishop in (1989).

12 This passage is from Davidson's reply to Bruce Vermazen in *Essays on Davidson: Actions & Events*, p. 221. In the relaxed sense I have in mind, it seems plain that Davidson's remarks represent a kind of conceptual truth for him.

13 For an incisive critique of the attempts by Alfred Mele and John Bishop to develop a positive account of 'causing in the right way,' see Sehon (forthcoming).

14 See especially the essay, "Mechanism, Purpose, and Explanatory Exclusion" in Kim (1993, 237–264).

15 An extensive presentation of the argument that these are the relevant options is given in Kim, *op. cit.* The popular option is, of course, the one that Davidson has defended.

16 I present examples of the kinds in question in Wilson (1989, 181–182).

17 I owe the term for and the idea of the significance of the composite view to Abraham Roth. The topic was raised in his "Teleology and Intentional Action," a paper he gave at the Pacific

Division Meetings of the APA in 1995. Remarks of Michael Bratman's were also very helpful in this regard.

[18] Hornsby (1993, 165, fn. 5).

[19] Discussion of strut behavior in Wilson (1989, 201–204). However, in that context, this example was used to illustrate a different but related point.

[20] For a simple exegesis of strut behavior and its explanation, see Salvadori (1990, 85–89).

[21] The present paper originated as a reply to Michael Bratman and Alfred Mele in a session on *Intentionality* at the Pacific Division Meetings of the APA in 1996. I am grateful to Michael and Alfred for their contributions to that pleasant session. As usual, I am greatly indebted to Mark Wilson – especially for his knowledge of the bizarre behavior of metal struts.

REFERENCES

Anscombe, G.E.M. (1963), *Intention*. 2nd Edition. Ithaca, N.Y., Cornell University Press.

Bishop, John (1989), *Natural Agency: An Essay on the Causal Theory of Action*. Cambridge, Cambridge University Press.

Davidson, Donald (1980a), "Actions, Reasons, and Causes" in *Essays on Actions and Events*. Oxford, Oxford University Press.

Davidson, Donald (1980b), "Agency" in *Essays on Actions and Events*. Oxford, Oxford University Press.

Davidson, Donald (1980c), "Freedom to Act" in *Essays on Actions and Events*. Oxford, Oxford University Press.

Ginet, Carl (1990), *On Action*. Cambridge, Cambridge University Press.

Hornsby, Jennifer (1993), "Agency and Causal Explanation" in J. Heil and A. Mele (eds.), *Mental Causation*. Oxford, Oxford University Press.

Kim, Jaegwon (1993), "Mechanism, Purpose, and Explanatory Exclusion" in *Supervenience and Mind: Selected Philosophical Essays*. Cambridge, Cambridge University Press.

Mele, Alfred E. (1992), *Springs of Action: Understanding Intentional Behavior*. Oxford, Oxford University Press.

Roth, Abraham (1995), "Teleology and Intentional Action," the Pacific Division Meetings of the APA in 1995.

Salvadori, Mario (1990), *How Buildings Stand Up: The Strength of Architecture*. New York, W.W. Norton.

Sehon, Scott R. (1994), "Teleology and the Nature of Mental States," *American Philosophical Quarterly* **31**, 63–72.

Sehon, Scott R. (forthcoming), "Deviant Causal Chains and the Irreducibility of Teleological Explanation," *Pacific Philosophical Quarterly*.

Stoutland, Fred (1976), "The Causation of Behavior" in *Essays on Wittgenstein in Honor of G.H. Von Wright. Acta Philosophica Fennica* **28**, pp. 286–325.

Stoutland, Fred (1985), "Davidson on Intentional Behavior" in E. LePore and B. McLaughlin (eds.), *Actions and Events: Perspectives on the Philosophy of Donald Davidson*. Oxford, Basil Blackwell, pp. 44–59.

Vermazen, B. and M.B. Hintikka (eds.) (1985), *Essays on Davidson: Actions & Events*. Oxford, Oxford University Press.

Wilson, George (1989), *The Intentionality of Human Action*. Revised and Enlarged Edition. Stanford, CA, Stanford University Press.

Woodfield, Andrew (1976), *Teleology*. Cambridge, Cambridge University Press.

RISTO HILPINEN

ON STATES, ACTIONS, OMISSIONS AND NORMS

I

Philosophers, lawyers and detectives have been puzzled by the problem of locating actions in time and space. The great detective Nero Wolfe observed (Stout 1935/1982, 16):

The average murder, I would guess, consumes ten or fifteen seconds at the outside. In cases of slow poison and similar ingenuities death of course is lingering, but the act of murder is commonly quite brief.

Wolfe seems to think that an act of murder by poisoning takes place at the time when the murderer (for example) pours poison into the victim's drink; the result which makes that individual action an act of murder may occur much later. The time of the poisoning is the time when the murderer interacts with the external world in a way which causes the victim to die. According to Wolfe, the act of murder *consists* in this case in the murderer's pouring of the poison into the victim's glass.[1]

If the spatial location of an action is determined in an analogous way, we should say that an act of murder occurs in the place where the perpetrator acts (for example, moves his hand), and this may be quite distant from the location of the victim's death. Questions concerning the location of actions are not always merely conceptual exercises, but can be of considerable practical importance, for example, when a court has to decide whether a given act has occurred within its jurisdiction. In 1859 a New Jersey court considered a case in which the victim died in New Jersey from blows struck by the defendant in New York, and decided that the state of New Jersey had no jurisdiction over the case, because "no 'act' of the accused took place in New Jersey" (Cook 1942, 9). Like Nero Wolfe, the New Jersey court identified the act with the agent's bodily movements. However, other courts have adopted a different view on this matter. In a case in which the accused stood on the North Carolina side of the state border, and shot and killed a person who was in Tennessee, a North Carolina court held that "in legal contemplation" the act of killing took place in Tennessee, because the action "became effectual" in Tennessee (*ibid.*, p. 12). This view seems reasonable insofar as the effect (or the result) required for the characterization of the act as a murder was actualized in Tennessee, even though the perpetrator pulled the trigger in North Carolina. "In legal contemplation", the act was not completed until the victim was dead. According to W.W. Cook (1942, 9), there seems to have been a time when, according to

G. Holmström-Hintikka and R. Tuomela (eds.), Contemporary Action Theory. Vol. I, 83–107.

the English law, a murderer could not be punished unless both the blow and the death occurred in the county where the defendant was prosecuted. However, Cook notes that "the accuracy of [this] statement is not entirely clear", and from the moral and legal standpoint this requirement would have been a highly unsatisfactory way of avoiding the problems of localizing actions. In judicial contexts it is reasonable to adopt the view that the location of the act can be determined either by the actor's bodily movements or by the legally relevant effects of such bodily action (Cook 1942, 10–12).[2] According to this view, the location of an act includes both the location of the actor's movements and the place where the action "takes effect", that is, where the result of the act is actualized. In the recent philosophy of action, many critics of the Wolfean view have adopted this conception of acts and argued that the location of an act includes the location of the event or events on the basis of which the act is described and identified (Thomson 1971, 116–119; 1977, 47–60; Thalberg 1977, 101–111).[3]

II

The problems mentioned above have reappeared in the recent formal theories of action. In his book *Norm and Action* (1963) Georg Henrik von Wright observes that actions (or acts) usually involve changes in the world:

> Many acts may ... be described as the bringing about or *effecting* ('at will') of a change. To act is, in a sense, to *interfere* with the 'course of nature' (p. 36).

von Wright notes: "To every act ... there corresponds a change or an event in the world", and adds:

> the terms 'change' and 'event' must then be understood in a broad, generalized sense, which covers both changes (events) and not-changes (not-events). (*Ibid.*, p. 39.)

By this he means that the change associated with an act need not be an actual change, but a merely possible change, that is, a change which would have occurred if the agent had not been active. Von Wright analyzes actions in terms of three world-states or *occasions*: (i) the *initial state* which the agent changes or which would have changed if the agent had not been active (had not interfered with the course of nature), (ii) the *end-state* or the *result-state* which results from the action (von Wright 1963, 28), and (iii) the *counter-state* which would have resulted from the initial state without the agent's interference, in other words, the state which would have resulted from the agent's passivity. The counter-state is needed for expressing the "counter-factual element" of action (von Wright 1968, 43–44).

The characterization of acts by means of three states or occasions makes it possible to distinguish $2^3 = 8$ different *modes of action* with respect to a single proposition or state of affairs p. These modes of action may be defined as follows: Let $W = \{u,v,w,\ldots\}$ be a set of possible world-states or occasions, and let us assume that the agent can be in a given state either active or passive. Let d be a function which assigns to each $u \in W$ a state which results from the agent's activity at u, and let e be a function which assigns to each $u \in W$ the corresponding counter-state. The truth-value of p at u is denoted by '$V(p,u)$', and (as usual) '$V(p,u)=1$' (where '1' means the value *true*) will be abbreviated '$u \models p$'. For example, if $u \models \neg p$, $d(u) \models p$ and $e(u) \models \neg p$, we can say that the agent *brings it about* that p or *produces* the state of affairs that p. In this case p becomes true as a result of the agent's activity: without the agent's action it would have remained false that p. The falsity of p at the initial state and at the counter-state constitute an *opportunity* for the agent to bring it about that p. On the other hand, if p is false at $d(u)$ under otherwise similar circumstances, we can say that the agent *omits* to bring it about that p. In this way we obtain the action possibilities presented in Table 1.

Table 1. The Main Action-Types according to von Wright.

	u	$d(u)$	$e(u)$	Mode of action	Action-logical expression
Act1	$\neg p$	p	$\neg p$	Bringing it about that p. (Producing the state that p.)	Bp
Act2	$\neg p$	$\neg p$	$\neg p$	Letting it remain the case that not-p.	$omBp$
Act3	p	p	$\neg p$	Sustaining the state that p.	Sp
Act4	p	$\neg p$	$\neg p$	Letting it become the case that not-p.	$omSp$
Act5	p	$\neg p$	p	Bringing it about that not-p. (Destroying the state that p.)	$B\neg p$
Act6	p	p	p	Letting it remain the case that p.	$omB\neg p$
Act7	$\neg p$	$\neg p$	p	Sustaining the state that not-p. (Suppressing the state that p.)	$S\neg p$
Act8	$\neg p$	p	p	Letting it become the case that p.	$omS\neg p$

For the sake of brevity, I shall sometimes speak about states of affairs as if they were objects, and say (for example) that the agent brings about or produces the state p, instead of saying that an agent brings it about that p.[4] In this simplified terminology, we can say that Act1 is an act of *producing* p, Act3 is an act of *preserving* p, and Act5 is an act of *destroying* p.

If $V(p,d(u)) \neq V(p,e(u))$, the truth-value of p depends on the agent's activity; in this case the agent is *active* with respect to p; otherwise the agent may be said to be *passive* with respect to p. The action-types in which $V(p,d(u)) = V(p,e(u)))$ are *omissions* (abbreviated 'om'). An omission should be distinguished from the non-performance of an act: an agent can omit an act only in a situation in which he has an opportunity to perform the act in question; thus an omission entails non-performance, but not conversely. If $V(p,d(u)) \neq V(p,e(u))$ and $V(p,d(u)) \neq V(p,u)$, the action in question is a *productive* or a *destructive* act, but if $V(p,d(u)) \neq V(p,e(u))$ and $V(p,d(u)) = V(p,u)$, the action is an act of *sustaining* or *preserving* some state of affairs.

III

According to von Wright, the truth-values of sentences, including those of action sentences, are relative to occasions or world-states (1963, 23). The interpretation of an action sentence involves three occasions, two of which (the initial state and the result state) are actualized in the course of the action, but the third one is a merely possible (counterfactual) occasion. Should an action sentence be evaluated as true or false relative to the initial state or the result state – does the action "take place" in the initial situation or the result situation? This is the action-logical counterpart of the philosophical problem of the time and the location of an action discussed in section I above.

In (1983) von Wright argues that the sentence

(1.B) $Bp \rightarrow p$

is not a logical truth on the ground that

> $Bp \rightarrow p$ would say that if a state is produced on some occasion then it *is* (already) there on this occasion. But this is logically false. (1983, 195–196.)

This suggests that the *initial* occasion should be regarded as the point of evaluation. An agent can bring it about that p only if p is false on the initial occasion. According to this view, we should define (for example) the truth of 'Bp' (the agent brings it about that p) as follows:[5]

(ABvW) $u \models Bp$ if and only if (i) $d(u) \models p$, (ii) $e(u) \models \neg p$, and (iii) $u \models \neg p$.

According to (ABvW), sentence (1.B) is logically false, whereas

(2) $Bp \rightarrow \neg p$

is logically true.[6]

Definition (ABvW) is not plausible if 'Bp' is read 'the agent brings it about that p', that is, if 'Bp' is regarded as a genuine action proposition which states that the agent *does* something. According to von Wright, an action changes a situation or a state in some respect or keeps it unchanged, and the state or 'world' u is understood here as the situation which either is or is not changed by the agent's action. It should be clear that 'Bp' cannot be regarded as part of the description of the very situation which is changed (or kept unchanged) by the action in question. It is convenient to say that the agent chooses to perform an action "at" the initial state (or situation) u: u is the state from which the action 'originates', but strictly speaking, the sentences 'Bp', 'Sp', '$omBp$' and '$omSp$' cannot be regarded as true or false at u – if they are understood as genuine action sentences.

IV

One potential source of confusion here is the possibility of understanding the expression 'possible world' in two different ways: it can mean either temporal world-states or world-histories, that is, sequences of world-states. In von Wright's approach, a 'possible world' is understood in the former way: it means a possible state of the world at a given moment, a world-state. If events are regarded as changes (or world state transformations) and an action is regarded as the bringing about of a change, we obviously cannot assume that action propositions are interpreted as sets of possible worlds: actions do not take place within possible worlds.

On the other hand, if possible worlds are understood as *histories*, as paths in a tree whose nodes are world-states, we can say that an agent performs a certain action *in* a possible world. For example, in his pioneering work on the modal logic of imperatives and action statements Brian Chellas (1969) defines the truth-conditions of action sentences for history-time pairs. He represents actions by means of an "instigative operator" D_a which may be read "a sees to it that ...", and presents the following truth-definition for D-sentences:

(AD.Ch) $h,t \models D_a p$ if and only if $h',t \models p$ for every history h' such that $R_t(h,h')$.

Chellas calls the relation R_t the "instigative alternativeness relation" between possible worlds. Thus he regards the concept of seeing to it that p as logically analogous to the necessity operator of modal logic: the truth of $D_a p$ at a given time t in a history h amounts to the truth of the proposition p at t in all "instigative t-alternatives" of h. R_t is assumed to be a reflexive relation; thus Chellas's semantics validates the action-logical counterpart of the principle T of modal logic,

(1.D) $D_a p \rightarrow p$.

Intuitively speaking, the truth of $D_a p$ at (h,t) means that what the agent does in h constrains the course of history in such a way that p is bound to be the case at time t. Chellas's analysis of action sentences does not contain a counterfactual condition.

According to Chellas, the t-alternatives of a given history h must have the same past as h, but may differ from h at t (Chellas 1969, 82; 1992, 490–491). If we let $h(t)$ be the state of world (history) h at t, Chellas's condition can be expressed by

(DR.Ch) $R_t(h,h')$ only if $h(t') = h'(t')$ for every $t' < t$.

If we assume that time is discrete and points of time are indexed by integers, the t-alternatives to a history h must (according to (DR.Ch)) coincide with h up to the instant t-1, but can diverge from h after that point. Thus they can be pictured by a cone of histories which has its apex at $h(t-1)$. (Cf. Segerberg 1992a, 372.)

In von Wright's terminology, we may say that, given the assumption of the discreteness of time, Chellas's theory makes a distinction between the initial state and the end-state (or result-state) of an action, and action sentences are evaluated at the end-state. If $h,t \models D_a p$, we may regard $h(t)$ as the end-state and $h(t-1)$ as the initial state *a*'s seeing to it that *p*.

In Chellas's semantics, a pair (h,t) represents the state of a world-history at *t*, that is, what has been denoted by *u*, *w*, etc., in our earlier discussion of von Wright's theory. Consequently Chellas's theory is subject to the same interpretational questions as von Wright's theory. Krister Segerberg (1992a, 373) has raised such questions in his comments on Chellas's analysis:

> Does the agent 'do' anything at $t-1$ [the immediate predecessor of the time of evaluation] to define a certain cone – does action consist in choosing or somehow committing oneself to a cone? Otherwise, where does action come from? And when does it take place – at $t-1$, at *t*, at the interval $[t-1,t]$, or what?

Since the cone of alternative histories (the *t*-alternatives to a given history *h*) represents a choice which is open to the agent in the situation $h(t-1)$, we obviously cannot say that the agent's action 'takes place' in the later situation $h(t)$, that is, at time *t*. It would be more plausible to say that the action takes place in the interval $[t-1,t]$, and that the pair $\langle h(t-1),h(t)\rangle$ *exemplifies* the action which ties the agent to the result. Thus it is misleading to read Chellas's D-sentences as action sentences of the form '*a* sees to it that *p*'; the D-formulas should instead be regarded as statements about agency, i.e., statements to the effect that a certain result *p* is due to an agent *a*. This point is illustrated by Chellas's justification of the principle '$D_a p \rightarrow p$' (1.D), the action-logical variant of the principle T of modal logic (1969, 66):

> One can see to it that such-and-such is, or be responsible for such-and-such's being, the case only if such and such is the case.

It is obviously false or misleading to say that one can see to it that *p* only if it is the case that *p*: as von Wright has pointed out, a person can bring it about that *p* only if it is *not* the case that *p*, and bringing it about that *p* may be a case of seeing to it that *p*.[7] On the other hand, it is correct to say that one can be held responsible for it being the case that *p* only if it is the case that *p*: statements about (causal) responsibility can be evaluated only at the end-states of actions. Thus we have to distinguish here between (present tense) action sentences and statements about agency. A person is an agent of a certain result only if he *has done* something which has caused the result.

Krister Segerberg (1992a, 373) has observed that Chellas's action semantics provides no picture of action itself and suggested that this failure may be related to the validity of the T-principle mentioned above. But von Wright's rejection of the T-principle does not make his theory superior to Chellas's theory in this respect; on the contrary, as we have seen, Chellas's theory can be given a reasonable (re)interpretation as a theory of agency statements, but von Wright's choice of the initial states as the circumstances of evaluation of action sentences excludes such an interpretation.[8] If Chellas's theory is understood in this way, the lack of a counterfactual condition seems to be a weakness, but such a condition can of course be added to his analysis (Hilpinen 1997b).

V

If actions are temporally indeterminate (to some degree) or extend over a stretch of time, any theory of action in which action sentences are evaluated at moments or instants of time is likely to have some counter-intuitive consequences. Von Wright seems to be partly aware of this difficulty; for example, he notes (1963, 27–28):[9]

> When we say that an individual event happens on a certain occasion, we may regard this happening of the event as constituted by two successive occasions for the obtaining of a certain state of affairs. Similarly, when we say that an individual act is done on a certain occasion, we may regard this occasion for the doing of the act as constituted by the two successive occasions for the corresponding individual event.

This suggests that von Wright's 'occasions' include not only world-states, but also ordered pairs of world-states, and that action sentences should be evaluated at such ordered pairs.[10] According to this view, action sentences and unmodalized sentences cannot be combined by means of truth-functional connectives to form 'mixed' complex sentences such as (1.D).[11]

One of the first philosophers who adopted this way of analyzing action statements seems to have been Lennart Åqvist. He interpreted generic actions as 2-place *relations* between possible situations, that is, as sets of pairs $\langle u,w \rangle$ (1974, 77). Åqvist's view was developed further in the dynamic logics of action (Segerberg 1980; 1992a; Czelakowski 1997).[12] This approach is a formal counterpart of the philosophical view that the (temporal or spatial) location of an action includes the location where the action "takes effect" and the result which identifies the action is actualized.

VI

The analysis of actions as world state transformations makes it possible to distinguish between several interesting modes of action and agency, but von Wright's formulation of this view has certain shortcomings (in addition to the interpretational problems discussed above). For example, his formulation of the counterfactual aspect of action seems unsatisfactory. According to von Wright, the agent's passivity at any given world-state u would lead to a single world-state (counter-state) $e(u)$: the functions d and e have as their values worlds, not sets of worlds. This means that the counterfactuals used in von Wright's analysis satisfy the following principle:

(CEM) Either: if the agent had been passive, it would have been the case that p, or: if the agent had been passive, it would have been the case that not-p.

(CEM) is an instance of a principle called the principle of Conditional Excluded Middle (Lewis 1973, 79); thus von Wright's theory is in effect based on a logic of conditionals in which the principle of conditional excluded middle is valid. This principle is not generally plausible,[13] and is not that in the present case: it is more plausible to assume that the agent's passivity at u might lead to various alternative world-states, depending on how u might change without the agent's interference. Thus the agent's passivity at u should be represented by means of a function which has as its value the *set* of those world-states which could result from the agent's passivity. Such a representation agrees with the analysis of counterfactuals based on set selection functions rather than world selection functions (Lewis 1973, 57–58).

Another weakness in von Wright's analysis is that the representation of the agent's activity by means of the d-function seems too restricted and uninformative. According to von Wright's analysis, the initial state u offers the agent two action possibilities with respect to any state of affairs p: to be active or to be passive. It would be more natural and realistic to assume that the agent can change u in different ways by undertaking different actions or by performing some action in different ways. We can enrich von Wright's analysis by assuming that the agent can perform in a given situation various actions $A,B,A_1,\ldots,$ each of which is represented by means of a function f which assigns to each situation u the set of world-states to which the action might lead the agent from u.[14] It is assumed that the world-states $u \in W$ form a treelike partial ordering $<$ of temporal precedence, in other words, for any u, v and w in W, if $u<w$ and $v<w$, then $u<v$ or $v<u$ or $u=v$; moreover, $w \in f(A,u)$ only if $u<w$. One of the action possibilities open to the agent is passivity. Let Z represent passivity (the 'zero action'), and let $z(u) = f(Z,u)$; $z(u)$ is the set of world-states that might result from u by the agent's passivity.

VII

If von Wright's analysis is enriched in the way suggested above, it can no longer be regarded as an analysis of the concept of action, but simply as an analysis of the phrases 'a brings it about that p', 'a prevents it from being the case that p', and related concepts of *agent causation*. The concept of action is used in this analysis as a primitive notion. If $w \in f(A,u)$ for some situation u, we say that the pair $\langle u,w \rangle$ *exemplifies* A or is an instance of A; this will be abbreviated below '$\langle u,w \rangle \models A$'. The semantical apparatus outlined above enables us to define several concepts of 'bringing it about that' and other concepts of agent causation. A familiar and often used notion of agent causation is expressed by the *sine qua non analysis*, according to which an agent causes a certain state of affairs (or event) only if that state had not actualized (or the event had not occurred) if the agent had not acted they way he did, in other words: a state of affairs p is due to (caused by) an agent only if there is some action A (performed by the agent) such that it would not have been the case that p if the agent had not performed A (if the agent had omitted A). (Hart and Honoré 1959, 104–108.)[15]

According to von Wright's analysis, this counterfactual should be formulated in terms of the agent's passivity. Thus we obtain the following version of the *sine qua non analysis* of the concept of bringing it about that p:

(AB1) $\langle u,w \rangle \models Bp$ if and only if there is an action A such that
(i.a) $w \in f(A,u)$,
(i.b) $w \models p$,
(ii) $z(u) \subseteq |\neg p|$, and
(iii) $u \models \neg p$.

Condition (i.a) says that the pair $\langle u,w \rangle$ is a (minimal) performance of A, that is, that the agent arrives from u to w by means of A without doing anything else. (ii) is the counterfactual condition: it says that if the agent had been passive, p would have remained false.

The corresponding analysis of sustaining action is obtained from (AB1) by replacing condition (iii) by the condition

(iii′) $u \models p$.

If condition (iii) is simply deleted, we obtain analysis of the concept of producing or preserving (the state of affairs that) p, expressed by 'D^1p':[16]

(AD1) $\langle u,w \rangle \models D^1p$ if and only if there is an action A such that
(i.a) $w \in f(A,u)$,
(i.b) $w \models p$, and
(ii) $z(u) \subseteq |\neg p|$.

This analysis corresponds to the simple *sine qua non* analysis of agent causation or the dependence of a state of affairs on an agent's action. Following Åqvist and Mullock (1989, 37, 93) and Belnap (1991, 792), we may call the conjunction of conditions (i.a) and (i.b) the *positive* condition of agent causation and (ii) (the counterfactual condition) the *negative* condition. Most analyses of agent causation follow this pattern and consist of a positive condition and a negative (counterfactual) condition.

VIII

(AB1) and (AD1) are not the only possible generalizations of von Wright's theory. We obtain a stronger concept of agent causation by replacing condition (i.b) by the condition

(AD2.ib) $f(A,u) \subseteq |p|$,

which can be taken to mean that the action *A necessitates* the result (that) *p* or is sufficient for *p*. Stig Kanger has defined the concept of *seeing to it that p* by means of a condition analogous to (AD2.ib).[17] According to Kanger, an action sentence of the form '*a* sees to it that *p*', abbreviated '$Do_a p$', can be regarded as a conjunction (Kanger 1972, 109):

(CDKa) $Do_a p \leftrightarrow D\acute{o}_a p \;\&\; D\grave{o}_a p$,

where '$D\acute{o}_a p$' and '$D\grave{o}_a p$' are understood as follows (Kanger 1972, 109 and 121):

(i) $D\acute{o}_a p$ = *p* is necessary for something *a* does,
and
(ii) $D\grave{o}_a p$ = *p* is sufficient for something *a* does.

The right-hand side of (i) can also read as "something *a* does is sufficient for *p*"; thus Kanger's Dó-operator expresses the sufficient condition aspect of action and agency, whereas Dò expresses the necessary condition aspect (or *sine qua non* aspect) of action: '$D\grave{o}_a p$' may also be read as 'but for *a*'s action it would not have been the case that *p*' (Pörn 1974, 95). Kanger presents for the Dó-sentences and Dò-sentences possible worlds analyses analogous to Chellas's condition (AD.Ch) (Kanger 1972, 121):

(ADó) $u \models D\acute{o}_a p$ if and only if $w \models p$ for every *w* such that $R_a(u,w)$

and

(ADò) $u \models D\grave{o}_a p$ if and only if $w \models \neg p$ for every *w* such that $S_a(u,w)$,

The relation R_a is analogous to Chellas's "instigative" alternativeness relation and S_a is another alternativeness relation between possible worlds. According to Kanger, '$S_a uw$' means that "the opposite of everything *a* does in *u* is the case in *w*" (Kanger 1972, 121). This characterization is not intuitively clear, because it is not clear how we should understand the 'opposite' (or the negation) of an action. However, we can say that the purpose of the S-relation is to enable us to refer to worlds in which the agent does not do any of the things he does in *u*. In the light of von Wright's analysis, we may take the *S*-alternatives of *u* to be worlds in which the agent is passive: if in *u* the agent sees to it that *p*, then *p* would be false in all such worlds, according to Kanger. In the interpretation and application of Kanger's semantics of action sentences, the possible worlds u, w, etc. should be regarded as world-histories and not as temporary world-states.

Ingmar Pörn (1974; 1977) has argued that we should accept instead of Kanger's Dò-condition only a weaker requirement, viz. '$\neg D\grave{o}_a \neg p$', abbreviated here '$C\grave{o}_a p$':

(ACò) $u \models C\grave{o}_a p$ if and only if $w \models \neg p$ for some w such that $S_a(u,w)$.

This condition can be read: but for a's action it might not have been the case that p (Pörn 1974, 96; 1977, 7). It means that it is not unavoidable for a that p. Lennart Åqvist (1974, 86) has defended a similar weak form of the counterfactual condition. According to Pörn and Åqvist, the negative condition should be formulated as a might-statement or a might-conditional, not as a would-conditional. In the state transition semantics outlined above, this analysis assumes the form:

(AD3) $\langle u,w \rangle \models D^3 p$ if and only if there is an action A such that
(i.a) $w \in f(A,u)$,
(i.b) $f(A,u) \subseteq |p|$, and
(ii) $z(u) \cap |\neg p|$ is nonempty.

Condition (ii) is again based on the assumption that the counterfactual condition refers to possible circumstances in which the agent is passive.

In their recent analyses of the concept of action and agency Nuel Belnap and his associates have followed Pörn's approach and defined the concept of seeing to it that p by means of conditions analogous to (ADó) and (ACò), that is, by means of a strong positive condition (a 'necessitating' condition) and a weak negative condition, according to which the agent might have avoided the result p by making a different choice at the initial state of the action (Belnap 1991; Belnap and Perloff 1990; 1992; Horty and Belnap 1995; Perloff 1991).[18]

IX

According to the definitions proposed above, 'p is due to (the agency of) a' means, roughly speaking, that a has done something (performed an action) which has caused p or has been sufficient for p.[19] The locution 'an agent sees to it that p' suggests agency as a sufficient condition, whereas the concept of bringing it about that p seems to express the necessary condition aspect of agent causation: there is a clear intuitive difference in meaning between the two expressions, even though philosophers have sometimes treated them as alternative readings of the same agency operator.[20] As von Wright has pointed out, a situation offers an opportunity to bring it about that p only if p is not true in that situation (on the initial occasion of action). The concept of seeing to it that is not subject to this restriction: it covers both productive and sustaining (preserving) agency. Another difference between the two concepts is that seeing to it that *p* normally entails ensuring that the result *p* will obtain, whereas bringing it about that *p* involves no such guarantees. When a person does something deliberately and with care, we can say that he 'sees to it' that a certain result will be actualized: in such cases his actions necessitate the result. The expression 'seeing to it that *p*' usually characterizes deliberate, intentional action, but 'bringing it about that p' does not have such a connotation, and can be applied to the unintended as well as intended results of one's actions, including unexpected and improbable results.[21]

It might be suggested that it is always possible to construct, for any state *p*, an action description *A* such that the performance of an action of kind *A* is sufficient for *p*, for example, 'to cause (it to be the case that) *p*' or 'to bring it about that *p*',[22] and that all instances of agent causation can therefore be regarded as instances of necessitating agency. To be able to distinguish different forms of agent causation from each other, we have to assume that the action descriptions *A*, *B*, etc. in definitions (AB1) and (AD1)−(AD3) identify action-types which are reliably performable by the agent or which the agent can choose to perform in a given choice situation *u*. Following Krister Segerberg, I shall call such action types *routines*: "To be able to do something is to have a routine available. To deliberate is to search for a routine." (Segerberg 1985, 188.)[23] The action routines available to an agent can be regarded as the tools which the agent can use for changing the world or keeping it unchanged. I assume that the routines can be characterized independently of the objectives or results which an agent tries to reach by means of his actions. For example, turning the ignition key of a car is a routine whereby one can (normally) bring about the state that the engine of the car is running. For many states *p*, the actions 'to bring it about that *p*' or 'to see to it that *p*' are impossible actions, that is, not performable by a given agent – or by any agent. For example, there are no routines for bringing it about that there are no wars in the world, even though we might think that the United Nations ought to bring about such a state of affairs.

X

If an action is regarded as an interference with a natural course of events (a course of events unaffected by agents), then the concept of passivity or 'zero action' is meaningful, and (AB1) and (AD1)−(AD3) seem reasonable analyses of the concept of agent causation. These definitions are based on the following ontology of action: an agent has in a given situation at his disposal a number of action routines *A*,*A'*,*B*,..., by means of which he can change the situation or keep it unchanged, or he can refrain from applying any of these routines, that is, be passive. Actions are regarded here as analogous to tools which the agent can use to work on a situation. If action situations are understood in this way, it is natural to assume that the *sine qua non* condition of causal dependence refers to hypothetical circumstances in which the agent is passive. However, this interpretation is not applicable to all action situations. There are situations in which there is no clear alternative of passivity and no alternative can be regarded as the 'natural course of events'. In such cases the counterfactual aspect of action (or an omission) cannot be analyzed by referring to situations in which the agent is passive. For example, if someone drives his car into a railway crossing and is knocked over by a passing train, we may say that the driver of the car caused the accident by his failure to brake and stop the car before the crossing; he satisfies the *sine qua non* condition 'if x had not driven into the crossing, no accident would have occurred'. In this case the antecedent of the *sine qua non* schema does not refer to situations in which the driver "is passive", but to situations in which he brakes and stops in time.

The plausibility of treating the omission of an action as passivity depends also on the assumption, made tacitly above, that an agent can perform in a given situation u only one of a number of alternative actions open to him, in other words, on the assumption that the situation u is represented as set of mutually exclusive action alternatives. In this case the omission of an action A means either the choice of any alternative to A or the choice of a specific alternative called 'passivity'.[24] If we assume that the agent can perform simultaneously several actions and the choices available to the agent are analyzed as action complexes, neither interpretation of the concept of omission seems correct, and it is no longer plausible to formulate the *sine qua non* condition in terms of the passivity of the agent, as in (AD1)−(AD3).

It is clear that the performance of an action A together with another action B can change the world quite differently from the performance of A or B alone. Thus, if we let $f(A,u)$ be the set of worlds to which the performance of A alone might lead from u, and let 'AB' represent the joint performances of A and B, $f(AB,u)$ is not determined by $f(A,u)$ and $f(B,u)$. I shall assume here that the action descriptions A and B can be joined together to form complex action descriptions, for example:

AB = A and B together (simultaneously),
$A+B$ = A or B, and
$A;B$ = A followed by B.

Here I shall consider only action complexes of type AB and $A+B$. I shall also consider the omissions of acts, abbreviated 'omA' (where A is an arbitrary action description). All omissions of A share the feature that they do not exemplify A; otherwise the character of omA depends on the complex action from which A has been omitted.

Let $g(A,u)$ be the set of situations into which the performance of A by itself or together with other actions may transform u. ($f(A,\_)$ represents the performance of A alone.) It is clear that

(3) $g(AB,u) = g(A,u) \cap g(B,u)$;

thus we may call AB the 'conjunction' of A and B.[25] Moreover, f and g should satisfy the following conditions:

(4) $f(A,u) \subseteq g(A,u)$ and
$g(AB,u) \subseteq g(A,u)$.

XI

The application of this semantical apparatus to the analysis of action situations can be illustrated by the following simple example. Let us assume that an old-fashioned safe-cracker called George wants to open a safe by means of suitably placed explosives. He wants to open the safe without hurting himself; thus he has to protect himself while detonating the explosives. We may assume that he can do this in some routine manner, for example, by using a protective shield or by hiding behind a desk. The states of affairs in which George is interested and the relevant acts available to him are described by the following (atomic) sentences and action descriptions:

(5) p = The safe is open.
q = George is alive and well.
A = (the action of) detonating the explosives,
B = (the action of) protecting oneself.

In the initial situation u, $\neg p \,\&\, q$ is true and George wants to transform this into a situation in which $p \,\&\, q$ holds. This would be a case of bringing it about that $p \,\&\, q$, because $p \,\&\, q$ is false in the initial situation. George can do this by detonating the explosives while protecting himself, that is, by means of an action AB. (It is of course essential here that he does these two things simultaneously.) If he does only A, he might be hurt by the explosion, and B alone as well as the zero action would preserve the initial state of the world. (In this example a clear alternative of passivity is available.) Thus the situation u and the results of the action possibilities open to George in u can be described as follows:

(6) $u \in |\neg p \,\&\, q|$,
$z(u) \subseteq |\neg p \,\&\, q|$,
$f(A,u) \subseteq |p \,\&\, \neg q|$,
$f(B,u) \subseteq |\neg p \,\&\, q|$,
$f(AB,u) \subseteq |p \,\&\, q|$.

Suppose that George hides behind a protective shield while detonating the explosives (in other words, he does *AB*) and manages to open the safe without getting hurt by the debris; thus he arrives at a situation *w* in which $p \,\&\, q$ is true. The following counterfactuals are true at *w*:

(7) If George had not detonated the explosives, the safe would not be open.

(8) If George had not protected himself, he would not be (or might not be) alive and well (without injury).

In other words:

(9) If George had omitted *A*, *p* would not be the case.

(10) If George had omitted *B*, *q* would not be (or might not be) the case.

But if George had been passive, *q* would still be the case: George would be unhurt, because there would not have been any explosion. The counterfactual (10) is not evaluated by considering courses of events in which George does nothing, but by considering omissions of the act *B*, that is, courses of events in which George does not protect himself, but which are otherwise maximally similar to George's actual behavior at $\langle u,w \rangle$. The antecedents of (9) and (10) refer to the past of the world-state *w*.

The similarity between individual courses of action can be represented in the same way as the similarity between possible worlds, that is, by means of a selection function *s* which selects for each action description *A* and each individual course of action, represented by a pair of world-states consisting of the initial state *u* and the result state *w*, those world-states which could have resulted from the initial state by a course of action which satisfies the action description *A* and is otherwise maximally similar to the actual course of action $\langle u,w \rangle$. This way of evaluating conditionals with action descriptions as antecedents is based on the general principle that conditionals should be evaluated by considering courses of events which satisfy the antecedent but are otherwise minimally different from the actual course of events. (Cf. Lewis 1973, 1.) The counterfactuals needed here for the analysis of the concept agency are defined by the following truth-condition:

(CCA) $w \models$ If *G* (had been chosen by the agent), then *q*, if and only if there is a situation $u < w$ such that $s(G,\langle u,w \rangle) \subseteq |q|$.

Above, '*G*' may represent either a positive action or an omission. If we assume that the similarity between complex actions depends only on the number of simple (atomic) actions shared by them, and $\langle u,w \rangle$ exemplifies *AB*, the *s*-function should in this example have the following properties:

(11) $s(om(AB),\langle u,w\rangle) = f(A,u) \cup f(B,u)$,
$s(omA,\langle u,w\rangle) = f(B,u)$,
$s(omB,\langle u,w\rangle) = f(A,u)$, and
$s(om(A+B),\langle u,w\rangle) = z(u)$.

According to (11), the conditionals (9) and (10) are true at the result state w.

According to (CCA), the concept of (*sine qua non*) agent causation can be defined as follows:

(AD4) $\langle u,w\rangle \models D^4p$ if and only if there is an action A such that
(i) $w \in g(A,u) \cap |p|$, and
(ii) $s(omA,\langle u,w\rangle) \subseteq |\neg p|$.

The corresponding concept of 'strong' or necessitating action (seeing to it that p) can be defined as follows:

(AD5) $\langle u,w\rangle \models D^5p$ if and only if there is an action A such that
(i) $w \in g(A,u)$ and $g(A,u) \subseteq |p|$, and
(ii) $s(omA,\langle u,w\rangle) \subseteq |\neg p|$.

If the negative condition is formulated as a might-conditional, we obtain the following generalization of (AD3):

(AD6) $\langle u,w\rangle \models D^6p$ if and only if there is an action A such that
(i) $w \in g(A,u)$ and $g(A,u) \subseteq |p|$, and
(ii) not $s(omA,\langle u,w\rangle) \subseteq |p|$.

In this example, we can say that George saw to it that he was not hurt by the explosion, and 'seeing to it that' can be interpreted by (AD5) or (AD6), depending on how the example is understood. We have to use the g-function and not the f-function in these definitions, because the agent can perform several actions in the initial situation, but the outcome p in which we are interested may depend on only one of these actions.[26]

XII

If George's action situation is analyzed simply as a choice between a number of alternative (mutually exclusive) action possibilities, we have to regard AB, A, B and Z as the alternative actions or choices open to George in the situation u. (We may also include in the set of alternative actions other possibilities which are completely irrelevant, for example, the action of praying that the safe would open by itself.) Under this analysis, the *sine qua non* condition 'If omA, then $\neg p$' can be understood in two ways:

(i) Some action alternative to A would (or might) have led to $\neg p$.
(ii) Passivity (in an earlier situation) would (or might) have led to $\neg p$.

If George does nothing in the initial situation in which $\neg p$ & q is true (or for example prays that the safe would open by itself), we should say, according to the first proposal, that the fact that the safe remains locked is due to (or caused by) George, because he could have caused the safe to open by detonating the explosives. We have seen earlier that the second account, based on the concept of passivity, also gives unsatisfactory results. Moreover, this account is inapplicable to the situations which do not include a clear alternative of passivity. According to the analysis proposed here, praying that the safe would open by itself does not make George the agent of the safe's being locked if he does nothing else in the situation, because in such circumstances the safe would have remained locked even if George had omitted to pray. In the present analysis, the concept of omission is indispensable, and can be regarded as a generalization of von Wright's concept of passivity.

In the collision example given earlier, the omission of the relevant act – driving into the railway crossing without stopping – consists in not driving into the crossing while deviating from the actual course of events in other respects as little as possible. The driver of the car satisfies the counterfactual condition and is therefore, according to (AD4), an agent of the collision.

XIII

All the analyses of agent causation considered above entail the following condition: *a* may be regarded as an agent of a result *p* only if *p* is *favored* by some action *A* performed by *a* in the sense that *p* is more likely as a result of *A* than as a result of *a*'s inactivity or the omission of *A*. The concept of probabilistic favoring is familiar from the theories of causation and explanation (Eells 1991, 1–5, chapters 2–3; Mellor 1995, 73);[27] thus the condition of favoring suggests the following connection between the notions of agent causation and explanation:

(CA.exp) *a* is an agent of the state of affairs that *p* only if *p* is explained by the actions of *a*.

The concept of probabilistic favoring is usually regarded (at least) as a *prima facie* criterion of agency and agent causation (Åqvist and Mullock 1989, 21–22). The variety of the concepts of agent causation resembles the variety of the concepts of explanation, and the conditions of agent causation discussed above have their counterparts in the theory of explanation. For example, the negative or counterfactual condition of agency can be regarded as a special case of the corresponding requirement for an adequate explanation. In the deductive model of explanation this condition is the requirement that the general laws in the *explanans* should be essential (necessary) for the derivation of the *explanandum* (Salmon 1989, 19–21). Most authors who have developed logics of action

– for example, Chellas, Kanger, Pörn, Åqvist and Belnap – have been mainly interested in actions which *necessitate* their results; in this respect these theories of action resemble the deductive model of explanation, according to which the *explanandum* of a good explanation should be a necessary consequence of the *explanans*. In the light of condition (CA.exp), it is clear that these analyses apply only to certain interesting special forms of agent causation.

XIV

It should be observed that agency or agent causation in the senses discussed here (as defined by (AD1)–(AD6)) is not a necessary condition of the moral or legal responsibility of a person for some state of affairs. Sometimes an agent is regarded as responsible for a state of affairs p because of his omission of an act A which would have prevented the result p, that is, because he has let it be the case p (has let p become or remain true). In these cases we should not say that the agent causes p (sees to it that p or brings it about that p), because then we should regard a person as an agent of any state of affairs which he could have prevented by choosing a different course of action in some earlier situation. The action routines $A, B, \ldots$, etc. mentioned in the definitions (AD1)–(AD6) should be positive actions, not omissions. In our ordinary moral thinking we make a distinction between activity and passivity or between action and omission;[28] the fact that there are borderline cases in which it is difficult to say whether a person does something or is passive (with respect to a certain result p) does not obliterate the distinction.[29] However, it is clear that letting something happen (being passive) can in some circumstances be morally or legally as objectionable as causing something by means of one's positive actions: letting an animal die may be as objectionable as killing an animal.[30] Thus we should say that an agent may be regarded as responsible for some result p if he has caused p or if he has failed (omitted) to cause (or see to it that) $\neg p$. For example, cases of negligence in which a person is regarded as an agent of a harmful result because of his omission of some required action are examples of the latter kind. (Cf. Hart and Honoré 1959, 121.) It is natural to say in such cases that the result is due to the agent, but such judgments of agency or agent causation depend on judgments of responsibility and not *vice versa*. In cases of negligence the agent usually satisfies the *sine qua non* condition that p would not be the case if the agent had not omitted A (for some A), but this is used as a ground for judgments of agency only in situations in which the agent was required to see to it that $\neg p$.

XV

In this paper, actions have been analyzed as world-state transitions or as relations between world-states. This model fits actions which can be said to lead to a certain result and characterized by means of their results, and it explains the temporal and situational indeterminacy of actions. According to this conception of actions, we have to distinguish action descriptions from 'ordinary' propositions which are interpreted as sets of situations; the latter include agency statements, that is, sentences which state that a certain result (a fact, a state of affairs) is due to the actions of a certain agent.[31]

The distinction between action descriptions and propositions underlies the traditional distinction between two kinds of *ought* (or two kinds of ought-statements), viz. the ought-to-be and the ought-to-do (between *Seinsollen* and *Tunsollen*).[32] An ought-to-do statement is a normative statement to the effect that a certain action is required (or obligatory), permitted or forbidden in a certain situation, whereas ought-to-be statements say that a certain state of affairs ought or ought not to obtain in a given situation. To represent this distinction in deontic logic, we need two kinds of deontic operators: the ought-to-do operators apply to action descriptions and turn them into deontic statements, whereas the ought-to-be operators turn 'ordinary' propositions into deontic statements. Georg Henrik von Wright's first (1951) system of deontic logic which started the contemporary development of the field was a logic of the ought-to-do: in this system the deontic operators were prefixed to expressions for action-types or (in von Wright's terminology) "act-qualifying properties", not to propositional expressions (statements).[33] However, in the subsequent work on deontic logic the deontic operators were usually construed as propositional modalities rather than action modalities.[34]

If actions are represented as binary relations between world-states or as transitions from one world-state to another, a simple semantics of directives (ought-to-do sentences) can be obtained by applying the basic ideas of the standard semantics of deontic logic to such transitions or ordered pairs of possible worlds (world-states). Instead of dividing world-states into deontically perfect (ideal) worlds and deontically imperfect (unacceptable) worlds, we divide the movements from one world-state to another into legal (or acceptable) transitions and illegal (unacceptable) transitions (Czelakowski 1997). The truth-conditions of deontic sentences can then be defined in the same way as in the standard system of deontic logic: an action A is obligatory (or required) in a given situation if and only if all legal transitions from that situation exemplify A, and A is prohibited if and only if all transitions which exemplify A are illegal.[35] The state transition semantics can be enriched and embellished in the same way as the semantics of the standard system, e.g., by defining in addition to the ideal transitions various "sub-ideal transitions" or by distinguishing between different degrees of deontic perfection. (Cf. Jones and Pörn 1985; Carmo and Jones 1993, 61–74.)

What is the relationship between the two kinds of ought? Von Wright (1996, 68) has argued that the norms that prescribe what ought to be (or may be) are more basic than the norms concerning actions, and that the latter depend on and are justified by the former. This view reflects a consequentialist conception of normativity. Perhaps this view is correct on some fundamental level of morality, but on the level of ordinary normative argumentation the justification can run in both directions. Sometimes we say that an agent ought to perform an action because it is necessary for a result which ought to obtain, or more likely to lead to such a result than the alternative actions; in other circumstances we may argue that a certain state of affairs *p* ought not to obtain (is normatively unacceptable) because it resulted from an illegal or immoral action, or that *p* ought to obtain because it would have been the result of an action (or actions) which an agent ought to have performed in an earlier situation. For example, a person's being rich is a normatively unacceptable (prohibited) state if the wealth has been obtained by theft, but normatively acceptable (permitted) if it is the result of honest work.[36] Thus the normative status of an action may be considered from a consequentialist viewpoint in the light of the interests and objectives of an agent or a norm-authority, and the normative status of a state of affairs may be considered deontologically on the basis of the actions which led to it or could have led to it.

University of Turku and
University of Miami

NOTES

[1] In the recent philosophy of action the Wolfean view has been defended by Donald Davidson (1980), who has argued that individual actions can be identified with the agent's "primitive actions", that is, bodily movements which are "intentional under some description".

[2] Cook (1942, 13–14) notes:

> On the basis of actual observation of what the courts have done and are doing, ... we may safely make the following generalization: Where *A* in state *X* sets in force a motion which injures *B* in state *Y*, and *B* goes to and as a result of the injury dies in state *Z*, either *X*, *Y*, or *Z*, if it gets its hands on *A*, can apply its own criminal law to the case.

[3] If individual actions are understood in this way, they are plausible candidates for *qua-objects* which are constituted by an object together with some property possessed by it. According to the doctrine of qua-objects, 'Socrates qua philosopher' refers to an object (a qua-object) distinct from Socrates (Fine 1982, 100; Bäck 1996, 489–493). For the application of this view to acts, see Kit Fine (1982, 101–104).

[4] Von Wright sometimes uses abbreviated expressions of this kind; see (1983, 174).

[5] The explicit reference to the agent can be omitted when the actions of a single agent are being considered.

6 Krister Segerberg (1992a) interprets von Wright's theory in this way: he regards (2) as a valid principle of von Wright's logic of action (p. 358).

7 We can say, of course, that an agent *can have seen to it* (or can have brought it about) that *p* only if it is the case that *p*.

8 Most versions of the state transition semantics of action and agency proposed in the recent years have followed Chellas's example in this respect; for example, Belnap (1991), Belnap and Perloff (1990; 1992), and Sandu and Tuomela (1996). Von Wright's logic of action can also be revised in this way and regarded (or reinterpreted) as a theory of agency statements; see Hilpinen (1997b).

9 See also von Wright (1983, 174, 195–196), where von Wright notes that an occasion on which a change takes place, for example, a state of affairs comes to obtain, should be regarded as involving two 'phases', a phase when the state of affairs is absent and a phase on which the state is present.

10 In (1996, 69), von Wright notes: "The fact that an agent performs a certain action is also a state of affairs of a sort." If the distinction between world-states and transitions is taken seriously, actions should not be assimilated to states of affairs; in the state transition semantics this assimilation is apt to lead to the confusions discussed above.

11 However, as will be seen later, we can form complex sentences from action expressions and propositional expressions by means of suitably defined intensional connectives.

12 Many philosophers have adopted this view of actions. For example, Leo Apostel (1982, 104) has observed that "an action is a transformation of nature in order to realize a purpose", and in his "action-state semantics" for imperatives C.L. Hamblin has analyzed actions or deeds in terms successive world-states (Hamblin 1987, 137–166). According to Ota Weinberger (1985, 311–314), "an action is a transformation of states within the flow of time" involving a subject (an agent).

13 For a discussion of the Principle of Conditional Excluded Middle and counterexamples to it, see Hilpinen (1981, 307–309).

14 This representation is equivalent to the representation of actions by binary relations on *W*; any binary relation on *W* defines a function from *W* into the power set of *W*; cf. Czelakowski (1997).

15 The *sine qua non* analysis is not without its problems; as Åqvist and Mullock (1989, 67) have observed,

> The *conditio sine qua non* is a perennial problem for all theorists of causation – no one is satisfied with it but it is hard to ignore.

For example, the *sine qua non* analysis gives rise to the familiar problems of causal overdetermination. A state of affairs *p* may be caused by an agent's actions without being dependent on them if another agent's actions would have caused *p* if the first agent had been passive. (Cf. Hart and Honoré 1959, 117–118.) The *sine qua non* analysis needs refinements, but in this paper I shall leave these problems and complications aside.

16 In my earlier paper (Hilpinen 1997b) I defined the agency operators as operators which turn 'ordinary' propositions into statements of agency evaluated at the result-states of the agent's actions. Here the D-sentences are action sentences proper, evaluated at world-state pairs.

17 In this respect Kanger's analysis agrees with Chellas's definition (AD.Ch) discussed above.

18 For a more detailed discussion of the work of Nuel Belnap and his associates, see Hilpinen (1997b).

19 The formulations of agent causation discussed here resemble Lars Lindahl's (1977) and Ghita Holmström-Hintikka's (1991) formulas for "instrumental action", '[an agent] *p* sees to it that *F* by performing action *A*' (Lindahl 1977, 69) and 'by means of *m*, agent *x* sees to it that *r*' (Holmström-Hintikka 1991, 37–38). Holmström-Hintikka does not distinguish action descriptions from propositions, but calls both *m* and *r* here "conditions" (p. 38); she regards both as propositional expressions.

[20] For example, Ingmar Pörn (1974) defines the concept of agency by means of a D^3-type modality, but translates his agency sentences by the phrase '*a* brings it about that ...', and notes: "It is a plain truth that if *a* brings it about that *p*, then *p* is necessary for something *a* does" (1974, 96). Pörn's concept is a concept of necessitating agency, and therefore the expression 'seeing to it that' fits it better than 'bringing it about that'.

[21] Lars Lindahl (1977, 70) has observed that the expression '*x* sees to it that *p*' characterizes sometimes merely an intention or preparedness to act in order to sustain the state of affairs *p* should the circumstances require it, and does not necessarily require any bodily movement. Lindahl calls such an action a "null action" (Lindahl, *ibid.*; Holmström-Hintikka 1991, 48). Lindahl's null action can be regarded as one of the action alternatives *A*, *B*, etc. used in (AD1)–(AD3), and should be distinguished from the concept of zero action or passivity used here.

[22] Krister Segerberg (1989; 1992b) has studied the logic of an 'action-forming' δ-operator which forms from a proposition *p* an action description δp with the reading 'the bringing about of *p*'. It is clear that an action of type δp necessitates *p*, because it is defined in terms of the result *p*.

[23] It is not entirely clear whether Segerberg wants to understand the concept of routine in the way intended here; thus my use of the expression may differ from his.

[24] G.H. von Wright has adopted the latter approach, Nuel Belnap (1991) and his associates the former.

[25] For a more detailed discussion of this way of analyzing actions, see Brigitte Buck (1987, ch. I), and Risto Hilpinen (1993a).

[26] It is clear that (AD5) and (AD6) define very strong concepts of necessitating (sufficient) action. I shall not try to analyze the concepts intermediate between (AD4) and (AD5)–(AD6) here.

[27] The view that probabilistic favoring is a sign of causation requires various well-known qualifications which need not be discussed here; see Eells (1991, 127–168).

[28] See Lucas (1993, 37–38). Lucas has argued that the failure to do justice to the distinction between action and inaction is one of the weaknesses of consequentialism.

[29] If actions are regarded as analogous to instruments or tools to be used for reshaping the world, the distinction between an action and an omission (or passivity) is clear.

[30] The philosophers who have rejected the moral significance of the distinction between killing and letting die have usually assumed that the distinction can be made (in most cases), and argued only that killing someone is not necessarily morally worse than letting someone die; see Rachels (1975) and Thomson (1985/1986).

[31] Hector-Neri Castañeda's (1981; 1985) distinction between *practitions* and *propositions* is analogous to the present distinction between action descriptions and ordinary statements (including statements about agency). For a discussion of Castañeda's theory, see Hilpinen (1993b).

[32] This distinction is closely related to but not the same as the distinction between impersonal and personal ought-statements (fiats and personal directives); see Hilpinen (1997a).

[33] In this respect von Wright's 1951 system agreed with the view adopted in the 17th and 18th century literature on normative discourse in which deontic concepts were regarded as action modalities; see Hruschka (1986).

[34] One exception to this trend was Hector-Neri Castañeda (1981; 1985), who was interested in developing deontic logic as a theory of the ought-to-do; he argued that directives and norms have non-propositional contents called *practitions* (Hilpinen 1993b, 88–89).

[35] However, the interpretation of action descriptions in terms of the *f*-function and the *g*-function makes it possible to make normative distinctions which are not possible in the standard system. For example, it is possible to distinguish between two concepts of permission, a *weak* permission and a *strong* permission: we can say that an act is weakly permitted in a situation *u* if and only if it is exemplified by some legal transition from *u*, and an act *A* is strongly permitted if and only if any transition which consists of *A* alone is legal. It is also possible to distinguish between different

concepts of prohibition. For the weak and strong concepts of permission and prohibition, see Risto Hilpinen (1993a, 310–311).

[36] In the same way, in the American judicial system a piece of evidence may not be admissible (permitted) in court if it has been obtained by illegal actions, regardless of the probative value of the evidence.

REFERENCES

Apostel, Leo (1982), "Towards a General Theory of Argumentation" in E.M. Barth and J.L. Martens (eds.), *Argumentation. Approaches to Theory Formation*. Amsterdam, John Benjamins B.V., pp. 93–122.

Åqvist, Lennart (1974), "A New Approach to the Logical Theory of Actions and Causality" in S. Stenlund (ed.), *Logical Theory and Semantic Analysis*. Dordrecht, D. Reidel, pp. 73–91.

Åqvist, Lennart and Philip Mullock (1989), *Causing Harm*. Berlin–New York, Walter de Gruyter.

Bäck, Allan (1996), *On Reduplication. Logical Theories of Qualification*. Leiden–New York–Köln, E.J. Brill.

Belnap, Nuel (1991), "Backwards and Forwards in the Modal Logic of Agency," *Philosophy and Phenomenological Research* **51**, 777–807.

Belnap, Nuel and Michael Perloff (1990), "Seeing to It That: A Canonical Form for Agentives" in H. Kyburg *et al.* (eds.), *Knowledge Representation and Defeasible Reasoning*. Dordrecht–Boston, Kluwer Academic Publishers, pp. 167–190.

Belnap, Nuel and Michael Perloff (1992), "The Way of the Agent," *Studia Logica* **51**, 463–484.

Buck, Brigitte (1987), *Eine deontische Logik auf der Grundlage dynamischer Aussagenlogik*. Dissertation, Universität zu Kiel, Kiel.

Carmo, José and Andrew Jones (1993), "Deontic Database Constraints and the Characterisation of Recovery" in A.I.J. Jones and M. Sergot (eds.), *ΔEON '94. Workshop Proceedings: Second International Workshop on Deontic Logic in Computer Science*. Oslo, Tano A.S., pp. 56–85.

Castañeda, Hector-Neri (1981), "The Paradoxes of Deontic Logic. The Simplest Solution to All of Them in One Fell Swoop" in R. Hilpinen (ed.), *New Studies in Deontic Logic. Norms, Actions and the Foundations of Ethics*. Dordrecht, D. Reidel, pp. 37–85.

Castañeda, Hector-Neri (1985), "Aspectual Actions and Davidson's Theory of Events" in E. LePore and B.P. McLaughlin (eds.), *Actions and Events: Perspectives on the Philosophy of D. Davidson*. Oxford, Basil Blackwell, pp. 294–310.

Chellas, Brian (1969), *The Logical Form of Imperatives* (Dissertation, Stanford University). Stanford, Perry Lane Press.

Chellas, Brian (1992), "Time and Modality in the Logic of Agency," *Studia Logica* **51**, 485–517.

Cook, Walter Wheeler (1942), *The Logical and Legal Bases of the Conflict of Laws*. Cambridge, Mass., Harvard University Press.

Czelakowski, Janusz (1997), "Action and Deontology" in Sten Lindström and Eva Ejerhed (eds.), *Logic, Action and Cognition*. Dordrecht and Boston, Kluwer Academic Publishers.

Davidson, Donald (1980), "Agency" in D. Davidson, *Essays in Actions and Events*. Oxford, Clarendon Press, pp. 43–61.

Eells, Ellery (1991), *Probabilistic Causality*. Cambridge and New York, Cambridge University Press.

Fine, Kit (1982), "Acts, Events and Things" in Werner Leinfellner *et al.* (eds.), *Language and Ontology: Proceedings of the Sixth International Wittgenstein Symposium*. Wien, Hölder–Pichler–Tempsky, pp. 97–105.

Hamblin, C.L. (1987), *Imperatives*. Oxford, Basil Blackwell.

Hart, Herbert L.A. and A.M. Honoré (1959), *Causation in the Law*. Oxford, Clarendon Press.

Hilpinen, Risto (1981), "Conditionals and Possible Worlds" in G. Fløistad (ed.), *Contemporary Philosophy: A New Survey*. The Hague–Boston–London, Martinus Nijhoff, pp. 299–335.

Hilpinen, Risto (1993a), "On Deontic Logic, Pragmatics, and Modality" in Herbert Stachowiak (ed.), *Pragmatik: Handbuch Pragmatischen Denkens*. Band IV: *Sprachphilosophie, Sprachpragmatik und formative Pragmatik*. Hamburg, Felix Meiner Verlag, pp. 295–319.

Hilpinen, Risto (1993b), "Actions in Deontic Logic" in J.-J. Ch. Meyer and R.J. Wieringa (eds.), *Deontic Logic in Computer Science: Normative System Specification*. Chichester–New York, John Wiley & Sons, pp. 85–100.

Hilpinen, Risto (1997a), "On Impersonal Ought-Statements and Personal Directives" in E.G. Valdes *et al.* (eds.), *Normative Systems in Legal and Moral Theory. Festschrift for Carlos E. Alchourrón and Eugenio Bulygin*. Berlin, Duncker & Humblot.

Hilpinen, Risto (1997b), "On Action and Agency" in Sten Lindström and Eva Ejerhed (eds.), *Logic, Action and Cognition*. Dordrecht and Boston, Kluwer Academic Publishers.

Holmström-Hintikka, Ghita (1991), *Action, Purpose and Will. A Formal Theory. Acta Philosophica Fennica* **50**, Helsinki, Societas Philosophica Fennica.

Horty, John and Nuel Belnap (1995), "The Deliberative Stit: A Study of Action, Omission, Ability, and Obligation," *The Journal of Philosophical Logic* **24**, 583–644.

Hruschka, Joachim (1986), "Das deontologische Sechseck bei Gottfried Achenwall im Jahre 1767," *Berichte aus der Sitzungen der Joachim Jungius Gesellschaft der Wissenschaften e. V.* **4** (2), Hamburg.

Jones, Andrew I.J. and Ingmar Pörn (1985), "Ideality, Sub-Ideality and Deontic Logic," *Synthese* **65**, 275–290.

Kanger, Stig (1972), "Law and Logic," *Theoria* **38**, 105–132.

Lewis, David (1973), *Counterfactuals*. Oxford, Basil Blackwell.

Lindahl, Lars (1977), *Position and Change*. Dordrecht and Boston, D. Reidel Publishing Company.

Lucas, J.R. (1993), *Responsibility*. Oxford, Clarendon Press.

Mellor, D.H. (1995), *The Facts of Causation*. London and New York, Routledge.

Perloff, Michael (1991), "*Stit* and the Language of Agency," *Synthese* **86**, 379–408.

Pörn, Ingmar (1974), "Some Basic Concepts of Action" in Sören Stenlund (ed.), *Logical Theory and Semantic Analysis*. Dordrecht, D. Reidel, pp. 93–101.

Pörn, Ingmar (1977), *Action Theory and Social Science*. Dordrecht, D. Reidel.

Rachels, James (1975), "Active and Passive Euthanasia," *The New England Journal of Medicine* **292**, 78–80.

Salmon, Wesley C. (1989), "Four Decades of Scientific Explanation" in Philip Kitcher and Wesley C. Salmon (eds.), *Scientific Explanation*. (*Minnesota Studies in the Philosophy of Science*, Vol. **XIII**), Minneapolis, University of Minnesota Press, pp. 3–219.

Sandu, Gabriel and Raimo Tuomela (1996), "Joint Action and Group Action Made Precise," *Synthese* **105**, 319–345.

Segerberg, Krister (1980), "Applying Modal Logic," *Studia Logica* **39**, 275–295.

Segerberg, Krister (1985) "Routines," *Synthese* **65**, 185–210.

Segerberg, Krister (1989), "Bringing It About," *Journal of Philosophical Logic* **18**, 327–347.

Segerberg, Krister (1992a), "Getting Started: Beginnings in the Logic of Action," *Studia Logica* **51**, 347–378.

Segerberg, Krister (1992b), "Action Incompleteness," *Studia Logica* **51**, 533–550.

Stout, Rex (1935/1980), *The League of Frightened Men*. New York, Bantam Books. (First published in 1935.)

Thalberg, Irving (1977), *Perception, Emotion and Action: A Component Approach*. Oxford, Basil Blackwell.

Thomson, Judith Jarvis (1971), "The Time of a Killing," *The Journal of Philosophy* **68**, 115–132.

Thomson, Judith Jarvis (1977), *Acts and Other Events*. Ithaca, Cornell University Press.
Thomson, Judith Jarvis (1985/1986), "The Trolley Problem" in J.J. Thomson, *Rights, Restitution, and Risk: Essays in Moral Theory*. Cambridge, Mass., Harvard University Press, 1986, pp. 94–116. Reprinted from *The Yale Law Journal* **94**, 1985.
Weinberger, Ota (1985), "Freedom, Range for Action and the Ontology of Norms," *Synthese* **65**, 307–324.
von Wright, Georg Henrik (1951), "Deontic Logic," *Mind* **60**, 1–15. Reprinted in G.H. von Wright, *Logical Studies*. London, Routledge and Kegal Paul, pp. 58–74.
von Wright, Georg Henrik (1963), *Norm and Action*. London, Routledge & Kegan Paul.
von Wright, Georg Henrik (1968), *An Essay in Deontic Logic and the General Theory of Action. Acta Philosophica Fennica* **21**, Amsterdam, North-Holland Publ. Co.
von Wright, Georg Henrik (1983), "Norms, Truth, and Logic" in G.H. von Wright, *Practical Reason: Philosophical Papers*, Vol. 1, Ithaca: Cornell University Press, pp. 130–209.
von Wright, Georg Henrik (1996), "Ought-to-be – Ought-to-do," in G.H. von Wright, *Six Essays in Philosophical Logic. Acta Philosophica Fennica* **60**, Helsinki, Societas Philosophica Fennica, pp. 63–70.

GHITA HOLMSTRÖM-HINTIKKA

ACTIONS IN ACTION

INTRODUCTION

This paper is a further development of a theory first presented in my book *Action, Purpose and Will* (1991). Here I continue to deal with the tripartition of agent causation: *mere causation*, *instrumental action* and *purposive action*. The concept of *goal directed will* is also subject for discussion. In this context, however, I shall bring these notions further in the direction of second-order actions and intentions. New in this regard are also attempted applications in computation as are investigations into instances of higher-order causations and actions with *separate* agents in particular the discussion on influence. As the logical foundations for the first-order cases are laid in my book I have no reason to go into detailed discussion here. I shall, nevertheless, for the sake of easier understandability collect the basic assumptions I make in an Appendix.

Although this paper is a systematic analysis of concepts, the systematization is obviously not a self-sufficient activity but shall form the foundation for philosophical comments or discussions of real life examples. In particular the notions of influence and derivatives thereof will be of interest. Modelexamples for these types of agent causation will be found in the interplay between agents – person with person, person with automaton, computer for instance, and automaton with automaton.

1. FOUNDATIONS

Actions are seen as performed by means of (or with the help of) some means or method, or they are seen as performed for some purpose (or with a specific intention). Some outcomes of an agent's activities may be the result of mere causation. These observations constitute the foundation for my action theory developed in Holmström-Hintikka (1991).

Thus, I distinguish two types of agent causations, (a) sufficient doing and (b) actions. In sufficient doing no intention is involved and it is therefore named (1) *mere causation* or pure causation, sometimes even *cause*. Actions fall into two kinds, (2) *instrumental* actions and (3) *purposive* actions. These three concepts together with the concept of an *agent* and of (4) *goal directed will* are the key concepts in this analysis.

G. Holmström-Hintikka and R. Tuomela (eds.), Contemporary Action Theory. Vol. I, 109–134.

a. *Terms and Concepts*

In order to make myself better understood, let me here introduce some technical terminology. Let $a,b,c,\ldots,x,y,z,\ldots$ be constants and variables for agents and let $m,n,p,q,r,s,\ldots$ be variables for conditions (states). Further, let '$\sim$', '$\vee$', '&', '$\rightarrow$', '$\leftrightarrow$' denote the common Boolean operators for negation, disjunction, conjunction, material implication and material equivalence. Likewise, $\exists$ and $\forall$ are the existential and universal quantifiers. We shall also adopt the signs '$\models$' and '$\vdash$' to indicate that what follows is an axiom or theorem derived from axioms or previous theorems. In addition, '*C*', '*E*', '*A*', '*W*' stand as operators for *causing*, for *instrumental* and *purposive* actions, and for *goal-directed will*. By means of these operators I can form the concept of

(1) *sufficient doing* (causing): $C(x,m,r)$
for x, m suffices to make sure that r

(2) *instrumental action*: $E(x,m,r)$
by means of m, x sees to it that r

(3) *purposive* action: $A(x,r,p)$
x sees to it that r for the purpose that p

(4) *goal-directed will*: $W(x,p,q)$
x wills that p aiming (with the further aim or goal) that q.

Further concepts and symbols may be added as we go along.

Conditions (i.e., states), including actions, may be replaced by other ones thereby constructing new conditions. Thus, for instance, $E(x,m,A(x,r,p))$ represents a condition obtained from (2) by substituting (3), a purposive action, for r. This reads "by means of m x sees to it that r for the purpose that p". Simple conditions are, e.g., "the sun is shining", "penguins are jumping around at the Antarctica".

The *agent* or agents are thought of as being individual persons, a robot, God, or a collective such as an institution, company, association etc. In the second-order action above – x sees to it that he sees to it – the agent variables may coincide or be distinct. If distinct one agent is seeing to it that another agent sees to it that a certain result occurs. In the expression above it is clearly displayed how an agent's action operates on his own action. From here it is easy to imagine two separate agents where one is seeing to it that the other is seeing to it that a particular condition is realized. For instance $E(a,m_1, E(b,m_2,r))$ may express the condition that I, by means of calling my husband, see to it that he, by cooking the food, sees to it that dinner is ready when I come home. The second- and higher-order actions shall be discussed later.

b. *Two-Place Relations*

By means of quantification I can define two-place expressions corresponding to the three-place relations above. The result is listed below:

(DfC) $C(x,r) =_{df} \exists mC(x,m,r)$
x causes it that r iff there is an *m* such that for *x m* suffices to make sure that *r*

(DfE) $E(x,r) =_{df} \exists mE(x,m,r)$
x sees to it that r iff there is a means *m* such that *x* sees to it that *r* by means of *m*

(DfA′) $A'(x,r) =_{df} \exists pA(x,r,p)$
x sees to it that r on purpose iff there is a purpose, *p*, such that *x* sees to it that *r* for the purpose that *p*

(Df′A) $'A(x,p) =_{df} \exists rA(x,r,p)$
x has the purpose that p iff there is an *r* such that *x* sees to it that *r* for the purpose that *p*

(DfW′) $W'(x,p) =_{df} \exists qW(x,p,q)$
x wills that p iff there is a *q* such that *x* wills that *p* aiming that *q*

(Df′W) $'W(x,q) =_{df} \exists pW(x,p,q)$
x has the goal that q iff there is a *p* such that *x* wills that *p* aiming that *q*.

Other possible readings may be

$C(x,r)$ *x* causes it that *r* – somehow
$E(x,r)$ *x* sees to it that *r* – by some means
$A'(x,r)$ *x* sees to it that *r* – for some purpose
$'A(x,p)$ *x* does something for the purpose that *p*
$W'(x,p)$ *x* wills that *p* – for some aim
$'W(x,q)$ *x* wills something for the goal that *q*.

c. *Basic Assumptions*

Mere causation may be thought of in terms of being a cause with an agent (but no intention, i.e., purpose) involved. Seven axioms accepted for this operator give us the limits within which we can move (see Appendix (C1)–(C7)). (For justification, see Holmström-Hintikka 1991, 30–32.) Based on those axioms we could show that mere causation, i.e., sufficient doing – as contrasted to actions – is a lattice (Holmström-Hintikka, 33–37).

One further assumption that is made is the equivalence relation adopted. This is taken to be an 'on-a-par' relation:

$$(\mathrm{Df}\sim_x)\quad p \sim_x q =_{df} (m)[C(x,m,p) \leftrightarrow C(x,m,q)] \;\&\; (r)[C(x,p,r) \leftrightarrow C(x,q,r)]$$

This is to say that, for instance

whatever x does, it suffices to make sure that x widens the door chink (p) iff it suffices to make sure that he opens the door (q) and whatever the result (r) is, x's widening the door chink (p) suffices to make sure that he reaches it iff x's opening the door (q) suffices to do so (Holmström-Hintikka 1991, 32).

The parity is agent related, indeed, because what suffices for one agent A to make sure that p, might not suffice for another agent B. Also, it should be noticed that parity is better defined in terms of causation than in terms of action (as in e.g., Holmström-Hintikka 1984, 1985; Kanger 1986). The reason is the absence of intentionality and the fundamental logic accepted. For basic logic and axioms accepted, please see Appendix.

d. *Bridging Principles*

As can be argued (see Holmström-Hintikka 1991, 69ff) if x by means of m sees to it that r then m suffices for x to make sure that r. Also x sees to it that r iff x sees to it that r for some purpose, i.e.,

(PEC) $\models E(x,m,r) \rightarrow C(x,m,r)$
(PEA) $\vdash \exists mE(x,m,r) \leftrightarrow \exists pA(x,r,p)$

which is the same as

(PEA.1) $\vdash E(x,r) \leftrightarrow A'(x,r)$.

Also, I argue that, by means of m, x sees to it that r iff x sees to it that r for some purpose and m suffices for x to make sure that r

(PEAC) $\models E(x,m,r) \leftrightarrow A'(x,r)\ \&\ C(x,m,r)$.

Moreover, x wills that p iff x does something for the purpose that p

(PWA) $\models \exists qW(x,p,q) \leftrightarrow \exists rA(x,r,p)$

which is the same as

(PWA.1) $W(x,p) \leftrightarrow {}'A(x,p)$.

This latter axiom is based on the observation that, as Harry Frankfurt puts it,

[An agent's will] is the notion of an effective desire – one that moves (or will or would move) a person all the way to action. (Frankfurt 1971, 7f.)

This is to say, that, if the agent wills that p then he does *something* for the purpose that p (is realized).

2. AGENT CAUSATION

Let us now imagine an agent, a, standing in a crossroad, o, wondering about where to go. He has three options (i) go to the left, r, (ii) go to the right, $\sim r$, (iii) stay where he is, o. Returning to where he came from is no alternative

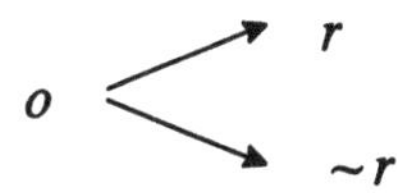

For some time he cannot make up his mind but stands where he is. This he does without reflecting upon it, in other words, without a purpose, i.e., non-purposely.

The best way to express this condition is to say that: doing nothing, $\top$, suffices for the agent to make sure that he stays where he is, o.

$$(2.1) \qquad C(a, \top, o)$$

The obvious outcome of this condition is o, i.e., that the agent stays where he is. This is quite in line with the axiom (C1) which states that for every agent, x,

$$(\text{C1}) \qquad \models C(x,m,r) \rightarrow m \;\&\; r,$$

hence

$$(2.2) \qquad \vdash C(x,m,r) \rightarrow r.$$

Being where he is means neither to go to r nor go to not-r. The fact that a remains where he is without reflection should therefore be expressed as (2.1) above.

Let us now imagine that the agent makes up his mind and *decides* to stay where he is. This time he stays where he is on purpose. So, two things can be observed: (1) a sees to it that he stays where he is (mirrored in (2.3)), (2) a stays where he is on purpose (mirrored in (2.4)). The fact that 'a sees to it that he remains at o', i.e., stays where he is, reflects a mental process. On the other hand there is some means by which he sees to it that he remains where he is. Thus

$$(2.3) \qquad \exists m E(a,m,o) \leftrightarrow E(a,o) \qquad [\text{DfE}]$$
$$(2.4) \qquad \exists p A(a,o,p) \leftrightarrow A'(a,o). \qquad [\text{DfA}']$$

The outcome obviously is the same, that a remains at o. In other words

$$(2.5) \qquad E(a,o) \leftrightarrow A'(a,o).$$

Let us now imagine that something makes the agent move towards r and actually reach r. This is nothing that he intends to or sees to on purpose.

Maybe he was pushed or maybe some other force made him move, an avalanche, a wave or what not. What has happened, then, is reflected in the expression

(2.6) $C(a,m,r)$
i.e., m suffices for a to make sure that r.

This may here be exemplified as the rolling of a wave suffices for a to make sure that he reaches r. In contrast the agent may move to r on purpose and he does so by some means, for instance by walking:

(2.7) $E(a,m,r)$
by means of m a sees to it that r.

This again is exemplified as by means of walking a sees to it that he reaches r.

If, again, he moves to r on purpose we have

(2.8) $A(a,r,p)$
a sees to it that r for the purpose that p.

This may in turn be exemplified as a sees to it that he reaches r for the purpose that he gets home.

Had his choice been $\sim r$, this would have been reflected in the formula by simply replacing r with $\sim r$ and for some purposes by the denial of the corresponding expression for agent causation C, E or A.

3. SECOND ORDER AGENT CAUSATION

Let us now imagine that another agent, b, influences a in some of the ways spelled out below:

(3.1) b holds a in a steady grip
(3.2) b pushes a
(3.3) b pursuades a.

Of these alternatives (3.2) in turn falls into

(3.2a) b pushes a non-purposely
(3.2b) b pushes a on purpose.

The various states of affairs or conditions above can now be spelled out.

3.0. *A Causal Chain*

Our first question will be whether one agent can cause another agent to cause a condition. To put it simple: Could b cause a to cause o? Certainly: To see this, the only thing we have to do is to substitute the sufficing condition, m_2, in

$C(b,m_2,r_2)$ by a similar clause with a as the causing agent, $C(a,m_1,r_1)$. This clearly gives us a mere causation of $C(b,C(a,m_1,r_1),r_2)$. More generally we shall write this in the form:

(3.0.1) $C(x,C(y,m_1,r_1),r_2)$.

We can obviously here identify a causal chain where, as it happens, human agents participate unintentionally in causing one another to cause a certain condition, new or *status quo*.

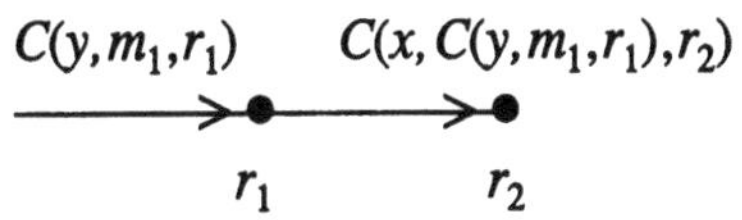

Various philosophical interpretations of this clause (3.0.1) may be possible although we shall not go into it here. The observation about the causal chain only spells out an old thought in the history of ideas concerning *initial*, or first, cause and proximate, i.e., *immediate*, or secondary, cause. In (3.0.1) we could think of the y-clause as presenting the initial cause and the x-clause as presenting the immediate cause of the outcome, that the condition r_2 is realized.

The philosophically interesting thought, much discussed in the Middle Ages, was how God as the initial cause with humans as immediate causes realized certain conditions, say s, in the world. Our concept (3.0.1) is not, however, the right one to spell out such an idea. More likely it was thought that God saw to it that humans saw to it that that particular condition, s, was realized. But this kind of agent causation is further analyzed in Section 3.3 – without further reference to historical problems, though.

3.1. *b Holds a in a Steady Grip*

The fact that b holds a in a steady grip can be looked upon from the perspective of either agent. From a's perspective what happens falls into

(3.1.1) $C(a,m_1,o)$
where m_1 stands for 'b holds a in a steady grip'. Thus

(3.1.2) $C(a,E(b,m_1,r_1),o)$
for a, the fact that b, by holding, sees to it that a stays where he is, suffices for a to stay where he is, or perhaps even

(3.1.3) $C(a,A(b,r_1,p),o)$
for a, the fact that b for the purpose that p sees to it that a stays where he is suffices for a to make sure that he stays where he is.

We might want to say that "the fact that b holds a in a steady grip, m_1, *causes*

a to stay where he is" as a synonym to the strict explication of $C(a,m_1,o)$ which is that "the fact that b holds a in a steady grip, m_1, suffices for a to remain in o".

From b's perspective this same thing looks different. In the first place what he does is two-fold and should be explicated either in the form of an instrumental action or a purposive action:

(3.1.4) $E(b,m_1,r_1)$
by holding a in a steady grip, m_1, b sees to it that a stays where he is, r_1.

Could we even say that

(3.1.5) $E(b,m_1,C(a,m_1,o))$
by holding a in a steady grip b sees to it that his holding a in a steady grip suffices for a to stay where he is, in o.

Yes, this is exactly what we should say, as I try to show later. From the above explications it is totally clear that the purpose or intention is only on the part of b.

Thus, the purposive aspect of b's actions looks as follows:

(3.1.6) $A(b,C(a,m_1,o),p)$
for the purpose that p, b sees to it that his holding a suffices for a to make sure that o.

From what has been said about b holding a and its possible "practical" implications we are ready to summarize and generalize the same to hold for all agents x and y, given that they stand in a similar relation to each other as do a and b in the various conditions above in (3.1.1)–(3.1.6).

The logical implications will again follow the general laws of the fundamental theory in Holmström-Hintikka (1991) collected in our Appendix. Be it enough to apply one of the axioms, e.g., (C1) together with (E1) to (3.1.1)–(3.1.3) to demonstrate their applicability to higher-order expressions. Due to the fact that both C and E are success operators on both conditions, m and r (in $C(x,m,r)$, $E(x,m,r)$) we can derive

(3.1.7) $\vdash C(x,E(y,m_1,r_1),r_2) \rightarrow E(y,m_1,r_1) \ \& \ r_2$.

From this it obviously follows that

(3.1.8) $\vdash C(x,E(y,m_1,r_1),r_2) \rightarrow m_1 \ \& \ r_1 \ \& \ r_2$

because

(C1) $\models C(x,m,r) \rightarrow m \ \& \ r$
(E1) $\models E(x,m,r) \rightarrow m \ \& \ r$.

This may seem trivial, but that is only due to the choice of axioms to apply (C1) and (E1).

Had a purposive action of the general form $A(y,r,p)$ replaced the instrumental action in (3.1.7) then the outcome would have been simply r_1 and r_2:

(3.1.9) $\vdash C(x,A(y,r_1,p),r_2) \rightarrow A(y,r_1,p) \,\&\, r_2$, but due to
$\models A(x,r,p) \rightarrow Er(x,r)$, and thus r, [A1]
$\vdash A(y,r_1,p) \rightarrow r_1$ only.

Simple as it may seem, the ancient and medieval discussions about *first*, initial, and *secondary*, not to mention *proximate*, immediate, cause show us the complexity of the problem. The second-order expressions in this section can be seen as a first attempt to spell out the elements in that overwhelming problem whether God has predestined human beings, as was claimed by, e.g., Thomas Bradwardine (1618) as reported by Calvin Normore (1982). I have, nevertheless, no intention to enter that discussion here.

At a closer look at the second-order expressions in (3.1), for each separate case one might have to decide whether the agents could coincide, can $x=y$? In our above example it does not make sense for a rational agent that "x's holding his own hand suffices to make sure that he stays where he is". Maybe our generalization has to spell out that $x=y$ or $x\neq y$ in $C(x,C(y,m_1,r_1),r_2)$ etc.

3.2. *b Pushes a*

As shall be seen later interesting aspects arise if we allow an automaton to take the site of either or both of the agents. I would like the reader to keep this option in mind as we proceed. Let us, then, move to the condition (3.2) where '*b* pushes *a*'. As was observed before this could happen either so that (a) *b* pushes *a* non-purposely or (b) *b* pushes *a* on purpose.

If (3.2a) is the case then this doing by *b*, pushing *a* non-purposely, should be interpreted as a sufficient doing on *b*'s part:

(3.2a.1) $C(b,m,r)$
b's pushing *a* suffices for *b* to make sure that *r*.

What then follows depends on what the variable *r* stands for. For our purposes, an action or doing with *a* as an agent is what we have in mind at this stage. We then have three options:

(3.2a.2) $C(b,m_1,C(a,m_2,s))$
(3.2a.3) $C(b,m_1,E(a,m_2,s))$
(3.2a.4) $C(b,m_1,A(a,s,q))$.

The first alternative causes no problems, *b*'s pushing *a* suffices for *b* to make sure that m_2 suffices for *a* to make sure that *s*. Here $(m_2=m_1)$ or

($m_2 \neq m_1$). This may be thought of as a chain reaction: m_1 makes b cause a to cause s by m_2.

The second alternative, (3.2a.3) where b's non-purposely pushing causes a to *see to it* that s by means of m_2 is not as clear but it should become obvious after some reflection. We could think that b's push is that impulse a needs to get started towards r. A similar explanation could hold for (3.2a.4) as well.

In case of (3.2b) b pushes a on purpose, this is just another example of the previously explained case which may be expressed in the general forms, or derivatives of them

(3.2b.1) $E(x,m,C(y,m,s))$
(3.2b.2) $A(x,C(y,m,s),p)$.

In this instance, as anybody can tell by now, by pushing y (= m), x sees to it that x's pushing y suffices for y to make sure that s. The second formula unfolds in a similar way. It is easy to imagine how this would apply to work on the computer. For instance, we can see that "by pushing the button x sees to it that his pushing the button suffices for the computer to start the program". We shall return to these later.

3.3. *b Persuades a*

Let us now move to the third condition, the one where b persuades a to either stay or to move. Before we go any further let us make some reflections about the very concept of 'persuasion'. Is it not the case that when we persuade somebody to do something, for instance a child to take her medicine, a friend to come and visit, a colleague to accept our viewpoint, we then make them (a) do what we ask, (b) do something they do not want to do, (c) do something they did not intend to do, (d) *want* what we want them to want, (e) *intend* what we make them intend, (f) *do* on purpose what we want them to do, etc.

I shall not at this point go into the discussion about belief change although it is a part of the process of persuasion. I shall stay much more simple minded and remain by agent causation. This does not of course rule out the fact that I at a later instance might identify some part of the agent causation with belief change. But here I want to keep it simple.

From the examples listed before we could observe that one aspect of persuasion is to make the other agent have the same purpose or intention as we have ourselves, or else as we intend or want him to have. When we persuade the child to take her medication and are successful therein, we

- make her do something on purpose
- make her do the thing with a particular purpose
- make her *do* what we ask her to do.

We can then ask

Does it have to be willingly? No. Think about the child and the medication.
Does it have to be with a purpose same as ours? No. The child might want to please us.
Can it be with the same purpose as ours? Yes.
Does it have to be on purpose? Yes, the child is not forced (only mildly) to take her medication. She sees to it that she swallows her pill for some purpose (to please her mother, to get out of the situation, to really get healthy).

It seems as if our persuasion was successful as soon as the other agent does what we ask him to do without the additional requirement of equivalent or coinciding purposes. However, if somebody, for instance the child, had purposes opposite to ours and negative wants about the action, to take the medicine, then the successful persuasion has been also on the part of the intention, i.e., purpose and the will.

If, on the other hand, we persuade a friend to come and visit us we can assume that he wants to do so from the beginning and we only need to make him do what he already wants to do.

Against these preliminary background observations, where for instance the concept of 'will' and its equivalence 'wanting' were not strictly defined, but taken for granted[1], we should be able to separate some instances of 'b persuades a'.

First we have become aware of the fact that persuasion is nothing accidental or unintentional, thus not some sufficient doing. On the contrary, b always has a purpose in mind which might involve a change of action on the part of the other agent, from either a non-action, state o, or the opposite action 'go to $\sim r$'. We cannot, however, without the addition of a time component express this change of action and intention as one instance of persuasion. Nobody can see to it that r and not see to it that r at the same time. As we are not going to introduce the time perspective into this discussion we simply have to leave it there for the time being.

There are, however, other aspects of persuasion which may be expressed in our language. For instance if a mother sees to it that her child takes the medicine this may be seen as an instance of persuasion. Both agents perform an instrumental action. Both agents therefore, as we saw, do what they do on purpose, with one purpose or other. The expression below is therefore seen as an explication of one kind of persuasion

(3.3.1) $E(b,m_1,E(a,m_2,s))$

or simply

(3.3.1') $E(b,E(a,s))$
i.e., b sees to it that a sees to it that s.

How does this differ from pushing? In particular how does it differ from the two instances of pushing where *b*'s pushing suffices to make sure that *a* sees to it that *s* by some means or alternatively for some purpose? This is exactly where it makes a difference: although pushing on *b*'s part might be on purpose, what the outcome seems to be on *a*'s part is *mere* causation, as expressed in (3.2b.1) and (3.2b.2). If, on the other hand, the pushing is non-purposive then the doing on *b*'s part is *mere* causation although the outcome could be an instrumental or purposive action on *a*'s part. This was the content of (3.2a.2)–(3.2a.4).

What we are looking at here is a condition where either an instrumental action on *b*'s part results in an instrumental or purposive action on *a*'s part as well; or alternatively a purposive action on *b*'s part results in an instrumental or purposive action on *a*'s part. Thus the options for what we here call *persuasion* are

(3.3.1) $E(b,m_1,E(a,m_2,s))$
(3.3.2) $E(b,m_1,A(a,s,q))$
(3.3.3) $A(b,E(a,m_1,s),p)$
(3.3.4) $A(b,A(a,s,q),p)$.

Any permutations or two-place derivatives of the above formulas are of course also candidates for persuasion.

4. MAN AND MACHINE

Let us now give names to the two agents, let '*b*' be Raymond and '*a*' his computer. We can then distinguish options of the similar kind as discussed above.

(4.1.1) By not turning it on Raymond sees to it that the computer remains shut off
$E(b,m,C(a,m,s))$

(4.1.2) $A(b, C(a,m,s),p)$ again expresses that
Raymond for the purpose that p sees to it that his not turning it on suffices for the computer to remain shut off.
(Here m stands for 'not to turn on'.)

Further we can distinguish the following cases

(4.2) Raymond pushes the button
(4.2a) Raymond pushes the button non-purposely
(4.2b) Raymond pushes the button on purpose

Depending on which button Raymond pushes accidentally the outcome s differs from either remaining shut off, or either r or $\sim r$ on the screen.

The first of the two may look as follows:

(4.2a.1) $C(b,m, C(a,m,s))$

Could it also be that

(4.2a.2) $C(b,m_1,E(a,m_2,s))$ or
$C(b,m_1,A(a,s,p))$.

Let us discuss this later.

What shows as r on the screen is a result of the computer processing along the path that results in r.

The notion 'Raymond pushes the button on purpose' shall be taken to mean that Raymond pushes a particular button on purpose. Referring to what was said before, then the following alternatives present themselves:

(4.2b.1) $E(b,m_1,C(a,m_2,s))$
(4.2b.2) $E(b,m_1,E(a,m_2,s))$
(4.2b.3) $E(b,m_1,A(a,s,p))$

or

(4.2b.4) $A(b, C(a,m,s),p)$
(4.2b.5) $A(b,E(a,m,s),p)$
(4.2b.6) $A(b,A(a,s,p_2),p_1)$.

The six alternatives above are the obvious outcomes of what Raymond does. Whether all of the alternatives can be philosophically accepted will be subject for further discussion at a later stage. We might also ask whether the following might be the case:

(4.2b.7) $E(b,m_1,A(a,s,p))$ & $A(b,A(a,s,p),s)$

where the second clause suggests that the computer has a purpose, p, different from Raymond's, s.

This too has to be discussed later, but before we reach that point let us follow Raymond's further activities:

(4.3) Raymond persuades the computer.

Like everybody else working with computers Raymond knows that this gadget has "a will of its own". So, when this monster refuses to follow his simple moves, instead of kicking and beating it up, Raymond patiently begins to persuade the machine. This is a very delicate thing to do because what it means is that he has to make this agent *want* the way he wants it to want. To be more precise, this means that in order to make it work Raymond has to see to it, by some means and on purpose, that this agent, his computer, on purpose sees to the outcome intended by Raymond.

Robots may be programmed in the same manner as are computers. As a matter of fact, they are often operating like computers and also operated by means of or by computers. Before deciding how Raymond should proceed let me spell out all options there are. Everything will then fall into places and we seem to return to our previous explications with one agent operating on another – on purpose or non-purposely.

Although the formal outlook might be the same in the explications below, the philosophical content changes drastically for instance with the switch of agent from human to non-human.

$$
\begin{array}{ll}
C(b,m_1,C(a,m_2,s)) & C(b,C(a,m,s),r) \\
C(b,m_1,E(a,m_2,s)) & C(b,E(a,m,s),r) \\
C(b,m_1,A(a,s,q)) & C(b,A(a,s,q),r) \\
\\
E(b,m_1,C(a,m_2,s)) & E(b,C(a,m,s),r) \\
E(b,m_1,E(a,m_2,s)) & E(b,E(a,m,s),r) \\
E(b,m_1,A(a,s,q)) & E(b,A(a,s,q),r) \\
\\
A(b,m_1,C(a,m_2,s)) & A(b,C(a,m,s),p) \\
A(b,m_1,E(a,m_2,s)) & A(b,E(a,m,s),p) \\
A(b,m_1,A(a,s,q)) & A(b,A(a,s,q),p).
\end{array}
$$

These eighteen alternatives are the outcomes of the positive actions and conditions. We must not forget that each condition, including actions may be denied. That gives us a rapidly rising number of options, options of abstaining, refraining and omission that we can easily imagine but shall not spell out here.[2] What needs to be done is to go through all the forms from $C(b,m_1,C(a,m_2,s))$ to $\sim C(b,\sim m_1,\sim C(a,\sim m_2,\sim s))$ and all the permutations in between, and then repeat the same for the other operators as well. But let Raymond leave that for his computer to do, or let the computer program the robot to perform all these various instances of agent causation. Our interest will remain on the philosophical aspects of influence.

Questions to Raise

Several questions present themselves at this stage. Can, for instance, a machine be programmed in such a way that it could intentionally, that is on purpose, perform certain moves? Could it for instance be that $E(b,m_1,A(a,s,q))$? Can it be programmed in such a way that it could on purpose program another machine, say a robot, on purpose to perform certain moves or is it all a matter of the programming human being's own purposes and further aims?

The interesting aspects referred to above arise when one or both of the agents are automata. Not unexpectedly, one automaton can cause another to operate in a certain way. Say a robot can cause a computer to perform a computational operation. Pushing a button on the computer suffices for the robot to make sure that the computer performs the operation. Both activities, the one of the robot and the one by the computer seem to be mere causations, i.e. they are non-purposive.

Questions of the kind just raised naturally arise in the framework presented, and let me stress that this framework helps to see the consequences of different answers. But these consequences have to be dealt with in another paper.

One more thing needs to be emphasized. This is that an automaton cannot be programmed to have purposes of its own. To see this, let us look at the following statement:

(4.4) $E(b,m_1,A(a,r,p)) \rightarrow A(a,r,p)$ [E1]

This may, for instance, be exemplified thus: by punching certain keys, Raymond sees to it that his computer stores the material, for the purpose of printing it later, which implies that the computer stores the material for the purpose of printing it later. But, just a moment. Although the computer stores the material in its memory for the purpose of reproducing it through the printer, this is *not* a purpose of the *computer*. It only stores in its memory what the operator commands, i.e., we have a situation of the form: $E(b,m_1, C(a,m_2,r))$ seen from the viewpoint of the computer. The computer has no further purposes or aims. The operator or programmer is the one who has further aims. Thus, it is *wrong*, after all, to prescribe the computer this capacity. It is wrong to suggest anything of the kind expressed by (4.4) as applied to an automaton. Even a complicated program contains only what was intended, or tacitly intended, by the programmer. Thus, in a straightforward case that we have been discussing, (4.4) should be replaced by either

(4.5) $A(b,C(a,m,r),p) \rightarrow C(a,m,r)$ [A1]

or

(4.6) $A(b,E(a,m,r),p) \rightarrow E(a,m,r)$. [A1]

The first of them may be taken to express the fact that, if Raymond, for the purpose of later printing the material, p, sees to it that his pushing the save button suffices for the computer to save the material, then, based on (A1), the pushing of the save button suffices for the computer to save the material.

The second clause, (4.6), suggests that instead of causing the storing of the material the computer performs an action, i.e., it sees to it by certain moves, that it stores the material. But again, if we hold that the computer itself performs an action, then we also have, implicitly given it the mental capacity of forming purposes (by PEA). This is, however, a matter which I strongly opposed just above. Computers have no intentions, bad or good.

5. INFLUENCE

One obvious application of the second-order action description with separate agents is in the area of *influence*. As soon as we open that door, however, an overwhelmingly wide range of possibilities opens up. Loyal to our three areas of accplication, viz. history of ideas, legal matters and computation, we would nevertheless seek to pick our examples from these areas. Before we do so, however, let us spell out what it really means for one agent to influence another.[3]

5.1. *The Concept of Influence*

Let us begin with some conceptual analysis. The clause

a sees to it that *b* sees to it that *r*

seems to grasp the most common, albeit not the only, form of 'influence'. Before we go on to discuss other ones, let us put this in a more general form and spell it out in the language provided before where $I(x,y,r)$ stands for 'x influences y to r'.

(DfI$_E$) $I_E(x,y,r) =_{df} E(x,E(y,r))$.

The obvious reading of this restricted definition is:

x influences y to r iff x sees to it that y sees to it that r.

Given alternative combinations of cause and action concepts we should clearly wonder why this particular constellation was singled out. Thus, could it not be the case that a combination of action and sufficient doing could grasp at least some aspect of 'influence'? Could

(5.1.1) $C(x,m,C(y,n,s))$
(5.1.2) $C(x,m,E(y,n,s))$ or
(5.1.3) $E(x,m,C(y,n,s))$

be candidates for any form of 'influence'?

I believe that we should separate *consciously* influencing from doing so *unconsciously*. If we make this distinction, then we have also drawn the lines between purposive and non-purposive influence. In this context my focus shall be on *conscious influence*. Having taken this stand I have thereby obviously ruled out (5.1.1) and (5.1.2) from the list of candidates for influence. Whether either of them could stand for unconscious, non-purposive influence is none of my concerns. The expression (5.1.3) may characterize some form of *coercion*.[4]

In our effort to try to find alternatives for the definience in (DfI_E) we should raise the question whether any locution containing purposive action would be suitable. The options then are

(1) $E(x,m,A(y,r,p))$
(2) $A(x,s,E(y,n,r))$
(3) $A(x,s,A(y,r,p))$.

As we saw before, a mother can see to it that the child takes her medicine for the purpose of getting well. In my mind, then, (1) is another suitable candidate for a concept of 'influence'. This should come as no surprise, however, when we keep in mind the bridging principles between the E and A operators.[5] Applied to this case we get

(5.1.4) $E(x,m,A(y,r,p)) \rightarrow E(x,E(y,r))$ [DfE, A1]

It seems, however, too strong to insist on (1) for the definience whereas the now accepted form, (DfI_E) captures all alternatives we want to include.

Why are not (2) and (3) admissible? The reason is simple. Both forms (2) and (3) express the second agent's purposive actions as the purpose of the first agent, x. To see how it unfolds we want to spell out (2):

(5.1.5) $A(x,s,E(x,n,r)) \rightarrow E(x,s)\ \&\ 'A(x,E(y,r))$.

The consequent shows that the agent x himself sees to it that s and that his purpose is that y sees to it that r.

This should make us raise the question whether one agent's purpose *vis-à-vis* another agent's action in any interesting way could be thought of as an influence. According to the foundations of the theory it is assumed that an agent x has the purpose that p iff he does something to fulfil this purpose:

(Df'A) $'A(x,p) =_{df} \exists r A(x,r,p)$.

Applied to our, perhaps not so influential agent, x, we could assume that if his purpose is that y sees to it that r, then he does *something* to fulfil that purpose. This, however, does not guarantee that the purpose really is fulfilled. It seems clear then that (2) falls short of meeting the requirements that "x sees to it that y sees to it that r". The reasoning concerning (3) goes along the same lines.

When it comes to one agent's influence regarding another agent's actions we have thus argued for the adoption of (DfI_E).

5.2. *Influencing the Will*

Influence clearly reaches further than from one agent to another agent's actions. We accept it as a fact that one can influence another's mind and will as well. Thus, when it then comes to the will, we have two options:

(1) $E(x,m,W(y,p,q))$

or

(2) $A(x,W(y,p,q),s)$

or some variants of these two.

Here, again, we can rely on one of the fundamental principles in Holmström-Hintikka (1991):

(PWA.1) $W(x,p) \leftrightarrow {}'A(x,p)$

which is to say that

> x wills that p iff x does something for the purpose that p.

From both (1) and (2) obviously follows that

(5.2.1) $E(x,W(y,p))$.[6]

Here some caution is in order. Notice that the clause $\exists rA(x,r,p)$, i.e., $'A(x,p)$, expresses a plain purpose (intention). The agent "does *something* for the purpose that p", it says. This is the reason why we have here the same concept as the two-place will $W(x,p)$, i.e., $\exists pW(x,p,q)$, which as we saw states that

> the agent wills that p iff he *does something* for the purpose of fulfilling that p.

If we want to spell out what it means for one agent to influence another agent's will, (5.2.1) is the clear interpretation of such an influence. This gives us a reason to return to (DfI_E).

In this definition, (DfI_E), we should really spell out what the term r stands for. Earlier, when we spoke about one agent's influence on the other to r we took r to be an instrumental or purposive action. Now is the time to realize that

> *r stands for that entity $\varphi(y)$*, which is influenced by one agent, x, in relation to another agent, y.

5.3. *The General Definition of 'Influence'*

As we saw, we have all reasons to expand our definition of 'influence' to cover all the areas of y's activities – including mental acts – that x might influence. This is to say that the third component, $\varphi(y)$, in an expanded form, $I(x,y,\varphi(y))$ could stand for any of the operators E, A, W, K, M, with y as the agent ($K(y,p)$ stands for 'y knows that p'). It is fully plausible that one agent influences not only another's actions but also his purposes, wills, knowledge and possibilities (in particular practical possibilities, i.e., what an agent can do; see Holmström-Hintikka 1991, 96–145).

We are now ready to formulate the definition of 'influence' in its general form:

(DfI) $I(x,y,\varphi(y)) =_{df} E(x,\varphi(y))$
x influences y with respect to $\varphi(y)$ iff x sees to it that $\varphi(y)$.

This definition clearly underlines the fact that x *consciously* influences y. If you then bear in mind that E is a success operator, it means that, according to this definition, every time x influences y to $\varphi(y)$ then $\varphi(y)$ obtains.

A few objections to the above view naturally present themselves.

5.4. *Comments on the Definition of Influence*

Among the strongest objections to the definition of influence, (DfI), one could imagine the fact that it may be impossible for y to $\varphi(y)$. In such a case it would be wrong to say that x influences y to $\varphi(y)$. This is quite correct. The following theorem spells this out:

(5.4.1) $\vdash \sim M(y,\varphi(y)) \rightarrow \sim M(x,I(x,y,\varphi(y))$
if y cannot $\varphi(y)$ then x cannot influence y to $\varphi(y)$.[7]

This may be spelled out for actions in the following way:

(5.4.2) $\vdash \sim \exists m M(y,E(y,m,r)) \rightarrow \sim \exists m \exists n M(x,E(x,n,E(y,m,r)))$.[8]

As 'cannot' expresses the same as 'it is practically impossible for the agent', we can say that

> if it is practically impossible for y to see to it that r then it is practically impossible for x to influence y to see to it that r.

One point where it becomes obvious how difficult it may be for x to influence y to $\varphi(y)$ is when we move to wills. Even if x might intend to influence y's will he might not succeed unless y could change his will at will.

Stig Kanger (1977) develops a preliminary logic for the concept of 'influence', preliminary in the sense that the relativized modality, $M(x,p)$ and its logic were not yet introduced. Also, Kanger's concept of 'influence' was limited to instrumental actions only. Nevertheless, a few of the axioms I adopted for practical possibility and capacity to will (1991) were based on Kanger's observation on actions (in my translation) that

> there are always means by means of which it is impossible to see to it that S [= r in my notation]. It is e.g., impossible to see to it that the lamp is turned off by counting to three. (Kanger 1977, 16)

This amounts, in my notation, to:

(K1) $\exists m \sim ME(x,m,r)$.

A second observation is that

(K2) $\sim M \sim E(x,m,r)$ is a contradiction.

It is easy to argue that these two axioms *mutatis mutandis* apply to practical possibility, capacity to will (= $\exists q M(x, W(x,p,q))$ and therefore also to the general concept of 'influence' as discussed above.

One further comment is here in order. The action theory outlined here allows for the possibility that more than one agent influences consciously another one. I shall not however carry out that discussion here.

6. APPLICATIONS AND SUMMARY

The action theory developed in Holmström-Hintikka (1991) and further in this paper has its applications in as different areas as in history of ideas, legal theory and praxis and computation. The same observation holds for the particular area connected to 'influence'. For the sake of brevity I shall choose only one example from the history of ideas and one from the legal domain. What was said about Raymond's activities by the computer may be taken as an example of influence as well. A few words should also be said about computer's capacity to influence other agents.

6.1.

It is well documented that Martin Luther (1483–1546) who so radically influenced European theology and philosophy, himself brought much of his foundations from the Augustinian tradition. A thorough analysis of the streaks backwards in history will reveal major similarities in various problem areas. One of the important issues for Luther was the free will problem and its connection to predestination and salvation. In tracing our way back in history we find that among others Gregory of Rimini and Thomas Bradwardine but in particular St. Augustine were influential in this regard. The theory at hand allows us to make comparisons between these thinkers and their aspects of for instance the problems of free will and predestination.

In our historical and comparative work we will find that God's influence on human beings, both with respect to their wills and their actions, is an important aspect of the free will problem. Stating that God is in command of the human will would be one way to explain this influence:

(6.1.1) $E(g,m,W(a,p,q))$
by first loving man God sees to it that man wills that he loves God aiming at being saved.

This example catches in a nutshell one basic thought of Luther's in his theological teaching. If accepted, this statement has consequences as to our belief in the freedom of human will. In more general terms, we should say that God's influence may be spelled out as: by means of *m* God sees to it that *a* wills that *p* aiming that *q*.

In the general clause we are free to wonder about what kind of entities *p* and *q* might be. Are they good or bad? If *p* is good, is the will then good? If *q* is bad, does it make the will evil? The importance of such questions can be seen from St. Augustine's acknowledgment that

> In his [God's] will rests the supreme power, which assists the good wills of created spirits, sits in judgement of the evil wills, orders all wills, granting the power of achievement to some and denying it to others... so he is the giver of all power of achievement, but not of all acts of will. Evil wills do not proceed from him because they are contrary to the nature which proceeds from him. (*De civitate Dei*, Book 5, Chapter 9)[9]

There are two options

(1) the will is good if the object, *p*, is good
(2) the will is good if the further aim is good.

Assuming these two options would give us one analysis of St. Augustine's statement, in the simplest possible form:

(6.1.2) p is good $\rightarrow E(g,m,W(a,p,q))$
(6.1.3) p is evil $\rightarrow \sim E(g,m,W(a,p,q))$.

A similar observation could be made for *q*.

A more interesting question, however, is how various philosophers have tried to explain God's influence on human will. If He is not the first cause of the evil will, where did it come from? If God influenced man to love Him by first loving her, what value is there in our love of God? In addition, is it not a matter of predestination that God chooses whom He influences to love Him?

As was shown in Holmström-Hintikka (1991) our tools are powerful enough to handle questions of this kind. Further attempts have also been made later. (See Holmström-Hintikka, "Questions about a Question in Ockham" (forthcoming), 1997 and "The Concept of Will in Augustine's *De libero arbitrio*, Book I" (forthcoming). See also Risto Saarinen 1993 and 1997.)

Analyzing these ideas and spelling out the results with the help of our method is a huge challenge and a long time project, which we shall not initiate here. Be it enough to emphasize that we have a framework at hand which can discover and explain these things in a better way than less sensitive and less developed methods.

6.2.

It takes little imagination to see what role influence can play in the legal field. In seeking reward or punishment for some action the chief executor, the judge or prosecutor is interested in who might have influenced the agent in which way. People are responsible for actions performed or not performed. Praise and blame is awarded according to rules or norms the agent or his actions are governed by. But, in all this, he might not be the only person responsible, perhaps not responsible at all. The influencing agent should at least share the blame or punishment.

As was seen second-order agent causation has branches which enable us to spell out the exact involvement by an agent. Was he pushed or persuaded? Was he made co-operate with unjust means? A close look at particular cases with this powerful method for the analysis of such and similar cases is a task for future investigations. Nevertheless, see also earlier attempts in this regard.[10]

APPENDIX

Basic Logic

Axiom Schemata

Here, φ and ψ range over arbitrary formulas, x, y, z are any agent variables, p, q are any propositional variables and u, v, w are any variable whatsoever, $\varphi(u/w)$ denote the result of replacing any free occurrence of v in φ by u.

(L1) All substitution instances of truth-functional tautologies

(L2) $\exists v\varphi \leftrightarrow -\forall\text{-}\varphi$

(L3) $\forall\varphi \rightarrow \varphi(u/v)$, provided that v does not occur within the scope of any modal operators in φ and u is a variable of the same sort as v which is free for v in φ

(L4) $\forall(\varphi \rightarrow \psi) \rightarrow [\forall\varphi \rightarrow \forall\psi]$, provided that v does not occur free in φ

(L5) $\varphi \rightarrow \forall\varphi$, provided v does not occur free in φ

(L6) $v = v$

(L7) $u = v \rightarrow (\varphi(u/w) \rightarrow \varphi(v/w))$

(L8) $M\varphi \leftrightarrow -N\text{-}\varphi$

(L9) $N(\varphi \leftrightarrow \psi) \rightarrow (\varphi = \psi)$

(L10) $N\varphi \rightarrow \varphi$
(L11) $N(\varphi \rightarrow \psi) \rightarrow (N\varphi \rightarrow N\psi)$
(L12) $MN\varphi \rightarrow \varphi$
(L13) $N\varphi \rightarrow NN\varphi$
(L14) $N\varphi \rightarrow N(x,\varphi)$
(L15) $M(x,\varphi) \leftrightarrow -N(x,-\varphi)$
(L16) $N(x,\varphi \rightarrow \psi) \rightarrow [N(x,\varphi) \rightarrow N(x,\psi)]$
(L17) $N(x,\varphi) \rightarrow \varphi$
(L18) $N(x,\varphi) \rightarrow N(x,N(x,\varphi))$

The analytic necessity operator, N, is an S5-operator while the agent relativized operator, $N(x,\varphi)$, satisfies the axioms of S4 (see, e.g., Hughes and Cresswell 1968).

Rules of Inference

(R1) If $\vdash \varphi$ and $\vdash \varphi \rightarrow \psi$, then $\vdash \psi$
(R2) If $\vdash \varphi$, then $\vdash \forall\varphi$
(R3) If $\vdash \varphi$, then $\vdash N\varphi$

Axioms

(C1) $\models C(x,m,r) \rightarrow m \,\&\, r$
(C2) $\models \exists p C(x,m,p) \,\&\, N(m \rightarrow r) \rightarrow C(x,m,r)$
(C3) $\models C(x,m,r) \,\&\, C(x,r,s) \rightarrow C(x,m,s)$
(C4) $\models C(x,m,r) \,\&\, N(r \rightarrow s) \rightarrow C(x,m,s)$
(C5) $\models C(x,m,r) \,\&\, C(x,n,s) \rightarrow C(x,m\&n,r\&s)$
(C6) $\models C(x,m,r) \,\&\, C(x,n,r) \rightarrow C(x,m \vee n,r)$
(C7) $\models -C(x,\top,r)$

(E1) $\models E(x,m,r) \rightarrow m \,\&\, r$
(E2) $\models E(x,m,r) \rightarrow E(x,m,m)$
(E3) $\models E(x,m,n) \,\&\, E(x,n,r) \rightarrow E(x,m,r)$
(E4) $\models E(x,m,r) \,\&\, E(x,n,s) \rightarrow E(x,m\&n,r\&s)$
(E5) $\models E(x,m,r) \,\&\, E(x,n,r) \rightarrow E(x,m \vee n,r)$
(E6) $\models -E(x,\top,r)$
(E7) $\models -E(x,m,\top)$

(A1) $\models A(x,r,p) \rightarrow E(x,r)$
(A2.a) $\models A(x,q,p) \,\&\, A(x,r,p) \rightarrow A(x,q\&r,p)$
(A2.b) $\models A(x,r,p) \,\&\, A(x,r,q) \rightarrow A(x,r,p\&q)$
(A3) $\models -A(x,r,\top)$

(W1) $\models -W(x,p,\top)$
(W2) $\models W(x,p,s) \;\&\; W(x,q,s) \rightarrow W(x,p\&q,s)$
(W3) $\models W(x,p,q) \rightarrow Mp$
(W4) $\models W(x,p,q) \rightarrow \exists yM(y,E(y,q))$

(N1) $\models N(x,p \rightarrow q) \rightarrow [N(x,p) \rightarrow N(x,q)]$
(N2) $\models N(x,p) \rightarrow p$
(N3) $\models N(x,p) \rightarrow N(x,N(x,p))$
(N4) $\models N(x,r) \rightarrow -E(x,m,r)$
(N5) $\models N(x,r) \rightarrow -A(x,r,p)$
(N6) $\models N(x,p) \rightarrow -W(x,p,q)$

(M1) $\models \exists mM(x,\varphi(x)) \rightarrow M(x,\exists m\varphi(x))$
(M2) $\models \exists q\text{-}M(x,W(x,p,q))$
(M3) $\models \exists p\text{-}M(x,A(x,r,p))$

Bridging Principles

(PEC) $\models E(x,m,r) \rightarrow C(x,m,r)$
(PEA) $\vdash \exists mE(x,m,r) \leftrightarrow \exists pA(x,r,p)$
(PWA) $\models \exists qW(x,p,q) \leftrightarrow \exists rA(x,r,p)$
(PEAC) $\models E(x,m,r) \leftrightarrow C(x,m,r) \;\&\; \exists pA(x,r,p)$
(PW) $\models W(x,p,q) \;\&\; \exists mM(x,E(x,m,p)) \rightarrow E(x,p)$

Boston University and
University of Helsinki

NOTES

1 For this concept, see Holmström-Hintikka (1991).

2 These concepts have been extensively discussed in Holmström-Hintikka (1991, 59–64, 74–76).

3 In his book *The Logic of Power*, Ingmar Pörn analyzes various aspects of influence based on his then accepted concept of two-place action $E(a,p)$. This action concept relies on a Kanger–Hintikka–Kripke type of possible world semantics. As this is not the foundation of my action theory, I shall not go further along this path, despite its valuable input to the theory of action.

4 It is my view, as spelled out in Holmström-Hintikka (1991) that if an agent is acting under coersion, this activity should be labelled *behavior* rather than action. Here I could even allow for *mere causation* rather than action.

5
$\exists mE(x,m,r) \leftrightarrow \exists pA(x,r,p)$ [PEA]
$E(x,r) \leftrightarrow A'(x,r)$ [PEA.1]
$A(x,r,p) \rightarrow E(x,r)$ [A1]
$\therefore\; E(x,m,A(y,r,p)) \rightarrow E(x,E(y,r))$
$E(x,E(y,r)) \leftrightarrow \exists mE(x,m,\exists n\, E(y,n,r))$

6
$$E(x,m,W(y,p,q)) \rightarrow E(x,W(y,p,q)) \quad [DfE]$$
$$E(x,W(y,p,q)) \rightarrow E(x,W(y,p)) \quad [DfW]$$
and
$$A(x,W(y,p,q),s) \rightarrow A'(x,W(y,p,q)) \quad [DfA]$$
$$A'(x,W(y,p,q)) \rightarrow A'(x,W(y,p)) \quad [DfW]$$
$$A'(x,W(y,p)) \leftrightarrow E(x,W(y,p)) \quad [PEA.1]$$

7 'Cannot' is equivalent to 'it is practically impossible for'.

8 For the discussion about the location of the quantifier and the fact that $\exists mM(x,E(x,m,r)) \rightarrow M(x,\exists mE(x,m,r))$, see Holmström-Hintikka (1991, 119). Be it enough here to emphasize that they do not commute.

9 The edition available for me was the Augustine, *City of God*, in translation by Henry Bettenson, 1972, Penguin Books.

10 In Holmström-Hintikka (1997) these matters were dealt with in connection to concepts of human rights and legal responsibilities. In a previous yet unpublished paper "Purpose and Legal Responsibilities" I outline the concept of legal responsibility again on the fundamental observation that human action is the main ingredient in matters of both moral and legal responsibilities and that purposes are in key position in the distribution of praise and blame. In yet another paper (1993) I have discussed connections between practical reason and law.

REFERENCES

St. Augustine (413–426), *De civitate Dei contra paganos*.

Bradwardine, Thomas (1618), *De causa Dei*. Edited by H. Savile (1618), London. (Reprinted, Minerva, 1964.)

Frankfurt, Harry G. (1971), "Freedom of the Will and the Concept of a Person," *The Journal of Philosophy* **68** (1), 5–21.

Holmström, Ghita (1984a), *Formell viljeteori* (A Formal Theory of Will). Licentiate Thesis. Department of Philosophy, University of Helsinki.

Holmström, Ghita (1984b), "Rights and Practical Possibilities" in A. Peczenic *et al.* (eds.), *Theory of Legal Science*. Dordrecht, D. Reidel Publishing Company, pp. 607–615.

Holmström, Ghita (1985), "Wills, Purposes and Actions" in G. Holmström and A.J.I. Jones (eds.), *Action, Logic and Social Theory*. Essays Dedicated to Ingmar Pörn on the Occasion of his Fiftieth Birthday. *Acta Philosophica Fennica*, Vol. **38**, Helsinki, Societas Philosophica Fennica, pp. 49–62.

Holmström-Hintikka, Ghita (1991), *Action, Purpose and Will. A Formal Theory*. *Acta Philosophica Fennica*, Vol. **50**, Helsinki.

Holmström-Hintikka, Ghita (1993), "Practical Reason and Legal Argumentation" in G. Haarsher (ed.), *Chaim Perelman et la Pensée Contemporaine*. Proceedings from the Chaim Perelman Memorial Conference, Bruxelles, 1991.

Holmström-Hintikka, Ghita (1995), "The Concept of Will in Ockham and Before" in *The Proceedings of the Ninth International Conference for Medieval Philosophy*. Ottawa, 1992.

Holmström-Hintikka, Ghita (forthcoming 1997), "God's Will and Human Action" in G. Holmström-Hintikka (ed.), *Proceedings from the International Symposium on Medieval and Contemporary Philosophy of Religion*. The Netherlands, Kluwer Academic Publishers.

Holmström-Hintikka, Ghita (forthcoming), "Questions about a Question in Ockham". Accepted for publication in the *Proceedings from the International Symposium on Late Medieval Philosophy*. Helsinki, 1994.

Holmström-Hintikka, Ghita (forthcoming), "The Concept of Will in Augustine's *De libero arbitrio*, Book I".

Holmström-Hintikka, Ghita (forthcoming), "Purpose and Legal Responsibility".

Hughes, G.E. and M.I. Cresswell (1968), *An Introduction to Modal Logic*. London, Methuen and Co. Ltd. (Reprinted 1972.)

Kanger, Stig (1963), "Rättighetsbegreppet" [The Concept of Right] in *Sju filosofiska studier tillägnade Anders Wedberg*. Filosofiska Studier utgivna av Filosofiska Institutionen vid Stockholms Universitet nr. **9**, pp. 79–102.

Kanger, Stig (1977), "Några synpunkter på begreppet inflytande" [Some Aspects on the Concept of Influence], *Filosofiska Smulor tillägnade Konrad Marc-Wogau. Philosophical Studies* **27**, Uppsala, Department of Philosophy, Uppsala University, pp. 12–23.

Kanger, Stig (1986), "Unavoidability" in M. Furberg *et al.* (eds.), *Logic and Abstraction*. Essays Dedicated to Per Lindström on his Fiftieth Birthday. *Acta Philosophica Gothoburgensia*, No. **1**. Gothenburg, pp. 227–236.

Normore, Calvin (1982), "Future Contingents" in Norman Kretzman, Anthony Kenny and Jan Pinborg (eds.), *The Cambridge History of Later Medieval Philosophy*. Cambridge, London, New York, Cambridge University Press, pp. 358–381.

Pörn, Ingmar (1970), *The Logic of Power*. Oxford, Basil Blackwell.

Saarinen, Risto (forthcoming 1997), "Augustine's Two Wills and Two Goals. Some Applications of Holmström-Hintikka's Formal Theory" in the *Proceedings from the International Symposium on Medieval and Contemporary Philosophy of Religion* (Boston, 1992). Dordrecht, Kluwer Academic Publishers.

Saarinen, Risto (1993), *Weakness of the Will in Medieval Thought. From Augustine to Buridan*. Dissertation, Helsinki. Later published by Brill.

ALFRED R. MELE

PASSIVE ACTION

Peter was placed – face down and head first – on a sled, and pushed from the top of a high, snow-covered hill. The brisk wind and flying snow swiftly awoke him. In moments, he had his wits about him and surmised that this early morning trip down the hill was part of his initiation into the SAE fraternity. Peter quickly surveyed his options. He could put an end to his trip by sliding off the sled, or by turning it sharply. He could grasp the steering handles and guide the sled down the slope. Or, in an effort at one-upmanship, he could pretend to remain asleep the entire time, lying still on the sled without grasping the handles or making any voluntary motions: what a coup it would be to convince his prospective fraternity brothers that he had been utterly unfazed by the prank, indeed, that he was never aware that it had occurred! Peter opted for the devious strategy. He was prepared to take control of the sled should disaster threaten: the rogues might have placed a log in the path of the speeding sled. But, as it happened, he had no need to intervene and simply allowed the sled to take its course.

If it is correctly held that Peter intentionally sleds, or slides, or travels down part of the hill, we have here a case of what might provocatively be termed "passive action." In a well known paper, "The Problem of Action" (1988, essay 6), Harry Frankfurt appeals to action of this kind in an attempt to undermine causal theories of action. I will argue that passive action does not constitute a special problem for a relatively standard causal theory of action.[1]

1. CAUSAL THEORIES OF ACTION

According to a popular view, actions are, essentially, events with a suitable causal history, a causal history featuring pertinent mental events or states. On the causal view of action to be considered here (*CV*), actions are like U.S. currency and sunburns in a noteworthy respect. The piece of paper with which I just purchased my Coke is a genuine U.S. dollar bill partly in virtue of its having been produced (in the right way) by the U.S. Treasury Department. The burn on my back is a sunburn partly in virtue of its having been caused by direct exposure to the sun's rays. A molecule-for-molecule duplicate bill produced by me with plates and paper stolen from the Treasury Department is a counterfeit dollar bill, not a genuine one. And a burn that looks and feels just like the one on my back is not a sunburn, if it was caused by exposure to a heat lamp rather than the sun. Similarly, on *CV*, a certain event occurring at *t* is my

G. Holmström-Hintikka and R. Tuomela (eds.), Contemporary Action Theory. Vol. I, 135–143.

raising my right hand at t – an action – partly in virtue of its having been produced "in the right way" by certain mental items. An event someone else covertly produces by remote control – one including a visually indistinguishable rising of my right hand not produced by an intention or desire of mine, or an associated mental event – is not a raising of my right hand by me, even if it feels to me as though I am raising my hand.[2]

CV is a nonreductive view of action. It does not identify actions with *non-actional* events caused in the right way (cf. Brand 1984, ch. 1). That would be analogous to identifying genuine U.S. dollar bills with pieces of printed paper that (1) are not genuine U.S. dollar bills and (2) are produced in the right way by the U.S. Treasury Department; and, of course, so identifying genuine U.S. dollar bills would be absurd. To say that an event E is an action partly in virtue of its having been produced in "the right way" is not to say that E is a non-actional event – any more than to say that a piece of printed paper P is a genuine U.S. dollar bill partly in virtue of its having been produced in the right way is to say that P is not a genuine U.S. dollar bill.

People may disagree about whether such things as ordinary, involuntary breathing, belching, and sneezing fall under some ordinary notion of action. I have no desire to argue about this. Plainly, they are not *intentional* actions; and I am concerned only with intentional actions here. I have no wish to argue, either, about whether actions are to be individuated finely or coarsely. On a fine-grained conception, x and y are different actions if, in performing them, the agent exemplifies different act-properties (Goldman 1970). Thus, if Ann turns on her VCR by pressing a button, her pressing the button and her turning on the VCR are two different actions. Alternatively, on a coarse-grained conception, Ann's pressing the button and her turning on the VCR are the same action under two different descriptions (Anscombe 1963; Davidson 1980, essays 1 and 6). On the latter view, unlike the former, the same action may be intentional under one description and unintentional (or nonintentional) under another, and an action is intentional *only* under a description. Thus, if Ann presses a button on a remote control device, intending to turn her television on, but turns on her VCR instead, her action is intentional under the description "pressing the button" but not under the description "turning on the VCR." I remain neutral on this issue.

Proponents of causal theories of action are not unanimous about the identity of the requisite mental causes. Popular candidates are reasons (construed as complexes of beliefs and desires), intentions, and events of intention-acquisition. I have taken a stand on this issue elsewhere.[3] Here I will leave the various options open.

Regarding causal theories of action, Frankfurt writes: "it is beyond their scope to stipulate that a person must be in some particular relation to the movements of his body *during* the period of time in which he is presumed to be performing an action. The only conditions they insist upon as distinctively constitutive of action may cease to obtain, for all the causal accounts demand, at precisely the moment when the agent commences to act" (1988, 70). However, some causalists about action have argued that the causal role of their favored mental items includes a sustaining and guiding function (see, e.g., Brand 1984; Mele 1992; Mele and Moser 1994). *CV* does not restrict the mental causes of action to triggering or initiating causes; sustaining mental causes fall within the scope of *CV*.

Three additional preliminary observations are in order. First, if, as I believe (Mele 1995, ch. 11), causation is not essentially deterministic, proponents of *CV* are not committed thereby to determinism. Second, libertarians accordingly are not committed to rejecting *CV*, unless they hold that even the nondeterministic causation of an action is incompatible with the action's being freely performed (or that all causation is deterministic). Finally, for the purposes of this paper, the reality of mental causation may be taken for granted. (I have defended its reality, under one interpretation, in Mele 1992, ch. 2.) The challenge to *CV* examined here is entirely consistent with there being mental states and events that play causal roles.

2. FRANKFURT ON PASSIVE ACTION

Frankfurt appeals to passive action in the following passage.

> A driver whose automobile is coasting downhill in virtue of gravitational forces alone may be entirely satisfied with its speed and direction, and so he may never intervene to adjust its movement in any way. This would not show that the movement of the automobile did not occur under his guidance. What counts is that he was prepared to intervene if necessary, and that he was in a position to do so more or less effectively. Similarly, the causal mechanisms which stand ready to affect the course of a bodily movement may never have occasion to do so; for no negative feedback of the sort that would trigger their compensatory activity may occur. The behavior is purposive not because it results from causes of a certain kind, but because it would be affected by certain causes if the accomplishment of its course were to be jeopardized. (1988, 75)

Frankfurt evidently has two different kinds of action in mind here. The driver's purposively coasting down hill exemplifies one kind. And he alludes to another kind in which "the causal mechanisms which stand ready to affect the course of a bodily movement . . . never have occasion to do so." Since Frankfurt represents this as a matter that is distinct from what transpires in the coasting scenario, by "bodily movement" here he must mean a kind of movement unlike the movement of the driver's body down the hill (as the driver is carried along by his car).

I start with the coasting scenario. In the absence of a desire or intention regarding "the movement of the automobile," there would be no basis for the driver's being "satisfied" with the speed and direction of his car. So we may safely attribute a pertinent desire or intention to the driver, whom I shall call

Al. What stands in the way of our holding that Al's acquiring a desire or intention to coast down hill is a cause of his action of coasting, and that some such cause is required for the purposiveness of the "coasting"? Even if Al passed out momentarily at the wheel and then, upon regaining consciousness, noticed that his car was moving smoothly down hill, his allowing this to continue to happen, owing to his *satisfaction* with the car's speed and direction, depends (conceptually) on his having some relevant desire or intention regarding the car's motion; and prior to his allowing the continuation he is not purposively or intentionally coasting down hill – he is merely being carried down hill. We are left with the same question.

Perhaps, unbeknownst to Al, the brakes, accelerator pedal, and steering wheel are no longer working, so that his car would continue moving as it is even if he were to lack the desire or intention in question. But then Al is not performing an action of coasting down hill – he is merely being carried along by a vehicle over which he has no control. And if he is performing no such action, he is not purposively or intentionally coasting, even if he thinks he is. (Notice that the claim that Al *is* purposively coasting in this case is at odds with Frankfurt's own position on purposive behavior; for it is false that Al would have corrected the car's course if he had deemed it unsatisfactory.)

So suppose that the car is in normal working order and that Al knows how to operate it, is not paralyzed, and so on. Then it is natural to say that Al is coasting in his car (or allowing the car to continue to coast, in the scenario in which he wakes up in a moving car) *because* he wants to, or intends to, or has decided to – for an identifiable reason (e.g., to conserve gasoline). And the "because" here is quite naturally given a causal interpretation. In a normal case, if Al had not desired, or intended, or decided to coast, he would not have coasted; and it is no accident that, desiring, or intending, or deciding to coast, he coasts. So, setting aside general worries about mental causation, it looks as though Al's coasting does have a mental cause.[4]

Frankfurt might reply that even if Al's coasting has a suitable mental cause, his coasting is purposive "not because it results from causes of a certain kind, but because it would be affected by certain causes if the accomplishment of its course were to be jeopardized." The idea is that what accounts for the purposiveness of the coasting is not any feature of how it is caused but rather that Al "was prepared to intervene if necessary, and that he was in a position to do so more or less effectively" (1988, 75).

The reply is problematic. Imagine that, throughout the episode, Al was satisfied with how things went and did not intervene. He decided to coast and the coasting was purposive. Imagine further that although Al intended to intervene if necessary, an irresistible mind-reading demon would not have allowed him to intervene. If Al had abandoned his intention to coast or had decided to intervene, the demon would have paralyzed Al until his car ran its course. The coasting is purposive even though Al was *not* "in a position to [intervene] more or less effectively." And this suggests that what accounts for the purposiveness of Al's coasting in the original case does not include his being in a position to intervene effectively. There are, moreover, versions of the case in which Al's coasting is purposive even though he is not prepared to intervene. Suppose Al is a reckless fellow and he decides that, no matter what happens, he will continue coasting. He has no conditional intention to intervene. Even then, other things being equal, his coasting is intentional and purposive.

Now, I myself do not think that it is sufficient for the coasting's being intentional that it is caused by Al's deciding to coast. Consider the following variant of the case. Again, Al decides to coast but is prepared to put an end to the coasting should danger threaten. Because he so decides, he coasts – for a time. At, and shortly after, the time of the decision (t), Al could have stopped his car. However, a little later (at t^*), matters were taken out of his hands: he became paralyzed. Al's deciding to coast was a cause of the coasting that occurred between t and t^*, and that coasting was purposive. But it was also a cause – a more remote one – of the coasting that occurred after t^*, and that coasting was *not* purposive. On my own view, among the roles intention plays in intentional action is a causal *sustaining* role (Mele 1992). For example, the acquisition of an intention to play a nine-iron shot now may initiate a golfer's backswing with her nine iron; but if she abandons her intention during her backswing (thinking, perhaps, that an eight iron would be better), she will halt her swing. The completion of her swing is causally sustained by the persistence of the intention. After t^*, the coasting is not intentional because it is not causally sustained ("in the right way") by Al's intention to coast.[5]

Is this last claim threatened by the version of the coasting scenario that features a noninterfering demon? In that case, Al's car would have continued to coast even if Al had not continued to intend to coast. Even so, his continuing so to intend was a causal sustainer of his actual continued coasting. That continued coasting was a willing coasting and an action. The counterfactual coasting sustained by paralysis is neither a willing coasting nor an action; it is not the same event as the continued coasting at the actual world. The continued coasting at the actual world is *motivated* – a causal phenomenon – by Al's persisting intention to coast. If Al were to abandon the intention, *that* coasting would cease.

I turn now to the other kind of action to which Frankfurt alludes in the quoted passage. Unfortunately, he does not provide an example. *Perhaps* he has something of the following sort in mind. Remove the sled from my initial scenario and suppose that Peter awakes to find himself rolling down a snow-covered hill. His prospective fraternity brothers, while he was sleeping, gave him a push from the top of the hill. Imagine that Peter, wishing to deceive the pranksters into thinking that he was not awakened by the stunt, decides to allow himself to continue rolling down the hill without making any effort to control the motions of his body. He is prepared, however, to put an end to the rolling should danger threaten.

Peter's rolling down hill is initiated by the push. Initially, his rolling is not an action. Later, seemingly, it is – once Peter awakes and decides to allow himself to continue rolling down hill. But, other things being equal, Peter's so deciding is plausibly regarded as a cause of his continued rolling, for reasons of the sort adduced in the coasting case. If Peter continues rolling because he decides to allow himself to do so, his so deciding certainly appears to be a cause of the continued rolling.

It may be replied that even if Peter's deciding to allow himself to continue rolling is a cause of his continued rolling, his continued rolling is purposive "not because it results from causes of a certain kind, but because it would be affected by certain causes if the accomplishment of its course were to be jeopardized." However, this maneuver failed in the coasting case, and it fares no better here.

Frankfurt articulates his own position on action in the following passage:

> The performance of an action is . . . a complex event, which is comprised by a bodily movement and by whatever state of affairs or activity constitutes the agent's guidance of it. Given a bodily movement which occurs under a person's guidance, the person is performing an action regardless of what features of his prior causal history account for the fact that this is occurring. (1988, 73)[6]

Again, for Frankfurt, a movement's occurring "under a person's guidance" does not require that the person actually exert any control or exercise any guidance in the situation. For example, in the case of the coasting driver (if that qualifies as a case of bodily movement), "what counts is that he was prepared to intervene if necessary, and that he was in a position to do so more or less effectively." (Notice that if this case does *not* qualify as a case of bodily movement, it falsifies the claim just quoted about "the performance of an action"; for the driver's intentionally coasting down hill is an action.)

Regarding an agent's actually guiding his movements, we can be sure that the view expressed in this passage is an alternative to causal theories of action only if some account of such guiding is provided that does not accord desires, intentions, or the like (or the physical realizers of the relevant mental states or events) a causal role in the guidance. Frankfurt does not offer a detailed account of guidance in "The Problem of Action"; but his discussion of passive action is supposed to help us understand how a person's "movements" may be under his guidance, and therefore be constituents of an intentional or purposive action, even though the person is not exercising any control or guidance over the "movements." However, here too there is a risk that a detailed version of Frankfurt's proposal would collapse into causalism. Part of what it is for a person's "movements" – occurring during *t* – to be *under his guidance* during *t*, even though he is not exerting any control over them during *t*, may be that he has some intention or desire regarding his "behavior," which intention or desire is causally sustaining that "behavior." Nothing Frankfurt says blocks this possibility.

Jennifer Hornsby distinguishes two senses of 'bodily movement': an agent's moving of her body ('movement$_T$') and a motion that a body undergoes ('movement$_I$') (1980, 2–3). Frankfurt certainly is not averse to using 'movement' in the second sense: he calls "the dilation of the pupils of a person's eyes when the light fades" a movement (1988, 73). In my discussion of a counterpart of the coasting case – a counterpart in which "the causal mechanisms which stand ready to affect the course of a bodily movement . . . never have occasion to do so" – I focused on movement$_I$. *If* Frankfurt meant (also) to include instances of movement$_T$ here, the following case may serve as an illustration.

Several hours ago, Ann sat down in her rocking chair and plunged into a fascinating book. Some time later, wholly engrossed in the book, she unknowingly began rocking gently in the chair. She is still gently rocking, unknowingly. Frankfurt *might* say that her rocking "is purposive not because it results from causes of a certain kind, but because it would be affected by certain causes if the accomplishment of its course were to be jeopardized." If, for example, Ann's chair were gradually to back up and eventually meet with an obstacle on the floor that impedes her rocking, she might take steps to continue rocking. However, if Ann is purposively (albeit unknowingly) rocking, she is doing so, it seems, even if, as it turns out, she takes no steps to continue rocking when she encounters an obstacle. Sometimes when I am knowingly and intentionally rocking, I simply stop when something gets in the way. That does not retroactively render it the case that I had not been purposively rocking. Further, even if it is true that Ann would take steps to continue rocking were she to encounter an obstacle, perhaps that is partly because she has (unknowingly) a desire to rock that is sustaining her rocking, a desire that would motivate an attempt to continue rocking were she to encounter an obstacle. Again, Frankfurt has not shown that the truth of counterfactuals of the kind at issue are not grounded in truths friendly to a causal theory of action.

3. NONCAUSALISM AND DE RE INTENTIONS

Another noncausalist approach to passive action merits discussion. A theorist might hold that Peter's rolling down hill while intending (*de re*) of his rolling that it occur is sufficient for his performing the action of rolling down hill, even if that intention is causally irrelevant to his rolling.[7] For example, it may be held that, given the presence of the *de re* intention, Peter is intentionally rolling even if the neural realization of his intention has been surgically separated from the rest of his motor control system. Similarly, in the case of the car, it may be proposed that Al is the agent of an action of coasting down hill in his car, provided that he intends of the car's downhill coasting motion that it continue, even if that intention is causally inert.

The proposals are unsatisfactory. If, for example, Peter and Al are paralyzed at the time, they are not agents with respect to the continued rolling and coasting – even if they have the identified *de re* intentions. Peter is simply being carried along by his momentum and Al is being carried along by his car.

The proposals may be modified to avoid this problem. Consider the following. (1) Peter's rolling down hill while intending of his rolling that it occur and being able to put an end to his rolling is sufficient for his performing the action of rolling down hill, even if the intention is causally irrelevant to his rolling. (2) Al is the agent of an action of coasting down hill in his car, provided that he intends of the car's downhill coasting motion that it continue and he is able to stop the coasting, even if the intention is causally inert. (Notice that (1) and (2) offer sufficient, not necessary, conditions for the pertinent actions. Someone may perform an action, *A*, even if she is unable to refrain from *A*-ing: imagine someone acting from an irresistible desire.)

Even these more cautious noncausalist proposals are unacceptable. As I am sitting here, thinking about actions and events, I reflect on my breathing, and I form an intention, of my breathing, that it continue as long as I sit here. Further, I am able to put an end to my breathing, both temporarily and permanently. But this is not sufficient to render my continued breathing an action of mine, any more than my satisfying parallel conditions concerning the beating of my heart would render its continued beating an action of mine. If my breathing continues in its normal way, unaffected by my intention, it continues to be nonintentional breathing. The same is true of the rolling and coasting at issue in (1) and (2). Satisfaction of the specified conditions no more makes actions of the continuation of the rolling and the coasting than satisfaction of the parallel conditions concerning my breathing makes an action of the continuation of my breathing. To be sure, if, intending to breathe in a certain distinctive way (e.g., the way a coach taught me to breathe when lifting weights), I were to take charge of my breathing and breathe in that way, that breathing would be an action. But it certainly seems to be breathing that is causally initiated and sustained by my intention.

Passive action, as far as I can see, poses no special threat to a causal theory of action like *CV*. The main threat to causalism is a general worry about the causal relevance of attitudes and attitudinal events. I have attempted to answer that worry elsewhere (Mele 1992, ch. 2), as have many others. My aim here was to disarm an apparent threat posed specifically by passive action.

Davidson College

NOTES

[1] In Mele (n.d.) I argue that causal theories of action survive threats apparently posed by cases featuring *mental* actions. Parts of my description of a causal theory of action in section 1 are borrowed from that paper. The causal theory to be sketched here is roughly what Brand calls "the Causal Theory" (1984, ch. 1).

[2] If *events* with a causal history "of the right sort" are actions, some *states* apparently are actions, as well. Consider a child playing hide-and-seek. She remains perfectly still for several minutes, wanting not to be found. Her so doing – that is, her intentionally remaining perfectly still for this period – is naturally viewed as an action. On *CV*, her remaining motionless at the time – a *state* – might be a major constituent of an action in virtue of its causal history. However, my concern here (like Frankfurt's in 1988, essay 6) is limited to actions that are events.

[3] I have argued that, in any case of overt intentional action, the acquisition of a "proximal" intention (an intention for the specious present) is at work (1992, ch. 10). I reject the thesis that intentionally *A*-ing requires intending specifically to *A* (ch. 8); but I have argued that some pertinent intention is required in any case of overt intentional action (ch. 10).

[4] Consider a scenario that differs from the preceding one only in the following respect and in ways entailed by the change. If Al had not decided to coast, he would have been utterly indifferent about the motion of his car – in which case he would have done nothing to alter the car's course and the car would have continued coasting. In this scenario, it is false that if Al had not decided to coast, the car would not have continued coasting. Even so, Al's deciding to coast is plausibly regarded as a cause of the continued coasting. Compare: *X* dialed *Y*'s phone number at t, but if *X* had not done so, *Z* would have done so (at t). *X*'s dialing is a cause of *Y*'s phone's ringing at t_1, even though the phone would have rung at t_1 if *X*'s dialing had not occurred.

[5] The coasting might be causally sustained in a *deviant* way by Al's intention to coast. Suppose that, unbeknownst to Al, a powerful mind-reading demon temporarily paralyzes him at t^* and intends to make the paralysis persist just as long as Al retains his intention to coast. Al's intention is a causal sustainer of the coasting: as long as it is present, it indirectly sustains the paralysis that sustains the coasting.

[6] Frankfurt seemingly has overstated his view in the first sentence of this passage. Surely, there are mental actions (e.g., adding numbers in one's head) that have no bodily movements as constituents, unless intracranial events are to count as bodily movements.

[7] Carl Ginet (1990, 136–150) and George Wilson (1989, chs. 8–10) advert to *de re* intentions for related theoretical purposes. For criticism, see Mele (1992, ch. 13).

REFERENCES

Anscombe, G.E.M. (1963), *Intention*, 2nd ed. Ithaca, Cornell University Press.

Brand, Myles (1984), *Intending and Acting*. Cambridge, MIT Press.

Davidson, Donald (1980), *Essays on Actions and Events*. Oxford, Clarendon Press.

Frankfurt, Harry (1988), *The Importance of What We Care About*. Cambridge, Cambridge University Press.

Ginet, Carl (1990), *On Action*. Cambridge, Cambridge University Press.

Goldman, Alvin (1970), *A Theory of Human Action*. Englewood Cliffs, Prentice-Hall.

Hornsby, Jennifer (1980), *Actions*. London, Routledge & Kegan Paul.

Mele, Alfred (1992), *Springs of Action*. New York, Oxford University Press.

Mele, Alfred (1995), *Autonomous Agents*. New York, Oxford University Press.

Mele, Alfred (n.d.), "Agency and Mental Action," *Philosophical Perspectives* (forthcoming).

Mele, Alfred and Paul Moser (1994), "Intentional Action," *Noûs* **28**, 39–68.

Wilson, George (1989), *The Intentionality of Human Action*. Stanford, Stanford University Press.

LENNART NORDENFELT

ON ABILITY, OPPORTUNITY AND COMPETENCE: AN INQUIRY INTO PEOPLE'S POSSIBILITY FOR ACTION

INTRODUCTION

What does it mean to say that a man is able to perform an action? Is it true, as the standard philosophical analysis of ability indicates, that this man is in a state which is such that he would perform the action if he were to try? Is the counterfactual conditional the proper form for the analysis of the notion of ability?

In this paper I shall seriously question such a contention and instead argue that there are various versions or layers of ability which are logically weaker than the counterfactual conditional suggests. At one level of analysis this is common knowledge. There is a traditional distinction between a person's internal possibility for action, his or her ability, and the person's external possibility for action, his or her opportunity. It is only when the person has both ability and opportunity, it is claimed, that all grounds are present for the counterfactual conditional to hold true. My purpose in this paper, however, is to question also this statement. I shall in particular argue that competence and skill are species of ability which do not fulfil the traditional conditions. During the course of this argument I shall also investigate the traditional distinction between ability and opportunity and point to the logical interdependence between these notions.

My discussion is focused upon ability in the context of intentional human action, but several of my observations can be shown to be valid for other notions of capability and power as well.[1] The notion of ability which is under scrutiny could then be formally characterised in the following way: A is able to perform φ (where A is a human agent and φ is an intentional action) if, and only if, A would do φ if A were to try to do φ.

SOME EXAMPLES OF ABILITY

At any moment of the day A and B think that they have the ability to do many things. A tells his mates that he can walk 25 kilometres in one day, that he can climb the mountain Kebnekaise, that he can count to a billion, that he can cook his own dinner without assistance and that he can win a lottery. B, on the other hand, claims that she can write a book about the notion of health, that she can

G. Holmström-Hintikka and R. Tuomela (eds.), Contemporary Action Theory. Vol. I, 145–158.

grant a licentiate's degree to her students, that she can play football and that she can feel anger.

Most of the things that these people can do qualify as intentional actions. The word "can" in the contexts of anger and of winning the lottery, however, is a "can" of mere possibility. The locutions can be translated into "it is possible that *A* will win in a lottery" and "it is possible that *B* will feel anger". *A* and *B* do not, however, (normally) intend to feel anger or intend to win a lottery.

Consider now the examples where the ability refers to intentional action. A quick glance then shows that the suggested analysis of "ability to perform an intentional action" is not adequate as it stands. Indeed, we may easily find interpretations of all the locutions such that the following holds: *A* or *B* would *not* do *X*, even if *A* or *B* were to try. It seems, however, still quite acceptable, according to these interpretations, to claim that *A and B have the ability* to perform their respective actions. Consider the following cases:

> *A* can walk 25 kilometres, but if he tries today he will not succeed because his boots are being repaired.
> *A* can climb the Mount Kebnekaise, but if he tries today he will not manage because he is 1000 miles away from the mountain.
> *A* can count to one billion, but if he tries today he will probably not succeed because he is so tired that he will fall asleep after having counted to a couple of thousand.
> *A* can cook his own dinner, but if he tries today it will not work because there is no food in the refrigerator.
> *B* can issue a licentiate's degree, but this term she is on a sabbatical leave so at the moment she is not entitled to do so.
> *B* can write a book on the nature of health, but she is at present not feeling well, so there is little chance that this book will materialise this year.
> *B* can play football but she has broken her leg so she won't play any football this month.

What then is the point of saying that one *is able* to do all these things? What is the information conveyed and in what way is this information related to the counterfactual: if *A* were to try to do φ, then *A* would do φ?

Part of the analysis here is, as I have mentioned, commonplace. The counterfactual constitutes the analysis of a very strong notion of "can", viz. the notion of *practical possibility*. This notion refers to the situation when all necessary conditions – which together with trying are sufficient for a particular action – are materialised. When it is practically possible for me to do φ, then it is true of me that, if I were to try to do φ, then I would do φ.

Obviously the "can" used in the above examples is a weaker version of "can". It shall be my particular task in this paper to distinguish between and analyse some salient variants of this weaker notion of "can". But let me first do some preparatory work and briefly introduce the theory of the stratification of actions.

FROM BASIC ACTIONS TO ACCOMPLISHMENTS. THE STRATIFICATION OF ACTIONS

We are all familiar with the idea that one can perform one action by performing another. One can travel to New York by taking a plane. One can greet someone by waving one's hand. This relation of "doing by" can be extended and sometimes be made very long. Consider the following examples:

> The driver started his car by turning the key; and he turned the key by twisting his hand.
>
> The teacher prevented a quarrel in the classroom by warning the pupils. She warned them by reminding them of the school rules. She reminded them by speaking in English. She spoke by using her speech organs.

This series of "by doing" is not infinite. There is always some action which initiates the chain; this is what action theorists nowadays call the *basic action*.[2] In the standard case the basic action involves the (intentional) movement of a part of the agent's body, but the basic action can also be constituted by omitting to move a part of one's body.

A chain of actions can be said to be generated by the basic action. Using one's speech organs may generate speaking in English; this action in turn generates the reminding of the school rules. The nature of this process of generation has been thoroughly analysed in contemporary action theory, in particular by Alvin Goldman.[3] He distinguishes between four kinds of level generation, viz. causal, conventional, simple and augmentative. The first two kinds are the most important and exhaust the vast majority of types of action-generation. Let me here briefly characterise them.

Consider first causal generation. When it is true to say that a person φ-s by ψ-ing and the generation involved is causal, then the end state of φ-ing is caused by the ψ-ing. When John starts his car by turning the key, then the turning of the key is the cause of the fact that the car starts. In conventional generation, the generation results from conventional stipulation. There is a socially determined rule that says: when a certain action occurs in a particular context, it should count as some other action. For example, lifting one's hat, when meeting another person, counts as greeting the person; making certain laryngeal noises in appropriate sequences can count as performing an action of speaking. In these cases the relation (of convention) can be said to hold between the actions themselves: a ψ-ing in a certain context is an φ-ing. Another way of putting it is to say that ψ-ing, given proper circumstances, generates the conventional result, which is the end state of φ-ing.

Every stage in a chain of generated actions requires conditions which are both internal and external to the agent's body and mind. The former are often said to constitute the person's *ability*, the latter, his or her *opportunity*. First, in order to perform a basic action the required physiological and neurological systems must be in order; there are also some mental requirements, to which I shall return below. But there is indeed also an opportunity requirement for the basic action. Bodily movements cannot be executed in any medium. They cannot be performed in concrete, nor can most of them be performed when there is a hurricane. Moreover, the movements must not be directly physically impeded.

Turning to higher-level actions in a generated chain we have to supplement this picture both on the ability side and the opportunity side. Concerning ability it is typical that the additional requirements fall into the mental category. First, the agent must know about the generating mechanism. In the case of starting a car the driver must know the mechanism by which the car is started, viz. that it requires that a key is put into the ignition hole. Moreover, the driver must be able to identify this hole. Concerning opportunity it is evident how the requirements expand radically. The driver needs a car, the engine of which is in order, and there must be no impediments outside the car which may prevent it from starting.

Some conventional actions require a particularly designated agent. Certain actions cannot be performed by other than a prime minister, a bishop, a professor or a customs officer, to take a few examples. In such cases we say that the designated agent has the *authority* to perform the action in question. The professor, in my example above, temporarily lacks the possiblity of issuing a degree. The reason is that due to her sabbatical leave she no longer has the authority to issue the degree.

Is authority part of a person's ability or of his or her opportunity for action, or is it a category of its own? I doubt that conceptual analysis can provide us with a definite answer to this question. It may be felt that ability should include only a person's "natural" properties, such as physical and mental capacities. Opportunities may on the other hand be conventionally determined. Following this intuition, authority may thus be an opportunity. One may argue, however, that authority is a property tied to the agent and not to the environment. Following this idea, it may be more reasonable to single out authority as a separate category. For the purposes of this paper I need not take a stand on this issue.[4]

THE DISTINCTION BETWEEN ABILITY AND OPPORTUNITY

We have found that ability and opportunity, and sometimes authority, are crucial notions for identifying various layers of a person's practical possibility of performing a certain action. Roughly, ability constitutes the person's internal conditions for performing an action and opportunity the external conditions for performing the same action. If both the internal and the external conditions are fulfilled it is practically possible for the agent to act.

Given this distinction some of the above examples can be easily analysed:

> *A* has the ability to walk 25 kilometres but does not have the opportunity. The necessary boots are not there.
> *A* has the ability to climb Kebnekaise but does not have the opportunity. Since he is miles away there is no opportunity for him to climb.
> *A* has the ability to cook, but does not have the opportunity. There is no food in the fridge.
> *B* has the ability to issue a licentiate's degree, but temporarily lacks the authority to do so, since she is on sabbatical leave.

But what is missing in the other cases? Can one say that *A* has the ability but not the opportunity to count, or that *B* has the ability but not the opportunity to write the book or play football? It seems not to be right to say so given the preliminary characterisation of opportunity as an external circumstance which enables a person to succeed in a particular task. There is nothing which externally prevents the person from counting. Likewise, there are no external impediments for the writer or the footballer.

It appears then that there are more layers and degrees of possibility of action which cannot simply be accounted for by the distinctions between ability, opportunity and authority. It shall be my next task to investigate these.

THE DISTINCTION BETWEEN A PHYSICAL AND MENTAL ASPECT OF ABILITY

Our task now is to answer the following question: How could we justify saying that the person who is to count, the potential author and footballer are able to perform their respective actions, and where are we to find the elements lacking for their successful performance of their tasks? I have suggested that ability is multilayered. An agent may fulfil the ability conditions in some of these layers but fail in respect of others. But which are the principal layers? Are there perhaps some fundamentally different senses of "ability" which play a part in this context?

In this section I shall test the hypothesis that there is a distinction between a person's physical and mental ability to perform an action. A person may be able to do something in a mental sense but not in a physical sense. Our hypothesis then is: the ability ascribed to the persons in our three examples is some kind of mental ability. They lack, however, the relevant physical ability for succeeding in their tasks. In testing this hypothesis I shall briefly investigate the mental conditions for the ability of performing a physical action. In this process

I shall argue that all abilities to perform a physical action have certain mental conditions.

Let me turn to the latter issue first. I think all actions, at least all action types, have a mental ingredient. This follows, I believe, from the fact, first, that actions are per definition intentional, and, second, that intending to do φ, entails believing that it is practically possible to do φ. A man cannot intend to travel to Brazil unless he believes that it is practically possible for him to make this journey. He may wish to do so, without the relevant belief, but intending is a much stronger species of will. (Observe that intentions are often the results of decisions, and decisions constitute the final stage of deliberation.)

Thus, if A is able to perform the intentional action φ, then he must be able to form the relevant belief concerning his or her possibility of performing φ. This holds for the simplest of actions, for instance the basic action of raising one's arm. An ability to form a belief is thus an element of all ability to be discussed here.

But this is not the whole story. An ability to perform a physical action presupposes some minimal perception and some bodily consciousness. The agent must have some perception of the environment and must know where he has his arm in order to direct his energy in the right direction. A further requirement is the ability to *identify* the opportunity of the action in question. All action, even the basic ones, presupposes, as I have said, an opportunity. The raising of one's arm presupposes that there are no impediments, nothing which actually prevents the movement of the arm. The person who sets himself to raise his arm must therefore identify the presence of the right opportunity.

Thus ability to perform a physical action entails the existence of a mental faculty in the sense that the agent must be able to form beliefs and that he or she must be a perceiving individual with a sophisticated bodily consciousness. If we leave the basic actions and turn to generated actions, the picture, as we have seen, becomes even more salient. The agent must know the generating mechanism and must identify the right opportunities for all the subactions constituting the chain.

Let me now return to my initial question and my examples: Is it true to say that the counting person, the author and the football player have the relevant mental ability for performing their respective actions but lack the relevant physical ability? The counter indeed knows the generating mechanism involved in counting; he knows how to generate a new number after having mentioned a certain number, but in our example he does not have the physical strength to continue after a while. Likewise, the author knows in principle what to do in order to write the relevant book, but she is not well and therefore lacks the necessary energy. Similarly, the football player knows how to play, but is impeded from playing by her broken leg.

As far as our observations go they seem to be correct. Claiming that the crucial distinction should go between the physical and the mental is doubtful, however. There are some mental elements which need not be relevant to the sense of ability which we are seeking, and, as I shall argue briefly, there are some physical elements which are relevant.

First consider some irrelevant mental ingredients. It is questionable whether fatigue is just physical. We often talk about mental fatigue. And the *feeling* of fatigue clearly is a mental property. The person who does the counting may very well stop counting because he feels tired. Still, we may say that he can count to a billion. A certain mental inability is compatible with his ability in the sense we are here trying to determine. Moreover, both the counter, the author and the football player may be inattentive when they try to perform their actions. They may fail to identify opportunities in their enterprises and thereby not completely succeed in completing their actions. Such mental inability, at least when it is understood as temporary, is compatible with the ability that we are seeking to identify.

Moreover, a person may through illness temporarily have lost his or her bodily consciousness and capacity to identify relevant opportunities but he or she may still have the ability in question. It seems, then, that the relevant condition for ascribing the ability we are seeking has to do with some more specific mental property. A very plausible hypothesis is that it has to do with the person's knowledge, in particular with what is often called his or her *know-how*.

ON ABILITY, KNOW-HOW AND COMPETENCE

The person who can count to a billion knows how to count; he knows all the rules concerning how to generate any number in the series of natural numbers. Similarly the author in our examples knows how to write a scientific book; she knows all the conventions and rules for producing a text acceptable to a scientific publisher. Similarly, the football player knows the rules of football and knows how to outplay the members of the opposing team. It is clear that knowledge is a very important element in the ability that we ascribe to the three agents under discussion. It is less clear that this knowledge has to be theoretical. Besides, it is quite doubtful that knowledge is all that is at issue.

Ever since Gilbert Ryle's famous essay it is commonplace to distinguish between theoretical knowledge, i.e. knowledge-that, and practical knowledge, i.e. knowledge-how.[5] In having a piece of theoretical knowledge one knows that a set of propositions is true. In having a piece of practical knowledge one knows how to perform an action or how to reach a goal. This distinction is fruitful but not entirely clear. A fully satisfactory application of it requires a number of further clarifications. Since my presentation does not rely on the distinction I confine myself to the following remarks. Knowing-that and knowing-how, however further clarified, must be related to each other. In some cases knowing that *X* may even be sufficient for knowing how to do φ, and in several cases knowing that *X* is necessary for knowing how to do φ. Among my three examples the relation between knowing that and knowing how is perhaps strongest in the case of the arithmetician. His knowledge of a set of mathematical truths may be sufficient for his know-how. In the case of the author there is still a strong relation, but it seems quite plausible that some of her know-how cannot be translated into true propositions. In the case of the football player, most saliently, most of her knowledge is of the practical kind and not translatable into theoretical knowledge.

But is knowledge, whether of the theoretical or the practical kind, ever sufficient for saying that the agent is able to perform a particular action? In answering this question, let me start with the football player, where the grounds for doubt are the strongest. Are we inclined to say that *B* can play football simply on the ground that she knows how to play football? Consider a former football player, a 75-year-old man, who has ever since his active years worked as a radio commentator on football and has supreme both theoretical and practical knowledge about the game. In a perfectly understandable sense this person knows how to play football. But clearly this man no longer has the ability to play football, in the sense we are seeking. He has, as we say, lost the relevant *skill*. He is no longer well-trained; he cannot move quickly enough, he does not react quickly enough and he no longer has the required physical strength.

Let me at this stage introduce what I take to be a crucial concept for my analytical task, viz. the concept of *competence*. The competent football player has both know-how and skill. In many areas of activity, perhaps ultimately in all areas, there is a combination of know-how and skill required for complete competence. This holds very clearly for painters, musicians and people who do handicraft. All these people need a skill to modulate and coordinate bodily movements which goes far beyond any kind of knowledge. But the same probably holds true to some extent for all enterprises.

It is important to let the notion of skill also enter the mental field. In fact the distinction between the mind and the body is hard to uphold here. In the case of painters and musicians, but similarly with athletes and circus artists, their training is equally much a training of the mind as a training of the body. Their skill comprises not only a trained body, that has strength, plasticity, and is capable of rapid movement, but comprises also a capacity of identifying more and more subtle nuances, whether it be in one's body, in one's task or in one's environment.

To summarise. I have identified an important notion of competence, constituted by know-how and by physical and mental skill. Supported by my examples I argue that the term "ability" and its verbal associate "being able" sometimes refer to competence and not to full ability. The counting person has the competence for counting to a billion, but since he soon gets sick and tired of counting, he does not succeed. The author and the football player likewise have the competence for their respective tasks, but fail to realise them because of lack of attention, fatigue, illness or injury.

It is typical that competence is a more enduring and basic state of the human being than full ability is. For temporary reasons, such as the ones mentioned above, the competence may be prevented from execution.[6] But when we look upon the situation precisely in these terms, i.e. as a situation of prevention from the execution of a competence, we say that the competence is still there. This statement is compatible with the recognition of the fact that also competence may get lost. There may, for instance, be cases of illness which permanently or for a long time destroy some basic properties of the person, including his or her competence to perform many tasks.

To say, then, that a person can perform φ, in the competence sense of can, is tantamount to saying something general and basic about this person.[7] It belongs to the same level of abstraction as describing the personality of the person. We say of a particular man that he is of the *kind* that can do such and such. But saying that a person is of such a kind does not entail that he will at any moment, when he tries and where the right opportunity is there, succeed in doing such and such. The general competence is distinct from present full ability.

THE MATCH BETWEEN ABILITY AND OPPORTUNITY

So far I have in a preliminary way accounted for the senses of ability given in my initial examples. A person can be said to have an ability although the opportunity is not present. A person can be said to have an ability although the authority is temporarily lacking, and a person can be said to have an ability in the competence sense although full ability is lacking.

So far the concept of opportunity has not been scrutinised in this discussion. Opportunity has, preliminarily, been characterised as a circumstance, external to the agent, which together with his or her full ability (and authority) constitutes the agent's practical possibility for action. The opportunity is there, I have said, in the case of walking 25 kilometres, if the agent's boots are at hand. The opportunity is there, in the case of mountain climbing, if the agent is placed at the foot of the mountain. The opportunity is there, in the case of cooking, if there is food in the refrigerator. For the rest of the examples I seem to have presupposed that it is easy to describe the opportunity. I shall now take issue with this naive presupposition and point to the interdependence between the notions of ability and opportunity.

THE IDEA OF INTERNALITY AND EXTERNALITY

According to my rough preliminary distinction between ability and opportunity, ability is a factor internal to the agent and opportunity is a factor external to the agent. But the question can now be asked: internal and external to what? Is the agent's body the criterion for the distinction? And in that case what belongs to the body? Or is the biological (and psychological) substance the criterion? One can, for instance, ask whether a pace-maker constitutes a part of the interior of a person or whether the pace-maker provides an opportunity for the person to act. But, assuming the latter alternative, is it reasonable to say that every piece of artificial stuff installed in a person's body, such as dental material or nails used in orthopoedic operations, provides an opportunity for action instead of contributing to the person's ability?

The question can be extended and we can ask whether glasses provide an opportunity for seeing or whether they constitute part of the bearer's ability to see. This example may give us a preliminary clue as to a fruitful demarcation line. It seems more natural to say that glasses constitute an opportunity for action than dental material does. Glasses can be easily removed and are much less part of the person than his or her dental metarial is. For certain purposes one choice may seem more practical than another. I think, however, that it would be futile to seek to find a metaphysical foundation for a particular choice. I shall therefore not dwell further on this issue here.

More challenging philosophically is the task of clarifying the *logical dependency* between the concepts of ability and opportunity. In my preliminary characterisation I have said that a full ability to perform φ plus an opportunity (and in some cases authority) to perform φ, constitutes a practical possibility of performing φ. But is there only one kind of full ability to perform φ and one kind of opportunity to perform φ which together constitute a practical possibility of performing the action φ?

That this is not so can be easily demonstrated. We say, for instance, of a man *A* that he can climb Kebnekaise. *A* happens to be a professional climber; he is well-trained and knows what necessities to bring with him when he starts climbing. His ability is constituted by his well-trained body, his fitness and his competence for climbing on foot. The opportunity is constituted by the nature of the mountain in question and by the weather conditions at the time of climbing, as well as by the fact that *A* stands at the foot of Kebnekaise. Consider now *C* who is also said to be able to climb Kebnekaise. *C* is not at all a well-trained athlete. He is a very ordinary city person but a very rich such person who owns a super-modern mountain scooter that can drive all the way to the top. So although *C*'s ability is different from *A*'s, and much less in a general sense, he can compensate for that by creating a very advantageous opportunity. Thus, in this case, the sum of *A*'s ability and opportunity is equal to the sum of *C*'s ability and opportunity. It is then easy to see that there is an infinite number of combinations between abilities and opportunities in order to create the practical possibility of performing a particular action.

From this observation follows something very important. There is, strictly speaking, no such thing as *an* ability to perform φ. (Remember that we are here talking about full ability and not just elements of ability as in the case of competence.) The idea of an ability is always related to the idea of a particular set of circumstances, in conjunction with which the ability constitutes a practical possibility of doing φ. This conclusion provides the ground for my introducing the notion of a pragmatic ability.

ON PRAGMATIC ABILITY

In spite of the observation in the previous section there is a lot of talk about a person's general ability to perform a certain action or engage in a certain activity. My initial examples illustrated this ordinary way of expression. But if a person's ability to do φ must always presuppose a specific set of circumstances to be intelligible, how can our ordinary mode of speech be at all successful?

A promising answer to this question is the following. When "ability" is used without reference to a particular opportunity there is a particular set of circumstances *tacitly* presupposed. The agent is considered to be able to do φ, given a set of tacitly presupposed circumstances. This set may vary somewhat. First, consider the following two alternatives:

a. the existing set of circumstances
b. ordinary circumstances.

The first alternative is straight-forward and the least problematic. It is, however, evident that this interpretation cannot be valid for all, nor even the majority of, uses. I only need to again consult my initial list of examples, where the existing sets of circumstances are completely ignored. Alternative b. covers much more and is much more promising. When I say that *A* is able to walk 25 kilometres I may very well mean that it is practically possible for him to do so under *ordinary* circumstances. These ordinary circumstances include the presence of his perfect walking boots.

The notion of an ordinary circumstance can have slightly different interpretations.[8] I shall here for the sake of simplicity interpret it in a frequency sense. The set of ordinary circumstances is then identified with the set which occurs most frequently or most of the time under consideration. I shall now contrast this with the following more normative notion, c. the notion of an *acceptable* circumstance.

By this I refer to the following kind of situation. A woman *B* may be said to be able to manage her job, where this does not entail that it is practically possible for her to manage it now under the given circumstances, nor under the most frequently given circumstances, but under the kind of circumstances which *ought to* be there, i.e. under the set of circumstances which are acceptable to *B* or some other person who judges whether *B* is disabled or not. It may for instance, be the case that *B* lives in a country at war. The state of war puts her under enormous pressure and also directly physically prevents her from doing her job properly. A person who judges whether *B* is unable to do her job properly may, however, find it unreasonable to judge her given the present situation. This may be so in spite of the fact that the state of war for a long time is the prevailing situation.[9]

But do these considerations suffice for giving an account of pragmatic ability? Consider again the case of climbing. We do say that *A* is able to climb the Kebnekaise. But as he lives in Stockholm there is no immediate opportunity for him to climb. He is at least a 1000 miles away. Nor is his being at the foot of Kebnekaise an ordinary circumstance, *A* is very rarely in Lapland. Saying that *A*'s being at the foot of Kebnekaise is normatively required is also odd indeed. The interpretation must then be the following:

d. circumstances provide both for *A*'s setting himself in the position for φ-ing and subsequently for performing φ or
e. given ordinary or acceptable circumstances *A* can both set himelf in the position for φ-ing and subsequently for performing φ.

It is true that *A* cannot immediately set himself to climb Kebnekaise but it is practically possible for him, given present, ordinary or acceptable circumstances, to travel to Lapland and to the foot of Kebnekaise. Moreover, given present, ordinary or acceptable circumstances, once he is there it is practically possible for him to climb the mountain.

SUMMARY

In this paper I have identified and characterised a number of conditions necessary for a person's successful performance of an intentional action. Many of these conditions are in the ordinary discourse referred to as "ability". A starting point for my discussion has been the traditional distinction between ability, interpreted as the agent's internal conditions for action, opportunity, interpreted as the agent's external conditions for action, and authority, interpreted as the agent's conventionally attributed power for action. My further analysis has particularly focused on the notion of ability and the logical dependency between the notions of ability and opportunity.

Within the concept of ability I have identified the important element of competence. Competence has been identified as a (normally) long-term property of a person, entailing know-how and skill, traits which typically are the result of systematic training. I have argued that the term "ability" is frequently used to refer to competence, without entailing the existence of full ability. Competence must in many cases be supplemented with attention, general fitness and health in order for complete ability to become realised.

In the second part of my analysis I have noted that even the notion of full ability is indeterminate. There is not a single set of bodily and mental properties which together constitute the full ability to perform an action φ. The reason why this is so is that the set of external circumstances can vary in an infinite number of ways. One set of internal properties constitute the ability to perform φ, only given a specified set of circumstances. Thus the concepts of ability and opportunity are interrelated. A consequence of this is that a locution which only mentions the ability term as in "*A* is able to do φ", must tacitly presuppose a particular set of external circumstances. I have given three examples of such presuppositions, viz. a. the existing set of circumstances, b. ordinary circumstances and c. acceptable circumstances. I have suggested that b. or c. are the presuppositions normally made.

Department of Health and Society
Linköping University

NOTES

[1] The notion of intention is left unanalysed in the text. In Nordenfelt (1974), however, I have proposed a dispositional analysis of intentions. An intention, according to this analysis, is a special sort of disposition to act. If *A* intends to bring about *P*, then *A* is in a certain way disposed to bring about *P*. The more specific analysis I wish to suggest is the following: *A* intends to bring about *P* (partly) means: For all actions φ, if *A* believes that doing φ is necessary for the realisation of *P*, and it is practically possible for *A* to do φ, then *A* does φ. (In the limiting case, when *P* is identical with φ there is only one action necessary for the realisation of *P*.)

[2] The term "basic action" was introduced by Arthur Danto in his (1965) and has subsequently been accepted by most authors in the field. It plays a particularly important theoretical role in Alvin Goldman's theory of action (1970).

[3] In the book *A Theory of Human Action* (1970) Alvin Goldman presents a comprehensive analysis of action and action explanation. He there systematically introduces the idea of action generation and the principles for such generation.

[4] A more complete analysis of the stratification of actions and the conditions for action is given in my (1995, 37–57).

[5] Gilbert Ryle's classic distinction was first presented in his article (1946).

[6] In (1975, 133), Anthony Kenny suggests, contrary to my analysis, that illness should be looked upon as a circumstance. He says: "illness, no less than imprisonment, may take away the possibility of my exercising some of my abilities without necessarily taking away the abilities themselves." It seems as if Kenny here by ability means what I call competence.

[7] There are similarities, but also genuine differences, between my analysis of ability and the one presented by Peter Morriss in his excellent book (1987).

Morriss there introduces a distinction between generic abilities and ablenesses (or time-specific abilities). His generic abilities are abilities which presuppose the existence of certain conditions, not necessarily external. Thus both my competence and full ability can qualify as generic ability. His "ableness" refers to a situation where there is a practical possibility for a particular action. *A* has ableness with relation to φ at t if, and only if it is practically possible for *A* to do φ at t.

[8] In (1995, 46–49), I introduce the notion of a *standard* circumstance. The standard referred to there is not a standard of frequency but a standard of convention. A similar notion is presented by Morriss (1987, 86).

[9] It is important to distinguish between two different notions of acceptable circumstance. In this context "acceptable circumstance" means a circumstance which is acceptable for the purpose of judging whether a person is disabled or not. In a more political context one often instead refers by this locution to a circumstance which is acceptable for the purpose of *enabling* a person to do what he or she wants to do. In modern policy-discussion about disability one frequently points out how environments can be disabling and be the real source of a person's disability or handicap. For a recent introduction to this area see, for instance, M. Oliver (1990).

REFERENCES

Danto, A. (1965), "Basic Actions," *American Philosophical Quarterly* **2**, 141–148.

Goldman, A.I. (1970), *A Theory of Human Action*. Englewood Cliffs, New Jersey, Prentice Hall Inc.

Kenny, A. (1975), *Will, Freedom and Power*. Oxford, Basil Blackwell.

Morriss, P. (1987), *Power: A Philosophical Analysis*. New York, St. Martin's Press.

Nordenfelt, L. (1974), *Explanation of Human Actions*. Philosophical Studies Published by the Department of Philosophy and the Philosophical Society, **20**, Uppsala, University of Uppsala.

Nordenfelt, L. (1995), *On the Nature of Health*. Second, revised, edition, Dordrecht, Kluwer Academic Publishers.

Oliver, M. (1990), *The Politics of Disablement*. London, Macmillan.

Ryle, G. (1946), "Knowing how and knowing that," *Proceedings of the Aristotelian Society*, **xlvi**, 1–16.

DOUGLAS WALTON

ACTIONS AND INCONSISTENCY: THE CLOSURE PROBLEM OF PRACTICAL REASONING

This article formulates a fundamental problem in the philosophy of action. It will become apparent that the same problem is also an abstract and general, but very important question for the field of artificial intelligence – and robotics in particular. As well, the nature of the problem, as revealed below, will make evident its importance in the field of logical evaluation of natural language argumentation. The problem is one of when a knowledge-based goal-directed inference leading to an action (or a recommendation for a course of action to be taken) may be said to be structurally correct (or closed), parallel to the sense in which a deductive argument is said to be valid (deductively closed).

Solving this problem will require a formalization of practical reasoning in the end, to be carried out in the way that the analysis of the problematic case developed in the article will indicate. However, being a philosophical contribution, this article will merely pose and sharpen the problem, making certain questions to be asked more precise. No claim is made that anything like a complete formalization of practical reasoning is given by the considerations brought forward in this article. However, by solving the philosophical and practical problem of closure, the way is opened to developing a formalization of practical resolving as a distinctive type of reasoning that can be evaluated as normatively binding on a rational agent.

A structure of practical reasoning is presented, and it is argued that the job of evaluating cases of arguments based on a criticism of inconsistency of actions, or "not practising what you preach", is best accomplished by applying this structure. In general, the task addressed by the article is one of evaluating the argumentation reconstructed from the text of discourse given in a particular case, and then using this evidence to judge whether the given argument meets the standards of practical rationality or not, as defined by the structures that should be used to judge such cases. Thus the goal of this article is seen to be one of applied logic, or as evaluating argument, as "correct" or "incorrect", as opposed to being a psychological inquiry into the agent's actual intentions, the motives of my particular person, weakness of will, or my other deeper psychiatric matters that lie behind a given case. It is not that these psychological or psychiatric questions are uninteresting. Indeed, the framework presented in this article could be used as a means of assisting empirical inquiries into them. But such a psychological investigation is not our goal. Our goal is that of evaluating a given argument normatively, based on the commitments of the participants,

G. Holmström-Hintikka and R. Tuomela (eds.), Contemporary Action Theory. Vol. I, 159–175.

as far as these propositions can be inferred from the text and context of discourse in a case where the argument was used.

1. THE CLOSURE PROBLEM STATED FOR PRACTICAL REASONING

Practical reasoning is often equated in philosophy with Aristotle's notion of *phronesis* (practical wisdom), as characterized in Book VI of the *Nicomachean Ethics* particularly. A good guideline to philosophical usage is the following entry in Honderich (1995, 709):

practical reason. Argument, intelligence, insight, directed to a practical and especially a moral outcome. Historically, a contrast has often been made between theoretical and practical employments of *reason. Aristotle's 'practical syllogism' concludes in an *action* rather than in a proposition or a new belief: and *phronesis* (see book VI of *Nicomachean Ethics*) is the ability to use intellect practically.

The ingredients of *phronesis,* or practical wisdom, as expounded by Aristotle, however, are complex. Hamblin (1987, 206) classifies them into four groups: (1) knowledge group, (2) art or skill, and cleverness, (3) deliberative excellence, including judgment, and (4) moral virtue. In this paper, a narrower view of practical reasoning is adopted, comprising primarily (1) and (3), but excluding (4). What will be called practical reasoning below could be described as instrumental or means-end reasoning. More fully defined (just below), it would be called goal-directed, knowledge-based, action-guiding reasoning. There is not meant to be any necessary implication that the goal is good (morally or otherwise), that the reasoner is a good person, or that he or she or it is basing her or his or its reasoning on good intentions (although traditional philosophy is certainly right to think that such ethical notions are closely connected to, and even based on practical reasoning).[1]

Practical reasoning is a goal-driven, knowledge-based, action-guiding species of reasoning that coordinates goals with possible alternative courses of action that are means to carry out these goals, in relation to an agent's given situation as he/she/it sees it, and concludes in a proposition that recommends a prudent course of action.[2] Practical reasoning is carried out by an *agent,* an entity with a capability for intelligent action. An agent does not necessarily have to be a person.[3] An agent is an entity that is a self-contained unit that has goals, and that is capable of autonomous action, based upon its ability to perceive its external circumstances, and modify its actions in accord with such perceptions. A higher-order agent can have some grasp of the consequences of its actions, and can modify its actions and goals in light of its perceptions of these consequences. This characteristic is called *feedback.*

A *practical inference* has basically two premises – one states that an agent has a particular goal, and the other cites a means whereby the agent could carry out this goal, in the agent's present situation, as it sees it. An additional premise states that if several such means are available, the means selected by the agent is the most satisfactory one, in relation to the agent's goals (and certain other factors that may be relevant, as indicated below). Practical inferences are chained together in practical reasoning.

The *closure problem* is that of determining the conditions under which an agent is bound (committed) to the conclusion of a practical inference, given that it is committed to all the premises, as holding in a given case. This problem can be usefully re-expressed as a negative question of defining *practical inconsistency,* the kind of situation where the agent is committed to a goal, and recognizes that a particular action is the most satisfactory means to carry out that goal in the given situation, but the agent is not committed to that action. The problem of closure then is one of determining the conditions under which one may correctly say, in a given case, that a practical (pragmatic) inconsistency exists. The problem is expressed below as one of determining when a conflict of commitments exists in the sense of Krabbe (1990).

The best way to pose this problem is to express it in an ordinary, and apparently simple kind of case where an agent maintains a stance that appears to be practically inconsistent. Using this case, some subtleties can be brought out, showing how an apparently simple case can conceal many subtleties in the chaos of everyday deliberations and arguments. But to frame the problem more sharply, it is useful to begin with the relatively well-defined idea of closure of a deductive argument.

The usual way to define deductive validity in logic is the following: an argument is valid if and only if it is logically impossible for the premises to be true and the conclusion false. An equivalent definition is given in the following entry in Honderich (1995, 894):

> 1. Deductive arguments, which are such that if the premises are true the conclusion must be true. Traditional logic studies the validity of syllogistic arguments. Modern logic, more generally, identifies as valid those arguments which accord with truth-preserving rules. (*Salva veritate.*) Any argument is valid if and only if the set consisting of its premises and the negation of its conclusion is inconsistent.

This negative way of defining deductive validity – by relating it to logical impossibility or inconsistency – is both instructive and useful, because it gives you an idea when *closure* has been achieved for a deductive argument, meaning that enough information has been given in the premises so that the conclusion may be inferred as following from those premises.

2. THE SMOKING CASE

To get a practical grip on the closure problem for practical reasoning, it is best to consider an ordinary and relatively simple kind of case. Consider the following example, sometimes called the *smoking case,* from Walton (1989,

141 – 142), which has the form of a dialogue.

Parent: There is strong evidence of a link between smoking and chronic obstructive lung disease. Smoking is also associated with many other serious disorders. Smoking is unhealthy. So you should not smoke.
Child: But you smoke yourself. So much for your argument against smoking.

The argumentation in this case is more subtle than it might appear at first sight. There are two sides to it. On the one hand, the parent may have cited good medical evidence that smoking is linked to lung disease, and her argument – that, therefore, smoking is unhealthy, could be (in this respect) a good argument. The child may be too hasty in rejecting this argument on the basis of his observations of the parent's actual practices.

On the other hand, the child does have a point worth considering, from his point of view, based on his observations. The parent smokes, and admits this practice. But at the same time, the parent advocates nonsmoking. Is this not inconsistent? It is not logical inconsistency, but it is inconsistency of a sort that might be called practical or pragmatic. And surely this practical inconsistency is a reasonable basis for the child's questioning the sincerity or the seriousness of the parent's advocacy of her own argument. If you look at it from the child's point of view, he is not really in a position to evaluate all this medical evidence, based on expert opinions he is not qualified to dispute. But he knows what he sees – the parent advocates non-smoking, but smokes, and admits it.

The kind of argument used by the child to question the parent's argument is not unfamiliar in logic. Traditionally, also, it has been called the circumstantial type of *ad hominem* argument. Traditionally, it has been categorized as a fallacious argument.[4] But is it really? Let us take a closer look.

If you take the conclusion of the parent's argument to be the proposition 'Smoking is unhealthy.' – that is, as an impersonal statement – then her argument could be quite reasonable. But the child's reply does not really seem to be challenging this argument. If the child's reply is a rejection of this argument, then indeed it could be a hasty or fallacious *ad hominem* argument.

But looking at the child's reply from a different angle, it represents a different line of argument, which could be expressed as follows, by extending the dialogue.

Child: You say that smoking is unhealthy. Does that mean you think that being unhealthy is generally a bad thing, or something to be avoided? Is being healthy a personal goal for you?

In answering this question, the parent needs to be careful. If she admits all the following propositions, her argument will potentially be open to a certain kind of criticism or attack.

1. Being healthy is a goal for me.
2. Smoking is unhealthy.
3. I smoke.

A critic can question whether a person who is committed to all three of these propositions might be showing evidence of a certain kind of conflict, which could be called a pragmatic inconsistency or conflict of commitments.

But one needs to be careful here to clarify the exact nature of the inconsistency that is claimed or perceived. It is not just the propositions 1., 2. and 3. that are at the heart of the conflict of commitments. For the parent (at this point) still has numerous replies to any claim that her reasoning is inconsistent. She could argue, for example: "Smoking is addictive. That is why you should not start smoking. I have tried to give up many times." She admits then she is weak-willed (akratic), but that is not the same thing as being pragmatically inconsistent, or exhibiting a conflict of commitments of the kind that makes your argument illogical or open to refutation as inconsistent. To get this kind of inconsistency, proposition 3. in the triad above needs to be changed to a stronger assertion which says something like, "Yes, I smoke and I'm proud of it." (meaning that I am committed to smoking as a practice or policy that I personally advocate or recommend).

But in what sense could this assertion, in the context of the case above, be open to refutation as inconsistent? The parallel is to a case of logical inconsistency, where an arguer is committed to the premises of a deductively valid inference, but then is also committed to the negation of the conclusion. But in this case, it is practical inconsistency, not logical inconsistency, that seems to be the root notion. To get closer to the notion of practical inconsistency, the form of practical inference must be more precisely expressed.

What is especially important to understanding practical inconsistency, and practical reasoning generally, is its relativity to a particular agent who is advocating a course of action as the practically rational thing to do for her (or for someone else, or for a group). The child only has a strong argument against the parent if the parent is expressing her own personal commitment to avoiding a practice that would endanger her own health. It is the first-person endorsement that makes the parent's practical reasoning binding on her as an agent that gives the child's criticism bite when he retorts that she smokes.

This special expressiveness of practical inferences in the first person, and its relation to expressive endorsements in the second and third person, has been pointed out by Clarke (1985). And in any analysis of practical reasoning, care must be taken to reconstruct any particular case in a way that makes clear the differences between first-person commitments and other kinds of commitments that may be binding only on another agent, or that may express a group involvement of some sort. Consequently, the analysis of the structure of practical reasoning given in the next section, will index a practical inference to a specified agent. In this key respect, practical inconsistency will be quite different from logical inconsistency (of the kind defined as a proposition conjoined with its negation, or another proposition logically implying its negation).

3. INFERENCE SCHEMATA OF PRACTICAL REASONING

According to Table 1 below, reprinted from Walton (1990, 48), practical reasoning is based on the following pair of inference schemata where an agent, represented by the first-person pronoun 'I' is contemplating bringing about a state of affairs $(A, B, C, \ldots)$.[5]

Table 1
PRACTICAL REASONING:
THE BASIC INFERENCE SCHEMATA

Necessary Condition Schema

(*N1*) My goal is to bring about *A* *(Goal Premise)*.
(*N2*) I reasonably consider on the given information that bringing about at least one of $[B_0, B_1, \ldots, B_n]$ is necessary to bring about *A* *(Alternatives Premise)*.
(*N3*) I have selected one member B_i as an acceptable, or as the most acceptable necessary condition for *A* *(Selection Premise)*.
(*N4*) Nothing unchangeable prevents me from bringing about B_i as far as I know *(Practicality Premise)*.
(*N5*) Bringing about *A* is more acceptable to me than not bringing about B_i *(Side Effects Premise)*.

Therefore, it is required that I bring about B_i *(Conclusion)*.

Sufficient Condition Schema

(*S1*) My goal is to bring about *A* *(Goal Premise)*.
(*S2*) I reasonably consider on the given information that each one of $[B_0, B_1, \ldots, B_n]$ is sufficient to bring about *A* *(Alternatives Premise)*.
(*S3*) I have selected one member B_i as an acceptable, or as the most acceptable sufficient condition for *A* *(Selection Premise)*.
(*S4*) Nothing unchangeable prevents me from bringing about B_i as far as I know *(Practicality Premise)*.
(*S5*) Bringing about *A* is more acceptable to me than not bringing about B_i *(Side Effects Premise)*.

Therefore, it is required that I bring about B_i *(Conclusion)*.

According to the representation in Table 1, the agent is represented as a solitary reasoner with a single goal who is aware of some aspects of its environment (called its situation or circumstances), and is making a decision to go ahead with a course of action or not, based on its knowledge (or informed but changeable opinion) of this situation.

Another useful (but more complex) way to think of practical reasoning is as a dialectical structure that takes the form of a deliberation on how the two parties (or one party who is "of two minds" on how to proceed) should reason in the face of some problem or decision which requires a course of action. This framework is one of multiagent systems (Singh 1994) for multigoal reasoning. In the simplest kind of case two agents are involved, and they can communicate with each other. Each agent can have more than one goal. According to one account (Walton 1990, 85), the type of practical inference used in such cases has the following form, called *the argumentation scheme for practical reasoning:*

(*SP*) *A* is the goal.
B is necessary to bring about *A*.
Therefore, it is required to bring about *B*.

Matching this argumentation scheme is a set of appropriate critical questions. Below, the fifth question has been added to the set of four given in Walton (1990, 85).

(*CQ*) Are there alternatives to *B*?
Is *B* an acceptable (or the best) alternative?
Is it possible to bring about *B*?
Does *B* have bad side effects?
Are there other goals that are in conflict with *A*?

The argumentation scheme and the matching set of critical questions are used to evaluate the practical reasoning used in a dialogue exchange in a given case as follows. The proponent advances (*SP*) to convince the respondent that *B* is a prudent course of action in the circumstances. This putting forward of an argument in the form (*SP*) by the proponent shifts the burden of proof in the dialogue to the side of the respondent. She is then obliged to accept *B* as having been shown to be a prudent course of action unless she can ask one or more of the set of critical questions (*CQ*). Unless the proponent can answer the question adequately, the presumption in favor of *B* supported by his prior argument is defeated.

In the dialectical model of practical reasoning using (*SP*) and (*CQ*), practical inference is seen as a defeasible type of reasoning – a presumption is lodged in place as tentatively acceptable (as a commitment in the dialogue, in the sense of Walton and Krabbe 1995). In the model conveyed by Table 1, practical reasoning is evaluated as an inference in which an agent is making a plan, or trying to devise a prudent plan of action to suit its own situation. Hence if all the premises are accepted by the agent, on the given information in its circumstances as it sees it, but it fails to accept the conclusion as a prudent course of action for it to adopt or carry out, then it may be said that this agent is practically inconsistent. This outcome does not necessarily mean that the agent is logically inconsistent, or that it has accepted a logical contradiction. But it does mean that its projected plan of action, as a whole, based on the situation as it sees it, does not represent a coherent chain of practical reasoning.

One reason there need be no logical inconsistency in such a case is that an agent's goals are normally stated at a level of abstraction that leaves room for intervening steps of reasoning between a goal and a specific course of action that would be a means (or part of a means) for carrying out that goal. Another reason is that an agent's estimate of a situation is typically based on presumptions that are not firmly known to be true (or false). But the most important reason is that the conflict or contradiction is relative to a particular agent who has expressed her personal commitment to the propositions that lie at the basis of the contradiction.

4. THE CLOSURE PROBLEM RE-EXPRESSED

The closure problem for the basic inference schemata of practical reasoning of Table 1 can be expressed by asking – what is meant by the word 'required' in the conclusion of the schemata? In this sense to say that B_i is required is to say that bringing about the state of affairs B_i is a prudent course of action for the agent in question, relative to the agent's goals, and the agent's knowledge of the circumstances, as stated in the premises of the inference. This is not to say that the agent actually will (or must) bring about B_i. For sometimes agents are weak-willed (akratic), or for whatever reason fail to act on their stated goals and assessment of a situation (in the case of a robot, it could be power failure). It is to say that bringing about B_i is the course of action that the agent is committed to, on the basis of its commitment to the premises of the inference. It means that given its acceptance of (commitment to) these premises, as applied to a particular situation as the agent sees it, on the basis of what it knows (or thinks it knows about the situation), the agent is committed to acceptance of the conclusion, i.e. to commitment to bringing about B_i as the course of action most appropriate for (or most practically reasonable in) this situation.

But, one may well ask – what kind of bindingness or closure is this? After all, presumably we are talking about some sort of real agent, whether it is a human being or not, that is acting in the so-called "real world." But the problem is that the real world is constantly changing. Moreover, an agent's knowledge or understanding of the situation it is in is (inevitably, in any realistic case) far from perfect. Questions can always be re-asked about whether another alternative might be better, or whether a proposed course of action might lead to consequences that have not been fully appreciated, or taken into account yet. After all, practical reasoning is about the future, and involves the possible future consequences of one's contemplated actions. Such contingent factors, in any realistic case, are matters of conjecture, and questions can continually be re-asked about them, requiring a re-assessment of a practical inference. If so, how could a practical inference ever really be closed?

Aquinas posed this question very pointedly in the *Summa Theologiae* (*Question 14,* Article 6; Blackfriars Edition, p. 155):

Article 6. May deliberation go on endlessly?

THE SIXTH POINT: 1. Yes, apparently, for it is about the particular things which are the concern of practical knowledge. These are infinite. Accordingly no term is to be set to the inquiry of deliberation about them.

2. Further, we have to weigh up not only what has to be done, but also how to clear away the obstacles. Now any number of objections to any particular course of action can be put up and knocked down in our mind. Therefore there is no stop to our questioning about how to deal with them.

3. Moreover, the inquiry instituted by demonstrative science does not lead back indefinitely, but arrives at self-evident principles which are altogether certain. Such certainty, however, cannot be found in contingent and individual facts, which are variable and uncertain. Deliberation, therefore, goes on endlessly.

Aquinas' solution to this problem is to be found in his characterization of deliberation (Question 14, Article 4; Blackfriars Edition, p. 151) as a kind of process that is useful or necessary only when we need to look into a matter we are doubtful about. When engaged in habitual or skilled actions, there may be no need to deliberate, or to raise questions about which is the best course of action, or the best way to do something. This account suggests that deliberation is a kind of process. What begins it is the raising of questions, the expression of doubts on how to proceed. What ends it is the answering of the question, or the resolution of the doubt. But exactly when is the question answered, or the doubt resolved? Do we need to make an assumption at some point in a deliberation that a decision is now called for?

Closing off the process of deliberation, as opposed to going on and on collecting information, or continuing to deliberate on the pros and cons of an issue, seems to be an important aspect of the closure problem of practical reasoning. The problem is one of when to terminate the process of deliberation and close off the collecting of new information relevant to a case. This problem of judging the sufficiency of evidence required for rational acceptance of a conclusion has been studied by Clarke (1989, 73–85) in cases of inductive reasoning.

Clarke takes a pragmatic approach, pointing out that practical matters – like the costs of continuing to search for information – are often relevant to acceptance of a conclusion and termination of an inquiry (p. 75). However, such pragmatic considerations can be easily overlooked, especially in the more traditional framework of decision theories, where optimizing (maximization) was stressed over more practical satisficing (Simon 1978) models of rational acceptance.

Using a pragmatic framework of the kind advocated by Clarke, one could argue with Aquinas that, in principle, deliberation in any real-life case could go on endlessly if one requires the best possible outcome, based on a maximizing principle of acceptance. But by a pragmatic standard of acceptance of a conclusion, clearly, practical matters, like the costs of continuing to collect information, ought to suggest closing off further deliberations, once a "good enough" solution to the problem has been reached. A "good enough" solution is one that solves the problem by arriving at a decision for a course of action that fulfills the goal, but also answers certain relevant questions in relation to what is known about the given situation, or alternatively recommends not taking action, on the grounds that one or more of these questions cannot be answered adequately.

5. THE CLOSED WORLD ASSUMPTION

Some complexities inherent in the closure problem are suggested by the observation that sometimes it is better to collect more information relevant to a situation, rather than rushing ahead with a decision to act on the presently known facts. The latter conclusion may be too hasty, and therefore may represent a significant type of failure of practical reasoning.

On the other hand, sometimes, doing nothing at all, while collecting more information, can be a bad sort of failure. One can overly research a problem while, in the meantime, the opportunity for optimally productive action has passed. Government inquiries and Royal Commission Inquiries, for example, can be used as stalling tactics to "study a problem to death," thereby putting off the need to move forward with any action.

A related complexity is the distinction between acts and omissions. In many cases, doing nothing at all can, in effect, be an action. Reason: doing nothing may have significant positive or negative consequences, in relation to a goal.

These complexities show that practical reasoning is very much a time-indexed kind of reasoning. The decision, in some cases for example, may be one between doing nothing now and doing something later. Or it may be one between doing something now, and doing something later (when more information has come in, and more is known about the situation).

Another complexity of the closure problem is that in some cases, trial and error is the most practical way to proceed, if a definite solution showing the best course of action is not yet apparent, and collecting further information would not be speedy enough to make for a better decision. If it is difficult to collect more information, and the consequences of acting on a trial basis are not likely to be disastrous, it may be that the best solution is to go ahead and try something, to see where that may lead. Such a decision may not be "hasty action" so much as "getting on with it," even if some risk is involved, and one does not know which alternative is best, or even whether any of the given alternatives will bring about the goal that is supposed to be the objective.

In cases of interest as representing deliberation of the kind that is so familiar to us in everyday actions, the premises of the practical inference and the way it operates generally, cannot be fixed or closed off, as if the circumstances of the agent in a given case were no longer subject to additional changes. In these cases, practical reasoning is better seen as based on tentative premises that lead by tentative inferences to tentative conclusions. Practical reasoning in such cases is a defeasible kind of argumentation, in that it is nonmonotonic in nature – subject to revision as new information concerning the agent's changing circumstances comes to be known.

However, for purposes of studying the closure problem, the premises of a practical inference can be fixed in some cases by assumption, relative to a given case, to determine what follows by practical reasoning from a given set of assumptions.

According to Reiter (1987, 158), the *closed world assumption* is the inference drawn that any positive fact not specified in a given database may be assumed to be false, on the basis that all of the relevant positive information has been specified. An example (Reiter 1980, 69) is the default inference drawn when scanning an airline monitor, when no flight is listed from Vancouver to New York. The closed world assumption is that all the relevant positive information about the flights one could take at this time are listed on the monitor. So if a Vancouver to New York flight is not listed, one may assume that no such flight is available.[6] This assumption can then function as a premise that leads, along with other premises as assumptions to a conclusion derived by practical reasoning. In some cases, the closed world assumption seems to be quite reasonable.

In *the blocks world* (Russell and Norvig 1995, 359), there are a set of blocks sitting on a table, and they can be stacked, one fitting on top of another. A robot arm can pick up one block at a time, so it cannot pick up one block that has another block on it. The goal is to build up a specified stack of blocks (specified by which blocks are on top of other blocks). Typical of the blocks world is a clearly stated goal, a small (finite) number of alternative means of implementing the goal, each of which is a definite series of steps that can easily be carried out by the robot, and an ignoring of any consequences of the robot's actions outside the blocks world. Also, there are no "outside forces" acting in the blocks world, e.g. to remove blocks or add new ones. The robot is the only agent being considered. Thus the blocks world is a simplified kind of case of practical reasoning.

In the blocks world, the closure problem is easy to solve. If the robot's goal is to achieve a particular stack of blocks, and the requirements of the given situation are such that it must take a particular step right away, e.g. picking up a particular block and putting it on the table, then any act (or omission) other than taking that particular step is a practical inconsistency.

By contrast, in the smoking case, the action of smoking, even given that one's goal is health, and one argues that not smoking is necessary for health, does not appear to (necessarily) constitute a practical inconsistency. It constitutes enough of a *prima facie* case for practical inconsistency that some sort of explanation or response is called for. But there does appear to be room for various kinds of explanations that could resolve the apparent inconsistency. The problem is that while, in a sense, actions do "speak louder than words," inferring commitment to a particular proposition on the basis of a perceived or acknowledged action is by no means straightforward or automatic. Because one smokes, it does not necessarily follow that one is committed to smoking as a general policy that one approves of, or is advocating.

The key to achieving closure in the smoking case (and comparable cases) seems to reside in questioning the smoker (or the agent) to try to get her to make verbal commitments to specific commitments, based on her perceived actions, and on what those actions may be assumed (subject to rebuttal) to imply.

6. PROBLEMATIC CASES

Aquinas was right to insist that in typical everyday deliberation, a case is never really closed, for practical purposes. As he put it, deliberation "goes on endlessly." But there often does come a time when it is practically useful and reasonable to bring the closed world assumption to bear, and arrive at a prudent (if provisional) decision for action based on what one presently knows, in line with one's present goals. Once the premises of a practical inference are provisionally fixed, in such a case, propositions can be evaluated as following from these premises by practical reasoning, or as being practically inconsistent with these premises.

In principle then, the structure of inference represented in Table 1 provides the means for solving the closure problem of practical reasoning. But as the smoking case already indicated, applying this structure to ordinary "real world" cases of deliberation is by no means straightforward.

In some cases, there really does seem to be a pragmatic inconsistency, and yet the inconsistency can be explained by the person involved, so that her stance does not appear to be illogical, meaning that her practical reasoning is defective. Examples of this sort of criticism, and responses to it, are very interesting to think about. One example is the case of a woman who had long argued that a certain type of income tax exemption ought to be abolished, but when an opportunity came by for her to take advantage of this exemption personally, in her tax return, she did it. But she argued that her position was not illogical, and that she continued to maintain that this exemption should be abolished legally. But she still argued that as long as the exemption was legally permitted for everyone, as a policy, she had every right to take advantage of it, along with everyone else. It is puzzling to understand her defence exactly, and some would not agree that it is legitimate. But it seems to turn on the distinction between laws that apply to everyone as public policy, and matters of individual conscience or personal conduct.

A similar case has been the subject of considerable controversy and analysis (Cuomo 1984).

A Catholic politician running for a high federal office declared that she supported freedom of choice on the abortion issue, even though, as a Catholic she personally opposed abortion. She argued that her personal views are not in conflict with her position on public policy. A Catholic bishop criticized this stance as illogical, replying that he did not see how a good Catholic, who should be against the taking of human life, could vote for a politician who supported abortion. She replied that as a Catholic she did not personally support abortion, but that she felt she had no right to impose that view on others, who might have different religious viewpoints. She stated that her political support of freedom of choice concerning reproduction was logically consistent with her personal opposition to abortion because of the separation of church and state (Walton 1989, 169).

In this case, the stance of the politician definitely does involve a pragmatic inconsistency, but her defence seems to explain the inconsistency in a way that takes the sting out of the criticism against her stance. Democratic politics being what it is, it seems that there will be cases where a citizen may support general policies that are supposed to apply to everyone, even if such a policy would support or sanction actions that she would be against, personally.

In this case, it does seem that there is a pragmatic inconsistency in the practical reasoning of the agent. But the inconsistency can be explained away, or resolved, by the group involvement of the agent in policies that affect the group as a whole. Even if an agent disagrees with the policy as an expression of her own personal goals, or standards of conduct, she may still have to support the policy as an expression of what is best for the group – even if, paradoxically, she is one of the individuals in the group.

In this kind of case, there is a kind of pragmatic inconsistency involved, but it can (arguably) be resolved or explained in a way that shows it not to represent a defect in the agent's practical reasoning. But this kind of case remains deeply problematic, and there is a lingering feeling that somehow the agent is compromised by voluntarily belonging to a group that lives by general policies that conflict with the personal goals of the agent.

This particular case, which, as many readers will know, is that of Geraldine

Ferraro, the vice-presidential nominee who in 1984, advocated the pro-choice position for women, while stating that she was personally opposed to abortion. In response to the subsequent criticisms of the Catholic bishops, a group of Catholic theologians, priests and nuns proclaimed in a full-page ad in the *New York Times* that a "diversity of opinion regarding abortion exists among committed Catholics." (Jonsen and Toulmin 1988, 1). Shortly afterwards, Vatican authorities issued a statement to the effect that the "direct termination of prenatal life is morally wrong in all instances." (Jonsen and Toulmin 1988, 2). One can see from the controversy generated by this case that the conflict at the basis of it is not an easy one to resolve, and has ethical implications.

One way to resolve the conflict is to draw a distinction between personal commitments and group commitments of a kind that arise from membership in a group. Tuomela (1992) makes a distinction between normative beliefs that involve a whole social group, and merely factual beliefs that relate only to personal beliefs an individual has. This analysis of group beliefs of the normative kind, as being distinct from personal beliefs, offers a way out of the conflict, by arguing that the perceived contradiction is based on an underlying ambiguity. Some would say, however, that holding political office creates a situation where the normative group belief overrides personal belief.

Some would say that when a person chooses to take up political office, he or she has given up the right to a private life, and should not complain if personal matters are reported – for example, by the media – and used in public deliberations on political issues. Others would say that it is a question of roles. As a public official who is a member of a group, like a political party, one has a role as a member of the group, and must base one's rational deliberations on what general policies to support this role. However, as a person with a conscience, who may, for example, have personal religious or moral convictions or codes of conduct, one has commitments based on a different role that may conflict with the other commitments stemming from the other role. One may, for example, be bound to vote for the acceptance of laws or general policies that are binding on a group – like a whole country or a state – that one may or may not feel obliged to follow as a private individual, who may have certain moral or religious views on a matter like abortion or joining the armed forces. In such cases, there can be an ambiguity involved in the different roles one is committed to play in a complex multiagent situation where one may be a member of different groups.

7. SOLVING THE CLOSURE PROBLEM

The solution to the closure problem is to be found in utilizing the structure for practical reasoning provided by the argumentation scheme (*SP*) and the matching set of critical questions (*CQ*). First, one has to relationize the decision in a particular case to the text of discourse given, representing the sequence of deliberations to that point in the case, and to what is known (or thought to be known) by the two parties (in the two-person multiagent dialogue) in that case. The agent (proponent) must formulate a goal, and a proposed means, according to the form of the inference (*SP*). If both premises are reasonably acceptable presumptions in relation to the information known in the case, then a weight of acceptance is shifted (defeasibly) towards tentatively moving by inference from the premises to the conclusion.

But once such a forward-moving shift of an inference of the form (*SP*) is put into place in a dialogue, the respondent is obliged to ask one or more of the set of appropriate critical questions (*CQ*). If the proponent cannot answer any one of the critical questions asked, the burden of proof shifts back to her side and the practical inference is defeated. But if the critical question is answered satisfactorily, the inference is restored as binding on both parties. But then if the respondent asks another of the critical questions, the inference is once again suspended until that question is replied to adequately. Acceptance or non-acceptance of the conclusion (based on acceptance of the premises and the structure of the practical inference) shifts back and forth from one side to the other during the sequence of deliberations in the dialogue. However, if the proponent has succeeded in answering all five critical questions adequately, and no new information has come into the dialogue in the meantime that is relevant to the problem (issue) being deliberated, then the line of practical reasoning is *closed*, meaning that if the premises are acceptable in the dialogue to both parties, then the conclusion (by inference from the premises) ought (practically) to be acceptable too. In particular, if the respondent accepts the premises, then as a collaborative participant in the dialogue he ought (practically speaking) to accept the conclusion as well.

In exactly this type of case, as described in the previous paragraph, if any party in a deliberation accepts all the premises that rationally require acceptance of a particular line of conduct as the inferrable conclusion by practical reasoning from the given premise she accepts or advocates, but then clearly indicates her commitment to an opposite line of conduct, then she is open to criticism as being practically inconsistent (as judged by her commitments reconstructed by the text of the discourse of the previous dialogue in the given case). The smoking case, as reconstructed in the extended dialogue above, in section two, is just such a case. Once the parent has advocated non-smoking as a policy, based on her premises that smoking is unhealthy and that health is a goal for her, then the child is justified in citing her practice of smoking as proving a putative practical inconsistency for her that needs to be questioned and resolved. The burden is then on the parent's side of the dialogue to answer to the charge of practical inconsistency. Only if she can answer the question adequately is the inference restored as practically binding.

The closure problem is thus solved, using the structures (*SP*) and (*CQ*) in a framework of deliberation, relative to the information given in a particular case. But a secondary problem is raised that we have not (at any rate, completely) solved. What are the allowable and adequate responses to a well-founded charge of practical inconsistency (once such a change is made in a given case)? This problem is left for another occasion.

The closure problem is solved because, in the smoking case, as the extended dialogue develops between the parent and the child, the child reconstructs the parent's argument against smoking as follows. The parent has expressed a personal commitment to the goal of being healthy, as well as making a general statement that health is generally a good thing for everyone. The parent has also expressed a commitment to the proposition that non-smoking is a necessary means to health. These two propositions, expressed as personal commitments by the parent, in her argument indicating to the child that he should not smoke, shifts a weight of presumption to the conclusion that not only is smoking imprudent (practically speaking, not a rational course of action) for the child, but for the parent as well. But by admitting to the practice of smoking herself, the parent gives the child grounds for questioning the sincerity of her own argument. In other words, the child uses the closure of the parent's practical reasoning to set up the charge of pragmatic inconsistency. From this practical point of view then, the child's circumstantial *ad hominem* argument against the parent's prior argument can be reconstructed as a reasonable argument.

University of Winnipeg

NOTES

[1] The author would like to thank the Social Sciences and Humanities Research Council of Canada for a research grant that supported the work in this paper. Dave Clarke sent a number of insightful comments on the paper (by e-mail) that threw new light on some aspects of a previous draft, and helped in making revisions. Also, this previous draft was presented at the University of Western Australia on September 27, 1996, and the following participants in the discussion made comments or criticisms that led to important improvements in the second draft: Guy Douglas, Michael Levinc, Barry Maund, Alan Tapper and Hartley Slater.

[2] This definition encapsulates the notion of practical reasoning analyzed in Walton (1990), but comparable accounts are given by Clarke (1985) and Audi (1989).

[3] To minimize gender babble, we frequently use the pronoun 'it' in the sequel. We are assuming generally that a practical reasoner can be either a human or a machine, but the frequent use of 'it' suggests the application to robotics.

[4] Looking through introductory logic textbooks that have a section on informal fallacies will tend to confirm this claim. Hamblin (1970) gives an outline of the standard treatment.

[5] A state of affairs can be thought of as a temporally indexed contingent proposition (neither a logical tautology or a logically inconsistent proposition) of the sort that, in principle, could be made true or false by an agent.

[6] This form of inference is called the argument from ignorance (*argumentum ad ignorantiam*) in logic.

REFERENCES

Aquinas, Thomas (1970), *Summa Theologiae*, vol. **17**. Trans. Thomas Gilby, Blackfriars Edition, New York, McGraw-Hill.

Aristotle (1954), *The Nicomachean Ethics of Aristotle*. Trans. and ed. by Sir David Ross, London, Oxford University Press.

Audi, Robert (1989), *Practical Reasoning*. London, Routledge.

Clarke, D.S., Jr. (1985), *Practical Inferences*. London, Routledge and Kegan Paul.

Clarke, D.S., Jr. (1989), *Rational Acceptance and Purpose: An Outline of a Pragmatist Epistemology*. Totowa, New Jersey, Rowman and Littlefield.

Cuomo, Mario M. (1984), "Religious Belief and Public Morality," *New York Review of Books* **31**, 32–37.

Hamblin, C.L. (1970), *Fallacies*. London, Methuen.

Hamblin, C.L. (1987), *Imperatives*. Oxford, Blackwell.

Honderich, Ted (1995), *The Oxford Companion to Philosophy*. Oxford, Oxford University Press.

Jonsen, Albert R. and Stephen Toulmin (1988), *The Abuse of Casuistry: A History of Moral Reasoning*. Berkeley, University of California Press.

Krabbe, E.C.W. (1990), "Inconsistent Commitments and Commitment to Inconsistencies," *Informal Logic* **12**, 33–42.

Reiter, Raymond (1980), "A Logic for Default Reasoning," *Artificial Intelligence* **13**, 81–132.

Reiter, Raymond (1987), "Nonmonotonic Reasoning," *Annual Review of Computer Science* **2**, 147–186.

Russell, Stuart and Peter Norvig (1995), *Artificial Intelligence: A Modern Approach*. Upper Saddle River, New Jersey, Prentice Hall.

Simon, H. (1978), "Rationality as a Process and as a Product of Thought," *American Economic Review* **68**, 1–16.

Singh, Munidar Paul (1994), *Multiagent Systems*. Berlin, Springer-Verlag.

Tuomela, Raimo (1992), "Group Beliefs," *Synthese* **91**, 285–318.

Walton, Douglas N. (1989), *Informal Logic*. Cambridge, Cambridge University Press.

Walton, Douglas N. (1990), *Practical Reasoning: Goal-Driven, Knowledge-Based, Action-Guiding Argumentation*. Savage, Maryland, Rowman and Littlefield.

Walton, Douglas N. and Erik C.W. Krabbe (1995), *Commitment in Dialogue: Basic Concepts of Interpersonal Reasoning*. Albany, State University of New York Press.

ROBERT AUDI

INTENDING AND ITS PLACE IN THE THEORY OF ACTION

The topic of intending is important in both the literature of action theory and, more generally, that of ethics and law.[1] In 1973, I offered an account of intending that has received much attention in the succeeding two decades.[2] Various elements in the account have been defended in print, both by others and by me,[3] but the account, like the subject in general, remains controversial. Even apart from what has been specifically disputed, there are unsolved problems. This paper is aimed at contributing to our understanding of intending in two ways: first, it will reinforce and clarify my original account of intending by bringing the account to bear on a number of important problems central for intending in particular and the theory of the will in general; secondly, it will reply to a number of objections to the account that have emerged or re-emerged in the past several years.

I. SOME BENEFITS OF THE COGNITIVE-MOTIVATIONAL ACCOUNT

My main concern will be simple intending, as opposed to, say, conditional intending, for instance intending to *A*, if *c*, where '*A*' ranges over action-types and '*c*' over circumstances of action. The account of simple intending from which I will work is this:

> A person, *S*, intends, at time *t*, to *A*, if and only if, at *t*, (1) *S* believes that *S* will (or that *S* probably will) *A*; (2) *S* wants, and has not temporarily forgotten that *S* wants, to *A*; and (3) either *S* has no equally strong or stronger incompatible want (or set of wants whose combined strength is at least as great), or, if *S* does have such a want or set of wants, *S* has temporarily forgotten that *S* wants the object(s) in question, or does not believe *S* wants the object(s).[4]

The only comment needed immediately is that incompatible wants are here construed subjectively and in terms of their objects: they are not, then, wants that cannot *coexist*; they are wants such that *S* has a belief to the effect that they cannot both be realized. Incompatible wants need not *compete*, as where one contemplates two things one wants about equally much, realizes that one cannot have both, and reflects on which thing to try to get. Incompatible wants will not compete at a given time if, at that time, at least one is temporarily forgotten.

G. Holmström-Hintikka and R. Tuomela (eds.), Contemporary Action Theory. Vol. I, 177–196.

Formation and Cessation Conditions

The rationale for an account of this sort will begin to emerge (for anyone to whom it is not clear) if we consider conditions under which intentions form. One path to intention formation is through practical reasoning. I am driving to a friend's home and must choose between a short, crowded route and an easier but longer one; I might judge that preserving my nerves is more important than promptness, conclude that the long route is better, and form the intention to take it. Another path to intention formation is decision that occurs without practical reasoning of which the decision is an upshot. Without engaging in practical reasoning at all, I could come to intend to take the longer route if, as I approach the intersection in question, against the background of my remembering the choice I earlier made there in favor of preserving my nerves, I simply decide, quite spontaneously, to take that route.

It is not necessary that intention formation be *reflective* at all. On a walk in the country, one may simply find a vista attractive, form the intention to walk that way, and immediately proceed to do so. In all of the cases I have considered, there is excellent reason to suppose that the agent has both the required want(s) and the requisite belief. It is useful to call the required motivational pattern *predominant motivation* and the crucial belief a *performance expectation*. What we intend to do we both want to do strongly *enough* relative to other things we want and, at least in some (weak) sense, expect to do.

These points help to explain two other phenomena that confirm the account. To begin with, notice that in each of the following two cases, (a) one of the main components of the account is present and one is missing, and (b) the occurrence of a change that supplies the missing component produces an intention – just as the account would predict.

The first phenomenon that confirms the account in this way is that, by the appropriate addition of a performance expectation, intentions can arise from desires, or from hopes, to *A* – where *A*-ing is something one would like to do. One may, e.g., pass from believing it unlikely that one will *A* to believing it probable that one will, where, given one's already wanting on balance to *A*, one thereby comes to intend to *A*. Here is a case of the kind in question: I may hope, but not intend, to meet you at the restaurant tomorrow if I believe you will very likely be committed to meeting someone else; later, when I discover that you will be free to see me, I immediately come to intend to meet you there. I may then phone another friend to cancel her plan to lunch with me elsewhere during the same hour.

Similarly – and here is the second genetic phenomenon that confirms my account – suppose I am half-hearted about visiting an aging uncle on Labor Day weekend and have a more attractive competing plan, yet believe that if only because of likely pressure from my family, I will eventually alter the plan and decide to visit him. The predominant want condition on intending is not satisfied, and I do not now intend to visit him. But if, as I think about how loving he is, visiting him gets more attractive to me and eventually becomes something I want more than to retain the competing plan, I may pass into a state of intending to visit him. The crucial change is the development of a predominant want of the kind my account posits.

It is worth noting here that I need not *decide* to visit him: if I am interrupted just as my balance of desires changes in favor of the visit, I may simply come away with a new overall attitude toward visiting him. If someone later asks what I intend to do over Labor Day, I may, without any need to review the matter, say that I intend to ("I'm going to") visit my uncle. The case thus shows not only that the appropriate addition of a predominant want to the performance expectation condition can yield intending, but also that an intention can form in one without one's having had to form it, say by making a decision or otherwise doing something through which one might be said to have explicitly formed the intention.

None of this entails that forming an intention – as opposed to causing oneself to form one or causing an intention to form in oneself – is a kind of action. I leave open that some instances of forming an intention might be actions, as where one takes a positive attitude toward an action and by thinking about its positive aspects volitionally endorses it, as it were. This (admittedly non-standard) way of forming an intention is a route to its formation quite different from, say, pushing a button that produces an intention in oneself by manipulating the volitional system irrespective of one's attitudes that might be a normal basis of the intention.

However we decide the question whether forming an intention is ever an action, surely *in* deciding to *A* I (at least normally) do form an intention to *A*, and there may be other things I can do, such as judge that I (morally) must *A* that result in my forming an intention to *A*. Intention formation is an important topic in its own right; my main concern here is simply to indicate how my account of intending is compatible with some of the most plausible and important facts about the formation of intentions.[5]

At this point it should be clarifying to note that there is a technical use of 'intending' which I do not pretend is addressed by my account. This is the use restricted to intending to do something "here and now," understood as (roughly) an endorsing (or assenting) thinking to oneself something approximating 'I shall *A* here and now'.[6] The notion in question is close to a major conception of volition, and I suggest that the notion is understandable largely in terms of a resolutive activation or similar conscious manifestation of intention, where the intention itself is understood along the lines of my account and with the proviso that the activation or manifestation need not always *precede* the formation of the relevant intention.[7]

Once the distinction between what we might call *standing intentions* and immediate intentions is understood, however, it is plain that an account of the former need only provide appropriate space for an understanding of the latter. This much my account of intending does. For one thing, it makes clear both how an intention can be formed without the occurrence of a conscious event of the kind some theorists call immediate intention (there may never be one, as in the case of intentions regarding the distant future that are abandoned long before the time in question). The account also indicates how an immediate intention can be conceived as grounded in motivation and cognition in a way that, largely through them, can give it the action-explaining power it possesses.

The quite different phenomenon of ceasing to intend is also well understood in the light of the account. If a snowstorm causes me to believe that I probably cannot get through to my uncle, I may well pass from intending to visit him to just hoping that I will. I may still intend to try to visit, but that is of course a different intention. Not only does it have a different object, it is also less definite, since many more kinds of actions can count as trying to *A*. Similarly, if I come to cease to want to see him as much as I want to do something I believe is incompatible with seeing him, such as go to an interesting conference, I may cease to intend to visit him. Moreover, I need not have "changed my mind," since the matter has never come before my mind.

As this case indicates, changing my mind is not required for *my mind's changing*, any more than my forming an intention (construed as an action) is necessary for an intention to form in me. If asked whether I intend to visit him, I may, on thinking for a moment, say that I do not though I did mean (intend) to in the past. This reaction need not derive from *now* changing my intentions. I might even be somewhat surprised at myself upon discovering this change in my intentions; I might have considered myself more dedicated.[8]

The Analysis of Action

There is not space here to treat in any detail the bearing of my account on the analysis of action, but it should help to note two prominent ways of conceiving action and how the account pertains to them. First, one might think of action as behavior that is intentional under some description (or other); on this view, action is roughly *intentional behavior*. Second, one might think of action as behavior that, under some description, is explainable (in the sense that the agent's performing it is explainable) by appeal to the agent's beliefs and wants; on this view, action is *motivationally explainable behavior*. Since beliefs and wants are both the chief elements in intending and capable of providing explanations of all intentional action,[9] their prominence in these conceptions of action (as most plausibly worked out) should pose no threat to my account of intending.

One might think, however, that an action must be not only intentional under some description or explainable by the kinds of attitudes that are components in intending, or both, but also *intended* under some description. Call this the *intendedness conception of intentional action*. On this strong view of action, my account of intending would be satisfactory as an adjunct to the analysis of action only if it allows us to posit the requisite range of intendings: at least one of them for every action we perform. I think that it might well allow this. For the likeliest way in which this intendedness conception of action, as opposed to an intentionality conception of it, could be true is by virtue of every action resting on some *basic* action that the agent intends to perform, i.e., roughly an intended action one does not perform *by* performing some other action.

Imagine this, however: I have just had surgery and strongly doubt I can move my right arm. Asked by my doctor to move it, I now hope to move it, but do not have an intention, as opposed to a mere hope, to move it. Yet if I succeed because, despite my grave doubts, I am in fact cured, my moving it is surely both an action and indeed intentional. If so, then neither intentional action nor even action simpliciter need rest on specifically intending some action, as opposed to being based on intentionality: roughly, on a relation to intentional attitudes, such as explainability in terms of wants and beliefs. There is no problem raised by such cases for the intentionality or cognitive-motivational conception; the trouble is for the intendedness view.

One might argue that what my case of unexpected recovery from paralysis really shows is that the performance expectation condition on intending is too strong. This move will be natural for some philosophers, but I shall shortly show how that very condition seems essential in accounting for an important role of intending in our lives. Speaking globally, however, I contend that to weaken this condition increases the agent's felt distance between intention and action in such a way that intending is no longer plausibly considered a "practical" state. What we do not expect to do may seem to us merely projected and is not a definite prospect in the way what we intend is.

Planning

Intending has at least four major roles in relation to plans: it may (1) cause their formation, (2) partially constitute them, (3) serve as a constraint, psychologically and normatively, on both their formation and their execution, and (4), by virtue of connections of content between plans and intentions, be a natural product of plans. Much could be said about each of these connections, but here I can indicate only how each one might be accommodated by the proposed account of intending.

(1) Plainly, if I intend to do something whose achievement is either difficult or complex, it is natural for me to make a plan as to how to proceed. The kinds of wants and beliefs that are, on my view, fundamental in intending explain this

naturalness at least as well as any alternative account can do. Indeed, if we do not take intending to require both predominant motivation and a performance expectation, the *need* for a plan in the kinds of cases in question will tend not to be as strongly felt. If, e.g., opposing motivation could be predominant over the motivation one has by virtue of intending an action, one would be less inclined to *frame* a plan for performing it and certainly less inclined to *adopt* one. If, moreover, one could merely hope to do the deed – as would be so if we significantly weakened the performance expectation as a requirement for intending – doing it could easily seem (say) far off or speculative or hypothetical, and there would not be the felt tension that easily results from expecting to do something requiring a plan, yet lacking a plan suitable for doing it.

(2) As to the constitution relation between intending and plans, it is plausible to hold that *having* a plan to *A* (in the sense of holding to the plan, not merely possessing one in the abstract) implies intending to *A*. Planning *to A* entails intending to do it; having a *plan for A-ing* does not. The former appears also to imply both wanting to *A* and believing (at least) that one will, or that one probably will, *A*. If one only hopes to *A*, one may have a plan for *A*-ing or for *how to A* (still another notion, applicable especially where the action involves complicated or unfamiliar steps); but one does not plan *to A*. Plans may also have as components both conditional intentions and also beliefs or wants that are not part of any intending. But clearly the way in which plans and planning processes depend on wants and beliefs is quite as one would expect given my cognitive-motivational account of intending.

(3) There are various ways in which intending constrains planning. What we plan to do is normally arrived at against the background of what we already intend to do. If I intend to be in Helsinki next week, I do not plan to visit New York during the very same time. Given my intention, forming such a plan would be neither rational nor at all psychologically normal for me. Granted, in making a plan, one may change existing intentions. But what one intends serves as an initial constraint on what one will plan to do at all, on how one will plan to achieve what one does plan to do, and on the rationality of both. The constraint is at once psychological and normative: I not only will not plan to go to New York during my intended visit to Helsinki, I would be irrational to plan to do so without at least suspending my intention to visit Helsinki. Now the expectation component of intending is crucial in accounting for this dual constraining role of intending: it places the action in question on one's actual future itinerary. The predominant want component is also important: it expresses a significant disposition to continue on that itinerary.

(4) That plans should produce intentions is also expectable on my account of intending. For naturally, if I plan to visit Finland I tend to come to intend to do what I believe is necessary for getting there. If planning to *A*, construed as entailing intending, did not imply a belief that one will *A* and a suitable desire

to *A*, then, other things equal, one would be less likely to form intentions to do things believed to be required for *A*-ing: one might either care too little about carrying out that part of one's itinerary or fail to take doing so to be realistically likely.

The Role of Intending in Selecting Act-Descriptions

It has often been noted that what we are doing has many descriptions and that there is a special significance in what we do intentionally, which is in turn sometimes taken to be what we do as an execution of an intention. Thomas Aquinas had a striking point along these lines: "moral acts take their species according to what is intended and not according to what is beside the intention, since this is accidental."[10] Similarly, Kant was concerned with whether an act is "done from duty" rather than merely in conformity with it, where by 'from duty' he meant something like 'with a suitably dutiful intention'.

I submit that these points are not a whit less plausible if intending is conceived as I propose. Indeed, if we adopt my account of intending and think of the deeds in question as bearing descriptions under which they are predominantly wanted, it is no wonder that these philosophers regard the deeds as highly significant conceived under those descriptions: the actions, so described, indicate what the agent is really "after" (or mainly aiming at); and if we think of the actions as expected by the agent, we can see how the agent may be plausibly thought to identify with them: they are envisaged as lying ahead on one's itinerary, not merely as possible objects of acquaintance if or when one's path should reach them. What we both predominantly want to do and expect to do are in a sense accountable for as items on our agenda – roughly, as prima facie contents of our will. This is what one would expect if that combination characteristically constitutes intending.

Intention as a Central Concept in Ethical Theory

Kant is widely known for his extraordinary claim, in the *Groundwork of the Metaphysics of Morals*,[11] that the only unqualifiedly good thing is good will. On one plausible reading, he takes good will to be constituted by the person's good intentions. That, in any case, is how good will is normally understood in appraising persons. Now surely there is much plausibility in so understanding good will in terms of intending construed as I explicate it. Indeed, my position has a special advantage here over competing views: in positing both predominant motivation and a performance expectation as essential in intending, the position makes it clear that one's will, conceived as determined by one's intentions, reflects both what one wants to do and what one believes one actually will do. What we intend is on our life itinerary, not just on a path we expect to traverse but are otherwise neutral about. It is thus something we are not only willing to do but in a sense *embrace*, and in that way it is a good basis for partially judging us.

The itinerary metaphor is misleading in one way: one decides on an itinerary, but may intend an action quite spontaneously and without deciding on it. Still, not every item of conduct expected and desired on the itinerary is separately considered, or need even be decided upon to be an object of intention. Intentions can arise by *diffusion* from a decision or from a choice or from plan formation. They need not arise from *deliberation* or even from the broadly deliberative origin of focal decision to perform the very action in question. Nor, by contrast, need they arise through the non-deliberate source of a spontaneous attraction to a behavioral option, as where a wild flower strikes one's fancy and one reaches out to pick it. The cognitive-motivational account of intending is compatible with the full diversity of routes to intention formation, and it helps to explain why some of these tend to have greater moral significance than others.

It is also instructive to consider intending in relation to the problem of formulating the maxims of our actions. These are the first-person principles of action that do (or should) govern them – which Kant says we must be able to universalize if we are acting rightly. As I have elsewhere argued,[12] the crucial element in framing the maxim is the intention(s) with which one has acted or, in the case of prospective decision, *will* act. The relevant intentions, then, are not just *to* do the deed; they are the explanatory one(s) underlying it (at least hypothetically, as where it is prospective). Thus, if I made a lying promise with the intention of getting money that I could not pay back, the content of this intention must go into my maxim.

Now it would be a mistake to think that it is easy to tell just what is the content of one's intentions in such difficult cases. But I think that the problem is no worse than that of determining the content of the appropriate want(s) and belief underlying each action in the way my account suggests. The lying promisor, for instance, presumably wants to bilk the creditor out of the money and believes the promise will accomplish this. (Note, incidentally, that where the promisor only hopes to succeed, there is no intention to accomplish this. My overall view allows that hopes *with which* one *A's* have a moral bearing similar to that of intentions to *A* in such cases. After all, wanting and believing are involved in hopes in a way similar to, if perhaps less far-reaching than, the way they figure in intending, though the difference may be significant in ways yet to be considered in the literature.)

Intentions as Rationality and Existence Constraints

One aspect of this topic has been covered: the way in which standing intentions are a constraint on the rationality of plans. Another aspect of it is the need to explain the conditions under which conflicting intentions are irrational. Clearly, if I should know that I cannot, or almost certainly cannot, both *A* and *B*, I should not form intentions, as opposed to hopes, to do both. It would also not be rational to plan to do both here. Moreover, if I should already have both intentions and then come to believe this incompatibility obtains, I should now give up at least one of the intentions (it may not even be possible to retain them both upon forming this incompatibility belief). These points are easily explained given the expectation condition on intention, since one cannot, at least normally, *expect* to do deeds one believes to be almost certainly incompatible (or flatly so) and one surely cannot rationally expect this.

Suppose, however, that the performance expectation requirement is mistaken and that (as some think) one could intend to *A* while believing *A*-ing to be improbable. Then, even if one believed one very probably cannot both *A* and *B*, it would be possible and conceivably rational to intend (separately and perhaps even conjunctively) both to *A* and to *B*, since one need not expect to do either and, wanting to do each, would be glad to achieve either one alone. I could intend to visit Helsinki on a given day and intend to visit New York on the same day. I could then wait for circumstances to force me to choose what plane ticket to buy. In reality, however, these two intentions are probably not even *possible* for someone who believes it is very probable that the goals are jointly impossible. The corresponding *hopes* are jointly possible, as are intentions to *try* to *A* and to *B*. But it is doubtful that one can intend to *A* and intend to *B* while believing (and not temporarily forgetting) that one very probably cannot do both.

The best explanation of this apparent impossibility seems to be that it is impossible for the two relevant performance expectations to coexist. But even where an expectation of *A*-ing does not preclude forming an intention to do something one believes highly unlikely given that one *A*'s, it would at least tend to be irrational to form the intention to do that other thing; and this is readily (and perhaps best) explained on the assumption that a performance expectation is essential to intending. If, in intending to *A*, I expect to *A*, it will tend to be at best irrational for me to come to intend to do something I believe I am highly unlikely to succeed in doing if I *A*.

Intention Transmission

It is surely both a truth of human psychology and a constraint on instrumental rationality that if one wants something, say *x*, and forms an appropriate instrumental belief, say that *A*-ing will definitely achieve *x*, one tends to want to *A*. A similar principle holds with intending in place of wanting, but the corresponding transmission tendency is stronger.[13] Such principles are quite expectable in the light of the conception of intending I have proposed: not only is wanting a constituent, but the wanting is predominant and there is also a belief that one will do the thing in question. The deed is, then, both backed by a certain motivational energy and envisaged as already on one's path.

To be sure, in discovering what one has to do to achieve an intended end one may be so put off that one ceases to have the intention. If, for instance, I realize that in order to invite Semantha I must invite her boorish partner, this may lead to my deciding not to invite her after all. But this too, is explainable on my account: the force of a contrary want overcomes the want to *A*, which either disappears, being as it were vanquished, or ceases to be predominant, being frustrated though not uprooted.

Conditionalization and Qualification

When we discover an obstacle to doing something we intend, we may not give up, but retreat, as it were, to a conditional intention, for instance the intention to visit New York *if* one can. Here the likely explanation of the change is that one came to believe that one could not both visit New York *and* do something more important to one; lacking an expectation that one will (definitely) *A*, one settles into intending to *A if* one can. Another possibility is that our intention becomes qualified. Discovering that if I simply *A* I will hurt Evelyn's feelings, I may decide to *A provided* she doesn't object; or I may simply come to intend to *A after she leaves town*.

Here the change from unconditional to conditional intention is best accounted for by two factors. First, I have desires that outweigh the original desire underlying the intention, for instance desires to protect Evelyn. Second, these are combined with my ability to form a new intention which incorporates a desire that preserves something of what was initially attractive to me (*A*-ing) while meeting the constraint set by the relevant new desire (not to *A* before she leaves). This constraint is brought into play by what I come to believe about how I can do the thing originally intended; specifically, I come to believe that *A*-ing without asking her first or before she goes will hurt her feelings. We may leave open how many actions figure in the scope of the resulting conditional intention(s) and how many conditional intentions are formed.

Sometimes conditionalization complicates one's intentions – many new intentions being needed to get as close as one can to what was originally intended unconditionally. Sometimes a single contingency, such as permission to *A* from some authority, is all that intervenes. The point is that conceiving intentions as I propose does just as well in accommodating these matters of the scope and number of new intentions as does any other plausible account.

To be sure, there is no sharp distinction (at least empirically) between (1) intending to *A* and (2) the pair of attitudes, (a) intending to *A* given *c*, and

(b) believing that c is satisfied. Suppose I want to dine with you, but leave the choice of restaurant up to you. I believe you will choose the Sushi place and want to eat there more than at any of the alternative places. Do I now intend to eat there or just to eat there if you choose it? It can be very difficult to tell, and an agent could even oscillate between these two intentions. Indeed, it is by no means clear that one could not have both, just as one can have both the belief that p and the beliefs that q and that if q then p. So far as I can see, my conception of intending provides conceptual space for us to use all of the resources we may plausibly draw on for distinguishing cases (1) and (2).

Social Action

The importance of intending for the theory of action is no less in the social case than for individual actions. Groups of agents (together) make decisions, have intentions, and perform actions. The distinction between the intentional and the unintentional applies here as in the individual case; there are plans, rationality constraints, conditionalizations, and so on. Here I must be content simply to point out that my account of intending seems to work at least as well as any alternative in explicating social action and the associated action concepts. In the most fully developed theory of social action available,[14] the most basic intention-concept needed in understanding social action is that of a we-intention, the kind each of us has *qua* member of a cooperating group, such as a university department, engaged in a common project:

> A member A_i of a collective G *we-intends* to do X if and only if [based on the (explicit of implicit) agreement concerning the joint performance of X made by the agents $A_1,\dots,A_i,\dots,A_m$,]
>
> (i) A_i intends to do his (agreement-based) part of X (as his part of X);
>
> (ii) A_i has a belief to the effect that the joint action opportunities for an intentional performance of X will obtain (or at least probably will obtain), especially that a right number of the full-fledged and adequately informed members of G, as required for the performance of X, will (or at least probably will) do their parts of X, which will under normal conditions result in an intentional joint performance of X by the participants;
>
> (iii) A_i believes that there is (or will be) a mutual belief among the participating members of G (or at least among those participants who do their parts of X intentionally as their parts of X there is or will be a mutual belief) to the effect that the joint action opportunities for an intentional performance of X will obtain (or at least probably will obtain).
>
> (iv) (i) in part because of (ii) and (iii).[15]

Joint intentions are constituted by we-intentions, and we-intentions (say to *A*) derive their central content from participants' intentions to perform their parts of the joint action in question (*A*-ing). Two further points are essential here. First, there is no reason why the notion of individual intention used here for each group member cannot be the one I have proposed. Second, it is noteworthy that the second and third clauses embody beliefs that seem to carry the expectation of performance, so that a we-intention is in effect distinguished from a we-hope. This is not to suggest that group intention and group action do not require far more for their explication than is required for the individual case. My point is only that my approach to conceiving individual intention seems to connect quite readily with meeting the constraint that social action must reflect individual intentions and individual beliefs related to those intentions.

II. OBJECTIONS AND REPLIES

This section will refine and develop my original account of intending by formulating and answering a series of objections. Most of these have been in the literature at one time or another, but some of them seem new or are interesting variants of existing objections.

Voluntariness and the Proper Objects of Intending

It has been widely presupposed that the objects of intending are actions. If action is construed with extreme breadth, however, this can lead to an objection to my account. For suppose I want to sneeze and believe that, since someone will blow pepper in my face, I will. It would seem that despite meeting the conditions of my account I do not intend to sneeze.[16] This case needs analysis. If sneezing is not an action-type – which seems correct – then the purported counterexample is inapplicable, since my variable '*A*' ranges over just those types. If, on the other hand, wanting to sneeze comes to wanting to *cause* oneself to sneeze, then no counterexample is achieved by the case.

I will not offer an account of an action-type, but I think that a necessary condition for a behavior-type to be one is the possibility of having tokens that are voluntary. I doubt, however, that sneezing behavior that is voluntary may be considered genuinely sneezing: it is perhaps pretending to sneeze, but it does not *befall* one in the way required for a genuine sneeze.

I am also happy to grant that sneezes may be *suppressible* at will; but suppressibility at will does not imply being an action. One might learn to suppress digestion at will; that would not make the process of digestion an action. If behavior is suppressible at will, then *letting it occur* may be an action; but letting a sneeze occur is by no means the same property type as sneezing. Even if sneezing can be an action, the example might be one of what I have elsewhere called passive intentions, roughly a kind the having of which is more a matter of willingness to behave in a certain expected way than the usual (but not essential) self-directness characteristic of intending.[17]

Intending and the (Subjectively) Inevitable

Consider poor Lauri, fearful that he may not wake up from some mandatory surgery. Still, he both wants to wake up and believes he probably will. Asked whether he intends to wake up, however, he might say no, but add that he certainly hopes to. Again, analysis is called for. If waking up is merely passing from sleep to waking, it is not an action-type. There is a use of 'intend to wake up at six' in which it means roughly 'intend to bring it about (say, by a resolution) that I wake up at six', but that is not the use in question here.

It might be objected that if waking up in the relevant sense is not an action-type, it should not be proper to say one hopes to "do it." I have two points. First, hoping clearly ranges over non-actions: one can hope that it rains, and even hope to warm up, or to levitate, or to disintegrate. So, hoping to wake up does not imply that waking up is an action-type. Second, the notion of an action-type cannot be captured by such a simple linguistic test: falling on the dance floor is something one might 'do' that embarrasses a companion, but is not thereby an action-type. Warming up after falling through the ice is another thing that can be "done" – and indeed be the object of propositional attitudes, yet it is not an action-type.

Suppose, however, that I think I will insult someone because I will be unable to resist a threat aimed at compelling me to do it, yet it turns out that I predominantly want to insult the person anyway. If this case meets my conditions, it is what I have elsewhere called a passive intention.[18] I am in fact internally motivated, as required, but because the threat will impose additional motivation on me, do not need to be internally motivated.

Let me stress, however, that my account does not imply that one can, in the normal way, *form* an intention to insult this person, since that presupposes taking oneself to have a kind of control (that I lack here) over whether one will do the thing. It may be the impossibility, in this case, of the kind of intention formation which would be normal for intending to deliver an insult that largely explains the inclination to think there is no intention here. But an intention to insult the person can, in the imagined case, still *form*. The relevant route to intention formation, however, is quite different from the common routes, as where we are planning our lives with the normal control over our actions. Perhaps, then, the irresistibility objection rests on assimilating conditions for the possession of an intention to conditions for its normal formation.

Another possibility is that the objection rests on taking the possession of an intention to require something like a presupposition that the action in question will be carried out *as* an *execution* of the intention, or at least intentionally. But this is too strong: granting that we (normal, articulate adults) are *disposed* so to view the actions we intend (and so will describe our expectations in this way if queried about how we will *A*), the concepts required for such a presupposition (or any similar attitude) are too complex for the simplest creatures (such as tiny children) who have intentions.

Even apart from this conceptual point, there is reason not to impose on the *having* of a conative attitude an expectation of conditions normally (or always) present in its typical *realization*. We form intentions, often, when a prospect seems sufficiently attractive to us in some way and is projected before us as on our path; we do not have to presuppose any definite way of traversing that path nor, as it were, assume that we will deliberately grasp the prospect as we get to it rather than simply run into it.

There is a related point that I should stress I am not denying. Perhaps we *do*, in holding an intention, presuppose something to the effect that we will be the same person, and presumably in some way the same *agent*, when we *A*; but this is a weaker presupposition deriving from our sense of agency rather than from intending as such, and it is perfectly compatible with my account.

Equidesirability (Buridan's Ass Revisited)

Imagine that you want to walk around a lake and can take the left path or the right one. They are equally attractive to you, but you know you must choose and you decide in favor of the right. Don't you now intend to take the right path? Yet you apparently do not want to any more than to take the left one. You would, for instance, shift to the left upon discovering it had the slightest advantage. You might also believe you will take the right path. It may thus seem that we have an intention here but, owing to the absence of predominant motivation, a counterexample to my account.

Let us distinguish between an *arbitrary choice* and *arbitrarily making a choice*. Where there is nothing to recommend *x* over *y*, the choice is arbitrary; but it may still be essential to make a choice, as it was for Buridan's Ass to choose between the two piles of hay, one or the other of which he needed to sustain him. Thus, one is not in such cases arbitrarily making a choice, as where one is indifferent between shark and salmon and simply plumps for the one nearest on the serving plate. Now unless it can be shown that an arbitrary choice cannot produce predominant motivation, it would seem that in choosing the right path I acquire somewhat more motivation to take it than to take the left.

Granted, I do not in any deep way render the chosen path *preferable* – this is why I would so easily change my mind if the other path turned out to have some advantage I had missed. But that may simply show the interesting result that I may rationally prefer x over y without taking x to be preferable (at least intrinsically preferable) to y. Preference need not be based on a believed superiority or even on a vague sense of preferability.

Monitored Intentions

When we think we are likely to forget to do something that we must accomplish as part of a plan, we often monitor ourselves. My plan to give a party requires a stop at a store I rarely go to, so I put notes out for myself. Still, I may think it unlikely that I can remember (and that I'll in the end have to make a special trip when reminded). It may seem that since stopping at the store is something I aim at as part of a plan and take pains to get myself to do, I intend to do it. Doesn't this imply that the performance expectation condition is too strong?

First, note how much like intending hoping can be and how natural it is, when asked if one intends to go to the store, to speak of hoping or trying – or trying to remember to – go there. Second, and more subtle, at the *time* one expresses an intention to go to the store one may believe that one is going to stop there: one may mentally see it happening and may not be not thinking of the tendency to forget such things. That belief may change as one does think of those things. So we might have a case in which the agent sometimes satisfies my account and sometimes does not. The general lesson here is that intending must not be taken to be *static*: as some of my examples have illustrated, we can quickly pass out of a state of intending and quickly pass back into it. It is a merit of my account that it explains how, by appeal to fluctuations in belief and desire (and in other ways, no doubt), this can be explained.

There are two other cases to be noted, in which, despite plausible appearances to the contrary, the agent satisfies the account. One possibility is this: I believe both that I probably will go to the store *and* that there is a significant chance of my forgetting to, and so I take steps to remind myself. Here the second-order, monitoring belief creates the appearance of one's lacking the performance expectation. A second possibility is that although the case is presented as one in which the agent's only relevant belief regarding the likelihood of the action is that it is unlikely, such cases are best read as involving a conditional belief such as this: if one's past behavior is a good guide, it is unlikely one will stop. One need not detach the second proposition from this context, and it is common for people not to make such detachments: even if I believe that if the weather report and lack of sun are good evidence, rain is likely, my optimism may prevent me from flatly believing that rain is likely. This can happen (at least in imperfectly rational people) even if one believes the weather report and lack of sun *are* good evidence of rain. Someone might thus believe that *given* the weather report and lack of sun, rain is likely, yet fail to believe rain is likely, or that given the extensive evidence, marital infidelity is very probable, yet not believe that it has in fact occurred.

We certainly cannot read off a person's first-order beliefs either from the person's higher-order beliefs about the propositions that are objects of the first-order beliefs or from conditional beliefs embedding high probabilities of those propositions. Thus, our agent may satisfy my conditions for intending after all. Quite independently of this, moreover, if, for the reason suggested in framing the example, the agent really does not satisfy the belief condition, then it is at least as plausible to describe such an agent as hoping or trying to *A* rather than as intending to *A*. Hoping can certainly account for all of the relevant behavior.

Acting Against One's Preferences

We do not always get our first choice. Suppose that what I most want to do right now is ski, but my driveway has not been plowed and I cannot get to the slope for two hours. My second choice for the next two hours is skating. Surely I can form the intention to skate for the next two hours, even though it is still true that I want more to ski in the next few hours. We can even imagine someone asking, "What are you doing here – didn't you want to ski this afternoon?" and my replying, "Skiing is what I really want to do, but I can't do it until four, so in intend to skate for two hours first."

I believe that if I speak strictly correctly, I will say that I want*ed* to ski now, or that I wish I could ski now, or that I would prefer to be skiing, but not that I want to ski now more than I want to skate. How can I want to ski now, when I believe this is impossible? I suggest that here *saying* that what I really want to do now is to ski expresses my general *preference* for skiing, which is roughly a motivational disposition such that, if offered the chance to ski now, say by a helicopter coming for me, I would, from that motive, take the opportunity.

There are, however, people who will insist that in such a plight one retains a stronger desire for something one sees is incompatible with what one is doing. Suppose I grant for the sake of argument that this is so. How, then, is my account of intending to be sustained? One response is to say that a desire one believes one cannot fulfill during a time is not *practical* during that time, and then restrict my original account to practical desires. There is plausibility in doing this in explicating intending because the latter is a paradigm of a practical attitude. Certainly the desire to skate is practical, being the motivational ground of my actually skating. And at present my desire to ski is only potentially practical (or is practical in a different way).

Another way to deal with the issue is to substitute, for the notion of an equally strong or stronger incompatible want, that of an equally strong or stronger *competing* want. Plainly, when I believe I can skate but that I cannot both skate and ski, my wanting to ski does not compete with my wanting to skate. This is indeed what seems to explain why I am calmly doing what fulfills a lesser goal. The resulting change in my account is small and certainly in the originally intended direction. Note, for instance, that (on the original account) a temporarily forgotten want does not compete with others, and if I temporarily forget that *x* and *y* are incompatible, then even if I want both, the two wants will not compete (which may of course cause me trouble later).

If this approach is sound, we could now simply say that *intending is a union of an agent's predominantly wanting to A and the agent's believing at least that A-ing is probable* – where predominantly wanting is understood in terms of the absence of an at least equally strong set of competing wants, and where the details of my original account are also taken to apply, with the minor change indicated by substituting the notion of a competing want for that of an incompatible one.[19] The notion of motivational competition is not easy to analyze; this remains a further project. But I see no reason to think that the way it turns out will undermine my basic account.[20]

III. CONCLUSION

If there is a quite general conception of intending that emerges from the points made here, it may be this. Intending is a predominant disposition of the will, where the will is understood as practical in a way mere desires are not: it is directed toward what the agent envisages as at least likely. If the notion of practicality will not appropriately bear this much weight, we might simply call intending *a predominant, expectant disposition of the will*, where the relevant kind of expectation is a matter of having a belief of one of the kinds we have discussed.

Another way to describe in very general terms the conception that has emerged is to say that intending is a *practical commitment of the will*. One reason for the plausibility of this idea is that we think of people who readily abandon their intentions without good reason as irresolute, where that notion is readily understood as suggesting too easy an abandonment of commitments. Another reason is that we tend to take or try to take means to doing what we intend to do: intentions, like commitments, tend to generate more of their kind.

This idea that intending is a practical commitment of the will is as instructive for what it does not say as for what it does: it does not speak of a practical commitment of the *agent*. Our intentions, unfortunately, can fail to reflect what we are, overall, practically committed to; weak-willed intentions are typically one kind of example.[21] To see the difference between the two kinds of commitment, think about the locution once common as a question put by subordinates to their superiors: What is your will? The force of this is roughly to get a statement of intention or something more of the same sort but emphatic, such as a directive or even a command, understood to reflect the intentions of the speaker. My will at a given time can, however, be a poor representation of what, overall, I am committed to. For any plausible notion of commitment, will, like desire, can easily go beyond – or fall beneath – one's overall commitments. Our overall commitments are a holistic matter that depends on the total force of our relevant desires, beliefs, and other elements; our will does not always conform to these elements: it may be misdirected, too weak, too strong, or deficient in other ways.

One reason why it is useful to conceive intentions as practical commitments of the will is that we can thereby discern why a "reductive" account like mine might be unnecessarily resisted. For intentions seem to be the most basic practical commitments, if not of the person, then surely of the will. Analyzing them in terms of wants and beliefs seems to make them *derivative*. That conclusion, however, does not follow, at least if taken to imply that intending is not the most basic kind of practical commitment. Intending may still be basic in this sense: the will is not committed to an action until we intend it; and when, under appropriate conditions, we resolve or promise or swear to do it, thereby acquiring a kind of practical commitment to do it, we also intend to do it.

I would emphasize, however, that even though intending seems to be the most basic practical commitment, it is not the most basic *practical attitude*. That attitude is wanting, in the widest sense. To see this, notice that wants can be reasons for intending, but intending – except insofar as it embodies wanting – cannot be a reason for wanting. Our wants are the typical grounds from which our intentions arise; the main exception to this seems to be the case in which both arise simultaneously from circumstances in which there is a disposition to intend, as where the hungry person unexpectedly sees attractive hors d'oeuvres and immediately comes both to want and intend to take some cheese and crackers. We can have wants without intentions, but not intentions without wants. If we wanted nothing, we would have no intentions.

My last point concerns the relation of intending to beliefs of a kind that many have taken to be possible grounds – and even producers – of intention even apart from desires. Nothing said here implies that certain beliefs – such as beliefs that something would be painful or believing (or judging) that something is one's overall moral obligation – cannot produce intentions, say intentions to avoid it. But surely *in* producing those intentions they also produce the constituent wants. It is, moreover, the desirability or undesirability of the state of affairs in question that makes it reasonable to form an intention to *A* on the basis of a belief that *A*-ing will *promote* that state of affairs.

Intending is a central concept of action theory. To treat it as understandable in terms of still more basic concepts in action theory and the philosophy of mind is not to detract from its importance. If, moreover, we can understand intending better so conceived than taken to be unanalyzable and sui generis, this approach may in the end do it better justice than the initially more flattering stance that it is in no way reducible.[22]

University of Nebraska, Lincoln

NOTES

[1] Aristotle's *Nicomachean Ethics* – though the standard translations do not use 'intending' as opposed, e.g., to 'desiderative desire'; Thomas Aquinas's *Summa*; in many modern philosophers, including Bentham, who is famous for his distinction between direct and oblique intentions, and Mill; and, in the Twentieth Century, a long line of writers beginning with G.E.M. Anscombe's *Intention* (Oxford: Basil Blackwell, 1956).

[2] In "Intending," *Journal of Philosophy* **LXX** (1973).

[3] For defense of one or another element in my account (but not the whole of it) see, e.g., Raimo Tuomela, *Human Action and Its Explanation* (Dordrecht: D. Reidel, 1977) and Wayne A. Davis, "A Causal Theory of Intending," *American Philosophical Quarterly* 21 (1984); and for some of my replies to critics, e.g., H. J. McCann, A. R. Mele, and J. L. A. Garcia, and extensions of the account see my "Wants and Intentions in the Explanation of Action," *Journal for the Theory of Social Behaviour* 9 (1980); "Intending, Intentional Action, and Desire," in Joel E. Marks, ed., *The Ways of Desire* (Chicago: Precedent Publishing Company, 1986); "Deliberative Intentions and Willingness to Act: A Reply to Professor Mele," *Philosophia* 18 (1988); and "Intention, Cognitive Commitment, and Planning," *Synthese* 86 (1991).

[4] This is the account I offered in Audi (1973). The variables have been altered. Only minor, stylistic changes have been made, such as alteration in the variables in the original account. I would now make explicit something only suggested in that paper: the agent need only believe at least that the action is probable – we need a *disjunction of beliefs* here not a *disjunctive belief*.

[5] In this context have in mind *intentionally* causing oneself to form an intention, not doing this in the way one does when, say by breaking a glass, one causes oneself to form an intention to clean up the fragments. One way to see that (intentionally) causing oneself to form an intention is different from simply forming one is to note how the former typically occurs: in artificial cases, as where one is paid to form a certain intention, such as to stand on one's head, hence takes a pill to produce it in oneself. Here one might have a reason to cause oneself to form the intention (that it will pay one) that is *not* a reason to *A*. But typically a reason for forming an intention to *A* is also a reason to *A*, for instance where it is in one's interest to *A* tomorrow, and one cannot *A* then without both forming the intention, now, to do so and making the preliminary steps one takes *A*-ing to require.

[6] A number of action theorists have spoken of such events as intentions, often following Sellars. Myles Brand, for instance, says "I shall follow Sellars in taking the proximate cause of action to be an intending to do something here and now. Let me call this 'immediate intention'. See *Intending and Acting: Toward a Naturalized Action Theory* (Cambridge, Mass: MIT Press, 1984), p. 35. For a detailed more recent discussion see Alfred R. Mele, *Springs of Action* (Oxford and New York: Oxford University Press, 1992), esp. Part II. Further development of Brand's view is given in his "Intention and Intentional Action," in this volume.

[7] This hypothesis receives some confirmation from considerations raised in my "Volition and Agency," in my *Action, Intention, and Reason* (Ithaca and London: Cornell University Press, 1993). That paper explores volition in relation to both intention and action and stresses the importance of volition as a candidate – like immediate intention – to serve as an event cause of action.

[8] An interesting theoretical question here is whether the motivational component of an intention must have a minimum absolute level. I leave this open, but am inclined to think that so long as we may truly speak of *S's wanting to A*, we may, when the other conditions are met, speak of at least a *weak* intention. That strength of intentions varies with want strengths in the way my account suggests is further confirmation of the account.
[9] Something I argue for in detail in "Acting for Reasons," *Philosophical Review* **XCV** (1986).
[10] *Summa* 2.2 q. 64, art. 7.
[11] See ch. 1. Note that he does not say (and I think did not believe) this is the only *intrinsic* good. This distinction in Kant is discussed in some detail in my *Practical Reasoning* (London and New York: Routledge, 1989), ch. 3.
[12] In *Practical Reasoning*, ch. 3.
[13] The matter is not simple, however; some of the complexities of the appropriate principles are discussed in my "Intention, Cognitive Commitment, and Planning," cited above.
[14] Raimo Tuomela's, esp. as presented in his *The Importance of Us* (Stanford: Stanford University Press, 1995).
[15] *Ibid.*, pp. 145–146.
[16] I take this example (which comes from a criticism Gilbert Harman made of Monroe Beardsley's account of intending) and nearly all of the following examples from a paper by Ann Bumpus, given at the Northern New England Philosophical Society Meeting in 1994, in which she summarized and developed a number of objections recently proposed to my account. The sneeze case also occurs in Michael E. Bratman's review of my *Action, Intention, and Reason*, *Ethics* **105** (1995), 928.
[17] See "Wants and Intentions in the Explanation of Action," *Journal for the Theory of Social Behaviour* **9** (1980). A similar example is discussed there; but the solution proposed here seems to me preferable for this case to the passive intention approach.
[18] In "Wants and Intentions," cited above.
[19] Here 'believing at least that' is short for (roughly) this: 'believing something, concerning the likelihood of *A*-ing, at least as strong as that', a formulation slightly broader than the original one.
[20] It might be noticed that I have made no specific mention of mental action; this is because I doubt that it raises any difficulties for my account that need special treatment here. For relevant discussion of how a causalist theory might deal with mental action, see A.R. Mele, "Agency and Mental Action," forthcoming.
[21] Not every weak-willed intention exhibits this property, however, as I have argued in "Weakness of Will and Rationality," in my *Action, Intention, and Reason*, cited above.
[22] This paper began as a reply to Ann Bumpus's presentation, made at the Northern New England Philosophical Society meeting in 1994, of a series of criticisms of my account of intending. Later, expanded versions of the paper were given at the University of Helsinki in 1995 and at Wayne State University in 1996. All three audience discussions were helpful, and for a number of critical responses I particularly want to thank Ann Bumpus, Hugh McCann, James Moor, David Sosa, and Raimo Tuomela.

MYLES BRAND

INTENTION AND INTENTIONAL ACTION

An adequate theory of human action will explain, among other things, how external events and the agent's recent psychological history initiates bodily activity, which, in turn, affects changes in the world. If we take the initiating event to be an intending and the resultant activity to be an intentional action, then any adequate action theory will explain the relationship between intending and acting intentionally. My goal in this paper is to partially specify this relationship.

An attractive approach is to identify the content of an immediate intention with the ensuing intentional action. In which case, a person intentionally *A*ed only if he had a present-directed intention to *A*. I intentionally ordered the burger only if, immediately prior, I had the intention to do so. This approach connects the initiating mental event and the action in a simple and straightforward manner.

Michael Bratman has labeled this approach 'The Simple View,' and he argues against it.[1] Others have criticized Bratman's argument and embraced the Simple View.[2] In the first part of this paper, I make the case that Bratman's critics are right to point out that his argument against the Simple View is unsound. Nonetheless, Bratman is correct to reject the Simple View, though for reasons he does not present.

Being clear why the Simple View is not acceptable requires an understanding of the nature of intending. In the second part of the paper, I provide a brief stretch of intending; and armed with it, I develop an account of the central feature of the relationship between intentional action and intention. Finally, I assess this account using several test cases.

1. THE SIMPLE VIEW

Let me begin by specifying more carefully the Simple View, which identifies the contents of intentional action and intention.

(I) If *S A*'s intentionally during *t*, then *S* intended to *A* immediately prior to or during *t*,

where here (and elsewhere) *S* ranges over subjects (that is, persons), *A* over act-types, *t* over temporal durations, and where universal closure is assumed.

Several explanatory comments are in order. First, and obviously, (I) provides only a necessary condition for intentional action. Another necessary

G. Holmström-Hintikka and R. Tuomela (eds.), Contemporary Action Theory. Vol. I, 197–217.

condition, which if understood in highly expansive terms, yields a sufficient condition, is that the world is friendly toward the agent's *A*ing. Second, temporal parameters play a crucial role. If one believes, as I do, that intention is the causally precipitating event of an intentional action, then the intention must begin prior to the intentional action. But note: the intention will continue through all or some of the time it takes to execute the action. I will say more about this part of the relationship between present-directed intention and intentional action later.

The Simple View is an instance of what Bratman labels 'the Single Phenomenon Theory.' This is the view that there is a common element to the intention and the ensuing intentional action. On the Simple View, this common element is identical contents. Metaphorically speaking, on the Simple View, the content of what goes on in the agent's head when he is immediately intending to act is the content exemplified by the ensuing intentional action. As will be discussed later, the Single Phenomenon Theory permits a relationship between the contents of the intention and the ensuing intentional act that is weaker than identity.

Observe that the Single Phenomenon Theory (and thereby the Simple View) is compatible with the relationship between intending and acting intentionally being causal, but it does not require it. The Single Phenomenon Theory by itself is silent as to what that relationship is. For instance, it is also compatible with the Single Phenomenon Theory that intending is part of acting intentionally, not distinct from it. In which case, an intending could not cause an intentional action because events are causally related only if they are distinct. Bratman adopts a version of the Single Phenomenon Theory; but in so doing, he leaves open the question as to whether a causal account best explains the relationship between intending and acting intentionally.

By contrast, I explicitly adopt a causal account. An intention to act becomes an immediate intention when there is an awareness by the agent that *now* is the time to act.[3] Immediately intending is a complex mental event, only part of which is cognitive. Likewise, an intentional action is, most often, itself complex, in that it consists of a sequence of bodily activities and their consequences. The intending is partly or wholly coincidental temporally with the intentional action, but nonetheless distinct from it. The intending, as it were, is what goes on in the agent's head prior to and during the time of action, but the action itself is the sequence of bodily movements and worldly effects. Again, intentional action is the output of immediate intending. I will say more about this causal approach shortly.

In addition to its straightforwardness, the Simple View also offers the prospect of shedding some light on the connection between moral responsibility, on the one hand, and action and intention, on the other. A precondition of the ascription of moral responsibility is that the agent acts intentionally within a social setting. That is, acting intentionally is not a necessary condition for the attribution of responsibility, since persons can be responsible for omittings and for the actions of others to whom they bear a special relation, for instance, being a parent, nor is it a sufficient condition, since one can act intentionally in isolation without anything happening of moral significance (as when I adjust my glasses while alone in my room). But, if a person acts intentionally and if the action affects more than one person, then, under normal conditions, he or she can be held morally responsible for doing it. Since by (I), intending is necessary for acting intentionally, it follows that a sufficient condition for the ascription of moral responsibility, under normal conditions, is that the agent realized his intention in acting and that that act occurred within a social setting.

However, despite any advantages to the Simple View, Bratman argues that it is untenable. His argument begins by observing that intention, including present-directed intention, must be strongly consistent with one's beliefs about the world. Someone cannot *intend* to leap tall buildings in a single bound, if he knows that it is physiologically impossible to do so. But there can be cases in which each of a person's intentions is rational, yet the contents of these intentions taken together are inconsistent with his beliefs. From this, Bratman concludes that the contents of one's intentions do not necessarily reflect one's intentional acts. That is, the Simple View is false.

Bratman uses an example involving video games to illustrate his point. Suppose that the objective of the game is to direct a (virtual) missile to a (virtual) target. Hitting the target is quite difficult, so our player – call him Mike – decides to attempt two such games simultaneously, one with each hand. Mike is ambidextrous, and by playing two games at once, he believes that he will increase his chances of success. There is a twist to the story: the games are so wired that if the missiles from each game simultaneously hit their targets, both automatically shut off, and Mike loses. Mike is aware of this added dimension to the games, but decides, apparently reasonably, that playing both games simultaneously will enhance his chances to win.

Bratman puts it this way:

> Suppose I do hit target 1 in just the way I was trying to hit it, and in a way which depends heavily on my considerable skill at such games. It seems. . . that I hit target 1 *intentionally*. So, on the Simple View, I must intend to hit target 1. Given the symmetry of the case I must also intend to hit target 2. But given my knowledge that I cannot hit both targets, these intentions fail to be strongly consistent. . . The Simple View imposes too strong a link between intention and intentional action, a link that is insensitive to differences in the demands of practical reason.[4]

My reading of the argument is that it requires the truth of two principles concerning intention. The first is that intentions are strongly consistent with the agent's beliefs about the world; that is,

Strong Consistency of Intention: If *S* intends to *A* at *t*, then *S* has beliefs about the world at *t* such that these beliefs entail that *S*'s intention to *A* at *t* can be realized.

Note that *A* here can be a complex intention involving more than one act-type. The second principle is that intentions are agglomerative, that is, the contents of multiple intentions can be brought together into a single intention:

Agglomeration of Intention: If *S* intends to *A* at *t* and *S* intends to *B* at *t*, then *S* intends to *A* and *B* at *t*.[5]

There are also several assumptions. First,

(A1) The games are symmetrical;

that is, whatever is true of one game is true of the other. And second,

(A2) It is not the case that Mike believes that he can hit targets 1 and 2 simultaneously.

Mike knows about the feature that if both targets are about to be hit simultaneously, both games shut down and he hits neither target.

Suppose now that Mike plays both games simultaneously at noon and

(A3) Mike hits target 1 intentionally at noon, thereby winning.

The argument can be stated as follows:

(1) Mike intends to hit target 1 at noon.
(from (A3) and (I))

(2) Mike intends to hit target 2 at noon.
(from (1) and (A1))

(3) Mike intends to hit targets 1 and 2 simultaneously at noon.
(from (1), (2) and the Principle of Agglomeration)

(4) If Mike intends to hit targets 1 and 2 simultaneously at noon, then he believes that he can hit targets 1 and 2 simultaneously at noon.
(from the Principle of Strong Consistency)

(5) Mike believes that he can hit targets 1 and 2 simultaneously at noon.
(from (3) and (4))

(6) Mike believes that he can hit targets 1 and 2 simultaneously at noon and it is not the case that Mike believes he can hit targets 1 and 2 simultaneously at noon.
(from (5) and (A2))

Bratman identifies the Simple View (I) as the culprit. He holds that there is an intending in the offering, but not the intention to hit target 1 or the intention to hit target 2. Rather, the intentions are more likely *to try to hit target 1* and *to try to hit target 2*.[6] In that case, the resultant conjoined beliefs would be:

(7) Mike believes that he can *try* to hit targets 1 and 2 simultaneously at noon and it is not the case that Mike believes that he can hit targets 1 and 2 simultaneously at noon,

and this statement is not inconsistent. Or, there may be some other, similar intentions in the offering, say, the intention to shoot the missile toward the target. When the agent's intention is not identical with what he does intentionally, no contradiction arises.

Various criticisms might be lodged. Exception can be taken to the Principle of Agglomeration because it is psychologically unrealistic. Persons do not and cannot always bring their intentions together. Sometimes persons have long-term intentions of which they are not aware at every moment and they may fail in fact to bring them together to form a single intention. In the extreme case, the Principle of Agglomeration permits combining all intentions into a single intention, and that surely is unrealistic. No one has a single master plan for all that they intend to do at every moment of one's life. Restricting ourselves to less complex and immediate intentions, there are cases in which bringing such intentions together can inhibit success. We can plausibly take the cognitive content of intending to be a plan. Assuming that the subject has the requisite skill, he or she must separate plans in some circumstances in order to complete them simultaneously, such as my simultaneous plans to rub my stomach clockwise and to rub my head counterclockwise. Some plans, of course, can be integrated. If I intend to purchase a book today at the local bookseller and I also intend to pick up my shirts at the dry cleaners, then it is not only possible, but prudent and rational to integrate these plans into a master plan. But, in general, there is a limitation to plan integration based on one's cognitive capacity.

As stated, then, the Principle of Agglomeration is untoward. The Principle, though, may be recast in a way restricted to those intentions where the cognitive contents (plans) can be integrated, given an individual's cognitive capacity. To develop this reformulation would take us too far afield, though I know of no good reason in principle that would dictate against there being a properly restricted principle of intention agglomeration that is psychologically realistic.[7] This reformulated principle would be weaker than the one used in the video game argument, but nonetheless it would be adequate for the argument. Presumably, Mike's intention to hit target 1 and Mike's intention to hit target 2 are sufficiently similar and complementary that an integrated plan can be formulated.

Another attack on the argument might focus on the Principle of Strong Consistency. There is reason to hold that the real culprit in this *reductio* is this principle, and not the Simple View (I). One way to make that point is to observe that the video game example yields a contradiction without an appeal to the Simple View. The argument's assumptions can be taken as (1) and (2), that Mike intends to hit target 1 and Mike intends to hit target 2, and not as derived from the other assumptions and the Simple View. Indeed, these two assumptions about Mike's intentions are natural because they represent Mike's psychological state when beginning to play the games. The argument then proceeds from (1) and (2), the Principle of Agglomeration (revised to be psychologically realistic), and the Principle of Strong Consistency of Intention directly to the contradictory conclusion. Surely, in this construal of the argument, it is the Principle of Strong Consistency that does the damage.

In defense of Bratman, it might be claimed that the new assumptions

(1) Mike intends to hit target 1 at noon

(2) Mike intends to hit target 2 at noon

do the damage. These assumptions do not adequately describe Mike's state of mind. Rather, his intentions are best represented by

(1′) Mike intends to hit target 1 at noon if he does not hit target 2 at that time;

(2′) Mike intends to hit target 2 at noon if he does not hit target 1 at that time.

These conditional intentions when agglomerated do not contradict Mike's belief that he cannot hit both targets simultaneously.[8]

This is a weak defense, however. First, it is highly plausible that Mike has the flat-out intentions (1) and (2). While he might have the conditional intentions (1′) and (2′) on another occasion, the case which we are considering is the one in which he plans to hit target 1 by manipulating the first game's joy-stick and he plans to hit target 2 by manipulating the second game's joy-stick. Second, even if, contrary to the case, Mike has the conditional intentions (1′) and (2′), that only serves to defend the Principle of Strong Consistency. The Simple View plays no role in the reconstructed argument, which starts with the assumptions of Mike's intentions rather than deriving them from the Simple View.

Hugh McCann also identifies the Principle of Strong Consistency as the problematic step in the argument. He says:

> It is important to realize that such cases [as the video game] need not be taken as refuting the Simple View. The alternative is to claim them as exceptions to the constraints of internal and epistemic consistency. Indeed, in Bratman's formulation both requirements carry clearly stated

ceteris paribus clauses, and he claims that both are defeasible, in that "there may be special circumstances in which it is rational of an agent to violate them" [Bratman 1987, 32].[9]

Basically, then, there are exceptions to the Principle of Strong Consistency that result when it is pragmatically advantageous to so plan. To adapt one of Bratman's examples, suppose a large log rolled onto my driveway because of last night's storm.[10] I believe that I cannot move a log of that size; yet, because of the critical need to get my car out of the garage, I intend to move it. I do not merely intend to try to move it; I intend to move the log, *flat-out*. I formulate a plan, which includes grabbing one end and moving that end, then grabbing the other end and doing the same, and so on successively. Much to my surprise, I succeed in moving it in this way. My moving the log is intentional, despite my initial belief to the contrary. Similar reasoning applies to the video game case. Despite Mike's beliefs to the contrary, he intends flat-out to hit target 1 and to hit target 2.

The Principle of Strong Consistency captures an important generalization about intentions and plans. Generally speaking, as Bratman points out, planning takes place in the context of an agent's beliefs about the world and about himself. We do not make our plans, nor form our intentions, without cognizance of the impediments and opportunities the world presents. Nonetheless, the Principle of Strong Consistency must be modified to permit intentions contrary to our beliefs in certain types of cases in order to ensure psychological realism. In sum, a properly revised Principle of Strong Consistency does not yield step (4) in the argument; and thus, the video game case does not present a problem for the Simple View.

McCann's criticism of the argument is undertaken in the service of a defense of the Simple View, as the cited passage makes clear. Here I disagree. While McCann is correct that the video game argument does not defeat the Simple View, there are other good reasons to reject it.

The Simple View, recall, is

(I) If *S A*'s intentionally during *t*, then *S* intended to *A* immediately prior to or during *t*.

The primary problem with (I), I contend, is that it fails to capture the differences in 'chunking' intentions and intentional actions. Our plans proceed at certain levels of generality because of our psychological limitations. Plans are stored in long-term memory, which places constraints on the complexity and structure of these representations. But individuation of intentional action depends, in part, on external, non-psychological constraints imposed on the action insofar as it is a precondition for moral responsibility.[11]

Suppose that I intend now to walk to the corner postbox to deposit a letter. How specific and detailed is my intention? Presuming this situation to be normal in all ways, my intention is rather undetailed. The cognitive content of my intention – my plan – includes several *nodes*, or key contained actions, that are constitutive of this overall action, namely my leaving the house, my walking, my arriving at the postbox, and my inserting the letter in the postbox. Each of these nodes, when completed, constitutes an intentional action, which the Simple View correctly yields. However, there are also intentional actions performed as part of the overall action of walking to the postbox that are not included in my plan. Each step I take is intentional. But taking intermediate, particular steps is not included specifically in my plan. Similarly, improvised actions, such as avoiding the potholes in the sidewalk, are intentional; but they too were not included in my overall plan.

A plan for even a relatively simple activity, such as walking to the corner postbox, cannot realistically include all the contained and improvised actions that are in fact needed to achieve the goal. Persons have limited cognitive resources. They are able to carry out their intentions successfully because their representations of future activity tend to be chunked macroscopically. If a person had to preconceive each minute, contained action and each possible improvised action prior to undertaking every activity, he would find himself constantly in the posture of Rodin's *Thinker*, merely contemplating what to do without ever doing anything.

Each node in a plan triggers a program for the performance of the contained, specific physical actions. The node for walking includes specific instructions for putting one foot in front of another. The precise placement of each foot is to be determined, in part, by the perceived state of the ground at those moments. The intention for the overall activity includes a monitoring and guidance mechanism for the agent's steps, but not prior representations of each step. It would be absurd to characterize my intention to walk to the postbox as including explicitly my putting my left foot in front of my right one on the 23rd step or my stepping around a pothole that was unknown when I began the walk.

Yet, each of the microscopically contained intermediate physical actions during my walk was intentional. None were accidental or haphazard. Specific actions contained within nodes of complex activities inherit their intentionality from these nodes. Intentionality is ascribed to action on the basis of what an agent can *in principle* be held responsible for. This ascription of intentionality depends, in part, on a schema for individuating action on the basis of social context. Since there is the possibility that the subject is to be held responsible for the 23rd step, for whatever reason, it is to be identified as an intentional action. By contrast, an agent's intention is limited by his cognitive capacity. There will be differences, then, in how we divide intentions on the basis of normal cognitive functioning and how we divide intentional actions on the basis of ascription in principle of moral responsibility.

It might be objected that, although I did not intend to take the 23rd step prior to my beginning the activity, and in that way taking the 23rd step was not part of my initial plan, I did form the intention to take that step immediately before doing so. Similarly, avoiding the pothole was not preconceived, but when I saw the pothole and stepped over it, I formed the intention at that precise moment to step over it.

This objection, however, confuses the monitoring and guidance function of intention with the planning function. There is a dual cognitive component of intending. Firstly, there is a high-level representational feature which consists in having a plan prior to and during the action. I have been stressing this cognitive aspect. But secondly, intending also involves monitoring and guidance, that is, feedback mechanisms that accompany the ongoing activity. But monitoring and guidance by itself is not sufficient for an activity to be intended. A person intends to do something only if he has a representation of it within one of his plans. The monitoring and guidance typical of ongoing specific physical actions is the running of a motor program, as it were, for successfully completing the intended action.

To sum up, the Simple View is not subject to Bratman's criticism. He argued, basically, that intentions, but not intentional actions, are subject to the constraints of agglomeration and strong consistency with beliefs. But these constraints do not hold universally for intention. Nonetheless, Bratman is correct in rejecting the Simple View. Intentions and intentional actions are chunked differently. Intentions are individuated in terms of cognitive representations, which because of realistic psychological capacity limitations, are macroscopic; intentional actions are individuated in terms of preconditions for the ascription of moral responsibility, which is a microscopic means of counting.

The Simple View, then, is unacceptable, in that the content of an intention is not identical to that of the ensuing intentional action. Nonetheless, there is always some intention in the offering when we act intentionally. I turn, now, to the manner in which that intention is to be specified.

2. THE RELATIONSHIP BETWEEN INTENTION AND INTENTIONAL ACTION

Bratman proposes that intention and intentional action are related by means of the 'motivational potential.'[12] I interpret his claim to be

(I*) If *S A*'s intentionally during *t*, then there is an act-type *B* such that *S* intended to *B* immediately prior to or during *t* and *S*'s *A*ing is within the motivational potential of *S*'s *B*ing.

I took the 23rd step intentionally because my doing so was within the motivational potential of my walking to the postbox. Note that (I*) permits $A = B$, in which cases (I*) yields the same result as the Simple View (I). It would appear that these instances are restricted to either basic actions, or cases in which *A* is itself the entire complex activity. Intermediate actions and improvised actions, cases which proved damaging to the Simple View, would presumably be accommodated by (I*).

They would be accommodated by (I*), that is, if there is a viable explication of the notion of motivational potential. Bratman provides the following:

(8) *A* is in the motivational potential of *S*'s intention to *B iff* given *S*'s beliefs and desires, it is possible for *S* to *A* intentionally in the course of executing his intention to *B*.[13]

But this explication is uninformative. It does not explain why those actions that, though not included within the agent's plan, are nonetheless to be included among his intentional doings. Put baldly, (8) begs the question. Bratman recognizes this problem when he says that his explication of motivational potential is a "theoretical placeholder."

Bratman's (I*) is an instance of the Single Phenomenon Theory of the relation between intention and intentional action. As in the case of the Simple View, the contents of the intention and the realized intentional action are identical. However, in the case of (I*), there can be an intervening, covering intention whose content connects to actions that are not explicitly preconceived.

The Single Phenomenon Theory, as noted earlier, is compatible with a causal theory of action, but is not committed to it. By contrast, I advocate such an approach. Although this is not the place to try to develop a fully articulated causal theory, let me add to the earlier sketch by saying something more about intending.[14] For this discussion, let us limit consideration to moderately complex actions performed under normal conditions.

Intending is the focal mental event in the causal sequence emanating in physical action. The full sequence starts with standing background conditions, including, but not limited to, the agent's personality traits, his long-term physiological and psychological needs, his emotional state, and his long-term beliefs, both dispositional and occurrent. These background conditions generate desire and belief matrices, which, when combined with current needs and perceptual beliefs, yield desires (or wants) and beliefs about undertaking a present course of action.

Desires and beliefs are intention-generators. I contend that an intention is not reducible to a combination of desire and belief, but rather derivative from them. Beliefs have the wrong cognitive structure to be action-initiators; for one thing, the representational complexity of a plan exceeds that permitted by the commonsense notion of belief. Desires, even one's strongest desires, are preferences; and preferences by themselves do not motivate action. But these claims are controversial and they need considerable defense.[15]

An intention is then generated. This prospective, future-directed intention has both cognitive and conative components. The cognitive component itself is dual. In part, it is the representation of a plan. This type of representation bears significant similarity to a story or episode in long-term memory, except that it is future-directed and necessarily the agent himself is the protagonist of the episode.

The conative component of intending is more difficult to explain. It is the motivational impetus that initiates and sustains the activity. Cognitive plans, like beliefs, are not themselves sufficient for action. A person may have a detailed plan to rob the First National Bank. But no matter how carefully this plan is formulated, unless the agent is motivated to act, he will do nothing. I would argue that motivation is rooted, somehow, in one's biological functions. Motivation to act appears to be derivative of the type of organism we are, with our particular bodily needs and drives.[16]

Intention, as already noted, is doubly temporally indexed. That is, the form of an intention description is

(9) At t_1, S intends to A during t_2,

where t_1 is the time at which the subject is intending and t_2 the time of the intended action. When $t_1 < t_2$, the intention is prospective or future-directed. As the differential between t_1 and t_2 decreases to zero, the intention becomes immediate, or present-directed. When that occurs, the conative (motivational) component of intending initiates the motor programs that are necessary for the bodily activity required by the plan. The running of these motor programs, complete with self-corrective feedback loops that monitor and guide the activity to completion, is the second part of the cognitive component. Immediate intention, that is, involves a cognitive feature associated with the monitoring and guidance of bodily activity, in addition to sustained plan representation which is the critical cognitive feature of prospective intention.

Returning now to the central issue of the relationship between intentional action and intention, intentional actions are those which are either explicitly planned or part of a pattern of planned activity. In walking to the corner postbox for the mail, nodal actions such as leaving the house and opening the postbox, are explicitly planned, in that they are included within my representation of what I will do. My taking the 23rd step is not explicitly represented in my plan; I do not have, in the normal case, a preconception of taking that step. But my taking the 23rd step is intentional in virtue of its being part of the pattern of planned activity I have undertaken. While not explicitly planned, my taking this step is triggered by the appropriate motor program and monitored and guided to completion. Similar comments apply to improvised actions, such as stepping over an unexpected pothole. The task then becomes to account for the inclusion of specific actions within a pattern of intended activity, when these actions are not explicitly part of the initial plan.

By way of illustration, consider my action of driving to the Indianapolis campus from Bloomington, an action that I have performed many times. The trip takes about an hour, and it includes a number of steps. Each step is a node in my routine for completing this activity, for example, drive on Route 37 until West Avenue. But a lot can happen on Route 37. Each time I step on the brake or gas, I am performing a necessary intermediate action. These contained actions are intentional. Suppose that Route 37 is blocked, and I must take an unexpected detour. This part of my trip is not planned, and I must substitute new actions for the planned ones in order to reach Indianapolis. Each of the substituted actions is intentional. Or suppose that midway into the trip a traffic blockage develops. I notice a restaurant at the side of the road, and I form a new plan to have coffee and pie while waiting for the traffic to dissipate. Finished with this treat, I resume the trip. Interruption to the original plan does not change the intentional status of those actions in the latter part of the plan. That is, in addition to nodal actions being intentional, those actions that are intermediate and those that substituted into the plan form part of the pattern of planned activity. Moreover, a plan can be interrupted without the loss of intentional status for the remaining elements of the plan. Intuitively, then, an action is intentional only if it is explicitly part of an agent's plan or it is part of the overall pattern of activity constituting the plan, where an action is part of this pattern of activity if it is an intermediate action or a substitutional action. An interruption to a plan does not, normally, disqualify the remainder of the plan from intentional status.

Let me try to state these intuitions somewhat more carefully. To begin, we need the notion of an action plan. A first approximation is:

(D1) P is an action plan for Aing *iff* P is a tree structure constructed from $(A_1, A_2, \ldots, A_n, A)$, where each A_{i+1} is dependent on A_i and A is dependent on A_n.

Each A_i is nodal action, and A is the plan's goal. This definition generalizes on the intuitive idea of an action plan, in that the tree structure can be branching, thereby permitting disjunctive plans involving decision points, and conjunctive plans, in which various segments go forward simultaneously. Note that this definition permits trivial plans involving only one nodal action.[17]

The notion of dependency between actions in this definition is to be understood in terms of a relation between events that encompasses causal necessity and conventionality. That is, for any event types F and G, F is dependent on G *iff either* there is a causal law that entails that it is causally necessary that, for every event x, if x is of type F, then there is an event y such that y is of type G *or* there is a convention such that, for every event x, if x is of type F, then there is an event y such that y is of type G. An example of conventionally related actions is Stravinsky's lowering his arm and Stravinsky's signaling to the cellos, where the convention is that a conductor signals to the musicians in the orchestra by the movement of his baton.[18]

Now, the principle governing the inclusion of intermediate actions within plans is:

(IN) *If* S has an action plan P such that (i) P includes S's $A_i$ing, S's A_{i+1}ing, but not S's A^*ing and (ii) S's A_{i+1}ing depends on S A^*ing and S's A^*ing depends on S $A_i$ing, *then* S's A^*ing is an intentional action.

(The temporal parameters are suppressed in these principles for simplicity.) For example, my stepping on the accelerator during a certain portion of my trip on Route 37 is not included in my original action plan, in that it is not represented as a nodal action, but nonetheless it is intentional because it is a necessary intermediary for completing the plan.

The principles governing substitution within an action plan are the following.

(S.1) S's A^*ing is a substitute action for S's $A_i$ing with respect to his action plan P *iff* S adopts an action plan P^* that differs from P only in containing his A^*ing where P contains S's $A_i$ing and where S is not able to A_i or S prefers A^*ing to $A_i$ing.

(S.2) *If* S's A^*ing is a substitute action for S's $A_i$ing with respect to his action plan P, *then* S's A^*ing is an intentional action.

For example, when I am forced to take a detour, and thus unable to follow Route 37, I alter my plan to include the detour trip. The drive during the detour leg, then, is intentional, despite its lack of representation in the original plan.

Two points need to be made. First, I leave the notion of adopting a substitute plan, or for that matter, any plan, at the intuitive level. Much can, and should, be said about the psychological conditions and rationality constraints of plan adoption. Second, principle (S.1) restricts substitution to cases in which the agent is unable to perform the planned action, in the sense that he lacks the opportunity or ability to do so, or he prefers at that time the substituted action. It might be argued that this principle should be strengthened so that substitution is permitted, not on the basis of preference alone, but only if the preference is the result of rational deliberation. Or, it might be maintained that this principle should be weakened so that adopting a new plan for any reason – or no reason at all – yields a substitute action. But here I pass no final judgment on these modifications of (S.1).

These three principles can operate in tandem. The principles affecting substitution apply only to nodes in the plan. Once one or more nodes are replaced by substitution, then new intermediary actions are identified as intentional by means of (IN).

Finally, consider plan interruption.

(INT) *If* S has an action plan P such that (i) S's $A_i$ing and his $A_j$ing are contained in P, but his A^*ing is not contained in P, (ii) S A^*s between or during his $A_i$ing and his $A_j$ing and (iii) S's A^*ing is dependent on either S's $A_i$ing or his $A_j$ing, *then* S's $A_i$ing and S's $A_j$ing are intentional actions.

That is, an action retains its status as intentional provided only that it is part of a plan, even if that plan is interrupted. The interrupting actions, of course, can be themselves intentional. Thus, my halting my trip temporarily for coffee and pie is intentional, and it does not disqualify the intentional status of the actions I performed when completing my trip. Principle (INT) differs from the previous principles in that it does not assign intentional status to actions initially not included in the plan, but rather preserves intentional status despite deviations in the plan.

These principles can be reiterated. But taken to the extreme, reiteration yields that an action plan can be wholly replaced by another plan and a plan can be interrupted indefinitely many times. Can these extremes be permitted, or are there points at which plans are no longer in effect? The answer, clearly, is the latter, that after a certain degree of substitution or interruption, either in the duration or quantity, the initial action plan is no longer operative. However, there does not appear to be any definitive point for all plans at which this change occurs. Rather, the point for each plan – or better, the range for each plan, since there will be gray areas – depends on contextual factors such as the complexity of the plan, its timeliness, the importance of its goal for other plans, the plans of others with whom the agent is interacting, and so on. If my plan to drive to Indianapolis dissolves into my traveling by train through a route that takes me to Chicago, then what I do is intentional, not in virtue of substitution into my original plan, but rather because of a new travel plan. Or if my drive is interrupted after a short time by other, pressing obligations that bring me back home, and I do not begin to drive to Indianapolis again for several weeks, my original plan has been abandoned and, at that later time, a new plan is followed. That is, these principles need to be supplemented by criteria that specify their limitations.

Intuitively, then, an action is intentional only if it falls within the scope of an action plan, which is the representational component of a prospective intention, or it falls within the pattern of activity for realizing that plan, which is controlled by the monitoring and guidance resulting from immediate intentions. To put the matter more carefully,

(I**) *If* S As intentionally during t, *then* S has an intention prior to or during t such that the cognitive content of S's intention is his action plan P, where either (i) S's Aing is contained in P or (ii) S's Aing satisfies (IN), (S.1) and (S.2), or (INT).

Again, an action is intentional in virtue of its relationship to the representational content of a prospective intention; or in those cases in which the action is not explicitly preconceived, it is intentional in virtue of its being part of the pattern of activity constituting the overall activity.

Bratman's attempt to extend the relationship beyond that provided in the Simple View appealed, if only loosely, to the motivational features of intending. By contrast, I have focused on the cognitive features. Motivation appears to be too undifferentiated to serve the function of specifying the scope of intentional action. The cognitive aspect of intention provides specific guides to discharging the motivation. As such, the cognitive aspect differentiates among actions, thereby providing a basis for the identification of intentional actions.

Do any actions fail to meet the necessary condition cited in (I**), that is, are all actions intentional? To answer, let us first be clear that we are talking about actions, and not mere bodily movements, such as those caused by muscle spasms and reflexes or cases in which someone or something moves our limbs. On the basis of (I**), an action that is not intentional is one that neither was planned nor within the scope of planned activity. The extent of intentional action, then, is quite broad; but, I suggest, it is not universal. Some actions are not planned; for example, in falling forward one puts one's hands in front to break the fall. There is no preconceived action plan that is brought to bear in this case. Similarly, impulsive actions, such as turning to look at an accident when driving, or highly habituated actions, such as tugging on one's ear, are not driven by action plans.

I contended earlier that all actions are caused by intentions. But not all intentions include action plans. Only prospective intentions and immediate intentions derivative from prospective intentions include action plans. Immediate intentions not so generated include a cognitive component involving the monitoring and guidance of the physical activity, but not an action plan. In the case of extending one's arms upon falling, agreeing for the moment that it is an action and not a mere instinctive reflex, the bodily activity is monitored and guided to completion, without there being a full-blown plan which the agent is following.

It might be claimed, however, that there is a plan, a representational structure, even in this simple case. That plan is embedded in episodic memory and it is retrieved on such occasions. In response, I would contend that there is a cognitive structure, a motor program, but not a plan, that is activated on this occasion. This type of cognitive structure, I speculate, is not stored in long-term memory, which is a central processing function, but rather as part of the action output system. In any case, an action plan is a representational structure to which one attends and about which one often deliberates; the motor program is not, normally, something to which one attends prior to or during a specific bodily activity, and it is not something about which one normally deliberates.[19]

Observe that, generally speaking, coerced actions satisfy the necessary condition cited in (I**). Suppose that I am threatened with mean and nasty consequences unless I open the safe. It is a huge safe, with complex combination locks. In order to open it, I must draw from memory the correct sequence of operations and then I must follow that routine. That is, I must have an action plan in order to open it. But clearly, from the fact that coerced actions satisfy the consequent of (I**), it does not follow that coerced actions are intentional. For (I**) does not provide a sufficient condition. There may well be other necessary conditions for an action being intentional that precludes coerced actions from that status.

Let me conclude the discussion of (I**) with several test cases. Consider accidents. Suppose that I reach for the light switch; but in doing so, I accidentally knock over the vase and shatter it. My reaching for the light switch is intentional, but my knocking over the vase is not. And that is what (I**) yields. Presumably I had a plan that included as a nodal action, flipping the light switch, but this plan did not include, nor did I have any other plan that included, my knocking over the vase. Nor does knocking over the vase fall within the pattern of activity I undertake. It is not an intermediate action, in that, although causally related to what I am doing at that time, it is not causally related to a later part of my action. It is also not something I substitute into my plan.

The same reasoning applies to 'happy accident' cases. Chisholm's well-known example concerns a nephew who wants to kill his rich uncle in order to inherit the family fortune.[20] He knows that his uncle is home today, so he gets into his car to drive to his uncle's house in order to undertake the dastardly deed. The thought of killing his uncle causes him to drive recklessly and he runs down a pedestrian, who, it turns out, is his uncle. Here the nephew intended to kill his uncle and he in fact killed him. But his action was not intentional; he killed his uncle by accident. And that is just what (I**) delivers.

The main point is that the nephews' plan for killing his uncle included driving to his house and undertaking the deed there and then. It did not include running down his uncle with his car. Furthermore, running down his uncle neither qualifies as an intermediate or substitutive action, nor as the completion of an interrupted plan. With respect to being an intermediate action, running down his uncle depends on an earlier node in the plan, driving to his uncle's house, but running him down does *not* bear a dependency relation to any next node in the plan, for instance, entering his uncle's house. With regard to being a substitute action, the nephew does not formulate a substitute plan in which he runs down his uncle. The nephew *might* have had a disjunctive plan in which he either went to his uncle's house to kill him or run him down in the street, whichever came first. But in fact he had only the single sequential plan that excluded his running down his uncle. Further, although the end-state of the plan was realized, it was not done by following a plan that was interrupted and then brought to completion. The nephew's running down his uncle in fact prevented him from completing his plan of killing him at home.

Action plans are representational constructs in 'the language of thought.' I will not speculate here about the proprietary vocabulary or the syntax and semantics of the language of thought, except to note that it is an intensional language. In particular, co-referring singular terms cannot be substituted *salva veritate*. This feature of our thinking has consequences for intentional action. Suppose that Susan wants to pay homage to Mark Twain by establishing a scholarship in creative writing at Indiana University. Her establishing a scholarship in honor of Twain meets the condition stated in (I**), and indeed this action is intentional. However, suppose too that Susan does not know that Mark Twain is identical to Samuel Clemens. Her establishing a scholarship fund, then, in honor of Samuel Clemens is not an intentional action; for her action plan does not include this act. The fact that Mark Twain *is* Samuel Clemens does not alter the situation. Susan's establishing a scholarship that honors Samuel Clemens is an accidental consequence of her intentionally establishing a scholarship in honor of Twain.

Not knowing that Clemens is the same person as Twain, Susan did not foresee this consequence of her action. However, it would appear that sometimes we do foresee the consequences of our actions, even though these consequences are not part of what we do, and thus not intentional. Bratman describes a case in which a runner intends to use a certain pair of shoes, which are family heirlooms, when competing in a marathon.[21] He holds that wearing down the rubber on the bottom of the shoes is foreseen by the runner, but his doing so is a consequence of his action, not part of what he did intentionally. Here my analysis may yield a different result. While it is true that wearing down his shoes is not part of the runner's plan, it does fall within the normal pattern of his activity. There are causal connections between each step and the removal of small amounts of the rubber. The necessary condition for intentional action stated by (I**) is, then, satisfied on the basis (IN). However, the final disposition of this case depends on whether there are other, unstated necessary conditions for intentionality which are unsatisfied.

Despite potential disagreement with Bratman about this example, there seem to be other instances of foreseen but unintentional consequences. Suppose that I pay a large tax bill on a particular occasion, not with great pleasure, but intentionally. A foreseen consequence of my paying this bill is that certain government programs of which I disapprove receive funding. I do not intentionally provide funding for these programs; rather, providing this funding is an unavoidable, but foreseen consequence of what I do intentionally. This case differs from the runner's wearing down his shoes in that removing minute amounts of rubber are necessary intermediate actions, which taken together constitute wearing down the shoes. Supporting the government programs is not an intermediate action, but rather a causal (or conventional) consequence of my intentionally paying the tax bill.

There will be difficult cases, and much gray area in determining which effects are merely foreseen, unintended consequences, and which are intentional in virtue of falling within the scope of the agent's planned activity. But we should not expect that there is a sharp psychological distinction between a plan and immediate foreseen consequences.

3. SUMMARY AND CONCLUSIONS

The Simple View relates intention and intentional action in a straightforward way, namely a person intentionally *A*ed only if he intended to *A*. Bratman argues that the Simple View is untenable because it conflicts with two principles governing intention, namely that separate intentions can be agglomerated into a single intention and that intention must be consistent with the agent's beliefs. He illustrates this argument by means of a video game in which the agent intends to perform simultaneous actions that he knows to be impossible to complete jointly. However, the problem to which Bratman points lies not with the Simple View, but rather the strong statement of belief and intention consistency. Put another way, Bratman's argument fails to show that the Simple View is false if the principles of intention agglomeration and consistency with belief are made psychologically realistic.

Even though Bratman's main argument against the Simple View fails, he is right to reject it. For the Simple View fails to take account of the fact that intentional action is more finely individuated than intention. Intentional actions are 'chunked' on the basis of being preconditions for responsibility. Intentions are individuated on the basis of our action plans. Given persons' normal processing limitations, these chunks may well be macroscopic as compared with his intentional actions.

Bratman adheres to the single Phenomenon Theory, in which there is commonality of content between intention and the ensuing intentional action. This approach is consistent with a causal theory of action, but it is not committed to a causal theory. By contrast, I suggest that the best way to understand the relationship between intention and intentional action is by means of a causal account.

Intending is a complex event involving a prospective cognitive component of having a plan and an immediate cognitive component of monitoring and guiding ongoing activity. In addition, intending has a conative, or motivational, feature derivative of our biology that yields fulfillment of the plan. Bratman suggests that a focus on the motivational aspect of intention provides an adequate successor to the Simple View. By contrast, I contend that it is the cognitive features of intending that play this role. In particular, an action is intentional only if it is part of the agent's plan or it falls within the pattern of activity that occurs in his executing the plan. To fall within this pattern of activity is to be an intermediary action necessary for the completion of the plan or an action substituted for a preconceived one because of an unexpected impediment or a preferred change. Further, plans can be interrupted, to some extent, yet be completed. Such deviations do not override the intentional status of the actions performed in following the plan. In general, this account of the relation between intention and intentional action flows from an understanding of the causal role of intention, in particular the cognitive component of intention that constitutes an agent's having a plan.[22]

Indiana University

NOTES

1 Michael Bratman (1987). See especially Chapter 8, "Two Faces of Intention."

2 For example, Hugh J. McCann (1991), and J.L.A. Garcia (1990).

3 Cf. Wilfrid Sellars (1966). Sellars calls the immediate intention generated by a prospective intention a 'volition.'

4 *Op. cit.*, 114–115.

5 These principles, and the discussion throughout, focus on conceptual truths about intention. Given Bratman's overall project to offer a rational planning theory of intention, he might be interpreted as providing constraints on the rationality of intention. Thus, the principle concerning consistency would be restated by something like the following:

> If S's intention to A at t is rational, then S's beliefs about the world at t are such that his intention to A at t can be realized.

I suggest that these principles go beyond constraints on rationality, and speak to the nature of intention. Intentions, unlike desires, are to be consistent with each other and with our beliefs about the world. (Bratman certainly appears to be talking about conceptual truths concerning intention on a number of occasions, e.g., Bratman 1987, 113). In any case, it is not merely rational constraints, but conceptual ones that matter in assessing the Simple View and its alternatives.

If, however, the proper reading of Bratman is that he is limiting the discussion to rational intentions and beliefs, then let us make the assumption, fully suitable for the purposes here, that our subject is rational and acts rationally, and that only rational intentions and beliefs are considered.

6 Bratman (1987, 120).

7 Bratman recognizes these points (1987, 134–138) and appears to opt for a restricted version of the Principle of Agglomeration.

8 Cf. Garcia (1990, 203–204).

9 McCann (1991, 28).

10 *Op. cit.*, 39.

11 See Brand (1984, Chapters 7 and 8) for a fuller discussion of the cognitive component of intention. Also, cf. Brand (1986).

12 Bratman (1987, 119–126).

[13] *Ibid.*, 119–120.
[14] See Brand (1984) for such a defense. Cf. Brand (1989).
[15] For a strong defense of the reduction of intention to desire and belief, see Robert Audi (1993). Audi too defends a causal theory of action.
[16] Drive and need are key constructs within neobehaviorist learning theory. However, I do not mean to evoke this approach, which is highly problematic, in basing motivation on physiological determinants. Cf. Brand (1984, Chapter 9).
[17] Initial work on action plans was done by Alvin Goldman (1970). Cf., too, Raimo Tuomela (1977). Also see Goldman (1976) for a discussion of the relationship between intentions and the intermediate actions.
[18] I have argued at length elsewhere that events (including actions) are to be individuated in a fine-grained way. See, for example, Brand (1984, Chapter 3) and (1977). Events resemble physical objects in that they are spatiotemporally located particulars. But they differ from physical objects in that they do not wholly occupy the spatiotemporal region in which they occur; two events, such as its growing dark in Bloomington and its becoming warmer in Bloomington, can occur at the same time and place. Thus, identity conditions for events must be stricter than those for physical objects. My view is that the identity conditions for physical objects are spatiotemporal coincidences and the identity conditions for events are necessary spatiotemporal coincidences. On this basis, Stravinsky's lowering his arm and Stravinsky's signaling to the cellos are distinct, for it is possible for one to occur in a spatiotemporal region without the other also occurring.
[19] Motor programs such as putting one's arms forward when falling appear to have features that make them modular: they are domain specific; their operation is mandatory; they are fast; they are associated with fixed neutral architecture; and they are informationally encapsulated. Cf. Jerry Fodor (1983). Fodor limits his discussion to input systems, such as vision. I take it that his points about modularity, to the extent that it is a useful notion, can be extended to output systems.
[20] Roderick Chisholm (1966, 29–30).
[21] Bratman (1987, 123). Cf. Garcia (1990, 204–205).
[22] I am grateful for the helpful comments of Robert Audi, Michael Bratman, Hugh McCann and Raimo Tuomela on drafts of this paper. I also appreciate the commentary of Dennis Senchuk and audience queries when the paper was presented at the Mind and Action Conference, Indiana University Bloomington, October 1996.

REFERENCES

Audi, Robert (1993), *Action, Intention and Reason*. Ithaca, N.Y., Cornell University Press.

Brand, Myles (1977), "Identity Conditions for Events," *American Philosophical Quarterly* **14**, 329–337.

Brand, Myles (1984), *Intending and Acting: Toward a Naturalized Action Theory*. Cambridge, Mass., MIT Press.

Brand, Myles (1986), "Intentional Actions and Plans," *Midwest Studies in Philosophy* **X**, 213–230.

Brand, Myles (1989), "Proximate Causation of Action," *Philosophical Perspectives* **3**, 423–432.

Bratman, Michael (1987), *Intention, Plans, and Practical Reason*. Cambridge, Harvard University Press.

Chisholm, Roderick M. (1966), "Freedom and Action" in K. Lehrer (1966), pp. 11–44.

Fodor, Jerry (1983), *The Modularity of Mind*. Cambridge, Mass., MIT Press.

Garcia, J.L.A. (1990), "The Intentional and the Intended," *Erkenntnis* **33**, 191–209.

Goldman, Alvin (1970), *A Theory of Human Action*. Englewood Cliffs, N.J., Prentice-Hall.

Goldman, Alvin (1976), "The Volitional Theory Revisited" in M. Brand and D. Walton (eds.), *Action Theory*. Dordrecht, Holland, D. Reidel.

Lehrer, K. (ed.) (1966), *Freedom and Determinism*. New York, Random House.
McCann, Hugh J. (1991), "Settled Objectives and Rational Constraints," *American Philosophical Quarterly* **28**, 25–34.
Sellars, Wilfrid (1966), "Thought and Action" in K. Lehrer (1966), pp. 105–139.
Tuomela, Raimo (1977), *Human Action and Its Explanation*. Dordrecht, Holland, D. Reidel.

HUGH J. MCCANN

ON WHEN THE WILL IS FREE

Defenders of libertarian free will are generally of the view that the sort of freedom they uphold attends most, if not all, of our decisions and actions. Exceptions, if any, are apt to be claimed only for cases of duress or compulsion, in which it might be thought that the will is somehow bowled over by the strength of a particular motive. Recently, however, Peter van Inwagen has suggested that libertarian freedom is a rare condition at best, one that can obtain only in unusual circumstances (van Inwagen 1989).[1] The reason is simply that in the great majority of situations of decision and action, what to do is absolutely clear to us; and, van Inwagen argues, when this is so we cannot do otherwise. This result is disheartening, the more so since it is also a common sense belief that most operations of the will are free. If, on an incompatibilist account of freedom, this cannot be, prospects for a convincing defense of libertarianism are considerably diminished. Accordingly, it is worth considering whether the challenge presented by van Inwagen's argument can be met. I shall try to argue that it can.

I. THE PROBLEM

The alternatives we face in deliberation are presented to us in our reasons. Desires and other conative states embody the objectives we deem worthy of pursuit, and our beliefs portray ostensible means to their achievement. The problem van Inwagen raises is simply that in a great many cases, only the course of action an agent actually chooses counts as a meaningful alternative. Others are either lacking entirely, or else have no conative backing. In such cases, van Inwagen urges, an incompatibilist ought to conclude we *must* act as we do (p. 415). The leading example in terms of which he argues for this conclusion is one in which "duty is unopposed by inclination" (p. 411). In van Inwagen's original discussion of the case (there is a variation to be considered later), the agent is a university professor, who is importuned by a colleague to lie about another professor's work, so as to block her appointment as chair of the tenure committee. Though he would prefer that the person in question not receive the appointment, the agent regards lying about another's work as reprehensible, and given the totality of information available to him, thinks the act would be indefensible in the present case. He also lacks any positive desire to do such a thing, says van Inwagen, and sees no objection to not doing it. In such a case, van Inwagen claims, the agent cannot in fact behave as asked, he cannot tell the requested lie.

G. Holmström-Hintikka and R. Tuomela (eds.), Contemporary Action Theory. Vol. I, 219–232.

The reason for this inability is that the agent has no choice either about what his motives and beliefs will be at the moment the request is made, or about whether he will follow them. On the first point, it is generally agreed that we have no direct voluntary control over our beliefs and attitudes. The best we can do is influence them indirectly, by subjecting ourselves to appropriate conditions. At any given moment, we simply find ourselves with certain beliefs and conative dispositions, and have to cope with them (p. 408). And in the case at hand, there simply is no basis for coping. Rather, says van Inwagen, it is a necessary truth that if an agent regards an action *A* as indefensible given the totality of his beliefs, and has no positive desire to *A*, then he will not *A* (p. 409). By way of argument, he cites the complete implausibility of someone claiming to have *A*'d voluntarily, yet to have thought throughout the performance that *A* was irremediably reprehensible, to have seen no excuse for *A*-ing, and to have had no desire whatever to *A*. This, claims van Inwagen, is absolutely impossible (p. 408), and he concludes that the agent in the example could not have lied: he was not going to do so, and he had no choice about the matter.

Van Inwagen proceeds to extend this result to a second kind of case, where "inclination is unopposed by inclination" (p. 411). The example here is Nightingale, a character in C.P. Snow's novel *The Masters*, who deeply covets membership in the British Royal Society, and who on the day of the election we imagine to be seated by the phone in his room, biting his fingernails and daydreaming about the perquisites of membership. Just then the phone rings. Nightingale lunges for it and shouts a deafening "Nightingale here," into the receiver. As with the previous case, van Inwagen argues that there is no possible world in which, given the frame of mind he actually had when it rang, Nightingale does not answer the phone. Thus, since he had no choice at that particular moment as to what his frame of mind would then be, Nightingale had no choice about answering the phone. He was powerless not to do so, and the same would hold in any case where an agent wants very much to *A*, and has no desire whatever that inclines him toward not *A*-ing (p. 412).

Finally, van Inwagen considers the many actions we perform each day with little or no reflection or deliberation, simply because they are the obvious thing to do in the circumstances. His example is answering the phone while one is seated at one's desk grading papers. As with the other examples, something might have occurred just at the moment of action that would provide a reason for not answering the phone. But in the normal case that is not what does occur: no special reason to ignore the ringing occurs to one, nor does he go berserk or have his mind taken over by alien forces. And in the absence of such events, says van Inwagen, it is incoherent to suppose one would not answer the phone (p. 413). Given the actual circumstances, one has no choice about the matter. Since, moreover, a great deal of our behavior falls under this third heading, it now begins to appear "that we have precious little free will" (p. 414).

As for when the will does operate freely, one might expect that if we are unfree when competing motives are absent, we will at least be free when the competition is a tie – that is, in so-called "Buridan's Ass" cases, where the alternatives are interchangeable. Choosing which of several descriptively identical copies of a book to purchase might be an example. In fact, however, van Inwagen denies freedom in these cases too, saying he can find no basis for claiming we have a choice in them. Also in this category are what he calls "vanilla/chocolate" cases, typified by the situation where one vacillates between flavors of ice cream. Here the alternatives are not descriptively interchangeable, but the very properties that constitute the difference between them are the objects of our conflicting desires (p. 415). And as with Buridan's Ass cases, van Inwagen sees no basis for freedom here. Rather, he thinks what happens in both types of case is a kind of internal coin toss, in which an inner, default decision-making process is allowed to have its arbitrary way. When this occurs, one has no choice about how one acts, just as one has no choice about whether a coin will land heads or tails (p. 417). Seemingly, then, balanced competition among motives offers no better guarantee of freedom than the complete absence of competition.

When, then, is libertarian freedom exercised? At best, van Inwagen suggests, the incompatibilist can hold that we exercise free will only on two sorts of occasion. First, there is the classic type of case, in which duty or some other matter of policy is opposed by desire. Often, such cases involve moral struggle, as when a young official has to decide whether to accept his first bribe. But morality itself need not be involved if, say, the case is one of keeping to a diet (p. 416). Second are cases of the sort described by Robert Kane (1985), in which a decision must be made between incommensurable values. The best examples here are choices of lifestyle or vocation, as when one must settle whether to live a life of selfishness or of sacrifice, or choose whether to be a lawyer or a pianist. What characterizes these cases is that they cannot be solved simply by maximizing some value such as wealth or happiness. The issue is not a matter of calculation. Rather, these are situations where one's values do not settle the issue, leaving one in a situation of indecision that can persist for some time. It should be noted, finally, that even in cases of these two types van Inwagen offers no guarantees. Rather, he holds only that they represent the largest class of cases for which a claim of libertarian freedom might be feasible. The main point to be gotten is that in the other cases we have mentioned, the wherewithal for such freedom is absent (p. 418).

II. EQUIVALENT ALTERNATIVES AND SELECTABILITY

How should a defender of libertarian freedom react to these considerations? One option is simply to acquiesce, on the ground that they do little serious damage to the libertarian cause. After all, van Inwagen does allow for at least the possibility of libertarian freedom in what seem to be the most important cases: those of moral choice, and selections of career, lifestyle, and the like. And as he himself points out, this will often permit us to hold people morally responsible for their behavior even in cases that fall into his categories of unfreedom (p. 419). For while we cannot exert direct control over the motives we experience at a given moment, we frequently influence them indirectly, through prior moral choices, voluntarily chosen programs of self-discipline, etc. As long as an agent's actions can be traced to such antecedent exercises of freedom, he may be held responsible even if in themselves the actions were involuntary. It is not clear, however, that this will work in all the cases we would want (Fischer and Ravizza 1992, 443–444), and even if it did, I think the libertarian should be dissatisfied. For although there is a certain plausibility to van Inwagen's examples, the conclusions he draws from them simply do not match what the libertarian takes to be our preanalytic intuitions about the frequency with which we exercise free will.

The plausibility of those conclusions depends in part on the status of the claim that when a decision or action *A* is decisively favored by the agent's reasons, and he has no motivation whatever in favor of any alternative, then he will do or select *A*. That this or some similar principle enjoys the status of modal necessity is, I think, a conclusion the incompatibilist should resist. There is, of course, no denying that the principle is a highly plausible one, to which even the libertarian would expect few if any exceptions. But the libertarian can provide an account of this which does not, in itself, invoke logical necessity. The operations of the will are, for him, exercises of practical rationality, in which the agent takes up a course of action for the sake of ends presented in his motives and beliefs. The reasoning that supports the agent's behavior can be portrayed in encapsulated form in a practical syllogism. Thus, if the issue is one of deciding whether to lie about a fellow professor's work, we would expect a positive decision to be the outcome of reasoning like this:

> Would that I prevent Smith's becoming chair of the tenure committee.
> I can prevent Smith's becoming chair of the committee if I lie about her work.
> Therefore, I shall lie about Smith's work.

What is cited as grounding the agent's decision here is not his mental *states* of desire and belief. It is, rather, the content of those states: the putative fact that lying would derail the appointment, and the felt desirability of this objective expressed in the major premise. Had the agent in van Inwagen's example decided to lie, we would expect his decision to be supported by premises like this, and to be subject to what amounts to a teleological explanation in terms of them. Suppose, however, that there is no major premise to call upon, as would happen if the agent had no motive whatever in support of lying. In such a case, no argument to ground the agent's decision in a reason for lying would be available to him, and this entire framework for rational decision making would fail. Small wonder, then, that we do not expect agents to pursue ends they have no motive for pursuing. From the libertarian's perspective, to do so would be to engage in an exercise of will that is not just irrational but nonrational: a decision or action founded neither in reasons nor in causes, but in literally nothing at all.

To say the least, such an exercise of will would be a stark event. But there is nothing in the above account to rule it out – nothing, that is, which makes it a matter of necessity that an agent lacking a motive for *A*-ing could not *A*, or decide to *A*. The most we are justified in claiming is that he could not do so *rationally*. But I want to set this issue aside for a moment, for the fact is that even if the stronger claim could be made, there are difficulties about how broadly it would apply. In particular, it does not apply either to Buridan's Ass or to vanilla/chocolate cases, for in neither of those is absence of motive the issue. Faced with five copies of the same version of the *Nicomachean Ethics* on the shelf at the bookstore, I have a motive for buying each of them: the enjoyment and learning to be gotten from reading it. What I lack is a motive in terms of which I can single out one copy as preferable to the others. Similarly, when torn between two flavors of ice cream I have a motive for choosing each: the pleasure to be gotten from tasting it. What I lack, again, is a principle of selection – a way of assuring myself that I have chosen the best, and so soothing my frustration at not being able to have both.[2] But there is nothing in the above account of libertarian willing that calls for this. What it requires is just that I have *some* reason for whatever selection I make – which, *ex hypothesi*, I do in both sorts of case. That being so, my decision will be an exercise of rationality no matter which way it goes. There will be a practical syllogism in which it is grounded, and the explanation it receives from the libertarian will not differ substantially from what it would be had I had a preponderant motive favoring just one of the options available. Libertarian explanations are not much concerned with preponderance of motives. On the contrary: they always leave open the possibility that the agent might have done otherwise – even in the face of stronger motives or better reasons.

There is, then, no reason for libertarians to accept the idea that when the alternatives faced in deliberation are valued equally by the agent, freedom somehow disappears. To do so is to treat rational decision making not as a matter of pursuing rationally grounded goals, but as one of maximization, in which unless a basis can be found for preferring one alternative to all others, one cannot proceed in a reasonable way. But if rational deciding is a maximizing process, it is not clear what the point of libertarianism is supposed to be. Surely it is part of the idea of freedom that compulsive concern with what is best will at least sometimes make deliberation *ir*rational rather than rational. Why, moreover, is it thought better that when deliberation results in a tie, we should revert to some process of vacillation, wherein the issue is settled in a way which, precisely because it is involuntary, is from the point of view of reason *utterly* arbitrary? Surely, from a rational perspective, a free choice among equal alternatives is better than a determined one. The former still counts as selection of an end for the sake of the goods it offers; the latter seems not to count as rational decision making at all. In short, there is no reason for the libertarian to think his position is better served by striking Buridan's Ass and vanilla/chocolate cases from the list of situations in which a free decision might be made. They are in any case independent of van Inwagen's other examples, and their intrinsic characteristics offer no special justification for taking them as deterministic.

III. THE AVAILABILITY OF MOTIVATED ALTERNATIVES

As for the other examples, the absence of a motive in favor of *A*-ing does, as we have seen, count as an impediment to choosing to *A*. By itself, however, this does not imply that there will be many instances in which an agent has no positive motivation at all for any but one of the alternatives available to him. This is especially true where moral considerations are at stake, since they are often strictly negative in import. Even if we assume that the agent in van Inwagen's example is unable to lie about his colleague, it does not follow that he has no free will. He may be motivated to pursue a number of other options: to simply be silent at the meeting, to speak in favor of another candidate, to denounce the person who asked him to lie, etc. If so, then he would be perfectly free to choose among them, even by van Inwagen's standards. In fact, however, we should not even grant the assumption that the agent lacks a motive to lie about his colleague, at least on the basis of van Inwagen's original description of the case. For on that description the agent does have a motive: to keep his colleague from becoming chair of the tenure committee, which van Inwagen says he would prefer not happen (p. 406). Surely a preference counts as a desire that his colleague not be appointed to the post, and if there is reason to think lying about the colleague's work would prevent that, then such a desire is a reason for lying, even if the agent claims he views the act as "indefensible." And if he has a reason for lying, then we have as yet no ground for thinking the agent cannot choose to do so, even if such a choice is profoundly unlikely.

As it stands, then, this particular example is not all that troublesome to the libertarian. A motive for *A*-ing need not, after all, be a desire to *A* for its own sake. If that were necessary, no one would ever adopt painful means to achieve desired ends – something we do all the time. Rather, what rational choice requires is just that the agent have *some* motive in favor of *A*-ing, some end he either desires or has a felt sense of obligation about, to which *A* might serve as a means. And as this version of the professor's case illustrates, that can occur even when *A* is viewed as morally indefensible. Perhaps, however, the example should be redrawn. Van Inwagen's real concern is clearly with cases where *A* is not just reprehensible, but is of no value at all to the agent, and so is supported by no motive whatever. And in a later discussion he himself notes the error of having the professor prefer that the colleague he is asked to lie about not become chair of the committee (van Inwagen 1994, n. 9), and revises the example so that the professor is not at all opposed to the appointment (*ibid.*, p. 100). But even with this adjustment, the example is not very persuasive. The request to lie, remember, comes from another colleague. And even professors who are not that moral know the value of cooperating with their fellow professors. In addition, morally good people, like van Inwagen's protagonist, almost always have a general desire to satisfy the requests of others when circumstances permit. Now of course the circumstances here prohibit compliance, normatively speaking, since the action requested of the protagonist is morally abhorrent to him. And since he is a moral man we would expect him to decide accordingly. Nevertheless, the very goodness that ultimately leads him to reject the request may well give the professor an initial motive for complying, and that is all that is needed for him to have a reason to lie.

The problem here runs deeper than a dispute over an isolated example. It is that courses of action we have no motive for pursuing almost never come up in deliberation, or if they do they receive no attention. Rather, the actions that occupy our deliberations do so precisely because if performed, they might satisfy one or another of our aims. There can be exceptions: perhaps someone might offer me a reward simply for deliberating about *A*-ing, whether I finally choose to *A* or not. But even when we consider a putative option only to determine whether it is real or not – that is, to see whether it would in fact lead to the outcome in question – that outcome is one we desire to achieve. In the great majority of cases, therefore, one's motives for considering *A*-ing are in fact motives for *A*-ing. This is true even when the option is proposed by someone else, and even when we consider it to be morally indefensible. Indeed, morally indefensible actions are often all too readily suited to our ends. The contention that we are not generally free to perform such actions is not, therefore, one to which the libertarian need accede, provided they gain any place at all in our deliberations. As in the case of the professor, the very fact that they are considered, however briefly, indicates there is something to be said in favor of them. And that is enough to make a decision in their favor an exercise in practical rationality, even if such a decision would be entirely unlikely, and even if morally it would be beneath contempt.

It does not appear, then, that in most cases where an action is consciously rejected as morally reprehensible, duty is unopposed by inclination. But what about cases where conscious attention is focused largely on other matters, and routine actions are performed with seemingly little or no deliberation? These, which make up van Inwagen's third class of examples, are founded in what we may think of as *standing intentions*: the familiar and often habitual plans, policies and practices that we follow in getting through the ordinary business of life. Obviously, such actions are very common; it could fairly be argued that they make up the great majority of what we do each day. And it is true that in most situations where such behavior occurs, what action is to be performed becomes apparent to the agent almost simultaneously with the circumstances that call for it, so that things proceed pretty much automatically. Thus if my standard policy is to answer my phone when it rings, I am likely to do so as soon as I hear it, with no independent deliberation or decision to do so. Are we to conclude, though, that libertarian free will cannot obtain in such cases? Again I think not, at least if the reason is supposed to be that in such cases we lack alternatives that have motivational support.

To see why, we must first realize that the policies and routines that form the content of our standing intentions have to allow for variation and adjustment at the moment of action (Brand 1984). If they did not – if, for example, the routines for driving did not permit response to changing road and traffic conditions – the result would be disaster. To allow such flexibility, standing intentions have to be schematic only: that is, they have to allow for final determination as to whether and how the plan will be executed to occur at the moment of action. And that is a job for the will. Even in the daily business of life, I have to be attentive to my options, and be ready to modify or even scrap my standard procedures in response to circumstances. I must balance haste against safety, efficiency against kindness, my own interests against those of others. Doing so need not require lengthy deliberation, or decisions that are independent of action. What is needed is often quickly obvious, and intentions can be formed by volition alone – that is, through the activity of willing by which we enter upon purposive behavior, and which is itself intrinsically intentional (McCann 1986). But this kind of flexibility does require legitimate options. I cannot adapt rationally unless I am aware of alternative courses of action, and these are supported by motives.

What might such options be like? In extended activities like driving, which cannot be done all at once, they are simply the various ways of *progressing* towards my goal that are available at any moment. They may involve things as simple as speed and timing: whether to take a slippery looking curve at normal speed or to slow down, whether to move into the exit lane now or after this truck passes. Or they could be more significant: whether to try to make it past the traffic signal on this cycle or wait until it turns green again, whether to change my route in the hope of finding less congestion. Alternatives like these represent variations on the basic scenario of activity by which I plan to reach my destination, and *all* find motivation in my desire to get there with reasonable safety and dispatch. Sometimes the alternatives stack up about equally in terms of this motive, and I wind up with a kind of vanilla/chocolate decision, aimed simply at settling the issue. In others, my desire for safety may favor one alternative and my desire for speed the other. Then I will face a small scale decision as to lifestyle: whether I will live safely or dangerously this morning. In still other instances further motives enter the picture: fear of the policeman who seems to have his eye on me, say, or a desire to allow a fellow motorist to cross an intersection first. The important point, however, is that in all these cases I must determine on the spot how I will behave. The issue cannot be settled in advance. And there is every reason to think that when I make such determinations, I have motives that favor each of the options at issue, not just the one I select.

Though not as complex, the case of answering the phone while grading papers is essentially the same. My policy of answering the phone is not so rigid as to admit of no exceptions, and in any case the policy needs to be put into effect when the phone rings. That is a matter of intentional action, and intentional action requires a reason – typically, in this case, a desire to communicate with whomever is calling. But there are also reasons on the other side: I am, after all, grading papers, and whatever motive prompted me to do that is a motive for continuing to do it, which I cannot while conducting a telephone conversation. Indeed, if I am not motivated to continue grading papers, then by van Inwagen's argument I ought to have quit long ago. Presumably, then, the wherewithal is available for a rational decision not to take the call, however unlike me such a choice might be. To be sure, I may not pause long or, for that matter, at all over the issue. It may be apparent to me immediately what to do, and the entire episode may pass so quickly that it barely enters my reflective awareness, so that later it is as hard to remember as so-called automatic driving. But that is only to say that the task of choosing moves quickly and easily in this case. It is not to say it is not there to be performed, or that I am not free in performing it. And it would strain credibility completely to say that we are not aware of our options in situations like this. That would be to claim, in effect, that while we are immensely competent at coping with the events of daily experience, their practical meaning is in fact all but lost to us, the routines of life being so fixed that any motive which does not command our full attention is not even present.

IV. FREEDOM AND COMPULSION

This is a good point to take stock. We have seen that in cases of motivational ties, where more than one alternative appears equally favorable to an agent, there is no reason for a libertarian to surrender to the claim that the will is not free. By his account, any choice among such alternatives will be rational; moreover, the explanation it receives will be of the same kind the libertarian would give had there been a slight imbalance of motives – which need not, of course, have favored the alternative actually chosen. As for cases where there is only one motivated alternative, they are at best far less common than van Inwagen's argument would suggest. The great majority of situations where an agent considers acting in a way he would view as morally reprehensible are in fact cases of moral temptation, in which he is motivated so to act. This is because deliberation is itself a voluntary undertaking, and it would ordinarily be irrational to deliberate over actions one has no reason to perform. As for the numerous actions that make up the common business of life, there is every reason to think they too involve motivated alternatives. We are constantly choosing among alternative means to desired ends, even in performing largely habitual activities. And the very fact that we must leave off one activity in order to take up another suggests there will often have been motives to continue doing what we were.

What, then, about the case of Nightingale, where inclination is supposed to be unopposed by inclination? I have saved it for last in part because it seems to be the least damaging of all. Nightingale's case is not one in which a motive of normal dimensions stands unopposed, and so wins the day. It is, rather, a case in which a very powerful motive comes to dominate – perhaps even to banish – all others, even motives of ordinary civility and discretion. But of course that makes this case one of precisely the sort libertarians have often tended to view as involving an impairment of freedom. It is a case of compulsive behavior – the kind where we are apt to blame the agent more for getting himself into the situation he did than for the way he acted once in it. The difference is that as described, this case is even worse than normal. Typically, agents engaged in compulsive or addictive behavior are aware of alternatives, and have motives for choosing them. The problem is simply that in the face of, say, the alcoholic's insistent desire to drink, all other motives seem to lose force. But what is claimed for Nightingale's case is that any motive other than those that support answering the phone has ceased to exist, at least for the moment. That makes this an especially egregious example of compulsion, and one the libertarian can easily accommodate: he can claim it is simply a relatively rare subtype of an already rare phenomenon, for which libertarians have long been inclined to make an exception.

If this is correct, then incompatibilist freedom seems to survive van Inwagen's attack more or less unscathed. There do not appear to be very many cases of decision or action in which the agent is presented with just one motivated alternative. Indeed, though they cannot be pursued here, there may even be arguments that would make such cases virtually impossible. For one thing, it might be that the moment an agent becomes aware that he has just one motivated option, the limitation on rational decision making implied in that situation would itself become a motive for choosing differently, so that any alternative would now have something in its favor, simply by virtue of being available (Fischer and Ravizza 1992, 433). To be sure, this line of thinking need not occur to the agent in all cases (van Inwagen 1994, 103). Still, it is hard to count a limitation on freedom as serious if the moment it is noticed by the agent it is prone to disappear. Furthermore, it might be argued that *any* alternative that presents itself in deliberation has at least one valuable feature: namely, that to choose it would be an exercise of autonomous agency on the part of the chooser. If we are inclined to think of autonomy along Kantian lines – that is, as valuable in itself – such a position is not at all implausible. If it can be defended, then we may well begin to doubt that there is such a thing as an unmotivated deliberational alternative.

But even if arguments like this fail, and agents do occasionally face situations in which only one available course of action has anything whatever to be said for it, the incompatibilist need not accept the claim that when this occurs, one cannot choose otherwise. Admittedly, we would be at a loss if, as in van Inwagen's example of the professor, an agent were to claim he had intentionally undertaken a course of action for which he had no positive motivation of any kind. The question, however, is what would have gone wrong if this were to occur, and here intuitions may differ. By van Inwagen's account such an occurrence is a logical impossibility, something that could not happen in any possible world (p. 407). But if that is so there should be a self-contradiction in the vicinity, and none that I can find makes choosing differently impossible in itself. It would, for example, be a contradiction to claim an agent had decided on a course of action that never even entered his mind. To choose implies prior awareness of the alternative selected, so that a completely blind choice would seem impossible. But cases in which only one alternative even occurs to the agent must be rare at best,[3] and in any case they are not what van Inwagen has in mind. The problem his agent's face is not lack of alternatives, but lack of reasons for adopting them.

A second kind of contradiction, which is indeed present in the scenario van Inwagen imagines, was alluded to earlier: it would be implicitly contradictory to say of an agent that he had *rationally* chosen to A if he did so in the absence of any motive whatever that favored A-ing. Rational choices are founded in reasons that explain them, and in the absence of any motive at all, one has no reason to A. That, I think, is what accounts for the complete implausibility of the situation in which an agent claims to have done what he took to be morally indefensible, though he saw no reason whatever to do it. The discourse of such a person seems rational enough, but the behavior he reports is not. The functional role of rational decision making is precisely to assist us in changing the world in ways we find valuable, and that function can only be frustrated if one decides to *A* lacking any reason to *A*. But though it would be a contradiction to call such a decision rational, I can find no contradiction in the idea of it merely occurring. Someone might think that in the absence of a motive either the action or the decision to perform it could never be intentional. But that would be a mistake. Intentions do not reduce to motives; rather, I intend to *A* provided only that I have a practical commitment to *A*-ing – the sort of thing I get by deciding to *A*. And as for deciding itself, it requires no underlying motive in order to be intentional, because it is intrinsically so: there is no such thing as accidentally or inadvertently deciding to *A*, or deciding to *A* without meaning to do so. Decisions are always intentionally undertaken, because they are by nature an exercise of the will. So it appears that I can come to intend to *A* simply by deciding to do so, and that I can intentionally decide to *A* whether I have a prior motive or not.

There is one last option to be considered. It might be claimed that the alleged impossibility of deciding to *A* in the absence of a motive is not logical but contingent – the sort of modality often held to be associated with scientific laws. That would be enough for an argument that we are not free so to decide. Moreover, such a position gains support from the case of Nightingale, since some libertarians may feel that although the will is normally free, it succumbs to causal necessity in cases of compulsion. It might be argued that just as Nightingale's will is overwhelmed by the force of his desire to become a member of the Royal Society, so the will of any agent must yield to the force of causation if only one of the alternatives before it is supported by a motive. For, the argument would run, the absence of opposition must surely result in the one available motive overwhelming the agent's deliberation, so that he could not decide against it. But even if this were right it would not change very much as long as unopposed motives are uncommon, and likely to generate opposition the moment an agent comes to feel his freedom is threatened by them. The libertarian can readily accept the few additions to the list of compelled actions such a result would demand.

But even this concession is not required, for the phenomenon of compulsion need not be handled as one in which voluntary power somehow succumbs to the power of causal necessity – if indeed there is such a thing. Again, space does not permit a complete argument, but agents are not rendered passive in the formation and execution of intention simply because one motive tends to dominate all others. Nor need they be understood to be so transformed should a motive stand alone. It is still an active step for the agent to move from the consideration of an alternative to its adoption and enactment. Nor is it clear that the phenomenology of these processes, on which claims of libertarian freedom are often at least partially based, is suddenly changed in cases of compulsion or duress. Deciding is not something that happens to us in such cases; it is something we *do*, and it may still be held to be free. If freedom is curtailed by powerful motives, this may only be because such motives tend so to obtrude on deliberation that the value of other courses of action is diminished or lost sight of, so that choices which otherwise would not be thought reasonable are made to appear persuasive. If so, it is only the rational exercise of freedom that is hampered in cases of compulsion: in principle, the agent in such situations is as free to choose differently as he is any other time. And the same would go for an agent presented with just one motivated alternative.

V. CONCLUSION

There is, I think, at least some implausibility in the idea of a phenomenon that is sometimes determined and sometimes not. For example, it would not make sense for us to conclude that the behavior of subatomic particles was in certain respects intrinsically indeterminate, and then proceed to look for ways of bringing the phenomena in question under control. And I suspect the same holds of the will. If libertarianism is true at all, it ought to be because there is something intrinsic to the operations of the will which precludes their being subject to causation. If so, then what the libertarian should expect is that however unlikely it might be that an agent faced with only one motivated alternative might choose against it, it would still be intrinsically possible for him to do so. But even if that is wrong, such cases need not be feared by the libertarian. If they occur at all, they are too few in number to justify the conclusion that we are unfree in most of our behavior.

Texas A&M University

NOTES

1 Page references in the text are to this source, unless otherwise indicated.

2 It is not clear, by the way, that in vanilla/chocolate cases, "the properties of the alternatives that constitute the whole of the difference between them are precisely the objects of our conflicting desires" (p. 415). One difference between chocolate and vanilla ice cream is that the former, but not the latter, is toxic to dogs. But that toxicity is not likely to be an object of desire in typical examples of this kind, even in agents who are aware of the fact. Rather, what seems to characterize such cases is that our motivational response to the alternatives at issue remains about equal, even after we have reviewed all the features we believe might influence us. If that is correct, it is hard to see how these cases differ in principle from those of choosing among incommensurable alternatives, wehere van Inwagen allows for the possibility of freedom.

3 In order for me to deliberate about A-ing, I need to be aware of the necessity of choosing or willing A in order to get it done. But if I am aware of that need, then I must be aware that I am not presently A-ing, in which case I am aware of an alternative.

REFERENCES

Brand, Myles (1984), *Intending and Acting*. Cambridge, Massachusetts, MIT Press.
Fischer, John Martin and Mark Ravizza (1992), "When the Will is Free" in Tomberlin (ed.), *Philosophical Perspectives, 6, Ethics*, pp. 423–451.
Kane, Robert (1985), *Free Will and Values*. Albany, State University of New York Press.
McCann, Hugh J. (1986), "Intrinsic Intentionality," *Theory and Decision* **20**, 247–273.
Van Inwagen, Peter (1989), "When Is the Will Free?" in James E. Tomberlin (ed.), *Philosophical Perspectives* **3**, *Philosophy of Mind and Action Theory*. Atascadero, California, Ridgeview Publishing, pp. 399–422.
Van Inwagen Peter (1994), "When the Will Is Not Free," *Philosophical Studies* **75**, 95–113.

GOTTFRIED SEEBASS

WHEN IS AN ACTION FREE?

I. STRONG ACCOUNTABILITY AND FREEDOM

It is a commonplace of European philosophy and Western thought that *praise* and *blame*, *reward* and *punishment* are just and justified only if men are *accountable* for what they do, and that men are accountable only if what they do is *free*. Theoretical statements to this effect are present in the Greek as well as in the Jewish-Christian tradition. Furthermore they have remained present in our moral and legal practice up to today.

Despite recent scepticism, formulated most radically perhaps by Nietzsche, I am convinced that this conception is sound in principle.[1] In this paper I shall not address the general question of accountability. Rather, I start outright from the supposition that there are good reasons for not confining ourselves to a *weak* form of imputation (used, e.g., in the law of tort), but for relying in addition on a stronger, more differentiated form (used predominantly in criminal law and morals). Following the lead of Aristotle this notion of *strong accountability* may minimally be defined by three necessary conditions, viz. *knowledge*, *will* or *want*, and *deliberation*.[2] For various practical and theoretical reasons there is no possibility, at least at present and for a very long time to come, that these conditions might become explicable in purely neurophysiological, or purely behavioral and/or dispositional terms.[3] Thus strong accountability remains bound up with its traditional, tried and tested use, which implies tracing actions and consequences back to intentional *mental* events, which in the last resort have to be identified in consciousness. There are well-known, substantial difficulties involved here, which may eventually become insuperable. In the normal case, however, they are not so great as to foil any attempt from the start. Provided radical scepticism is excluded, strong accountability is ruled out neither by practical and empirical reasons nor by deeper, theoretical ones.

This brings me to my main topic. Granted that strong, no less than weak accountability is a desirable as well as theoretically tenable notion, the question arises of whether, and in what sense, it is also dependent on a condition of *freedom*. To the first part of this question most people will give an affirmative answer. Let us call this the thesis of the criteriality of freedom for strong accountability, or simply the *"criteriality thesis"*. Assuming this thesis to be true in *some* sense of "freedom", the crucial question to be addressed is in *which* sense an action must be free, if it is to be strongly accountable.

To this a first, partial answer seems easy. Approaching the subject from

G. Holmström-Hintikka and R. Tuomela (eds.), Contemporary Action Theory. Vol. I, 233–250.

common sense, one might expect that the most obvious condition of freedom required is *lack of external control*, i.e. the fact that the actor must not be subject to the overwhelming causal influence of another actor. However, this obvious and apparently innocent move turns out to be controversial if it is looked at from a philosophical point of view. Of course, nobody will deny that the condition under consideration is requisite to *weak* accountability. Moreover, many philosophers will not want to deny that it seems strange to hold a man *strongly* accountable for something for which he may not be weakly accountable, too. For isn't weak accountability implied by strong accountability, *a fortiori*? Yet, at least with regard to the relevant conditions of freedom, this seemingly natural implication is denied implicatively by a position widely held in modern philosophy and most influential here.

II. FREEDOM OF ACTION

Asked under what conditions a man acts freely, most contemporary philosophers will refer initially, many even exclusively, to a concept of freedom according to which a man is free just in case he can do what he wants or wills to do. Let us call this *"freedom of action"* in a terminological sense, abbreviated *"FA"*. *FA* has a long philosophical history. In analytical philosophy and in the English speaking countries generally, its origin is often ascribed to Hobbes, Locke or Hume. However, it is in fact much older. Prior to the British empiricists *FA* had long been invoked by Christian theology, beginning perhaps with Augustine. It is useful to bear this in mind. For as will be shown presently, *FA* is the conceptual key to the separation of strong from weak accountability mentioned above. Within the Jewish-Christian tradition, this separation is highly interesting on theological grounds. So it may well be that its attractiveness as a conceptual tool depends entirely on the relevant theological reasons, or their secular counterparts, and begins to vanish as soon as these reasons are uncovered.

Before we come to a discussion of this point, let us note some relevant characteristics of *FA*. Firstly, as an attempt to specify the conditions of free action, *FA* implies a significant shift in focus. First and foremost it is the *actor*, not the action, that is called free. An *action* is free just in case it is performed by an actor possessing *FA*. This conceptual ordering, inherent already in Augustine and pointed out most emphatically by Locke,[4] is well-taken and will not be called into question here. Secondly, whether or not a person possesses *FA* is not simply a matter of yes or no, but a matter of *kinds* and *degrees*. A man may be free as regards one particular action, action-part, or action-type without being free with regard to another. Strictly, then, we should say that a man is free only *in so far* or *to the extent* that he can do what he wants or wills to do. In continuing to speak of *FA* simply I take it to be understood that this has to be expanded eventually into a form of talk containing relevant gradations and specifications.

A third characteristic is more problematic. According to *FA*, freedom is a *modal* notion pertaining not only to actions that *are* part of the real world, but to actions that *can* be. Sometimes this is contested. Yet little reflection is needed in order to realize that one is well-advised to include a modal characteristic. Nonmodal descriptive criteria such as absence of conditions like "Mistake of Fact, Accident, Coercion, Duress, Provocation, Insanity, Infancy"[5] are conditions of *freedom* only because they have a direct bearing on the number of *options* open to a person at a particular time. Surely you are not free to win the jackpot in a lottery at will; but this is not merely because you don't know the numbers that will be drawn, but because this lack of knowledge makes it impossible for you to choose the winning numbers. Similar things may be said of the other conditions. Therefore the fact that *FA* is concerned not only with the questions of what a free actor actually does or what is descriptively true of him during his action, but also with the question of what a free actor can do, certainly is no defect of *FA* but a qualifying mark adding to its acceptability as an adequate notion of freedom.

Still, this leaves room for various *modal interpretations*. Depending on whether the defining "can" is taken in a stronger or in a weaker sense, *FA* itself appears as a notion of varying strength. Traditionally the proponents of *FA* have favoured a rather *weak* interpretation, in fact a *very weak* one. Most often their interpretation is not even bound to the absence of external control, thus enabling the separation of strong from weak accountability mentioned earlier. So it is not *FA* as such, but its weak modal interpretation, that leads to this separation. More specifically, it is the result of two general theoretical tenets associated with *FA* traditionally, viz. (I) that *FA*, though modal, does not imply the existence of *alternate possibilities* in the actual world and therefore does not rule out *determinism*, and (II) that the relevant "can", though not identifiable outright with descriptive conditions, may well be *theoretically* reducable or explicable in *nonmodal* terms. Let us look more closely at these two tenets, beginning in the next section with tenet (I).

III. STOIC FREEDOM

Consider the following example adapted from Locke.[6] While you are engaged in reading an interesting book, a person who wants you not to leave the room for the moment locks the door from outside. So it is ensured that you stay in by the external causal intervention of some other actor. Accordingly, one would expect that you cannot be weakly accountable for remaining in the room. However, remaining indoors while reading is exactly what you knowingly want to do anyway. Let us assume, moreover, that you have noticed the act of locking but have decided to ignore it and to continue. Thus the minimal conditions of being strongly accountable seem to be met by you. If so, do we not have a clear example of *strong* but *not weak* accountability here? And given the criteriality thesis, wouldn't we have to say also that a person in a position like yours is *free*?

The point is controversial though. Locke among many others answered the last question in the negative, thus following common sense. The Stoics, however, and quite a number of successors up to the present have given an affirmative answer.[7] If what you do accords with what you want or will and is determined by your wanting or willing, your action counts as free even if the result in question is determined by some other factor at the same time. To act freely in the Stoic sense, you do not need to have the objective, counterfactual possibility of acting otherwise if you were to want to. This is hard to accept, even in undramatic and harmless cases like our example from Locke. Surely we would not hesitate to say that in deliberately deciding to stay inside you did so on your own considered will. Perhaps we would also grant that this fact may be sufficient even to hold you "strongly accountable" for that action in some sense. But most of us would not say that you were free to stay where you were. At any rate, this interpretation would be rejected outright in more dramatic and harmful cases. If everything you do, e.g., is going to be controlled by a diabolical neurosurgeon, independently of your thought and will, you certainly will not say that your actions will be free whenever your informed, considered will happens to be in accord with what that devil has ordained!

The Stoic conception of freedom is not wholly absurd, however, but it gains the plausibility it may have from an important tacit assumption. The Stoicist wisely recommends that we no longer want or will things against what is determined independently of us. This recommendation, however, makes sense only if there is *one* realm at least that remains undetermined, viz. the deliberate *formation* of the beliefs, wants or volitions in question.[8] If the Stoic conception of freedom is convincing at all, its negation of alternate possibilities must be confined to *basic actions* and their *consequences*, whereas the underlying *mental events* are still affirmed to be unfixed, at least with regard to their determination by other actors. Thus even the very weak notion of Stoic freedom, which is unacceptable to common sense and many philosophers anyway, does not show that the modality of *FA* can be interpreted in a way that does not imply the existence of alternate possibilities and the rejection of determinism. Consequently, the first tenet associated with *FA* appears unconfirmed so far. Moreover, the exclusion of the determining influence of other actors appears to be *identical* with the condition of freedom required for weak accountability, viz. lack of external control. So what about the claim made in section II that *FA* is the conceptual key to a *separation* of strong from weak accountability?

IV. DOUBTS ABOUT FREEDOM OF WILL

Now, the use made of the criterion of lack of external control in strong as against weak accountability includes one important shift. In weak accountability it is applied not to preceeding mental events, but to *actions* and *consequences* of actions directly. In strong accountability, however, it is applied first and foremost, or even exclusively (as in Stoic freedom), to relevant *mental events*. Among these the central element which has attracted most attention traditionally is *volition*. Thus the exclusion of external control or external determination in general amounts predominantly to a requirement regarding *"freedom of will"*. Henceforth I shall concentrate on this topic. This concentration is justified also by the fact that the dominant role of volition derives mainly from its position *between* practical deliberation and action, thus *depending* on antecendent mental events of other various types. However, one should bear in mind that questions similar to those which will be raised with regard to will and volition arise with regard to the other elements, too: *want* that does not have the additional qualifications of will,[9] *knowledge*, *belief*, and *deliberation*.

The general question of whether or not volition is free is not bound to the specific question concerning its external determination. Yet it is mainly discussed within this latter context. And, as we have just seen, it is this connexion which seems to bring in the condition of freedom characteristic of weak accountability, viz. lack of external control. Consequently it is the combined problem of *"freewill and determination"* that is the target of those proponents of *FA* who favour a weaker interpretation of the relevant "can" and therefore, implicatively, the separability of strong from weak accountability. Today many even believe that the problem has long been settled and does not need any further discussion.[10] What are the reasons for this? Certainly one would not think that the description given, e.g., by von Wright shows that the problem is misguided from the start or ready for oblivion:[11]

> Granted that action is free when in conformity with our will, what then of the will itself? Are we free to will what we will? Or is the will determined by something else? If the will is not free, action determined by the will can be free at most in some relative sense, it seems.

Obviously, this is no senseless or patently disinteresting series of questions. If it is possible to dismiss them, there must be strong, general reasons for this. More specifically, there must be some argument to the effect that, when considered more closely, the problem turns out either to be *unanswerable* in principle or to provide its *own answer*. Both forms of argument have been propounded.

The first form is exemplified predominantly by the argument that the question of freewill leads into a *vicious regress*. Suppose von Wright's second question receives an affirmative answer. Then we are "free to will what we will". But what about the second "will" in this clause, which is simply taken for granted and has not been shown to be free yet? Couldn't we ask the same question with regard to this second "will", too? Obviously we could. An affirmative answer to this question, however, would amount to something like our being "free to will what we will to will", i.e. an answer still dependent on some volition whose freedom is unproven. So it becomes evident that the relevant question may be reiterated *in infinitum*. Yet if a question can never find a decisive answer, it seems to be senseless. Consequently, the problem of freewill may be dismissed including, of course, its traditional connexion with the question of determination. This knock-down argument is the standard move of those proponents of *FA* who try to show that the concept of freedom applies not to volitions, but only to actions and actors. The argument has played a particularly dominant role in modern philosophy. Thus it is present in thinkers as different as Hobbes, Locke, Leibniz, Edwards and Schopenhauer, or more recently Ryle and Kenny.[12] Many others rely on it, explicitly or implicitly.

Nevertheless, on closer inspection the argument does not show what it is intended to show. Firstly, the mere fact that an operation may be repeated indefinitely is no proof that its *finite* application is senseless. Formally, "x wills that [p]" is a sensible recursive function no less than "$n+1$" or the syntactical rule for inserting relative clauses into English sentences. Moreover, Augustine and more recently Moore and Frankfurt have argued plausibly that there are situations in which the question whether we are "free to will what we will to will" has clear empirical meaning.[13] What is shown by the argument is no more than that in applying the recursive question we will have to stop *somewhere*, i.e. we will have to accept some volition of second or higher order which we cannot demonstrate to be free any more by showing that it may be generated or cancelled in accordance with a volition of a still higher order.

Yet this is no serious objection. For secondly and most importantly, there is no reason to think that the *only* way to show that something is free is to show that it is dependent on or (as in Stoic freedom) merely in accord with a relevant prior *volition*. The regress argument relies on the tacit assumption that "freedom of will" cannot be understood other than in strict analogy to the formal structure of *FA*, viz. "x can --- what x wants or wills to ---". But this exclusiveness is wholly unwarranted. Instead of taking the vicious regress derivable from that structure as evidence that the *question of freewill* is senseless, one should have argued exactly the other way round. As it seems clear that the question of whether we are free in willing what we will at a particular time may sensibly be asked in many cases, a regress resulting from a certain form of analysis is sufficient to show that this *analysis* cannot be correct. We can rely on the structure contained in *FA* in part, viz. in cases where higher order volitions actually are involved. But in order to get a complete, positive answer, we have to develop a different way of understanding freedom of will.[14] And it has surely not been proven by the regress argument that such a way is inexistent.

Hence the *first* of the two forms of argument mentioned above, which are intended to show that the freewill problem may be dismissed as *senseless* and *unanswerable* in principle, is unconvincing and gets its apparent plausibility merely from a reduced conception of the question at stake. This result may be generalized. It is extremely unlikely that one might ever find a knock-down argument of the kind intended, as it actually seems quite clear that the question of free volition has a comprehensible empirical meaning. Even if higher order volitions could be left out of consideration completely, there would still remain a vast number of cases which have long been considered instances of "unfree volition" in criminal law and morality and which it indeed makes sense to distinguish from other cases, e.g. physical threat, blackmail, addiction, hypnosis, psychosis, and above all volition formed under conditions of restricted information. Cases like these, it seems, will have to be taken account of anyway. If there is any general reason to dismiss the "classical problem" described by von Wright, it must come from the *second* form of argument mentioned, viz. from an alleged proof to the effect that it is unnecessary to deal with it, since, if answerable at all, it will receive an *answer of itself*.

V. THE AUGUSTINIAN SOLUTION

In some way or other this form of argument must be relied on by all proponents of *FA* who do not trust the force of the regress argument (or some similar negative argument) but are nevertheless convinced that, in order to call an action or actor "free" in a sense strong enough for strong accountability, it is *not* necessary to invoke a notion of freedom *other* than *FA itself*, a conviction, which extends to the needlessness of entering into the traditional problem of "freewill and determination". Often the dependence on the second form of argument is not explicit, but there are cases where it is evident. Locke is perhaps the most prominent example for this. Just before invoking the objection of the vicious regress, he argues thus:[15]

> to ask, whether a Man be at liberty to will either Motion, or Rest; Speaking, or Silence; which he pleases, is to ask, whether a Man can *will*, what he *wills*; or be pleased with what he is pleased with. A Question, which, I think, needs no answer [, since it] carries the absurdity of it so manifestly in it self, that one might thereby sufficiently be convinced, that Liberty concerns not the Will.

According to this argument, being concerned about freedom of will is absurd, because in some sense the *mere fact* of willing is evidence that it is free. Some argument to this effect, or to a similar one, is needed if one wants to be content with *FA* as a sufficient answer to the question of when an action is free. However, is it convincing?

Obviously, the cogency of Locke's argument depends on interpretation. If "can" means no more than "possibly true", it is indeed absurd to ask "whether a Man *can will* what he *wills*", as this is true *a fortiori*. Yet this cannot be the interpretation in question. Otherwise *FA* itself would be unnecessary to freedom, too, since it is equally true *a fortiori* that what is done involuntarily "can" be done in this weak sense. But if "can" has another sense, is it still true that the mere fact of willing provides evidence that it is free? Is there any interpretation of "can" strong enough to be relevant to practical freedom, but still weak enough to be implied by willing as such? Historically there is an analysis purporting to give this result, advanced by Augustine long ago. The impact of Augustinian thought on the later conception of the problems of will and freedom can scarcely be overrated. So we may well expect that Locke and other modern proponents of *FA* are dependent on Augustine, not only with regard to *FA* itself, but also with regard to his analysis of the practical "can". In fact, it is probable that none of the later thinkers would have hit upon the idea that one might be content with *FA* and dispense with problems of freewill and determination completely, could he not have relied, explicitly or implicitly, on the wide acceptance and seeming force of the Augustinian solution.

The conceptual key to the solution is a *non-modal, conditional analysis* of the practical "can". This analysis is well-known in analytical philosophy from its presentation by Moore and the ensuing critical discussion.[16] But this is merely the most recent stage of a long history. In modern philosophy it may be traced back, e.g., to Schopenhauer, Hume, Leibniz and Hobbes.[17] In Christian theology its history is even longer. Thus the analysis in question was articulated quite clearly, e.g., by Anselm of Canterbury.[18] Its origin, however, is in Augustine.[19] Whereas the first of the two theoretical tenets traditionally associated with *FA*, its separation from alternate possibilities and lack of external control, can be traced back to the Stoics or even to Aristotle, the second tenet concerning the nonmodal explicability of the relevant "can" seems to have been introduced as a corollary of the Augustinian solution.

Reformulated with the help of logical variables, Augustine's analysis of the practical "can", i.e. of something's being "up to us" (*"in potestate nostra"*), is the following. A certain state of affairs "p" is not up to a certain person "x" if and only if it is the case either that "x wills that [p] & $-p$" or that "x wills that [$-p$] & p". To get the definition of "p is up to x" we have to negate this disjunction of two conjunctions. If we transform the result in accordance with well-known principles of propositional logic into a conjunction of two negated conjunctions and then transform the two conjunctions into material conditionals we get a nonmodal conditional variant of *FA*, henceforth abbreviated *"CFA"*:

> x is free with respect to p (= x can bring it about that p / = p is up to x) if and only if:
> (1) if x wills that [p], then p, and:
> (2) if x wills that [$-p$], then $-p$.

This definition differs from Stoic freedom in that it seems to include the alternate possibilities of both "p" and "-p", although their actual realization is *conditional* on the respective forms of will. More precisely, they depend *solely* on the corresponding volition. According to *CFA*, a man is free vis-a-vis "p" (and "-p") if and only if he is in a situation in which the background conditions, including external opportunities as well as internal abilities, are such that no more than his willing "p" or "-p" is needed to determine that "p" or "-p" will be the case. Thus the two possibilities in question are entirely "up to his will".

As a general analysis of the practical "can", *CFA* is clearly insufficient, but I shall waive this point here as it is irrelevant within the present context.[20] The critical point is this. While it seems to include alternate possibilities with regard to its *conditioned* states of affairs, *CFA* certainly does not include this with regard to its *conditions*. So it may well be that the actor's "willing that [*p*]" is determined antecedently and from without, e.g. by a second actor controlling him. If so, "p" itself is determined, given *CFA*. Consequently, the alternation of "p" and "-p" is lost, and the introduction of the antecedent conditions seems to be no more than a small prolongation of the action chains under consideration. Nobody would believe that a sentence like "if domino *A* falls so will domino *B* and if *A* does not fall, *B* will not fall either" tells us anything about the freedom of dominos. So why should this be different if domino *B* is replaced (say) by a bodily movement and domino *A* by a corresponding volition? Why should we believe that *CFA* gives a sufficient specification of free and strongly accountable action, whereas the condition of weak accountability, lack of external control, and with it the traditional problem of "freewill and determination" may be dismissed?

Now, the Augustinian solution purports to demonstrate why. Augustine's trick is an early use of the principle of substitution in propositional logic. Insert "*x* wills" for "p" in *CFA*, he argues, and you will find that the two clauses of the definiens, viz. (1) and (2), become true trivially. For, isn't it just a tautology to say that "if *x* wills that [*x* wills], then *x* wills"? Consequently, if, but only if, the analysis of the practical "can" and "free" contained in *CFA* is applied to volition itself, the question as to its freedom receives an affirmative answer of itself. Will, and will alone, is shown to be free *per se*.

Tricky as this may, be the argument is not sound. There are two big mistakes in it. Firstly, the tautology does not result in the negative case, viz. clause (2). It would result only if, instead of (2), one had:

(2′) if it is not the case that *x* wills that [*p*], then -*p*.

But in this form *CFA* is no plausible analysis at all, since (2′) is much stronger than called for. In short, Augustine has blurred the distinction between *negative volition* and *volitional indifference*. Secondly and most importantly, "*x* wills" is no adequate substitute for "*p*" in *CFA* but must be completed to "*x* wills that [*q*]". Taken in this form, however, even clause (1) will not result in a tautology any more. Or it will result in a tautology only if Augustine's solution is taken to rely on the tacit assumption of the following principle as a third defining clause of *CFA*:

(3) For every *x* and every *q*: if *x* wills that [*x* wills that (*q*)], *x* wills that [*q*].

That is, one would have to introduce a *reduction formula*, by means of which higher order volitions can be reduced to first-order volitions. Yet this is no plausible psychological principle. Moreover, it is strange for Augustine to rely on it, as he himself recognizes the relevance of higher order volitions for the freewill problem elsewhere (cf. note 13). Therefore, this argument fails because of two fatal defects at least.[21]

The Augustinian solution, then, is a pseudo-solution. There is no argument to the effect that *FA*, explicated by *CFA*, is a sufficient account of freedom and is not dependent on a solution to the problem of "freewill and determination" because freedom of will may be affirmed trivially. Accordingly, the attempt to separate strong from weak accountability on the basis of *FA* turns out to have failed throughout. Given this failure, one might well ask why that idea arose at all. Here we have to remember that *FA*, *CFA* and the argument that will is free *per se* were invented and applied first by *theologians*. This is no accident. According to Jewish-Christian monotheism, the world is ruled by God, who is considered omniscient as well as almighty. Hence God has everything under control including, of course, human volitions and all other mental events relevant to human actions.[22] But among these are cases of sinful thought and decision. So one might think that God is the responsible actor and thus the author of sin himself. However, if the mere fact that an action is dependent on will suffices to make the willing individual strongly accountable for it, quite independently of the question of whether his will is determined from without, God's innocence is restored. Therefore keeping human freedom within the confines of *FA* or *CFA* is a welcome conceptual tool in the hands of theologians anxious to cut off disquieting questions concerning theodicy.

VI. HIDDEN AUGUSTINIANISM IN MODERN PHILOSOPHY

Whether they like or are aware of it, or not, modern philosophers adhering to the idea of defining human freedom solely in terms of *FA* or *CFA* stand on the shoulders of their theological predecessors. Some things have changed of course. Two claims essential to the Augustinian solution usually will not show up in a modern philosophical context any more, viz. (i) the claim that strong accountability of human actors is not denied by the fact that volitions or other relevant mental events are determined completely by *another person*, i.e. God, and (ii) the claim that volition is *free per se*. Yet it is questionable what this really means. It is far from clear in particular that the philosophical positions in question must not and do not rely covertly on secular counterparts of (i) and (ii) in order to get the result they want. Accordingly, let us look at both claims more closely in turn.

Is (i) dispensable? To be sure, with the exception of Leibniz and perhaps a few others, God plays no essential role in the account of free action given by modern philosophers. However, they all share the conviction that the fact that volitions and other mental events are, or might be, determined from without does not affect the question of whether the ensuing actions are free and accountable.[23] The only difference here is that determination resulting from God, or some other person, is replaced by determination resulting from impersonal fate (as in Antiquity and Buddhism) or simply from the laws and given facts of nature (as in mechanistic determinism). Now, the absence of personal control *is* considered an essential difference by philosophers, who try to differentiate between *undetermined* action and action free from *compulsion* or *violence*, adding the latter, but not the former, as a defining mark of freedom over and above simple *FA* or *CFA*.[24] Hence some variant of (i) seems still to be present. Yet on what grounds is personal determination distinguished from impersonal determination here? The only obvious difference is that connected with weak accountability (used, e.g., in the law of tort), viz. ownership of costs and benefits to be distributed: persons normally qualify in this respect, fate and nature do not. But this is relevant only for the imputation of actions *weakly*, not *strongly*, whereas it is the latter we require. Is there any significant difference that would justify a fundamental distinction between personal and impersonal determination from the point of view of strong accountability, too?

I do not think there is. From the point of view of the acting individual, it is certainly irrelevant whether what I think, want and come to will is forced on me by a personal or impersonal power, given that its influence is overwhelming. Moreover, criteria like compulsion or violence are significant to freedom *below* the level of determination. Even a man at gunpoint is not *determined* to what he finally does. The freedom of his deliberation and resulting will is not completely annihilated, even in this extreme situation, although it is reduced severely because the options left open to him are drastically *restricted*. Consequently, if people can be strongly accountable in spite of their relevant mental events being determined from without, this must be on other grounds than the mere difference of personal and impersonal antecedents.

Now, in the original Augustinian solution, this gap is filled by (ii). Without Augustine's claim that volition is free *per se*, claim (i), concerning human accountability in the face of divine control, would be entirely unconvincing. Accordingly, we may expect that his modern, secular successors rely, implicitly or explicitly, on some analogue of (ii), too. And this turns out to be the case. The point can be nicely seen in a striking terminological irony, which is inherent in relevant parts of modern philosophical usage, perhaps most saliently visible in Hume. As is well known, Hume rejects indeterministic "liberty of indifference" and tries to show that liberty, explicated in terms of *FA* or *CFA*, is compatible with the fact that in performing a given voluntary action "we were govern'd by necessity, and that 'twas utterly impossible for us to have acted otherwise".[25] Now, this latter notion of freedom is termed "liberty of spontaneity" by Hume.[26] The terminology sounds strange, though, as "spontaneity" and "spontaneous" derive from the Latin *"sponte"* which means, as noted correctly e.g. by Hobbes, "done by a man's own accord."[27] Moreover, "sponte" in Latin and French as well as "spontaneous" in English and "spontan" in German are the modern philosophical translations of Aristotle's *"hekusios"* up to the 18th century, including of course his criterion of a "beginning from within".[28] Hence one would precisely expect that a "spontaneously free" action *cannot* be necessitated from without in such a way as to make it impossible for the actor to act otherwise. Obviously, if Hume's terminology in the *"Treatise"* is to be more than an accidental and ironic mistake, it must be backed by additional, substantial assumptions which he does not mention because he takes them as self-evident.

Now, there is and has long been a derivative, weakened use of *"sponte"* which can be traced back not to *"hekusios"* but to the Greek *"automatos"*. To avoid any misleading ambiguity, Kant distinguished explicitly between the notion of "simple spontaneity" (*"spontaneitas simpliciter talis"*) and the weakened notion of "conditional spontaneity" (*"spontaneitas secundum quid"*), which also applies to machines (called *"spontaneitas automatica"* here) and is exemplified by self-moving missiles, clocks and turnspits.[29] Conditional spontaneity is compatible with external necessitation and determination to one possibility, of course. Applied to human actions, this would mean that, in principle, these are considered as automatic as the movements of missiles and turnspits. Some advocates of conditional spontaneity as an adequate means of interpreting *FA* or *CFA* have been willing to draw the consequence that human actors *are* automatons, including the mind and the mental events relevant to strongly accountable action.[30] Most of its advocates, however, have been unwilling to do so. They thought it would be possible to *maintain* the usual connotations of human freedom by interpreting it in terms of conditional spontaneity. Yet how could they do this? One might think, as Kant certainly did, that the use of "spontaneity" by philosophers willing to accept the external determination of all relevant mental events is but an evasive verbal manoeuver invented to cover up their wretched picture of human action, which they nevertheless allege to be strongly accountable. However, I think there is a better, more favourable explanation.

As a key to this, consider the following, telling remark of Hobbes'. Having argued first that, following Greek and Latin usage, "spontaneous" may refer only to actions with no perceived cause, he goes on to describe the fallacy of theorists like his opponent Bramhall thus:[31]

because the causes of the will and appetite being not perceived, they supposed, as the Bishop doth, that they were the causes of themselves.

Clearly, this is a *non sequitur*. Lack of perceived external causes is no proof that such causes are inexistent. Still, their assumed inexistence explains why Hobbes' opponents think that the ensuing voluntary actions are done "of the actors' own accord" and therefore "free" in the usual Aristotelian sense. However, if one follows Hobbes and the other advocates of mere conditional spontaneity in the conviction that there *are*, or *must be*, external causes necessitating the will, one needs an alternative explanation for *not* giving up the traditional Aristotelian talk of spontaneous, externally unnecessitated voluntary action. And if there is such an explanation, it can only be the conviction, equally traditional after Augustine, that human volitions do not *need* any further proof of their being free, i.e. being done of the actor's own accord, because they are free *per se*. But where Augustine had tried at least, if even unsuccessfully, to found this conviction on argument, his later theological as well as philosophical followers simply rely on it, most often tacitly.

The same result may be reached from another side. It is not easy to see how the *modal "can"* contained in *FA* could be reducible or explicable in *nonmodal* terms. Thus, on what grounds could thinkers as different as Augustine, Anselm, Leibniz, Hume, Schopenhauer, Moore and many others come to believe that *CFA* offers a way of doing so? Certainly, the mere fact of the conditionality of the two defining clauses does not show this, at least if the conditionals are taken to be *material*. Suppose, then, that the conditionals in *CFA* are *subjunctive*, telling us, e.g., that instead of the factual sequence "willing [*p*] & *p*" there could have occurred counterfactually the alternate sequence "willing [–*p*] & and –*p*". Let us waive the question of whether this really will enable a *nonmodal* reduction. The much more critical question concerns the *meaning* of "could" in the counterfactual part of that sentence. Obviously it must be a "could" adequate to the explication of the *practical* "can", but not many obvious senses are likely to qualify.

The Leibnizian proposal to insert *logical possibility* here is ridiculous. It is not logical impossible that I reach out for a glass of water I desperately long for, although I certainly cannot do this if I am in the hands of someone torturing me by starvation. Moreover, the same example makes clear that it will not help to change logical into *physical possibility*, *compatibility with the laws of nature* or similar notions. Equally *ability* or *opportunity*, if taken in isolation, do not qualify. Disabled by a torturer, I cannot reach out for a glass of water, even if I have the opportunity to do so, and vice versa. To shorten my argument: try whatever interpretation of "could" you have and you will find that no interpretation is relevant to the practical "can" that does not give you an open alternative option *in* the situation in which you make a concrete decision.[32] Now, this seems evidently to *exclude* your being determined antecedently to one option. How then could the proponents of *CFA* mentioned ever come to believe that this condition is irrelevant, or to be content with interpretations of "can" which little reflection shows to be wholly inadequate or even ridiculous? Again, I think, the reason is hidden Augustinianism. Augustine tried to show by his tricky argument that "the will has power over itself" such that, however a certain volition has come about, it will *imply analytically* that the willing man *can* will what he wills. Only if *CFA* is backed by some argument to the same general effect may it seem a plausible device for the explication of the practical "can" at all. If such arguments are lacking, one has to give up that idea and to accept another, stronger explication.

VII. CONCLUSION

These problems might be avoided, of course, if we were willing to confine ourselves to imputing human actions *weakly*. However, there are good reasons not to give up the traditional concept of *strong accountability*. This implies that actions can be traced back to a number of relevant mental events which include wants and volitions. Also it can reasonably be assumed that strong, no less than weak accountability depends on a certain condition of *freedom*. Traditionally, *FA* or more specifically *CFA* have been considered the adequate conceptual tool for giving an explication of this condition by the majority of both philosophical as well as theological thinkers. Moreover, it has been thought that *FA* and *CFA* are sufficient theoretical tools to dispose of the traditional problem of "freewill and determination". I have argued that this is a mistake in principle. The question of whether or not volition or, more generally, all relevant mental events are free is still as urgent as it has ever been. Quite to the contrary, *FA* and *CFA* themselves *rest* on the presupposition that the volitions in question are free, although this fact has often been overlooked by modern advocates of that conception. Accordingly, their dismissal of the freewill problem is unjustified.

The theoretical background for this is a tacit, and most often totally unnoticed, reliance on the fallacious Augustinian proof that the will is free *per se*. However, it is more than doubtful that there will ever be found a cogent theoretical substitute for it. Once this is realized and it is also realized that the theological reasons underlying Augustine's argument and his introduction of *FA* and *CFA* in general can no longer carry philosophical conviction, the attractiveness of this model vanishes. One becomes free for a fresh start to specify the condition of freedom required for strong accountability, independent of the conceptual bonds of *FA*, *CFA* and Augustinianism. This may be hard for philosophers, predominantly those in English-speaking countries, who have been brought up in the conviction that Hume's distinction between "liberty of spontaneity" and "liberty of indifference" contains an answer to the freewill problem that is decisive in principle. To these philosophers my advice is simply to take Hume seriously. The Humean conception is incomplete without a specification of the notion of *"spontaneity"*. This notion should be explicated – thoroughly, consequently and without tacit evasions to Augustinianism. Having done this, however, one may well find that Hume's "liberty of spontaneity" is *liberty* of spontaneity only because it *is*, or *entails*, "liberty of indifference".

Universität Konstanz

NOTES

[1] I have argued for this in Seebass (1993a, chs. I and VI).

[2] Of course, the deliberation required may be reduced to its minimum, which I believe to be this: Any state of affairs or proposition "*p*" which belongs to the action and is known, or required to be known, by the actor in advance is strongly accountable only if the actor has given, or should have given, some thought, however brief, to the question as to whether it should be the case that "*p*" or "*–p*", and has taken a decision.

[3] See Seebass (1993a, esp. pp. 45–47, 91–106, 170–181, 185ff.). My objections cover both explications in terms of "attitudinal dispositions" as proposed, e.g., by Smith (1987; 1994, ch. 4), and full-fledged behaviorist analyses such as Bennett (1976, ch. 2).

[4] See *Essay*, II, 21, 14ff.

[5] Thus Hart (1948–49, 179); see also Nowell-Smith (1954, ch. 20); Berlin (1969, 118ff.).

[6] See *Essay*, II, 21, 10.

[7] See Epictetus, *Discourses*, IV, 1, and for a recent successor Davidson (1980, 74f.).

[8] If it is determined that you are to attain a Stoic frame of mind anyway, the recommendation is *superfluous*. If you are determined to the contrary, it *cannot help* you. Stoic advice would make a difference only if it were in itself sufficient to *determine* the minds of its audiences in the way recommended. But this is patently not the case.

[9] I take it that *volition* has to be analysed as a species of *want* marked by characteristic *motivational qualifications*. The relevant qualifications are specified and discussed in detail in Seebass (1993a, ch. IV, 1 and 6). A detailed account of wanting is given in ch. IV, 2–5 including (in IV, 5) relevant motivational aspects of *mere* wanting.

[10] See e.g. Schlick (1962, 143); Strawson (1974, 1ff.); Davidson (1980, 63).

[11] von Wright (1985, 110).

[12] See Hobbes, *The English Works*, ed. Molesworth, vol. IV, 69, 240; Locke, *Essay* II, 21, 23, 25; Leibniz, *Nouveaux Essais* II, 21, 23 and *Theodicy* § 51; Edwards, *Freedom of the Will*, II, 1–2, 4–5; Schopenhauer, *Preisschrift über die Freiheit des Willens*, sect. III; Ryle (1949, ch. III, 2); Kenny (1975, 13f., 26, 147f.).

[13] See Augustine, *Confessiones* VIII, 10ff., *De Trinitate* X, 11, and *Retractationes* XII, 5; Moore (1965, 93–95); Frankfurt (1971).

[14] This is also acknowledged by Moore (1965, 95) and Frankfurt (1971, 13, 16f.), although they do not present an alternative. However, Frankfurt's talk of a person "identifying himself decisively" with certain desires points in the right direction.

[15] *Essay* II, 21, 25; cf. II, 21, 48. – Actually the sentence after the square brackets (relocated by me to make the argument more conspicuous) occurs in Locke's text immediately before the sentences cited first here. The regress argument occurs in § 25 for the first time in the fifth edition; in the earlier editions it was already introduced in § 23.

[16] See Moore (1965, ch. VI and 1968, 623–627). Austin (1970) has been the most prominent critic. Most analytical philosophers, however, have taken the side of Moore.

[17] See Schopenhauer, loc. cit. (note 12); Hume, *Enquiry Concerning Human Understanding*, sect. VIII/1; Leibniz, *Philosophische Schriften*, Berlin Academy edition, vol. I, 541; Hobbes, *De Corpore*, chs. 9–10, ch. 25, 13; *De Homine*, ch. 11, 2; *The English Works*, loc. cit. (note 12), IV, 239f., 263, 275.

[18] See *Cur Deus Homo* (1093–1098), II, 1.

[19] See *De Libero Arbitrio* (388–395), III, 14–41; *De Civitate Dei* (413–426), V, 9–10.

[20] The difficulties of *CFA* are discussed more fully in Seebass (1994).

[21] A further objection would be that the Augustinian solution, like the regress argument, relies on the assumption that the freewill problem can arise *only* in the form of a question as to whether a *lower order volition* depends on a *higher order volition*.

[22] This is maintained not only by quite a number of biblical passages and radical Protestant theologians like Luther, Calvin or Edwards, but also by the leading Catholic authorities such as, e.g., Thomas Aquinas in *Summa Contra Gentiles* III, 88–91 and *Summa Theologica* I q.23a.5. Theologians holding an indeterministic conception of human will and freedom were condemned officially. Therefore, it is somewhat strange to find Kant's conception of indeterministic, transcendental freedom dubbed as "the Christian-Kantian thought" in Williams (1973, 228) and Bennett (1980, 25ff.).

[23] I avoid dubbing them *"compatibilists"*, since I believe that the opposition of "compatibilism" and "incompatibilism" is terminologically ill-conceived. It gives the misleading impression that one and the same *thesis* is affirmed by the former and denied by the latter party. The real dispute, however, concerns the *interpretation* of the practical "can" and "freedom", which allows, of course, for many more theoretical alternatives than merely two. The point is discussed at length in Seebass (1993b, 14ff.).

[24] See e.g. Hume, *Treatise* II, 3, 2; Schlick (1962, 148ff.); Hayek (1960, 11f., 20f., 133ff.).

[25] See *Treatise* II, 3, 2. In quoting this passage in this way, I take it that commentators like Penelhum (1975, 122) are correct in affirming, and commentators like Stroud (1977, 144) wrong in denying that Hume is willing to *accept* the impossibility of acting otherwise as a consequence of his causal theory of motivation.

[26] This holds for *Treatise* II, 3, 2 only where "liberty of spontaneity" is defined by *negative* criteria like absence of force, violence and constraint. In the *First Enquiry* VIII the dominant criteria are the *positive* characteristics of *FA* or *CFA* and the term "liberty of spontaneity" is dropped. This may be taken as evidence that Hume himself had become aware that his earlier terminology, taken over from "the schools", sounds ironic in his interpretation and is understandable only with regard to the negative criteria used, not with regard to the positive analysis of freedom given by *FA* or *CFA*.

[27] See *The English Works*, loc. cit. (note 12), V, 79. The English derivations seem to have emerged in the middle of the 17th century (see *Oxford English Dictionary*, vol. IX, 659f.). Hobbes himself believes that "spontaneity" and "spontaneous" are neologisms "not used in common English" and introduced only by his opponent, Bishop Bramhall, to fog the problem of freewill (loc. cit. 47, 91, 350f., 400).

[28] For example the Latin translation of *Nicomachean Ethics* 1111a 22ff. by Dionysius Lambinus (Paris 1558, 546b) has *"sponte"* for *"hekusios"* explicitly. The classic philosophers of the modern age focus on the criterion of "acting from an inner principle" e.g., Hobbes (loc. cit. 92f., 400),

Leibniz (*Theodicy* § 290, 301) and Kant (Prussian Academy edition, vol. I, 40; vol. XXVIII/1, 267f., 285).

[29] See Kant's *Lectures on Metaphysics* (1778–80), Prussian Academy edition, vol. XXXVIII/1, 267f. The general concept of "spontaneity" is still defined by the Aristotelian criterion of "proceeding from an inner principle" (see loc. cit. 285 and Prussian Academy edition, vol. I, 40). But in the case of "conditional" or "automatic spontaneity", this is identified simply with some built-in motor-drive or (in the missile example) even with the possession of impulse.

[30] See e.g. Leibniz, *Theodicy*, § 52, 403 and Baumgarten, *Metaphysica*, 7th edition 1779, § 705. For Kant (Prussian Academy edition, vol. V, 97), this terminological consequence of his predecessors amounts to a *reductio ad absurdum*, of course.

[31] See *The English Works*, loc. cit. (note 12), V, 92f., cf. 400.

[32] An argument to this effect is developed more fully in Seebass (1994, 217ff.). My conclusion is similar to that of Chisholm (1966 and 1976) and van Inwagen (1975, 1983 and 1989). The difference is that I try to *argue* for the necessity of a specific interpretation of the practical "can". By contrast, van Inwagen merely *presupposes* a certain interpretation of "can" which, to my mind, is the main reason why his (formally sound) argument has not impressed his "compatibilist" opponents very much.

REFERENCES

Austin, J.L. (1970) [orig. 1956], "Ifs and Cans" in J.L. Austin, *Philosophical Papers*, 3rd Edition. Oxford, Clarendon Press, pp. 205–232.

Bennett, J. (1976), *Linguistic Behaviour*. Cambridge, Cambridge UP.

Bennett, J. (1980), "Accountability" in Z. v. Straaten (ed.), *Philosophical Subjects*. Oxford, Clarendon Press.

Berlin, I. (1969), *Four Essays on Liberty*. Oxford, Oxford UP.

Chisholm, R.M. (1966), "Freedom and Action" in K. Lehrer (ed.), *Freedom and Determinism*. New York, Random House, pp. 11–44.

Chisholm. R.M. (1976), *Person and Object*. London, Allen & Unwin.

Davidson, D. (1980), *Essays on Actions and Events*. Oxford, Oxford UP.

Frankfurt, H. (1971), "Freedom of the Will and the Concept of a Person," *The Journal of Philosophy* **68**, 5–20.

Hart, H.L.A. (1948–49), "The Ascription of Responsibility and Rights," *Proceedings of the Aristotelian Society*, vol. **XLIX**, 171–194.

Hayek, F.A. (1960), *The Constitution of Liberty*. London, Routledge.

van Inwagen, P. (1975), "The Incompatibility of Free Will and Determinism," *Philosophical Studies* **27**, 185–199.

van Inwagen, P. (1983), *An Essay on Free Will*. Oxford, Clarendon Press.

van Inwagen, P. (1989), "When is the Will Free?," *Philosophical Perspectives* **3**, 399–422.

Kenny, A. (1975), *Will, Freedom and Power*. Oxford, Blackwell.

Moore, G.E. (1965) [orig. 1912], *Ethics*. Oxford, Oxford UP.

Moore, G.E. (1968) [orig. 1942], "Replies" in P.A. Schilpp (ed.), *The Philosophy of G.E. Moore*, 3rd Edition. London, Cambridge UP, pp. 623–627.

Nowell-Smith, P.H. (1954), *Ethics*. Harmondsworth, Penguin.

Penelhum, T. (1975), *Hume*. London, Macmillan.

Ryle, G. (1949), *The Concept of Mind*. London, Hutchinson.

Schlick, M. (1962), *Problems of Ethics*. Trl. D. Rynin. New York, Dover.

Seebass, G. (1993a), *Wollen*. Frankfurt, Klostermann.

Seebass, G. (1993b), "Freiheit und Determinismus," *Zeitschrift für philosophische Forschung* **47**, 1–22, 223–245.

Seebass, G. (1994), "Die konditionale Analyse des praktischen Könnens," *Grazer philosophische Studien* **48**, 201–228.
Smith, M. (1987), "The Humean Theory of Motivation," *Mind* **96**, 36–61.
Smith, M. (1994), *The Moral Problem*. Oxford, Blackwell.
Strawson, P.F. (1974), *Freedom and Resentment*. London, Methuen.
Stroud, B. (1977), *Hume*. London, Routledge.
Williams, B. (1973), *Problems of the Self*. Cambridge, Cambridge UP.
von Wright, G.H. (1985), "Of Human Freedom," *The Tanner Lectures on Human Values*, vol. **VI**, Cambridge, Cambridge UP, 107–170.

JOHN BISHOP

NATURALISING MENTAL ACTION[1]

I. INTRODUCTION: THE PROBLEM OF MENTAL ACTION AND ITS CONTEXT

This paper concerns the general problem of explaining how personal action can belong to the natural causal order, and the specific difficulty posed by the need to accommodate *mental* actions for such "naturalist" or "naturalising" accounts of agency.

I believe that the best (and quite probably, the only) candidate for a naturalist theory of action is a Causal Theory of Action (a "CTA"), according to which what makes something count as an action is its having the appropriate kind of causal history. The burden of developing a CTA is thus to specify *what* kind of causal history is the appropriate kind. Roughly, the idea is that behaviour counts as action if and only if it is caused in the right kind of way by mental antecedents which constitute the agent's own reasons for the action. To defend CTA is to flesh out this rough idea.

The attempt to develop a satisfactory CTA faces the following point of tension. On the one hand, it is clearly important that the specification of the kind of causal history needed for behaviour to count as action should not require any essential reference to causal antecedents which *themselves* have the status of action. For, if such reference did turn out to be necessary, causal theories of action would exhibit a circularity which would count as vicious, at least so far as their use in naturalising personal agency is concerned. Yet, on the other hand, there seems to be some truth in a "volitionist" type of position. For, mental actions are often, if not universally, involved in the causal antecedents of overt actions. Indeed, it seems to be *essential* to the character of *fully free and autonomous* actions that their antecedents do include mental actions. And so the problem on which I wish to focus in this paper is the question of whether a CTA can provide an adequate naturalisation of personal agency, while accommodating the existence of mental actions, and the essential role which they appear to play in the aetiology of fully autonomous actions.

Before I attempt to formulate more precisely the problem which mental action poses for a CTA, I wish (by way of further introduction) to say more about the context in which this problem arises. In particular, it will be useful to comment further about what it means to have a "naturalist" theory of personal action, why such a theory might be thought desirable, and how a Causal Theory of Action might successfully naturalise action.

A naturalist theory of action would be desirable because it would resolve the

G. Holmström-Hintikka and R. Tuomela (eds.), Contemporary Action Theory. Vol. I, 251–266.

tension between two important perspectives which we adopt in understanding ourselves, namely the ethical and the natural scientific perspectives. For, a naturalist theory of action would be a theory which succeeded in showing that the presuppositions of these perspectives are indeed compatible with one another. (Achieving a naturalist theory of action might well be a requirement of a *general* programme of philosophical naturalism. But one could think it important to naturalise agency without being committed to any such general programme: one might be a naturalist about agency without wanting to be a naturalist about numbers, for example.)

What *is* the tension between the ethical and the natural scientific perspectives? It amounts, I think, to this. From an ethical perspective we think of ourselves as sometimes morally responsible for our behaviour and its consequences. Now, for a person to be responsible for a given outcome, that outcome must have come about through that person's exercise of control. And this seems to entail that *the person* caused the outcome, or, at least, caused some event or state of affairs which, in turn, caused the outcome. It seems then that, to be morally responsible, agents must sometimes originate or cause certain events or states of affairs. Moral responsibility, we may say, requires *agent-causation*, i.e., the causing or bringing about of events or states of affairs by agents.[2] The natural scientific perspective, however, has no use for agent-causation. According to this perspective, everything that is caused to happen is caused to happen by prior events or conditions, and not by agents. So there is an apparent clash between the ethical and the natural scientific perspective. And this clash is apparent whether the natural world is deterministic or indeterministic, since, in either case, there remains the problem of trying to fit agent-causation into a world understood purely in terms of *event-causation* – of causal relations amongst events and states of affairs.

This apparent clash between our ethical and natural scientific perspectives would be resolved by a successful defence of a CTA. For, the basic idea behind a CTA is that a perspective dealing in agent-causation may be reconciled with a perspective that deals solely in event-causation for the very simple reason that *agent-causation turns out to be just a special kind of event-causation*. When people act they do so with some intention, or – to put it another way – for some reason, which is *their* reason for acting as they do. The nub of a CTA, then, is to suggest that actions are simply behaviour which is both made reasonable and caused by the agent's reasons. Since an agent's reasons for an action consist in certain kinds of mental states which the agent is in (in particular, desires and beliefs), a CTA ontologically reduces actions to causal relations between states and events – a kind of causal relation which is entirely admissible within the natural scientific perspective.[3]

Defending a CTA is not straightforward. In previous work (Bishop 1987; 1989, Chapters 4 and 5; 1990), I have paid special attention to one particular problem proponents of CTA face, namely the problem of causal deviance. It is clear that an agent's reasons causing her to behave in the rationally motivated way is *not* sufficient for the agent to be performing her own intentional action. There can be deviant cases where such a causal link obtains yet there is no action of the relevant kind. To illustrate this, philosophers have gone in for bizarre inventions – although some widely discussed examples do have a certain air of realistic horror to them. (Consider, for instance, Davidson's famous case of the nervous climber who wants to be free of the weight and danger of holding his colleague on the end of a rope and believes that all he has to do to satisfy this desire is to let go, and is then made so nervous by having this reason for letting go that he loses his grip (Davidson 1980, 79).) But it is certainly easy to get the impression that recent discussion of causal deviance is simply an esoteric game of conceptual analysis with little external motivation.[4] This impression is, however, quite mistaken. Dealing with the problem which causal deviance poses for a Causal Theory of Action is an important philosophical task. For, those "agent-causationists" who think that agent-causation is not ontologically reducible to event-causation, and that agency cannot therefore be naturalised,[5] could seize on the possibility of causal deviance as a way of arguing that a CTA cannot succeed. They could argue that the deviant cases show that there has to be more to genuine action than the agent's mental states causing matching behaviour. And what more could this be but *the agent's causing* of that behaviour? What's absent from the nervous climber case which, had it been present, would have made it a case in which the climber performed his own action of letting go? Simply *the climber's bringing it about* that his grip is released, something which (in the case as described) was pre-empted by the onset of his nervousness.[6] If a CTA is to succeed, then, there has to be an answer to this agent-causationist challenge. And it matters whether a CTA succeeds or not, because it matters whether we can reconcile the presuppositions of our ethical perspective with those of our current natural scientific perspective.

II. CAMERON'S FORMULATION OF THE PROBLEM OF MENTAL ACTION

I believe that it *is* possible to specify the right sort of causal links between "rationalising" mental states and overt behaviour without making any implicit appeal to ontologically irreducible agent-causation. I have sought to justify this defence of a Causal Theory of Action elsewhere,[7] and I shall not here attempt even to summarise my position, for the simple reason that the problem which mental actions seem to pose for the CTA applies *even if it is conceded* that the problem of excluding deviant causal chains linking mental states and behaviour has been overcome. J.R. Cameron provides a useful statement of this view and the reasons one might have for adopting it:

> Among the mental causes of action Bishop (like Davidson) includes beliefs, judgments and intentions. We clearly regard judgments as actions; and when we are considering any belief or intention as related to an action, we regard it, if not straightforwardly as an action, then as something for which we hold the person responsible. ... Thus the naturalistic account which Bishop assumes can be given will itself have to include another analysis of agency, or something very close to agency, in the mental realm. Indeed it is this analysis which will lay bare the heart of agency; for it is *because* I am responsible for my intention, for example, to shake my head, that my shaking my head is an action. The decisive battle to make sense of action has to be fought on another part of the front from that in which Bishop locates it. (Cameron 1991, 242–243)

I take Cameron to be making the following three claims:

(1) Action cannot be naturalised just by defending a CTA for the case of bodily actions, since moral responsibility applies to mental goings-on, as well as to bodily goings-on, and so the case of mental action – or something mental which is very close to action – would have to be covered by a successful naturalist theory.

(2) Therefore, if agency is to be naturalised, a CTA will, at least, have to be supplemented by *some other* naturalist theory of mental actions.

(3) Indeed, the *main* focus for a naturalist theory of agency will have to be on mental action (and so the project of defending a CTA turns out to be rather peripheral). And Cameron has an argument for this third claim. He holds, in effect, to the volitionist doctrine that *overt behaviour has the status of action only in virtue of the fact that it is caused by mental going-ons which themselves have (near enough) the status of action.*

If these claims are correct, then indeed it does follow that the success of a causal theory of bodily action would fall seriously short of the goal of a naturalisation of personal agency. We would then have to consider whether such a naturalisation can be achieved through some alternative or additional naturalist theory of agency which does "fight the battle on the right front", by dealing directly with mental actions, or whether the moral is anti-reductionist: i.e., that the centrality of mental action shows that ontologically reductive causal theories of action cannot succeed.

I believe, however, that Cameron's claims are not correct – or, at least, not wholly correct: a CTA may yet have the potential to achieve the naturalisation of personal agency. I do agree with Cameron's claim (1): there *are* mental actions, and a naturalist theory of action has to accommodate them. But I reject the inference from claim (1) to claim (2). Certainly, we need to naturalise mental actions. But it does not follow that we therefore need some other theory apart from CTA. And my principal aim in the present paper is to develop a suggestion for establishing that a CTA can be applied to mental actions too. So I straightforwardly disagree with claim (2).

I also disagree with claim (3) – but not quite so straightforwardly. In what follows, I will reject the volitionist thesis: it is not *universally* the case that behaviour counts as action only if caused by certain kinds of mental action. But I will concede that something close to the volitionist thesis *is* true: namely, (a) that *significantly free* actions count as such only because they are caused by certain sorts of mental actions; and (b) that persons count as significantly free agents only if they have the capacity to perform certain kinds of mental action. These concessions to the centrality of mental action do not, however, render the defence of CTA peripheral to the project of naturalising agency, for, as I shall argue, both these claims can be accommodated by a CTA without any threat of vicious circularity.

III. DRETSKE'S "TRANSITIVITY" ARGUMENT

But *why* am I prepared to make these concessions as to the centrality of mental action? What's wrong, really, with a causal model which firmly eschews mental actions in favour of understanding agency in terms of belief/desire sets non-deviantly causing matching outcomes?

One good way to explain what may be wrong with it is to look at an alleged problem for causal theories of action recently raised by Fred Dretske (1992). Dretske intends his argument to show that we must abandon causal theories as altogether too reductionist to account for genuine agency, and adopt, instead, a "component theory" of action. I shall reject these conclusions. But I shall concede that Dretske's argument can legitimately be construed as issuing a challenge to the effect that a CTA will somehow need to accommodate mental actions if it is to provide a naturalist ontological reduction of paradigm cases of *significantly free* intentional agency.

Dretske develops his argument by considering a particular example: Suppose that I offer Jimmy $1 to wiggle his ears. This causes Jimmy to believe that he will obtain $1 if he wiggles his ears. Given that he wants $1, he thus comes to have a reason for wiggling his ears. And (we are to suppose) he acts on that reason: he wiggles his ears. Now, Dretske argues, if a CTA is correct, Jimmy's reason (his desire for $1 plus his belief that he will get it if he wiggles his ears) causes his ear-wiggling behaviour. Yet, since I caused Jimmy to have this reason, given transitivity of causation, it follows that I caused Jimmy's ear-wiggling behaviour. But this conclusion, Dretske thinks, is problematic: if I caused Jimmy's ear-wiggling, then, surely, I *made him* wiggle his ears, and that does not seem to be consistent with *Jimmy's* wiggling his ears. Jimmy wiggles his ears, "as we like to say, of his own free will" (p. 3). Yet adopting a CTA (granted the transitivity of causation) makes it puzzling how this can be so. CTA seems to be too reductionist to supply the resources to explain how it is that, in this case, Jimmy does indeed "act of his own free will".

Dretske takes his example of Jimmy and the ear-wiggling as a paradigm case of freedom of action: "Here, if anywhere," Dretske says, "freedom of action is on display" (p. 3). Yet it is easy to raise doubts about *just how free* Jimmy is in the situation described. Jimmy's action may be more or less free, depending on the details of the case. If Jimmy is a senior colleague of mine, and I offer the $1, jokingly, in the course of a casual discussion about the genetic basis for ear-wiggling and tongue-curling, then, in all probability, Jimmy's action in wiggling his ears *is* significantly free. But suppose that Jimmy is a young boy. Then I'm paying him money for him to please me by putting on a bodily display, and, though the case is rather trivial (by comparison with other unmentionable cases of the same general sort), there is yet a faint suggestion of abuse about it. Boys usually lack the capacity to make fully autonomous responses to adult bribes.

What *is* true is that, whatever the further details may be, Jimmy exercises his own agency, his own intentional control. (The case is importantly unlike ones in which I get Jimmy's ears to wiggle by direct stimulation of the appropriate efferent nerves, or simply by manhandling him.) So perhaps the right way to construe Dretske's "transitivity" argument is that it is meant to show that a CTA cannot account for the fact that Jimmy's behaviour is an exercise of his own control: that a CTA cannot provide an adequate account of free action even in this, most fundamental, sense of the term.

Dretske takes his argument to show that "contrary to orthodox theory, reasons do not cause the actions they explain" (p. 6). If reasons do not cause actions, then, in the interaction between Jimmy and me, there is no scope for applying transitivity of causation to yield the allegedly problematic conclusion that I cause Jimmy's action of wiggling his ears.

Dretske thinks that he can defend Jimmy's freedom of action in this case by appeal to a "component theory" of action.[8] This theory depends on the familiar distinction between an action and its intrinsic event.[9] (For example, my arm's going up is the event intrinsic to my raising my arm, etc.) An action, Dretske observes, is distinct from its intrinsic event, although the occurrence of an action does "necessarily *involve*" the occurrence of its intrinsic event, which is a "*part* or *component* of the act" (Dretske 1992, 8).

Now, Dretske's component theory proposes that what agents' reasons cause are not their actions, but, rather, the intrinsic events of their actions. Return to Jimmy and me. I cause Jimmy to have a reason for wiggling his ears, and this reason does indeed cause Jimmy's ears to wiggle, but it does not cause Jimmy's *action* of wiggling his ears, and so I *do not* "make him" wiggle his ears. True, by transitivity of causation, I *do* cause Jimmy's ears to wiggle, but (hey presto!) Jimmy's freedom of agency is rescued. His *action* of wiggling his ears, since *it* is not caused by his reasons, is thus safeguarded from counting as something caused by me.

It is hard to see how this theory could provide a real solution to the problem allegedly posed by Dretske's transitivity argument. To the extent that it is problematic how Jimmy can perform *his own action* of wiggling his ears if *I* give him his reason for doing so, it seems equally problematic to maintain that what I cause, by transitivity of causation, is the wiggling of his ears. What use can it be to have it turn out that Jimmy's *action* is not caused by me, if it then emerges that *the event intrinsic to his action* (without which, *necessarily*, his action could not have occurred) *is* caused by me? Dretske's theory has no resources to explain why, if I make Jimmy's ears wiggle (which he concedes) I do not thereby pre-empt Jimmy's doing so, and, thereby, Jimmy's action.

Dretske's own theory, then, does not seem to deal with the difficulty his transitivity argument raises. So *how are we* to deal with this difficulty? One response is to claim that there is no difficulty, and that Dretske's argument simply begs the question against a CTA. A CTA says that if Jimmy's reason for wiggling his ears non-deviantly causes his ears to wiggle, then he performs his own intentional action of wiggling his ears. And this is so, the proponent of CTA will claim, quite independently of who or what has caused Jimmy to have his reason for wiggling his ears. In the case as described, I cause him to have this reason, and so, indeed, I cause him to act. But this is not inconsistent with his exercising his own control. Sometimes what one person causes a second person to do counts as that second person's action, and sometimes it does not. And a CTA has a way of characterising the difference: the difference consists in whether or not the causal chain the first person initiates passes through the relevant mental states of the second person and then non-deviantly from them to his matching behaviour. So a CTA *does* have the resources to preserve the intuition that, in the case as described, Jimmy is "exercising his own free will", even though I cause him to.

This response makes an important point. But it is not fully adequate. As I have already remarked, there are several variations on the Jimmy scenario. In all of them Jimmy exercises his own control when he wiggles his ears, but in some of them he does so quite unfreely, while in others he does exercise a significant degree of freedom, and, in yet others, he acts with full autonomy. Now, the problem is that it looks as if the causal theory's account of Jimmy's action is enough to cover cases only at that end of the spectrum where the action is just a bare exercise of control. For, if the wiggling of Jimmy's ears is a non-deviant causal consequence of his reason for wiggling them, then, according to a CTA, Jimmy's ear-wiggling is a genuine action of his. But this is consistent with Jimmy's response to coming to believe that he will get $1 by wiggling his ears being very unreflective and immediate – and hence, *relatively* unfree. His disposition to oblige when offered cash may be very readily triggered – on the offer of another dollar, he will be likely to curl his tongue, etc. etc. A CTA may be enough, then, to get us a naturalist ontological reduction of certain simple cases of an agent's own exercise of control, but it does not secure anything more than that. Much personal action, however, *is* more than that: it possesses a degree of freedom and autonomy which goes beyond a bare exercise of one's own control.

And this *could* be true, of course, of the Jimmy scenario. What would have to happen for Jimmy to be acting with significant freedom in this situation? Well, on coming to believe that he will get $1 if he wiggles his ears (given the standing desire for $1) Jimmy *is going to have to do more* than simply wiggle his ears. He is going to have to perform *certain mental actions*. For example, he might first consider how much he wants $1, given that, to get it, he has to behave in what he might feel to be a rather undignified way. So he has to make a judgment – and, as we are supposing, he does judge that he wants the $1 more than he fears to seem undignified. And so he forms the intention to earn the $1, infers that, therefore, his ears need to get wiggled, and so forms and carries out the intention to wiggle his ears. If this is what happens, then Jimmy is exercising his own control with a significant degree of freedom: indeed, granted the satisfaction of certain other conditions – of the sort which are highly likely to be satisfied if we switch to the case where Jimmy is my senior colleague – this may even be a case of a fully autonomous free action.

Now, here is the crunch question: how will a CTA provide the resources to deal with such cases of significantly free action? If we stick with a causal model under which agency is constituted by mental states non-deviantly causing matching outcomes, then we seem to leave out something which seems essential for significantly free action, namely *the agent's own exercise* of certain mental capacities.

What are these mental capacities? One is *the capacity to form intentions*. It is one thing to have a desire, and another to set out to satisfy it – to intend to achieve its object. Desires arise independently of our direct control: we are sometimes able *indirectly* to cause ourselves to have certain desires, but their formation never counts itself as a basic action.[10] However, we can (often, anyway) *directly* control whether we form the intention to satisfy a particular desire. Indeed, agents do not count as genuinely free unless they can exercise this capacity – the capacity either to take or not to take the imperative content of a given desire as a premise in their further practical reasoning. For example, I may desire, on a whim, to stroke the beautiful hair of the person in front of me on the bus, but it is up to me whether I form the intention to satisfy this desire. If this were not so, then I would lack significant freedom, and would be suffering from a compulsion.

This desire/intention distinction needs to be paralleled for cognitive states. The formation of beliefs is never itself a basic action – it is never directly under an agent's control. (Though it may be under an agent's *indirect* control. Consider, for example, Pascal's advice to those convinced by his "Wager": that they should induce belief in God by adopting a policy of acting *as if* they believed. "Go, then, and take holy water, and have masses said; belief will come and stupefy your scruples."[11]) But having a belief does not *compel* the believer to use its content in practical or theoretical reasoning. As L. Jonathan Cohen (1992) argues, we have the capacity to *accept or not to accept* what we believe. A person may, for example, be disposed to hold racist beliefs – and the triggering of this disposition may not be under his direct control: for instance, he may automatically be suspicious of any dark-skinned strangers he sees in his neighbourhood. Yet it usually will be within his control whether he accepts the content of his racist belief as a premise for his practical reasoning and acting. He may have enough critical awareness of the racist character and origin of his belief that this dark-skinned stranger is not to be trusted to restrain himself from accepting its content in his further thought and action. This capacity, too – the capacity to accept or not to accept the content of a given belief – seems essential to being a free agent.

And one may continue. Free agents must be able to form evaluative judgments about what it is all-things-considered best to do. They must be able to form intentions by practical inference from prior intentions and relevant beliefs whose content they accept. The capacity for these kinds of mental action (and, certainly, for more kinds than I have mentioned) seems clearly essential for an agent to count as genuinely free.

So, the upshot of this examination of Dretske's transitivity argument seems to be the following. If, with a wary eye on avoiding circularity, we seek to stick with a CTA which construes actions as constituted by outcomes caused by mental *states*, then it seems we get a naturalist theory which covers only the more impoverished kinds of actions, which are mere exercises of control without any significant degree of autonomy. Significantly free actions seem to have to involve certain types of mental action; and agents do not count as significantly free agents unless they have the capacity to perform these types of mental action. So, a CTA will not be able to provide an adequate naturalisation of significantly free actions, *unless* it can successfully be applied (without circularity) to mental actions, and specifically to those mental actions which are essential to the antecedents of significantly free action.

IV. THE PROPOSED SOLUTION: APPEALING TO HIGHER-ORDER INTENTIONS, CONSTITUTIVE OF RATIONALITY ITSELF

I shall now try to show that a CTA *can* be successfully applied to mental actions, and that it can accommodate the truth behind volitionism – namely that mental actions do belong essentially to the causal history of significantly free actions.

For a CTA to apply to a given mental action, that action will have to count as done for a reason. How can this be? Can mental actions be shown to fit the pattern of behaviour both caused and made reasonable by antecedent mental states? I think they can. Let me return to Dretske's case of Jimmy and me, and to the kinds of mental actions Jimmy would have to perform for his ear-wiggling to count as something he does with a significant degree of freedom. Jimmy would have to do at least the following. He would have to (i) form an evaluative judgment as to whether he should, all things considered, wiggle his ears for me, given his desire for the dollar, and other perhaps conflicting desires which he may have. And then, having made this judgment, he would have to (ii) form the intention to wiggle his ears, and (iii) carry that intention out. So let us see how a CTA might deal with these three actions.

The last of these actions is unproblematic. Jimmy's carrying out his intention to wiggle his ears *just is* his intentionally wiggling his ears, and a CTA will maintain that this is simply constituted by a non-deviant causal relation between Jimmy's intention to wiggle his ears and the wiggling of his ears. But how may a CTA be applied to the two previous actions in the sequence, which are *mental* exercises of control?

Consider Jimmy's mental action of forming the intention to wiggle his ears. How could a CTA apply to this? First, we must identify the event which is intrinsic to this action. I suggest that this is simply the formation of an intentional state with the content "let it be that I wiggle my ears", which is itself going to be constituted by a neural state which instantiates the intending-to-wiggle-one's-ears-here-and-now functional role. (If we adopt the Language of Thought hypothesis, then this will amount to a Mentalese sentence with the content <let it be that I wiggle my ears> coming to be in the appropriate part of Jimmy's cognitive architecture – call it his "immediate bodily output" box.) Jimmy could not form the intention to wiggle his ears here and now without this event occurring, but this event could occur (otherwise caused) without Jimmy performing the mental action of forming this intention.

Second, we must supply this event with a causal history involving mental states which constitute Jimmy's *reason* for forming his intention to wiggle his ears. In order to do this, we have to be prepared, I believe, to posit higher-order intentions.[12] It is constitutive of being an intentional agent that one has certain standing higher-order intentions classifiable generally as *intentions to act in accordance with the canons of practical rationality*. The member of this general class which is relevant here is the intention to form intentions consistently with one's all-things-considered judgments about what it is best to do (that is, to conform to what Davidson has called "the principle of continence"[13]). Granted that Jimmy has this higher-order intention, we can give a causal analysis of Jimmy's mental action of forming the intention to wiggle his ears as follows: his intention to conform to the principle of continence, plus his judgment that it is best to wiggle his ears non-deviantly causes the occurrence of the content <let it be that I wiggle my ears> in his immediate bodily output box.

Can we achieve similar success in applying a CTA to the first of the mental actions which Jimmy performs, namely his judging that it is all-things-considered best for him to wiggle his ears? The intrinsic event here is the mere occurrence of the judgment that it is best for him to wiggle his ears. For this occurrence to come about through Jimmy's action, it will need to be suitably caused by mental states which also make it reasonable. Now, my suggested strategy is to appeal to higher-order intentions which belong constitutively to practical reasoners. One of these is the intention to make *reasonable* judgments about what it is all-things-considered best to do – a highly general intention which will need to be broken down into a whole set of particular intentions to follow specific canons of practical evaluative rationality (and, of course, it is far from straightforward to provide a theory of what these canons are).

But is this really going to work, at the required level of detail? If Jimmy is acting significantly freely, one crucial aspect of his making a judgment about what it is best to do will be to decide whether he desires the dollar more than he desires not to behave in an undignified fashion, not to be someone else's to command for trivial sums of money, etc. And this seems to be a mental action – the action of setting an order of priority amongst his conflicting desires. In the case as given, he does this in favour of satisfying the desire for the dollar. How will the appeal to higher-order intentions to follow the canons of practical rationality enable a causal theory to be applied to this mental action?

Perhaps it will be suggested that agents constitutively intend to set priorities amongst competing desires in accordance with their fundamental values. And then, maybe, we can take the mental action of giving first priority to a given member of a set of incompatible desires to be constituted by a suitable causal relation between this higher-order intention, the agent's awareness of his fundamental values, and the event which consists in his forming the intention to seek to satisfy the favoured desire (an event which will itself be understood in terms of the relevant content, or Mentalese sentence, getting into the agent's "intention" box).

But this is unsatisfactory. For one thing, it simply shifts the problem back one stage, since an agent's fundamental values are far from static: free agents sometimes find they have to decide how to set priorities amongst what they had heretofore thought of as their fundamental values. So the problem of providing a causal ontological reduction of mental actions in which agents set priorities amongst their basic values would still remain. But, anyway, this picture is phenomenologically implausible. We do not *first* settle our fundamental values, and *then* adjudicate conflicts amongst our desires in relation to them. Rather, it is through the process of practically dealing with conflicts amongst our desires that we come to establish and develop our allegiance to fundamental values. It may be only when Jimmy is actually faced with my request to wiggle his ears for a dollar that he discovers that there is something about this prospective performance which he does not like, and that he does have some degree of desire not to let himself be used in this kind of way. And (a familiar existentialist point!) it will be *in* settling the conflict between his desire for a quick dollar and his desire not to be used that he will develop his own system of fundamental values.

I consider, then, that there is not much hope of providing the sought-for ontological reduction of the mental action of giving the satisfaction of one desire priority over another by seeing this as caused *inter alia* by a general intention to adhere to one's established fundamental values.

So how could we apply a CTA to cases where agents, discovering that satisfying one desire will require doing something which, to some extent, they desire not do, are faced with the need to determine an ordering amongst their desires, in order to settle their intentions as to which desire or desires to seek to satisfy? The only hope, I think, is to stick with my general approach, and to look for higher-order intentions to follow certain norms of practical rationality, which may plausibly be presumed to belong to the agent, *qua* practical agent. Now, I suggest that one (easily overlooked but vitally important) practical rational norm is that, when I find I have conflicting desires, I should *somehow* determine an ordering amongst them. Clearly, it is fundamentally in my interests that I should not simply "seize up" in circumstances of conflict. One way to obtain the required ordering, of course, would be to derive it from a more fundamental set of my desires or values which are already well-ordered – and, in that case, the decision is made for a reason, and it becomes possible to apply CTA. But, as already observed, this cannot be the *only* way in which agents decide how to order conflicting desires, since there can be conflicts amongst *underived* desires. So it may seem that some setting of priorities is done, but not done for a reason – and thus that there is a kind of mental action which cannot be given an ontological reduction along CTA lines.

But let the proponent of CTA not panic! Making such decisions can, I think, yet be seen to be intentional. Clearly, such decisions are not made *for the reason that they conform to already established systems of priorities* amongst more fundamental desires. But it does not follow that they are not made *for any reason at all*. The practical agent must, as I have suggested, intend that conflicts amongst desires be resolved *somehow*. If they cannot be resolved by derivation from more fundamental well-ordered desires, then they will have to be resolved some other way. One way would be to settle the ordering at random. Another would be to let (how shall I put this?) the emotional colour of the conflicting desires settle it. It feels good to be making easy money, and, though the idea of mildly prostituting oneself has a distasteful aspect, it is somehow exciting to be the object of this kind of attention. So, go with the flow, and let the desire for the money become the intention to get it. So we have available the following kind of account, which does meet the requirements of a CTA. What happens in Jimmy's case is that his desire for the dollar does get transformed into an intention to obtain it. He recognises that he has some desire not to let himself be used in this kind of way. He has the general constitutive practical intention to settle such conflicts somehow, and (we may suppose) cannot settle them by derivation from more fundamental, well-ordered, desires or values. This general intention, plus his monitoring belief that he does indeed need to resolve a conflict amongst his desires, then non-deviantly cause the translation of the content <would that I have a dollar> into his intention box. And all this realises his deciding to satisfy the desire to have the dollar rather than to preserve a view of himself as someone who cannot be used for money, and coming to intend accordingly. Of course, the ordering of his priorities which is involved here might well soon be overturned: when Jimmy discovers how other people respond to his willingness to let himself be another's plaything for money, he might find that he values maintaining his self-respect above easy money, and may then decide accordingly on all similar future occasions of conflict. So, though agents may sometimes have no reason for setting their priorities *a certain way* – especially when first faced with a particular kind of conflict amongst their desires – they may still resolve the conflict by forming an intention, and the forming of that intention may itself count as done for reason – as a mental action capable of a causal analysis.

V. COMMENTS ON SOME POSSIBLE OBJECTIONS TO THE PROPOSED SOLUTION

So much for a sketch of how I think the appeal to higher-order intentions allows the kinds of mental action which seem necessary for significant freedom to be brought within the ambit of a CTA. I will conclude by commenting briefly on some possible problems with this approach.

First, is circularity avoided? I think so. Appealing to higher-order intentions need not threaten circularity, provided we may defend the view that the formation of these high-order intentions does not *itself* have to count as an exercise of the agent's intentional control. This condition is, of course, meant to be satisfied by maintaining that the possession of these higher-order intentions is *constitutive* of being a rational agent. An individual's having these intentions is, simply, part of that individual's nature (and there will, presumably, be an evolutionary account of how creatures with such natures came to exist). To be free (even in the fullest sense), it is not necessary for agents to have exercised control over the formation of the very conditions which constitute them as practical agents in the first place.[14]

It might be argued that, even though the formation of these higher-order intentions does not itself have to count as the agent's own intentional action (so that circularity is conceded not to be introduced *that way*), nevertheless, for these states to count as intentions at all, there has to be *some* reference to active capacities implicit in their attribution (and so circularity still rears its ugly head). If it is *just in our nature* to operate in accordance with certain principles (which then get honorifically described as "the canons of practical rationality"), how can it be justified that we understand these operations as *our own actions*?

I envisage two lines of reply – not, perhaps, entirely consonant with one another. One is to adapt the insight of Lycan-style homuncular functionalism,[15] and admit that the most basic sorts of actions, both bodily and mental – such as making straightforward inferences, forming intentions from all-things-considered best judgments, carrying out intentions to perform here and now bodily movements within one's repertoire of basic acts – *are* pretty automatic and stupid, but that flexibile practical intelligence and genuine freedom of action emerges from the right sort of functional concatenation of these elements. The other line of reply is to argue that, though we do, so to speak, come already equipped with these higher-order intentions (and would think defective a person who lacked them), we are nevertheless able to repudiate them. We do not *have to act* in accordance with the canons of rationality, though if we do set ourselves not to act rationally, what we do will still turn out to be done for a reason, and will be intentional under some such description as "behaving counter-rationally".

Second, this solution is going to work only if it can be extended to *all* the kinds of mental action which may be needed for fully autonomous action. For example, it seems clear (and I am thinking here of the work of Harry Frankfurt[16]) that, to act fully freely, an agent must not be alienated from his or her own motivating reasons. But, as Velleman has observed (1992, 474), this condition may be thought to conceal a mental action – the action of "identifying" with one's reasons for acting. Velleman thinks he can overcome this objection by appeal to higher-order motives. I am inclined to think that it is a mistake to regard this kind of identification as an action at all. But, whichever of us is right, the CTA is secure.

Third, my suggested solution will also require defending the view that one can have, and act on, intentions of whose content one is not consciously aware – since it would, of course, be ridiculous to maintain that, in performing mental actions of judgment, decision and intention-formation, agents are in general aware of the higher-order intentions with which (on my theory) they are in fact acting. I do not think this is too serious an obstacle, though one does have to develop an account of when it is and when it is not warranted to appeal to the existence of unconsciously held mental states. My hope would be that such an account can be developed by appeal to what one might call "consciousness-raising" counterfactuals, about agents' dispositions to accept or not accept that they are acting on certain higher-order intentions when the question is put to them whether they are, in fact, doing so.

The University of Auckland

NOTES

[1] An earlier version of this paper was given as the Presidential Address to the May 1994 Conference of the New Zealand Division of the Australasian Association of Philosophy held at the University of Auckland.

[2] Note that I am here using the technical term "agent-causation" in what might be called a naive sense, *just* to mean a causal relationship between an agent (as cause) and an event or state of affairs (as effect). Thus, in using the term I am not endorsing Roderick Chisholm's (1966) position, according to which it is essential to agent-causation that what is agent-caused is not event-caused. My naive use of the term "agent-causation" does, of course, leave this possibility open. But, as is apparent from the account I am here giving of how a CTA would naturalise personal agency, it also leaves open the possibility that agent-causation should turn out to be ontologically reducible to a type of event-causation.

[3] It is important to emphasise that the reduction of action which a CTA proposes is an *ontological* reduction, and not a conceptual one. CTA is not committed to the (rather obviously false) claim that *all it means* to perform an intentional action is for relevant mental states to cause suitable behaviour. For further discussion, see Bishop (1989, 95–98).

[4] Perhaps this is what Paul Snowdon was suggesting when he described my *Natural Agency* as addressed "to the *aficionados* of deviance theory"? (Snowdon 1990)

[5] Unless, that is, irreducible agent-causation were to be reintroduced into our natural scientific ontology.

[6] Roderick Chisholm argued along just these lines in his influential (1966) paper, at the outset of recent discussions of causal deviance in action theory.

[7] For my attempt at a causal account of basic intentional action which excludes the deviant cases, see Bishop (1989, Chapter 5). My final proposal for an adequate definition is on p. 172.

[8] As developed in Dretske (1988).

[9] Dretske calls it the action's "associated result". I myself avoid this terminology because it might misleadingly suggest that a (causal) consequence of the action is being referred to, which is not, of course, what is intended.

[10] Following Arthur Danto (1965), I mean by a "basic" action, an action which is *directly* under the agent's control – which does not have to be performed "by" doing something else.

[11] William James's translation (James 1956, 6).

[12] I have floated this suggestion previously (Bishop 1990, 182). The idea has recently been developed by J. David Velleman (1992).

[13] Davidson (1980, 41).

[14] I am inclined to believe (but reserve the argument for another occasion) that it is the failure to recognise this point which is the fundamental flaw in most libertarian views of free action.

[15] See Lycan (1987).

[16] See "Freedom of the Will and the Concept of a Person", "Three Concepts of Free Action", "Identification and Externality", "The Problem of Action" and "Identification and Wholeheartedness", all collected in Frankfurt (1988).

REFERENCES

Bishop, John (1987), "Sensitive and Insensitive Responses to Deviant Action," *Australasian Journal of Philosophy* **65**, 452–269.

Bishop, John (1989), *Natural Agency: an Essay on the Causal Theory of Action*. Cambridge and New York, Cambridge University Press.

Bishop, John (1990), "Searle on Natural Agency," *Australasian Journal of Philosophy* **68**, 282–300.

Cameron, J.R. (1991), "Review of John Bishop, *Natural Agency*," *Philosophical Books* **32**, 241–243.

Chisholm, Roderick (1966), "Freedom and Action" in K. Lehrer (ed.), *Freedom and Determinism*. New York, Random House, pp. 11–44.

Cohen, L. Jonathan (1992), *An Essay on Belief and Acceptance*. Oxford, Clarendon Press.

Danto, Arthur (1965), "Basic Actions," *American Philosophical Quarterly* **2**, 141–148.

Davidson, Donald (1980), *Essays on Actions and Events*. Oxford, Clarendon Press.

Dretske, Fred (1988), *Explaining Behavior*. Cambridge, Mass., M.I.T. Press.

Dretske, Fred (1992), "The Metaphysics of Freedom," *Canadian Journal of Philosophy* **22**, 1–14.

Frankfurt, H. (1988), *The Importance of What We Care About*. Cambridge, New York, Melbourne, Cambridge University Press.

James, William (1956), "The Will to Believe" in *The Will to Believe and Other Essays in Popular Philosophy*, New York, Dover Publications.

Lycan, William G. (1987), *Consciousness*. Cambridge, Mass., M.I.T. Press.

Snowdon, Paul F. (1990), "The Will and the Way," *Times Literary Supplement*, 9th February, 1990.

Velleman, J. David (1992), "What Happens When Someone Acts?," *Mind* **101**, 461–481.

DAVID-HILLEL RUBEN

DOING WITHOUT HAPPENINGS: THREE THEORIES OF ACTION

There seems to be a distinction of some sort between my actions on the one hand, like my bending my finger and my raising my arm, and mere 'passive' events that occur to my body on the other, like my finger's bending and my arm's rising. My finger can bend without my bending it; my arm can rise without me raising it. What are actions, if not events?

Some find that *sui generis* actions would be something of a mystery, although events themselves, whether *sui generis* or not, are not similarly mysterious. There are two current theories about action which attempt to illuminate what action is by identifying every token action with an event token of some kind: the Causal Theory of Action (the CTA); and the Agent Causalist Theory (the ACT). One might be forgiven for thinking that any such view about action would be implausible. After all, bodily events like the ones I enumerated above are passive, since they merely happen or occur. How can some events be actions, which, if anything is, are active? That is the question both theories must answer: How can activity 'emerge' from, or supervene on, the passivity of events? Let us call this 'the problem of passivity'.[1]

According to the CTA, each token action can be reductively identified with a token movement or event (some non-actional item), but only with one which is caused in the right way by a rationalising mental state (a belief and a desire pair or perhaps an intention). So, on this view, the action, my bending my finger is, after all, the event, my finger's bending, when that bending is caused, for example, by my desire for something and my belief that my finger bending will satisfy that desire. The CTA must admit psychological states like belief and desire or intention into its scheme of things, but of course it is free at a later stage to be reductive about them in turn, identifying them with states of the brain. I do not consider this further move here.

The idea of rationalisation in play here is the old Humean idea of reason as the slave of the passions. Suppose I desire some end or goal, g (perhaps, I want to impress you), and I believe that only by engaging in action A (perhaps, bending my finger) will I obtain g. My doing A (my bending my finger) is thereby rationalised. For my action to be rationalised, it is not required that I consciously engage in such practical or instrumental reasoning, but it certainly is required, at the very least, that I do actually have the belief and desire in question, if they are to be causes of my behaviour and be responsible for 'upgrading', as it were, the finger's bending, to the level of action, my bending my finger.

G. Holmström-Hintikka and R. Tuomela (eds.), Contemporary Action Theory. Vol. I, 267–286.

The requirement that the mental states rationalise is added by the CTA to the requirement that they cause the event, and is intended to solve the problem of passivity. Causation alone cannot solve this problem. The reply of the CTA to the problem of passivity is that the activity of an action can be located in the type of causes it (or equivalently, the event with which it is identical) has. When my finger bends as a nondeviant result of my rationalising belief and desire, or intention, that is agency enough, says the CTA; an event so non-deviantly caused just is an action. I desire *g*, and I believe that only by bending my finger will I get *g*, so when that desire and that belief (or, my intention to bend my finger) jointly cause in the right way the bending of my finger, such a bodily movement is my action, my bending my finger.

It should not be imagined that any version of a CTA can jettison or weaken the rationalising requirement in any way. There is no chance at all of locating action or agency simply in bodily or other events, as and when driven by just any old psychological cause or other, if the latter is non-rationalising. My eyelids flutter, and the fluttering is caused by my desire for something or by my irascible temperament. I cannot always get agency (my fluttering my eyelids) out of the passivity of events (the fluttering of my eyelids) and their psychological causes (the desire for something or my irascibility). The fluttering of the eyelids might only be a reflex effect of that desire, like the dilation of my pupils is to the absence of light. What is missing in these examples, according to the CTA, is that such psychological causes (irascibility; a fleeting, embarrassing thought; desire-without-belief) do not rationalise as well as cause.

So even if mental events like beliefs and desires were in turn to be reduced to physical ones, the CTA is committed to finding, at the level of folk psychology itself, some mental occurrences that cause and rationalise each token action.

Assuming that we engage in a great deal of genuine activity, the demands of the CTA will also require of agents an implausibly rich mental life, over full of reasons, beliefs, desires, and intentions. The CTA must inflate the mental, as a precondition for reducing action. Its slogan might be: no (action) reduction without (mental) inflation.

In this way, the CTA is engaged in dramatic mental overpopulation. I count myself amongst the friends of mind and action. In my view, the friendliest thing one can do in the case of action is to prune (but not, of course, to eliminate) the mind's contents. If the CTA can be said to inflate the mind, in order to reduce action, I prefer to deflate the mind's contents, to preserve action's integrity. So, as a friend of action, I wish to practice some form of mental birth control. Mental life, on my view, is simply not rich enough to insure that there are sufficient mental states on hand to meet the requirements for the reduction of action, like those advanced by the CTA.[2]

What grounds do I offer for thinking that the CTA overinflates the mind? I grant the CTA its right to postulate all sorts of dispositional, subconscious, and unconscious mental states; the mental states it hypothesises need not all of them be open and transparent to consciousness. However, there will still be insufficient mental material, whether episodic or dispositional, conscious or subconscious, explicit or tacit, to make the CTA plausible for many cases of action.

Others have pointed out alleged examples of action for which the positing of causing and rationalising mental states (especially, beliefs) seems to be implausible. Brian O'Shaughnessy focuses on sub-intentional acts, like tapping one's feet to music and moving one's tongue in one's mouth. I do not dispute his examples, but one might hold, though, that such cases constitute relatively peripheral examples of action. Rosalind Hursthouse has also offered examples of action in which she claims that the relevant belief is missing. Her examples are cases in which the action is explained by the presence of emotion(s).[3]

The cases I have in mind are uncontroversially nonperipheral cases of action, and, unlike Hursthouse's, do not involve the emotions. I want to concentrate on stretches of activity which are made up of a large number of actions. Paradigm cases include front-crawling across a swimming pool, ice-skating around a pond, taking a walk around the block. The CTA does not have much trouble with the whole stretch of activity, the 'large' act as we might call it. I desire to get to the other side of the pool. I believe that if I front-crawl across the pool, I will get to the other side, so I front-crawl across the pool. So far, so good.

But the CTA is a theory that is meant to apply to all our intentional actions. In front-crawling across a pool, for example, I perform many actions: I raise my left arm out of the water, while pushing my right arm back, then I bring my right arm out of the water, while pushing my left arm back, and so on. These actions, along with many others, go to make up what it is to front-crawl across the pool. I desire to front-crawl. If I had the belief that I need to lift my left arm out of the water in order to front-crawl, that belief and desire would rationalise my so lifting. But I may not have any such belief.

When I learn to do such things, the specific guidance that directs these stretches of activity certainly has to be hard-wired in, in some way. But there might fail to be any appropriate beliefs, or any informational items at the level of folk psychology. We can describe the difference between hard-wired guidance and belief by using a distinction due to Daniel Dennett, between personal and subpersonal states of a system.[4] Intentions, beliefs, desires, even volitions and tryings, are states of a person, which have conceptual content. The concepts so contained are the concepts belonging to that person; they are 'available' to him, ones which he must be able to grasp.

In the absence of 'personal' beliefs, there may still be causally effective representational states, but these will be physical states of a subpersonal system (e.g., an appropriate brain state), and hence will have no location within folk psychology. Such neurophysiological states may be representational, that is, they may encode information about various matters, but are neither conceptual nor personal.[5] The information they encode may not, even in principle, be available to the person; they may not 'contain' concepts which he can grasp.

Such subpersonal states are really no more than physical states that confer on a person certain of the abilities that he may have, to do various things. They have no place within common sense psychology, nor are they states of the agents which are candidates for rationalising and controlling agency. The person has the ability to front crawl, produce certain sounds, ice-skate, and does so. A person may have, in virtue of his hard-wiring, an ability to, say, do *A* which he cannot conceptualise or represent in any way to himself. Whatever such an ability is, it is not a rationaliser. The ability to do *A* cannot rationalise doing *A*; mere physical abilities have no place in the folk psychological arena which includes rationalisation, and mental states with conceptual content.

A person may just know how to do something, having watched and emulated, without being able to say what he does, or without even having available the concepts with which to express this information. Notice that this point, if it works against ascribing belief and desire to the agent in such cases, also works against ascribing corresponding intentions to him. Intentions also require conceptual content. No one can have an intention to do something for which he has, in principle, no concepts. And where nothing with conceptual content, no propositions and hence neither inference nor practical syllogism. And without rationalisation, the case for the CTA offering an adequate analysis of action simply collapses.

There are two responses here that the CTA might make: (1) that it is not required to find beliefs that rationalise the actions I have mentioned; (2) that there are appropriate beliefs or other appropriate rationalising mental states even in these cases. Let me take each response in turn.

(1) One line of defense (I call it 'the whole-part strategy'), that might be used by the CTA, is suggested by remarks of Adams and Mele made in discussing a somewhat different issue (they call this 'the status of subsidiary actions'), and indeed follows the outline of an earlier suggestion by Alvin Goldman.[6] As Goldman argued, my mental states can rationalise my taking twelve steps in all, without a separate and distinct mental state rationalising every single step included in those twelve. Goldman's view may reflect common sense, but I do not believe that it is a view that is available to the CTA.

Let us distinguish between actions and their parts. If the actions which are preceded by no belief or desire are such that they are parts of larger actions which are so preceded by a suitable desire and belief pair (or intention), then it may be that the former qualify as actions simply in virtue of being parts of actions which qualify in their own right. So, the idea would be that there may be action parts for which we have no relevant beliefs or desires (or intentions), but these are merely parts of larger actions, and we can always find relevant beliefs and desires for the later. I must have, let us suppose, a relevant mental state whose content concerns the whole stretch of activity, front-crawling across the pool, but, the reply might continue, I surely need not have a distinct belief whose content concerns only lifting my left arm out of the water, another only for pushing my left arm back, another only for lifting my right arm out of the water, and so on.

The main difficulty with the whole-part strategy is this. In the course of my 'large' action, like my front crawling across the pool, two sorts of 'things' happen: (a) I act (like my lifting my left arm out of the water); (b) events may occur to me (like my getting water in my eyes or losing my goggles). Both (a) and (b) will occur as proper parts of my front-crawling across the pool, in one perfectly acceptable sense of 'part'.

The idea is that the overall whole-front-crawl-involving belief and desire cover, by extension as it were, the rising of my left arm, and so convert the event, the rising of my left arm, into the action, my lifting my left arm, but do not so cover my getting water in my eyes or the loss of the goggles, for these latter are not actions at all. If the belief were to cover the latter in the same way as the former, they too would be 'converted' into acts that went to make up my front crawl, which they are not. But I do not see how to distinguish between acts which are proper parts of the front crawl and non-actional events which are also proper parts of the front crawl, unless we already have the distinction in place between actions and non-actional events.

It is not my view that we do need to postulate beliefs that specifically involve each of these subacts; such a view would be clearly absurd. I do not doubt in the least that, in many cases of action, the action I perform can be broken up into smaller action units, concerning which I have no specific beliefs. But this perfectly acceptable thought is of no help to the CTA, since those smaller actions do not acquire their status as actions by being parts of the large action of which they are parts, which is what the defense on behalf of the CTA that we are imagining would require.

My argument is only that, if the CTA were to be taken seriously, it could not rely on the distinction between acts and events but must explain that distinction. Therefore, what the CTA needs to say is that, since it is an action, the lifting of my left arm out of the water, but not my getting water in my eyes or losing my goggles, is rationalised by the mental events that cause it (and not just caused by those beliefs and desires that cause and rationalise the large act of which they are both equally proper parts). So we are back, on the CTA, to the need for left-arm-lifting-beliefs after all, and not just whole-front-crawl-involving ones, and that seems to me to rule out this line of argument in its defense.

There are two sorts of replies that might be made in defense of the CTA's whole-part strategy: essentiality and the by-relation. First, essentiality. I said earlier that both lifting one's left arm out of the water and getting water in one's eyes will occur as proper parts of my front-crawling across the pool, in one perfectly acceptable sense of 'part'. That may be so, but there is perhaps another sense of 'part' which distinguishes them. One's lifting one's left arm out of the water is in some sense (yet to be specified) essential to the front-crawl, whereas getting water in one's eyes is not similarly essential.

But how are we meant to understand 'essential' here? No token left arm lifting is essential; the front-crawl across the pool could have been accomplished by the occurrence of some other token of the same type. I might have lifted my left arm from the water just a second sooner or later; I might even have managed to omit any left arm lifting between the previous and subsequent right arm lifting and still managed my front crawl. So the token left arm lifting seems no more essential to the front-crawl than does the token getting water in one's eyes.

Perhaps the difference between essentiality and inessentiality comes at the level of types. One can front crawl in the absence of any tokens of the type, getting water in one's eyes, but one cannot front crawl across a pool in the absence of any tokens of the type, lifting one's left arm out of the water. That supposition may be true, but is of no help in the defense of the CTA. The CTA is required to account for what makes some token event an action. Knowing that some action type is essential to the whole activity won't help us in accounting for why, concerning some token item, it is or is not an instance of that (or, any) action type. Knowledge that that item is or is not an action must come from elsewhere; if it is an action, the type of action of which it is a token may be essential to the whole activity, but, even if so, that fact has no bearing on whether it, the token, is an instance of that type.

To see this more clearly, suppose that in the course of the swim, my muscles seize up and my left arm rises from the water as a automatic response. That nonactional rising of my arm might look indistinguishable from what my action of lifting my left arm out of the water would have looked like, had the latter occurred instead. Although my lifting my left arm out of water is an action type essential to my front-crawling, that fact is irrelevant in determining whether the actual token arm rising that has just occurred is an instance of that action type or not. The CTA would seem to mistakenly convert both the token getting water in one's eyes and the nonactional token rising of my left arm out of the water (due to my muscles seizing up) into token actions, since both are as much a part of the swim as are the genuine tokens of the action type, my lifting my left arm out of the water.

The second defense of the CTA's whole-part strategy focuses on the by-relation. I front crawl by lifting my left arm out of the water, but I do not front crawl by getting water in my eyes. In the sense of 'action part' the CTA requires, *a* is a part of *b* only if one does *b* by doing *a*. If *b* is an action, then everything that is a part of *b* in only this sense is also an action. Lifting my left arm from the water passes this parts-test; getting water in one's eyes and losing one's goggles do not.

The difficulty with this suggestion is that some nonactions pass this test. Recall the nonactional rising of my left arm out of the water as a consequence of muscular seizure. It may be that this nonactional rising was accidentally effective in the context of the whole swim; it may indeed have been stronger than a typical case of my lifting my arm, and hence propelled me especially well. So I have accomplished my front-crawl in part by the nonactional rising of my arm out of the water.

Of course, there is a technical use of 'by' in the literature on action theory such that the by-relation holds only between actions and in this technical sense it is not true that I have front-crawled by my left arm rising (since the latter is not an action). But, the use of that technical sense of 'by', restricted as it is to actions, presupposes that we already know, concerning the relata that it relates, that they are actions rather than nonactional events.

I conclude that there is no way available to the CTA of getting parts to inherit the property of being an an act from the wholes of which they are the parts.

(2) If the whole-part strategy fails, the CTA might try another. A second line of defense is to try and specify beliefs after all that will rationalise and cause my lifting my left arm out of the water, and so on. The parts will get rationalising and causing beliefs all their own, and not merely rely on the whole stretch of activity having them. There are three thoughts here: (a) that the beliefs might be unspecific; (b) that they might be indexical; (c) there are standing intentions directing the whole activity and which rationalise the actions in question.

(a) The CTA needs to rationalise my lifting my left arm out of the water. I do not have the specific belief that I need to do just that, but perhaps I have the unspecific belief that I need to do something with my body that is appropriate to accomplishing the front-crawl, and so I lift my left arm out of the water. It is not entirely implausible, perhaps, to attribute to me this rather vague, unspecific belief.

Now, there are intentional and nonintentional descriptions of my actions. The CTA cannot be asked to rationalise an action under any of its nonintentional descriptions; *ex hypothesi*, no action can be rationalised in the appropriate sense under any nonintentional description. But what the rationalisation must do is to 'catch' the action under its full intentional description. If the complete intentional description of my action is that I *A*-ed, then the rationalisation must be about *A*-ing, and nothing more or less. The CTA requires not just a rationalising of my doing something, if what I did intentionally was lifting my left arm out of the water, even if my doing something was my lifting my left arm out of the water.

(b) The second idea is that my rationalising mental state might be indexical: I believe that I must do just this (said or thought just as I do it), and that indexical belief rationalises my doing this, 'this' referring to the token, my lifting my left arm out of the water. The difficulty with the suggestion is this: if 'this' occurs as part of the content of the mental state, the mental state must be simultaneous with the action which 'this' picks out in that context. If so, then the mental state cannot cause the action as well as rationalise it, as the CTA requires, since causes must precede their effects.

(c) Finally, there is a literature on standing intentions, and their role in guiding and monitoring just such stretches of ongoing activity, like that of buttoning a shirt, that might be thought to be of help in addressing these issues.[7] In fact, some of this literature makes just the opposite point. Intentions, like beliefs and desires, are part of folk psychology. An agent's intention is associated with a plan of action, itself available to his consciousness, and which must include beliefs of various sorts about that behaviour. But if there are no appropriate beliefs about the various actions that make up the whole stretch of ongoing activity, it cannot be standing intentions, via an action plan, which are doing the monitoring and guiding.

But it does not follow that there is no monitoring and guiding going on. Mele speaks of the role of 'intention-external representational states' in this connection, and Brand, following Stitch, talks in terms of 'subdoxastic states'. This fits in well with the view developed here. The monitoring and guiding of the agent through such stretches of activity depends on a whole host of informational and quasi-perceptual mechanisms, none of which may surface, as it were, as folk psychological items which are states of a person with conceptual content in principle available to that agent.[8] It is these mechanisms, whatever they may be, that play a role without requiring populating the mind with corresponding beliefs, action plans, or other folk psychological items.

Still, even if my claim that the CTA requires folk psychological mental states in these cases but that there are none available is correct, the victory might seem to ring hollow. Why not invent a new relation, rationalises*, such that one's nonconceptual, subpersonal representations and one's desire together rationalise* action? Doesn't my argument merely call for a trivial rewording of the CTA? Perhaps animals can act, in the full-blooded sense, without being able to grasp concepts and propositions; if so, their movements might count as actions in virtue of the nonconceptual, subpersonal representational states they are in, rationalising* those movements that they cause.

I think that this manoeuvre is altogether implausible. To see why, I want to introduce a piece of science fiction. I am not claiming that the story I now wish to tell is empirically cogent in the slightest; we simply do not know enough about the parts of the brain which control action to know whether they are discrete in the way the following story assumes. But I believe that my story is logically possible, and as such helps us to appreciate the conceptual links, or lack thereof, between belief and agency.

Suppose that you know how to front-crawl or ice-skate, but that I do not. That ubiquitous friendly neurophysiologist (well-known from his recent work with the brain-in-the-vat on Alpha Centauri) hooks me up, with the appropriate electrodes, to the informational storage systems in your brain, with a long lead so that I can move about freely. He provides me with an on-off switch, so that I can switch the wiring on and off when I want. The point of insisting on the on-off switch is to make it clear that I remain in control of what I do.

The wiring goes from your informational states direct to my motor apparatus, by-passing my brain, but allowing your information, along with my desire (say, to front-crawl), to jointly cause my action (like lifting my left arm out of the water). It is important to the examples that the wiring does not work by duplicating in me the same states that exist in you. I make direct use of your states, but have none of my own relevant to the details or specifics of the activity in which I am engaging.

One possible reply to this little story is to question why these information states, or beliefs, count as yours rather than mine, in spite of not being duplicated in me. What, after all, is the criterion for an information state or belief belonging to one person rather than another? If physical location were the correct criterion, they would be yours, as I am assuming, since housed in your brain. But I would agree that that suggestion is wrong; there is nothing conceptually impossible about my beliefs or information being realised in your body. On the other hand, if the correct criterion were causal role leading to action, then the beliefs or information would be mine, contrary to my view, since they are causally connected to my action.

But I do not think that that second suggestion is right either, since the information states or beliefs might be causally connected to both my and your action. The most plausible criterion, it seems to me, is this: they are the states of that person such that, if they were salient to consciousness at all, they would be salient to that person's consciousness. If it is your beliefs I am using, they are yours and not mine because they are in principle available to your consciousness, not mine. If it is your subpersonal information states I am employing, then this counterfactual is true: had they been available to consciousness, it would have been to yours and not to mine. So these are your states, not mine, as my story presupposes.

Variations on the same theme are possible, but all make the same general point. A famous ice skater, or an Olympic swimmer, or an English teacher, sells a programme, and a piece of hardware which straps onto one's back. With it operational, I can ice skate or front crawl as well as he can. My technique is as good as his, and unsurprisingly so, since I am utilising his information on how to do what I am doing. I can turn the device on and off. Let us call these cases 'prosthetic cases', whether the prosthesis is a mechanical or electronic aid or another person.

There is no doubt that in these prosthetic cases, it is I, not you, who am acting. Action must be under the agent's own control. Although I utilise your informational states, what I do is under my control. I control the back-pack module, or the wiring system that links me to your brain. Now I too can ice-skate or front-crawl professionally, by tapping into your informational states.

It does not really matter, when the agent acts, whether these subpersonal informational states that he requires are actually in him at all. It does not matter whether I take advantage of your information or of my own. I could find myself skating or swimming professionally, surprised at my marvellous technique, and unable to say how or why I do what I do.

But there is, in these sorts of cases, no plausible kind of rationalising, or rationalising*, going on, that will be of any use in explicating the agency involved in the act-parts of skating or swimming. Your neurophysiologically hard-wired information, along with my motivational states, cannot be whatever it is that confers agency on my movements. On the CTA, the states which are the causers have to be the same states as the states which are the rationalisers. One of the causers of the my lifting my left arm out of the water is your information state. But there is no such thing as a practical syllogism which is trans-personal, in the sense that one of its premisses is about one person's information states and its other premiss and conclusion are about another person's motivational states and action, respectively. That combination rationalises, or rationalises*, nothing whatever.

One critical response that might be made to the story is this: the story may leave a person in overall control, just insofar as he can turn the switch off and on, so that he can stop and start what he is doing. But the story involves a lack of control over the parts of what he does. The phenomenology of such a case leaves the person a stranger to, and with no sense of control over, the details of what he is 'doing', and as such there is reason to doubt that this is genuine agency at all.

I think that such a critical response would be misguided. To imagine what agency would 'feel like' in the science fiction story, imagine some skill that is innate but which develops only at a specific time in the life cycle of an organism. Imagine that you are a large bird living in your parents' nest, and one day you feel the urge to flap your wings. Before you know it, you are flying. You seem to know just what to do-how fast to beat your wings, how to position yourself for take-off and landing, and so on. All of this comes as a surprise to you. You would be in control of all of what you did, and feel yourself in control, even if you had no idea of what to do next or why you were doing it (although you might be able to gain this understanding after ex post facto reflection). You would be no stranger to what you were doing; you would feel that sense of intimacy with the details of your flying that is characteristic of agency.

There is no reason to think that agency in my science fiction case would feel any differently than this. How could the difference of where, in which person, the hardwired information is stored, make the phenomenology of agency different in the two cases?

There is action without rationalising, folk psychological mental states; no need to overpopulate the mind by inventing psychological states like beliefs, or like intentions, when none are required. The CTA fails in its account of agency.

The second theory about action is the Agent Causalist Theory (hereafter, the ACT).[9] The ACT disputes a central contention of most views about causality, namely, the thesis of event causation: (TEC) the causal relation always relates events (or, states of affairs, or facts, these differences being unimportant in the present context). Of course, even the event causation thesis can accept that statements like the following are meaningful (truth, of course, being a different question): 'John caused me to leave the party'; 'The brick broke the window'; 'G-d created the Universe'. These three statements seem to attribute causal efficacy to substances or agents. What the event causation thesis requires is that such statements be equivalent to some statement which asserts that some event involving the substance or agent (perhaps, John's obnoxious behaviour, the brick's striking the window, G-d's willing there to be a universe) caused the party leaving, the window breaking, and the creation of the Universe, respectively.

For the ACT, on the other hand, there is, in addition to event causation, another quite distinctive kind of causation, namely, agent causation: a person can cause or bring about something, in a sense irreducible to event causation. The ACT asserts that there are, or can be, true assertions which attribute causal efficacy to persons, and that such assertions cannot be understood in the reductive way which the TEC requires.

On the ACT, actions can be understood using this idea of agent causation: an action is an event brought about or caused by a person. (On some versions, an action is an event a person brings about on purpose.) An agent, I take it, just is a person who is acting. So now we can distinguish between the (mere) event of my finger's moving and my moving my finger. According to the ACT, the latter, but not the former, is an event that I (and not just one of my rationalising mental states) bring about. My bringing about an event must be sharply distinguished from my brain state bringing it about, or even my belief and desire or intention bringing it about. In action, I, but no proper part of me like a brain or mental state, is causally responsible for the event. The ACT does not have the problem that the CTA has, in explaining activity on the basis of the apparent passivity of events; the idea of an agent making something occur is intended to capture the idea of activity and hence to dispose of the problem of passivity.

The greatest difficulty with the ACT seems to me to be this. For the sake of argument, I assume that what a person agent-causes is, for example, the movement of his hand. (It will not make any difference if what the person agent-causes is only his own cerebral activity.) Since the hand movement which is his moving his hand is an action, it must be, for the ACT, agent-caused. It is also an event; so, is that hand movement also event-caused, in addition to being agent-caused?

If it is event-caused as well as agent-caused, it will be causally overdetermined, having a cause of each of the two kinds. We seem to be landed, on this horn of the dilemma, with an odd form of causal overdetermination in the case of every action. Every action would be overdetermined, since the movement that the person agent-causes will be both agent-caused and event-caused. It is no longer clear what intellectual work agent causation is doing, on this view, if we could explain and predict every action by its prior (and sufficient) event causes alone.

The alternative course would be for the ACT to deny that the hand movement is event-caused, since it is agent-caused. On this horn, the two forms of causation compete; nothing can be both agent-caused and event-caused. The problem with taking this course is that it leaves the theory a hostage to empirical fortune. We believe that, as a matter of fact, there are, in his cerebral activity, event-causes for a person's hand movement. Is it that the cerebral activity at some time t is allegedly agent-caused, and hence has no event-cause? This seems merely to leave the theory a hostage to empirical fortune at an earlier point.

Let us pause and take stock. We have found reason to reject both leading theories of action: the causal theory of action and the agent causalist theory. Might it be that, in spite of their differences, they share a common feature which makes them more similar than one might otherwise have supposed, and which accounts for the defects in both?

In my view, such indeed is the case. The CTA asserts that every token action is identical to a token event with a certain causal history in terms of the agent's folk psychology; the ACT asserts that every token action is identical to a token event which is brought about directly by a person on purpose. Notice the shared assumption: (a) every token action is identical with a token event of some kind or other. That is, on both theories, an action is an event of some type. Once (a) is granted, the dispute between the CTA and the ACT seems somewhat local; they disagree on how to characterise that event type.

If (a) were true, then a fortiori so would be (b): whenever anyone acts, it follows that an event occurs. It is (b) on which I wish to concentrate. (b) is weaker than (a); (b) is an assumption made not only by theories like the CTA and the ACT which identify the particular action with an event, but also by theories which identify that action with anything (like an ordered n-tuple) which includes an event, or with an instance of a relation, whose relata are events.[10] Someone who holds (b) might or might not identify the action and the co-occurring event.

Most standard accounts of the problem of action build (b) into the very way in which action is understood, even before developing any positive theory of action. That is, most accounts assume (b) above, for all cases of action. Particular examples of action, when given, are meant only to be illustrative of the general point. The necessarily co-occurring event is often called the action's event-result. For example, David Hamlyn says that '... it is undeniable that, when we make a bodily movement [i.e., when we act], a bodily movement in the intransitive sense [an event] occurs; when we move an arm certain arm movements take place.'[11] Jennifer Hornsby says that 'If John $moved_T$ his body, then his body $moved_I$'.[12]

Let us call the event whose co-occurrence is supposedly entailed by the action, the action's event-result. Events which are results of some action and events which are consequences or effects of that action should be sharply distinguished. There are at least two ways in which to draw this distinction: in terms of necessity and contingency; in terms of the a priori and the a posteriori. Event-consequences of an action are contingently related to that action, or it can only be known a posteriori what they are (e.g., the effects of my raising my arm might be that a plate is overturned, the soup is spilled, my trousers soiled, and the dry cleaner enriched); on the other hand, event-results of an action are necessary (but, on some theories, insufficient) for that action, or it can be known a priori what they are (e.g., the result of my spilling the soup is that the soup is spilled).[13]

The action's result is not amongst the action's effects or consequences; it is not a contingent consequence of my spilling the soup, or only knowable a posteriori, that the soup is spilled, but the necessary or 'internal' result of that action, or knowable a priori. The views I am considering claim that, if an action occurs, it follows that its event-result does, and hence (b) that an event does, and (for the CTA and the ACT at any rate) also (a) that the action is identical to that event.

What I want to deny is what Hamlyn called 'undeniable': that whenever an action takes place, so does an event (in any interesting sense). I am not just denying the identity of the action and the event; I deny that an event must have occurred at all if an action has. That is, I deny (b). Of course, if no event has occurred when an action takes place, then there can be no event with which the action is identical. A presupposition of both the CTA and ACT will have been shown to be false. I do not attempt to 'prove' my view, whatever that might mean, but merely to show that the view is coherent, that there is a place in logical space for it. The view I am defending was held by von Wright, although, as far as I know, he did not develop it or explain the motivation for it: 'It would not be right, I think, to call acts a kind or species of events. An act is not a change in the world. But many acts may quite appropriately be described as the bringing about or effecting ... of a change.'[14]

I do not say that, for example, when Anna moved her hand, that her hand also moved, but that Anna's moving her hand is distinct from her hand moving. That would yield an implausible dualism of token-action/token-event to which I do not subscribe. We would have Anna's moving her hand and, in addition, her hand moving. Rather, my view is that, when Anna moves her hand, there is no such event at all as that hand of hers moving. All that there is, is the action.

Consider a child playing a game of hide-and-seek. She remains perfectly still for several minutes, wanting not to be found. Her intentionally remaining perfectly still for this period is naturally viewed as an action. But her motionlessness is a state rather than an event, so all theories, the CTA, the ACT, and any other, must accept that there can be some doings without happenings. I neglect this complication in what follows. Call her remaining motionless, if an action, a negative action. My thesis is that there are positive actions, positive doings, without events.

Let me say something about the above qualification to my denying that whenever an action takes place, so does an event, namely, 'in any interesting sense'. There are three types of accounts that might be given to the idea of an event, and on two of them both my thesis and (a), the assumption common to both the CTA and ACT, will be trivial – either trivially true or trivially false. The first type of account will characterise events in such a way that it will follow, as an immediate and trivial consequence of that account, that items such as runnings, jumpings, and throwings count as events, along with volcanic eruptions, sneezings, and hurricanes. I call this first type of account 'a wide account' of events. Every explicit theory of events with which I am acquainted yields this wide and undifferentiated notion of an event. Suppose, for example, that one thinks of an event as an exemplifying of a property at a time by an object. Since properties can be both static (e.g., owning a car) and dynamic (e.g., running a race), and since the objects that can exemplify such properties may include persons,[15] a wide account of events trivially includes actions. On this type of characterisation, the action, Sophie's raising her arm, counts as an event.

On this first type of account, it is then trivially true (a) that every action is identical to an event, or (b) that an event occurs whenever an action does, since every action is identical to itself and co-occurs with itself. My denial of (b) would therefore be trivially false. But this is of no help for the CTA or ACT, for, if this were all that there were to it, part of their case would be assured not by honest philosophical labour but by classificatory fiat.

There is a second type of account of events, which I call a narrow account of events, and on which it follows as an immediate and trivial consequence that actions do not count as events. For example, such an account might characterise an event as, inter alia, a non-actional or passive, item. On this account of an event, (a) and (b) would be trivially false, and hence my denial of (b) trivially true. But again, the result would not be by honest philosophical labour but by classificatory fiat.

But if the CTA and the ACT are worthy of consideration at all, there must be a third account of events, such that the question of whether, for every action, there is some event with which it is identical, is a non-trivial question. Let us call this type of account 'a neutral account'. Once one possesses such a neutral account, it will be clear in very many cases which items are in the extension of 'event' (otherwise, the account would not be offering any stable, core meaning to 'event' at all). Consider the set α of those items which are clearly events on such a neutral account. It must then be a matter of further philosophical reflection whether every action is identical to some event in set α. I deny that (a) and (b) are truths, and that every action has an event-result, when 'event' is given its meaning by such a neutral account.

The idea of an event in the sense given by some neutral account is conveyed by means of examples. Items which are explicitly included as events in this sense are: the eruption of the volcano, the bursting of the pipe, my finger's moving, my hand's waving, my eye's blinking, my arm's going up. On the other hand, the following items would be neither explicitly included nor explicitly excluded: my blinking my eye, my moving my finger, my waving my hand, my raising my arm. If the four latter items are to be included as events, it is not an explicit matter of classification but a matter of philosophical argument, by identifying some events in α with which such actions are identical. This must be how the CTA itself conceives the issue. Proponents of the CTA do not argue that my raising my hand is an event on the grounds of self-identity; they argue that my raising my hand is an event because identical to my hand rising when the latter is appropriately caused.

So, once we fix the core extension of 'event' in the neutral sense, we ask whether actions can be identified with any events clearly in that core. If so, then actions are events in the neutral sense. If not (as I have argued above), then actions are not events in the neutral sense. Of course, one can continue to think of events as the union of the core events and actions unreduced, but that is to switch from 'event' in the neutral sense to 'event' in the wide sense.

So, what I deny is that an event (as specified by some ideal neutral account) necessarily occurs if an action does. When Sophie moves her hand, it is false that Sophie's hand moved. Her hand did not move, since she moved it. Henceforth, I intend the meaning of 'event' to be fixed by some neutral account, unless otherwise specified, and I assume that the result of the ensuing argument is that there is no event in this sense with which any token action is identical.

I take this point to be standard fare in philosophical arguments about identity, whenever the identities are not intended as analytic or apriori truths. Consider for example a token-token mind-body identity theory. It says, roughly, that for every mental state, there is some physical state with which it is identical. What is the meaning of 'physical' here? If the physical is given a narrow account, so as to exclude the mental by definition, the thesis will be trivially false. If the physical is given a wide account (e.g., whatever a true science assumes to exist), the thesis will be trivially true, because mental states are assumed by psychology, and every mental state is identical to itself.) One will need a neutral account of the physical, so that whether or not every mental state is a physical state is a non-trivial question, answerable only upon further philosophical or empirical reflection. Tim Crane and Hugh Mellor have made us aware just how difficulty it may be to produce an account of the physical that will not yield at once a trivial answer.[16]

But surely, someone may say, when Simon moved his hand, his hand changed its place. And when his hand changed its place, it moved. So, when he moved his hand, his hand moved. And his hand's moving is an event. Who can deny that? My reply is predictable. When Simon moved his hand, his hand did not move (or anyway, so I assert, and the point is that my assertion is neither trivially true nor trivially false). So, if one's hand changed place, it does not follow that it has moved, since it might change its place because one has moved it. 'His hand moved' (where a movement is an event in the neutral sense) is made true by an event, but by no action; 'He moved his hand' is made true by an action, but by no event in the neutral sense. In that sense, when Simon moved his hand, it is false that his hand moved, true only that he moved it. 'His hand changed place' is made true by the disjunction: either he moved his hand or his hand moved in the neutral sense.[17]

My account of action can provide a plausible alternative to the volitional theory of action (at least to Hugh McCann's version of this theory). The volitional theory, like mine, is or can be non-reductive regarding action. It need not try to make agency 'appear' out of the mere passivity of events. The volitional theory claims that every action basically is, or is caused by, an act of willing or trying. It is from willing or trying that all other cases of agency stem. It locates basic action 'inside' the agent, in his mind or brain. Assuming that there are lots of things an agent does, there will have to be, on this theory, an awful lot of tryings or willings around as well.

Wittgenstein asked: 'What is left over if I subtract the fact that my arm goes up from the fact that I raise my arm?'[18] Recall that actions typically (although I have argued, not always) have event-results as well as event-consequences. Whenever an action has such a result as well as a consequence, Wittgenstein's question arises. My giving the signal is, on this view, just the event-consequence that a signal has been given, brought about by some action of mine, like my raising my arm.

But what about the action, my raising my arm? For any theory which accepts that that action too has an event-result, namely, my arm's going up, there must be some more basic action, or logically more basic description of that action, such that the event of my arm's going up is an event-consequence of that more basic action (or, of the same action under its logically more basic description). (I am assuming that the CTA's and the ACT's replies to Wittgenstein's question have already been dismissed. I am engaged here in an argument between two theories, McCann's volitional theory and my own, both of which regard agency as irreducible.)

So, if (i) every action has an event-result as well as event-consequences, and (ii) whenever an action has an event-result, it cannot be basic (or cannot be basic as described), there would be an infinite regress in the analysis of action. To avoid this, we shall have to find 'basic' actions, or basic descriptions of action, which have no event-results whatever, and which bring the regress set up in trying to answer Wittgenstein's question to a halt.

On the volitional view, then, there must be some acts, namely, the basic ones, with no event-results whatever. With this much, I am in agreement. That is, in my terminology, when such an act occurs, it does not follow that any event does. My view and the volitional view agree that (a) and (b) are false, and agree that some actions, although they may have contingent (or knowable only a posteriori) consequences, must themselves be resultless.[19]

But, according to the volitional theory, no physical action can be basic, since 'bodily actions like moving a finger always have results: that of moving a finger is that the finger moves.'[20] Basic actions, or actions under their basic descriptions, will turn out to be mental acts of thinking or willing, basic because resultless: 'That acts of thinking do not have results means there can be no action-result problem about thinking. If there is no result to be distinguished from the action, there can be no question as to what makes it a result.'[21] On this view, no physical action can be a basic action, or no action can be basic under any of its physical descriptions. No doubt some event occurs in the brain whenever there is a mental action, but the brain event will not qualify as the mental act's result, since its connection with that act is contingent or a posteriori rather than necessary or a priori (or anyway, so their story goes).

I do not dispute that there are mental acts, like thinking, trying and willing, but, other things being equal, it is unattractive to have to hold that, on every occasion on which I act, I basically am engaging in some mental act (or, an act under a mental description), as this view requires. This would lead to the sort of mental overpopulation I have already described. The volitional theory overpopulates the mind as much as does the CTA.

One way to break the hold this picture of action has on us, that leads to a volitional theory, is to distinguish between physical actions like giving a signal and physical actions like raising one's arm. In the case of my giving a signal, there is something I do, raise my arm, whose event-consequence is that a signal is given, the latter being the event-result of my giving a signal.

But the same pattern of analysis does not always apply to a physical action like raising my arm. We need not, on my theory, be driven inside the agent to find an act of will as a stopping place to account for action. In this case, description would make a bad guide to metaphysics. Normally when I raise my arm, there is no event-result like my arm's rising that occurs (since (b) is false), and so a fortiori it is not the case that there is something more basic that I must do which has my arm's rising as an event-consequence either (in the neutral sense). If no event-result for my raising my arm, then Wittgenstein's question will not even arise: in the normal case of my raising my arm, there is no event, my arm's rising, whose occurrence needs to be explained as a consequence of something I do, in order to elevate its status to that of an action.

So, my view, the denial of (a) and (b) for the cases in which I move parts of my body, permits preservation of the idea that some physical actions may be basic actions (or, basic as so described). Recall that many writers in action theory hold that there is an entailment of 'an event occurs' from 'Someone acts'. In the neutral sense of 'event', I agree that this entailment holds if restricted to nonbasic physical action, but it does not hold for basic physical action. The descriptions of basic physical actions, like one's raising one's arm, do not 'contain' event-results, for when one engages in basic physical action, it does not follow that any event (in the neutral sense) occurs. (b) is false.

In conclusion, let me sum up what I think I have shown. I have rejected two theories of action which I have found wanting, by rejecting an assumption that both share and which, I think, explains at least in part where they both go wrong. My theory leaves action unreduced, as a basic type of item in one's metaphysics of the world. Perhaps such a simple position should not be called a 'third theory' of action, and to that extent my title may be misleading. There are many questions left for me to answer, of a metaphysical, conceptual, and epistemic nature. I would, for example, wish to see to what extent my views on actions and events, and the so-called disjunctive theory of appearance, are two examples of a much more general strategy that can be extended to many areas of philosophical inquiry.

London School of Economics

NOTES

[1] An interesting discussion of this point is to be found in J. David Velleman (1992, 461–481).

[2] I want to flag a problem here, that I shall not further discuss. I will be taking the terms 'mental' and 'folk psychological' as more-or-less synonymous. I do not in fact believe that this is so. For any object *x*, *x* is either mental or not mental. Not so for the folk psychological; the term is vague. This is a problem for the CTA to address. My discussion of the CTA assumes that the extension of this term has been fixed in some principled way, but does not itself participate in that fixing. It seems to me very difficult to draw a sharp, nonarbitrary line between cases of a person being in a folk psychological state like belief (even if that psychological state is identical to some brain state), but of which he is unaware, and cases of his not being in that sort of state at all, but only in a neurophysiological or brain state. Nor do I think that there is any reason to draw such a sharp line. But I do think that there are clear cases of action which are preceded by no relevant belief or desire on the part of the agent, however those terms are to be construed.

[3] Brian O'Shaughnessy (1980, Chapter 10). Rosalind Hursthouse (1991, 57–68).

[4] See also Christopher Peacocke (1992, Chapter 3).

[5] An even stronger case is made by Wakefield and Dreyfus, who claim that there are cases of action preceded by no representational states of any kind whatever. Their examples, like mine, are of skilled activity. They, unlike me, may be thinking of physical states as necessarily nonrepresentational. Jerome Wakefield and Hubert Dreyfus (1992, 263–266).

[6] A. Goldman (1970, 88–91). Frederick Adams and Alfred Mele (1989, 511–532).

[7] See for example Alfred Mele (1992, 136–137, 221–222); Myles Brand (1984, 153–159), who draws a very different conclusion from the absence of belief than I have.

[8] It is as subpersonal neurophysiological states that I understand the effective and receptive representations of Kent Bach's theory. He claims that, in the case of many actions, there will be these 'representations', but the agent may have no intentions or beliefs about that which is so represented. Bach says that these representations are characteristically 'not conscious' (p. 367). Indeed, there seems to me, in spite of Bach thinking of them as unconscious sensuous awarenesses, nothing lost if one merely thinks of them as subpersonal representational states, neurophysiological states which have no place in folk psychology itself. I assume that, given an acceptable, principled fixing of the extension of 'folk psychological' by the CTA, Bach's effective and receptive representations will fall outside that extension, in the same way in which I have argued that subpersonal neurophysiological representational states do. Kent Bach (1986).

[9] E.g., Roderick Chisholm (1966, 28–44); Richard Taylor (1966). For useful discussion, see Irving Thalberg (1976, pp. 213–238), and John Bishop (1983, 61–79).

[10] Kent Bach (1980, 114–120).

[11] David Hamlyn (1990, 130).

[12] Jennifer Hornsby (1980, 2). Think of an action as what makes a sentence with the form 'aV_Tb' true ('Simon moved his hand'), and an event as what makes a sentence with the form 'bV_I' true ('Simon's hand moved'). '*a*' names a person, '*b*' an object, '*V*' stands for a verb, and the subscripts '*I*' and '*T*' for intransitive and transitive occurrences of the verb respectively.

[13] Notice that the event-consequence need not be a causal consequence. It may be a conventional consequence, as in the case of a signal being given by my raising my hand. See A. Goldman (1970, Chapter 2).

[14] Georg Henrik von Wright (1963, 35–36).

[15] Cynthia Macdonald has suggested to me that if this account of events as property exemplifications were to exclude persons as appropriate exemplifiers, this might be the account I need. Certainly many examples which seem to make persons as exemplifiers are better construed as making parts of their bodies as the real exemplifiers: Sophie's bleeding is merely some part of her body's bleeding. But there are recalcitrant cases: Anna's hiccuping seems to make Anna the

exemplifier, and no proper part of her, and yet hiccuping is an event that happens to Anna.

[16] Tim Crane and Hugh Mellor (1990, 185–206).

[17] The analogy between my view of action and the Hinton–Snowden–McDowell disjunctive theory of experience will be apparent. See J.M. Hinton (1973); Paul Snowdon (1980–1, 175–192); John McDowell (1982, 455–479). The last two are reprinted in J. Dancy (ed.) (1988), *Perceptual Knowledge*, Oxford University Press.

[18] Quoted in Hugh McCann (1974, 451–473).

[19] The only discussion I know of this occurs in Stewart Candlish (1984, 83–102).

[20] McCann (1974, 456).

[21] *Ibid.*, p. 465.

REFERENCES

Adams, Frederick and Alfred Mele (1989), "The Role of Intention in Intentional Action," *Canadian Journal of Philosophy* **19**.

Bach, Kent (1980), "Actions Are Not Events," *Mind* **89**.

Bach, Kent (1986), "A Representational Theory of Action" in M. Brand and R. Harnish (eds.), *The Representation of Knowledge and Belief*. University of Arizona Press.

Bishop, John (1983), "Agent-causation," *Mind* **XCII**.

Brand, Myles (1984), *Intending and Acting*. Cambridge, Mass., MIT Press.

Candlish, Stewart (1984), "Inner and Outer Basic Actions," *Proceedings of the Aristotelian Society*, n.s. **LXXXIV**.

Chisholm, Roderick (1966), "Freedom and Action" in Keith Lehrer (ed.), *Freedom and Determinism*. New York, Random House.

Crane, Tim and Hugh Mellor (1990), "There is No Question of Physicalism," *Mind* **99**.

Goldman, Alvin (1970), *A Theory of Action*. Princeton, Princeton University Press.

Hamlyn, David (1990), *In and Out of the Black Box: On the Philosophy of Cognition*. Oxford, Blackwell.

Hinton, J.M. (1973), *Experiences*. Oxford, Oxford University Press.

Hornsby, Jennifer (1980), *Actions*. London, Routledge & Kegan Paul.

Hursthouse, Rosalind (1991), "Arational Action," *The Journal of Philosophy* **LXXXVIII**.

McCann, Hugh (1974), "Volition and Basic Action," *Philosophical Review*.

McDowell, John (1982), "Criteria, Defeasability, and Knowledge," *Proceedings of the British Academy* **68**.

Mele, Alfred (1992), *Springs of Action*. Oxford, Oxford University Press.

O'Shaughnessy, Brian (1980), *The Will: A Dual Aspect Theory*, Vol. 2. Cambridge, Cambridge University Press.

Peacocke, Christopher (1992), *A Study of Concepts*. Cambridge, Mass., Bradford Books, MIT Press.

Snowdon, Paul (1980–1), "Perception, Vision, and Causation," *Proceedings of the Aristotelian Society* **81**.

Taylor, Richard (1966), *Action and Purpose*. Englewood Cliffs, N.J., Prentice-Hall.

Thalberg, Irving (1976), "How Does Agent Causality Work?" in M. Brand and D. Walton (eds.), *Action Theory*. Dordrecht, Holland, Reidel.

Velleman, J. David (1992), "What Happens When Someone Acts?," *Mind* **101** (403).

Wakefield, Jerome and Hubert Dreyfus (1992), "Intentionality and the Phenomenology of Action" in E. Lepore and Robert van Gulick (eds.), *John Searle and His Critics*. Oxford, Blackwell.

von Wright, Georg Henrik (1963), *Norm and Action: A Logical Enquiry*. London, Routledge & Kegan Paul.

FREDERICK ADAMS

COGNITIVE TRYING

1. WHY AN ACCOUNT OF TRYING?

People do things (walk, talk, plan for retirement). People also try to do things (to quit smoking, to time the stock market, to preserve their marriages). Doing and trying are very basic activities, ranging from the simple (a baby grasping a toy, a toddler trying to walk) to the sublime (attempting to capture the beauty of a sunset on Waikiki, trying to reduce mathematics to logic and set theory). Surprisingly, or at least surprising to me, there are many interesting philosophical issues that converge on the topic of trying. For instance, Ken can unintentionally do something (offend someone, perhaps), but Ken cannot unintentionally try to offend someone (by mimicking them, say). Why is that? What is it about trying such that one cannot do it unintentionally? Also, can only creatures with minds or the making of minds try to do things? Or can trees or bacteria try to do things? If not trees or bacteria, why not? What do minds contribute to trying? Or is it the other way around – is the ability to try an ingredient in the makings of having a mind?

Similarly, trying is often closely related to moral responsibility. If one does an action unintentionally (accidentally breaks the precious glass figurine) and could not have foreseen this action, we are inclined to go easy or withhold blame. However, if one genuinely tries (to break the figurine), whether one succeeds or not, we are likely to heap on the blame. Why are intentional attempts and acts so closely tied to moral praise or blame?

In addition to these general issues that converge on the topic of trying there are also some specific claims that philosophers recently have made about trying that require a closer look at the nature of trying in order to evaluate. Alfred Mele (1990, 1991) claims, although not everyone agrees (Adams 1995b), that one can try to do something without wanting or desiring to do it. Why would that be so? The answer that Mele gives is that it is possible to *try* to do something *A*, *wanting* only *to try* to do *A*, not wanting actually *to do A* (the idea being that one may want only to try to win the race, say, but not actually want to win it, during the attempt). Is that really possible? Isn't winning the race what you want *while trying* to win the race? Whether what Mele claims really is possible depends on the nature of trying.

Kirk Ludwig (1992) has claimed, although not everyone agrees (Adams 1995a), that it is possible to try (and do) something that one believes to be impossible. This may seem easier to accept initially than Mele's claim. For it

G. Holmström-Hintikka and R. Tuomela (eds.), Contemporary Action Theory. Vol. I, 287–314.

is very common for us to try to lift a heavy object, say, that we think we may not be able to lift, or to try to climb a mountain that we fear we may not be able to climb. So, initially it may seem quite plausible that one may be able to try to do what one believes to be impossible. Still, whether it is possible depends on the nature of trying. There may be constraints upon what one must believe in order to be able to get oneself to try to do something. These constraints may only become apparent once we look more closely at the nature of trying. For instance, if I really believe that it is not possible to lift the object or to climb the mountain, perhaps all I am really trying to do is to pull up as hard as I can or to climb as far as I can (I may not be trying *to lift* the object nor *to climb* the mountain to the top). Whether Ludwig is right depends upon the nature of attempts and what they do and do not permit.

Michael Bratman (1987) maintains, although not everyone agrees (Adams 1986, 1989), that it is possible to *try* to do what one may not be able to *intend* to do. Why might this be so? Bratman maintains that there are rationality constraints on intentions that do not apply to attempts. One should only intend or plan to do things that are consistent with one's other intentions. However, Bratman thinks one may attempt to do several things simultaneously, even while knowing that doing them all is an impossibility. Why would this "rationality constraint" apply only to *intentions* and not to *attempts*? The answer depends upon the nature of trying (and, in this case, intending).

There are, I submit, enough issues tied to the notion of trying that it is worthwhile to have an account of trying. Therefore, I propose to develop such an account here and to bring that account to bear on the above issues.

2. A COGNITIVE ACCOUNT OF TRYING

Before we get too far along, let me acknowledge that there is a difference between mental trying and bodily trying. I do not propose to make a fuss over this distinction. When I try to print a document on my computer, I point and click my computer mouse at an icon of a printer. This would count as a bodily trying. When I try to remember the 800 number for AT&T[1] credit card calls, this would count as a mental trying. I don't intend to make a fuss about this traditional distinction because, being a physicalist, I believe that all mental events or states are physical events or states of some kind or other (token identity, if you will). So mental tryings will involve relevant mental states (beliefs, desires, or intentions, that are token identical to some physical states of the brain or central nervous system) causing some other mental states (also token identical with physical states).

Suppose my attempt to remember the 800 number for AT&T involves my attempt to visualize my AT&T calling card and to visualize the telephone number on the back of the card. I certainly have beliefs, desires, and intentions in the background of this mental attempt. These states are all relevant somehow to my trying to remember the number. For now, it is not important just how they are relevant. The point is that the event of mentally trying to remember involves some mental states that cause other mental states (states such as images coming before my mind's eye, the AT&T 800 number coming to me, and so on). Thus, a mental trying involves some physical states of the brain and central nervous system causing other physical states of the brain and central nervous system (states with which the relevant mental states are token identical).

In bodily trying, the main difference is that the relevant states caused by similar inner mental states extend to the body (extend outside of the head). That is, my attempt to print my document involves relevant inner mental states causing my bodily movements of pointing and clicking with my computer mouse. What makes one attempt mental and the other bodily is merely how far out the causal chain extends. If it literally does not go outside the head it is a mental trying. If it goes out to other regions of the body and to the world (via the body), then it is bodily trying. If there were such a thing as telepathy, and I could move my computer mouse without moving my body, then perhaps states of my brain could send mysterious waves directly to the computer mouse, click on the "print" icon, and print my document. This would be a new category of trying, I suppose, because it would leap over the bodily step that now mediates my attempts to print documents. I would be able to interact in new ways with the world. Perhaps we would call it 'direct' or 'telepathic trying'.

At its most basic level, trying involves one thing's causing another thing for a reason – a teleological causing. Whether it be mental or bodily trying, this causing begins with internal states of the brain or central nervous system – cognitive states. Our attention now turns to what it is about those internal states that create attempts. Not just any old internal cause yields a trying. A brain tumor (mysteriously) may cause me to remember AT&T's 800 number without that being a mental trying. An electrode strategically planted in my brain may cause my arm to move and click on my computer mouse, in turn causing my computer to print a document, without its constituting a bodily trying on my part (I'm not thereby trying to print a document). So the nature of the internal causes is crucial to their being components of genuine attempts.

Perhaps it will also help to be up front that I accept a component theory of action and attempts. On this view, let M be a cluster of relevant mental states that cause a bodily trying. Let B represent the bodily movements that are involved in the attempt. On a component view of trying, this attempt would consist of M's causing B ($M \rightarrow B$). Neither M nor B alone is the trying. It is the complex causing that is the trying with each component, M and B, being components of the attempt (Thalberg 1972; Thomson 1977; McGinn 1982;

Dretske 1988). In cases of mental trying, trying would look like this: $M1 \rightarrow M2$.

Now as we proceed we can tease out at least two questions for an account of trying. Into the schema *S tried to do A*, we can substitute various actors for "*S*" and various deeds for "*A*". In asking what makes something an attempt to do *A*, we can disentangle two contrastive questions:

1. What makes something an *attempt* to do *A*?
2. What makes something the attempt *to do A*?

Let's take up question (1). What makes the attempt to do *A* an *attempt*? An attempt is not a propositional attitude, such as a belief, desire, or intention[2]. Hinckley may desire, hope, plan, intend, and believe it is possible to shoot Reagan, but he has not attempted to shoot Reagan until these relevant mental states cause the relevant activity (in this case, pointing and shooting a gun at Reagan). So attempts cannot be states of mind that we can wait for some future science of psychology to functionally characterize. They cannot because attempts go beyond propositional attitudes. In the case of bodily trying, attempts involve relevant mental states causing bodily activity, for a reason.

Attempts do have intentional objects. Attempts are always attempts at or towards achieving some goal or end. So it is very likely that they acquire their intentional objects from propositional attitudes (or similar intentional states).

If we are right so far, an attempt is constituted by a mental state's causing another mental state (mental trying) or causing a bodily state (bodily trying), and causing this for a reason[3]. How do mental states cause things for a reason? They do so when they cause things in virtue of their representational contents (Dretske 1988; Adams 1991). How do they do this? We must turn to neuroscience for the neurophysiology or neurochemistry of this, but the explanation of how they do it is likely not to be at that level of explanation anyway. Consider mental trying. I don't have to know how my mind does it chemically or physically to know that when I cannot remember something (say, where I parked my car in a large parking lot), if I picture myself driving into the lot or walking to the office from my car, the activity of picturing sometimes jogs my memory about where I parked. Knowing from experience that thinking about or picturing one thing can lead to remembering another thing can lead to my trying to remember where I parked my car by picturing myself driving into the lot or walking to the building.

The picturing is *M2*, but what is *M1*, if *M1*'s causing *M2* is an attempt to remember where I parked? Surely remembering the whereabouts of my car is a goal to be accomplished. So *M1* will include mental states directed at the goal of remembering – states with that goal or intentional object.[4] Some mental state will represent my goal of remembering where I parked my car. Thus, mental states with the cognitive function of representing goal-states of affairs will be involved in *M*1. But that alone won't get me to start picturing myself driving into the lot or walking into the building. I must also be moved by the right conative state. I must be motivated to act upon the goal of remembering where I parked my car. I have many goals, not all of which are currently causing me to act or try to act. So something like a desire to remember the whereabouts of my car must be involved in engaging my cognitive states to cause things, in concert with my desires. Also, I must have some reason to think that trying to picture my driving in to campus or walking in from the lot will help me remember. I must have beliefs about how one thing may lead to another. Some would add that an intention is involved (McGinn 1982; Bratman 1987; Mele 1992) in initiating and sustaining the attempt, as well as in co-ordinating this attempt with other attempts in which I may also be engaged (bodily or mentally). An intention may be the thing that settles upon which of my desires or goals I will act upon now and in the immediate future. So *M*1 is either a complex of mental states, such as beliefs, desires, and intentions, or it is a state causally influenced by these states, perhaps a willing or a proximal intention that triggers *M*1's causing *M*2.[5]

A similar scenario is true of bodily trying. The bodily part of my attempt to print my document consists of my hand's pointing my computer mouse at the printer icon on my computer screen and clicking. If that is *B*1, what is *M*1, when my trying is *M*1's causing *B*1? If *M*1 is causing *B*1 for a reason (or goal), then *M*1 must contain a representation of the goal to be achieved – in this case the goal of a printed document's being produced.[6] In addition to containing a representation of this type of state of affairs (the document's being printed), M1 must contain a desire to bring about that goal, and perhaps an intention to bring it about now (for, I know my document can be printed even when I don't desire that it be printed or am not attempting to print it). Also, *M*1 must contain some beliefs or other cognitive states that represent the relationship between clicking on the icon and a document's being printed. Otherwise, why is *M*1 involved in causing the computer mouse to click on the icon, rather than causing something else? Background beliefs about causal relationships in one's environment, must be stored and influence *M*1's causal role. Finally, something must determine which things I am attempting now or in the near future – something like a plan or an intention must help coordinate matters and put it all into action.

If we are on the right track, what makes something an *attempt* is that it is a causing by relevant mental state (or complex of states) *M*1 of a relevant mental state *M*2 (mental trying) or bodily state *B*1 (bodily trying), for a reason. That it is a causing "for a reason" entails that the causing is sensitive to the cognitive (representational) and conative (motivational) content of *M*1 (or related states). Thus, something is an attempt only if it has the right causal history. It has to be nested within the appropriate cognitive and conative circuitry, if you will. Therefore, although attempts are not themselves propostional attitudes or functionally characterizable mental states, they are causings that are influenced by and nested within such states. Therefore, we would expect a futuristic science of psychology to be able to functionally characterize the role of beliefs, desires, and intentions (and perhaps, volitions, though I am skeptical of the latter), in the production of attempts.[7]

Now let's take up question (2). If we now have an account of what makes something an attempt, what makes it the attempt *to do A*? What makes something the specific attempt that it is and not another attempt? The view I wish to defend is that an attempt to do *A* is caused by, sustained by, and controlled for the end or purpose of doing *A*. That one has the goal of doing *A* is the reason *M*1 is causing what its causing, if you will. The easiest or simplest way for this to be the case would be for *M*1 to be causally sensitive to whether it has or has not caused a state of affairs of type *A*. This would be the case if something in state *M*1 means "do *A*" and its having that meaning causally explains why *M*1 causes *B*1 (since *B*1 is thought either to constitute the doing of *A* or to have doing *A* as a consequence). *B*1 may or may not lead to one's actually doing *A*. Some attempts fall short of their mark. Still, the fact that something that means "do *A*" is causing, sustaining, and monitoring what *M*1 is causing, monitoring for bringing about the doing of *A*, makes what *M*1 is causing the attempt to do *A*. If *M*1 were the intention to print my document and *B*1 were my bodily movements of clicking of the computer mouse on the print icon, then *M*1's causing *B*1 would be my attempt to print my document *because M*1 was my intention to print my document. That is, the intention (*M*1) with the content *to do A* causes the relevant state (*B*1) that constitutes the other component of the *attempt to do A*. It is the match between the content of the intention and the descriptive content of the attempt that makes it the attempt it is (*to do A*), when the attempt succeeds. It is that the attempt was launched and sustained via the content "*do A*" that makes it the attempt it is, even when the attempt fails. This answer to question (2) is simple, elegant, and, I think, correct. However, we will face disagreement below.

Equipped with answers to questions (1) and (2), we have the beginning of an account of the nature of trying. Eventually we need to compare this account with the kinds of things that recently have been said about trying (specific claims mentioned in the opening remarks). Some of those claims disagree with this account. Some will require elaboration of the account in order for it to apply to them. At stake is whether this theory has a coherent, consistent, and plausible defense when it comes into conflict with recent dissenting claims about the nature of trying.

3. TRYING AND DEVIANT CAUSAL CHAINS

Before attempting to apply this theory to puzzle cases, rudimentary as it still is at this stage, let me fill one obvious gap. So far I have said nothing about causal deviance, and yet I am clearly constructing a causal theory of trying. The theory should face the usual types of causal deviance (Brand 1984; Mele 1987; Adams 1989). Take the case were *M*1 causes a deviant causal state *D* which then causes *B*1 (bodily trying). So I intend (*M*1) to click the computer mouse on the "mail" icon of my word processor on my computer screen. This will cause my computer to send my e-mail editorial to the school paper (where it will be printed for all at the university to see). In the editorial I rail against the stupidity of the President's plan to academically re-organize the colleges of the university and merge my department with another. That I intend to send such a radical protest to the paper for all to see so unnerves me that I begin to panic (*D*). My panic causes my finger to click the computer mouse on the "mail" icon (*B*1). I thereby mail the scathing editorial to the school paper.

Many would say that I sent the editorial, but did so unintentionally because of the causally deviant link (*D*) (Mele 1992, 202).[8] But did I try to send it? And, if trying is essentially intentional, then I could not have tried to send it unintentionally. Did I intentionally try to send it?

On the one hand, our account of trying so far says that when *M*1 causes *B*1 for a reason, a teleological causing, as it were, then we have a case of trying. If *M*1 was the intention to do *A* and *B*1 is or causes an *A*-ing, then we have a match of content (*to A)* with the outcome of *A*-ing (*M*1 caused something designed to bring about *A*-ing) and we have an attempt to do *A*. So without deviance we have an attempt to do *A*, and an intentional attempt at that.

On the other hand, here we have a deviant causal chain. So we must decide if that changes whether *M*1 is causing *B*1, for a reason (or for the right reason). Certainly, it is the intention *M*1 and its content that triggers or kicks off the causal chain leading to *B*1. If I had not intended to actually send the blasted editorial and to send it RIGHT NOW, I may not have panicked. But my plan was not to panic nor to have the panic cause the appropriate clicking of the mouse. Indeed, my plan was not very explicit about how I would click the mouse. I suspect that a presupposition of the plan included that I would click the mouse in the normal, calm way, though this was never made explicit or brought to consciousness.

In this particular case, one may be torn between saying that I did not try to send the editorial to the school paper and saying that I tried, but my attempt when awry. There are reasons for saying both. For saying that I did not try, there is the fact that, once the panic sets in, I have lost control of what my intention causes. Before that I could have aborted the attempt. Normally any time during the movement of my hand toward the mouse and the pointing of the cursor arrow on the "mail" icon, I could have aborted the attempt, had I changed my mind. However, once the panic set in it caused my clicking on the "mail" icon. My movement of clicking on the icon (*B*1) at that time was not under the control of my intention (*M*1) even though, indirectly, via the panic (*D*), it caused it. If *M*1's causing *B*1 at that time was not under my control, then it was not causing it in the right way to be intentionally done. And, if trying is essentially intentional, then I did not try to send the editorial. I certainly didn't intend to send it in just that way.

For saying that indeed I did try to mail the editorial, there is the consideration that my intention to send it caused quite a bit of arm movement in the direction of the computer mouse prior to the onset of the panic and prior to the clicking of the mouse. Only after the panic set in did my bodily movement fall beyond the recall of my intentions, had I changed my mind. Only then did my movement *B*1 go ballistic. Was I not trying to e-mail my editorial all the while that my arm was moving toward the computer mouse? Surely, it seems that I was. So it seems that an attempt was made but went awry with the onset of the panic.

To resolve this type of problem, some (Brand 1984; Mele 1992) suggest that the intention must directly and proximately cause the relevant activity which constitutes the attempt.[9] The idea would be something like this: the intention to click on the mouse here and now must proximately cause the neural signals running down the efferent pathways and eventuating in the bodily movement of clicking the mouse on the "mail" icon. This effectively eliminates room for the deviant cause (*D*) from the picture. I suppose we could handle this type of causal deviance this way.

While I think this way of handling deviance may work, I am inclined to think that control, not proximity, is the key to cases of deviance, generally. I am inclined to think this because there are other cases of deviance (Brand's "consequential" and Mele's "tertiary" waywardness) that are not handled by considerations of proximity. These other kinds of deviance do seem to be handled by considerations of control (Adams 1989). Also, under quite extraordinary circumstances, it may well be possible to have one's intentions cause bodily movements, but not cause them proximately, and still be intentional attempts.[10] Suppose I know that a scientist has wired my brain so that when I form the intention to move my index finger *right now* the intention activates a computer program before efferent signals start down neural pathways to my muscles. The computer program then prosthetically sends electrical signals to my finger and stimulates the muscles in my finger and arm and causes my finger to move in just the way required to satisfy my intention to move my finger. Now my intention's causing the relevant finger movement would not be proximante, but I believe I could try, and succeed in moving my finger intentionally in this case (especially if I am wise to the set up). What could be easier? All I would need to do is form the intention to move my finger now.

This would constitute my part in the trying (*M*1). The scientists' set up would take care of the rest (*M*1 would cause *B*1 via the mediated set up).

These sorts of consideration lead me to believe that control by intentions (and relevant planning), not proximity of cause by intentions, is the key to solving the deviance problems. Let's say that *B*1 (bodily movements involved in clicking the computer mouse on the "mail" icon and e-mailing my editorial) stretch over many temporal stages. This helps. For now when we ask whether I tried to mail the editorial, we can ask whether my intention *M*1 has caused any of the temporal stages involved in the set that is *B*1. If it has, my attempt has begun. Also, we can ask whether *M*1's causing these stages was under my control. If so, then clearly my attempt began and was intentional. Suppose the intention *M*1 forms, causes the panic immediately (*D*), prior to its causing any temporal stage in *B*1. Then has my trying to mail the editorial begun? No. However, suppose instead that *M*1 has caused several stages involved in *B*1. In fact, as my finger comes close to clicking the mouse on "mail", it is the fact that I am so close to doing the deed that causes the panic (*D*), which causes the completion of the remaining temporal stages in *B*1. Then I think it is clear that I have lost control of my attempt. I did attempt to mail the editorial. Only at the point that the panic takes over did I lose control of my attempt. At that point I stopped trying and my actions become unintentional (even though intended). My attempt is cut short, once the panic kicks in.

But what of the case I presented above where the intention to move my finger activates the computer which stimulates and moves my finger? How is this under the control of my intention? It is under the control of my intention because the scientists so rigged the set up so that it faithfully executes what I intend. And if my intention does not form, it does not move my finger. There are no deviant causal chains in the scientists set up that correspond to the panic in the other example. Of course, there could be deviance, and if there were, then my attempt, even in that weird set up, would end at the point that the wayward cause kicked in. However, in the set up I've described, we can think of the causal pathway as reliable and non-deviant, though certainly unusual.

There is another form of causal deviance that confronts intentional action, but not trying. This is where *M*1 causes a relevant *B*1 (in bodily trying) and *B*1 is supposed to cause some goal *G*. The connection between *B*1 and *G* is deviant (not expected, not the norm, and not one that could be counted on again...not reliable). So the deviant cause *D* comes between *B*1 and *G*, not between *M*1 and *B*1. Say that Quickdraw intends to kill Speedy in the battle of fastest gunslingers. Quickdraw intends to kill Speedy (*M*1). *M*1 causes his set of bodily movements involved in aiming, pulling the trigger, and firing a gun at Speedy. The gunshot causes an avalanche (*D*) which kills Speedy (*G*). Many would say that Quickdraw killed Speedy, but not intentionally. This may be so. I won't argue for or against it here. For our purposes, it is nonetheless true that

Quickdraw intentionally tried to kill Speedy. Quickdraw had control over his trying. So this type of deviance ("consequential") is not a problem for our account of trying.

Within attempts, intentions not only initiate (trigger) their effects, but they sustain and causally structure their effects. It is this idea that I will attempt to capture by saying that the intention exerts some degree of control over the effect that it produces in an attempt. It is this feature of control, along with the feature that what makes the attempt the attempt to *do A* is that doing *A* is the content of the intention, that helps to explain why all trying is intentional. It is intentional because at the point one would lose control, one's attempt ceases or fails to begin. In so far as the appropriate mental states are planning, guiding and controlling the relevant outcomes, the attempts are fully intentional and purposive. So when in an attempt a relevant internal state is causing some appropriate outcome for a reason, it must also be causing it in the right way...a controlled way.

4. TRYING, DESIRE, AND DESIRING TO TRY

Let's now turn to some of the specific claims about trying in the recent literature. Take Mele's (1990, 1991, 1992) claim that one can try to do an action *A* wanting only *to try to do A* not *to do A*. We shall see that this view is inconsistent with the view we are developing here. Let's see the type of example that Mele has in mind, so that it will become clear why his view is at odds with the present account.

Mele's example is as follows. Brett will pay Belton fifty dollars if Belton tries to solve a mate-in-two chess problem within five minutes. Belton is very bad at solving this type of chess problem and he knows this about himself. Brett assures Belton that Belton need not actually solve the problem. To get the money, Belton must only try to solve it. Further, Belton is convinced that Brett can read minds and can tell whether Belton has tried, independently of his succeeding. Based upon this example, Mele claims that Belton can try to solve the puzzle (*A*), even if Belton is 'absolutely indifferent to his actually solving the puzzle' (to his actually doing *A*) (Mele 1991, 225). Thus, we are to conclude that Belton can try to do *A* while not wanting or desiring to do *A* – indeed, while being absolutely indifferent to his doing *A*.

Why is this at odds with our account? Surely someone may try to do something either half-heartedly or with little confidence of success. Isn't this what Mele's example implies? I don't think so. Here is why. Let us say that the attempt to solve this puzzle is a case of bodily trying. One must actually move the chess pieces around, let us say, not just try to solve the problem in the mind's eye. We could consider this to be a case of mental trying, for the points would be the same, but it will be easier to mentally picture the attempt, if we make it a case of bodily trying. Let *M*1 be the intention that causes the relevant bodily movements (*B*1). For the moment, let's not specify the content of the intention.[11]

Let *B*1 be a complex set of bodily motions over time <*b*1,...,*bn*> (plus moved chess pieces), as we decided that we needed to do when discussing deviant causal chains. Then an attempt to solve the puzzle is *M*1's causing elements of set *B*1. The movements in set *B*1 by themselves do not constitute an attempt. That is, we agreed that *M*1 must cause *B*1, *for the right reason* for its causing *B*1 to be an attempt. *B*1 alone is just a set of bodily movements. By themselves these movements are not an attempt. If we stimulated one's arm with electric probes, for no good reason, and coincidentally the arm made these movements, *B*1 would not constitute an attempt to solve the puzzle. *B*1 may consist of movements one would make, were one trying to solve the puzzle, but unless these movements have the right etiology and teleology, they are not parts of an attempt to solve the puzzle. *B*1 alone does not constitute an attempt.

So far, Mele would agree. He would also agree that Brett must desire something and have beliefs about which bodily motions (*B*1) are involved in an attempt to solve the puzzle. Then Brett's beliefs (about what to do) and his desire (to try to solve the puzzle) lead to his intention to move the chess pieces here and now (*M*1). The question, for our purposes, is about what Brett must desire for it to be true that he is trying to solve the puzzle. What must be the intentional object of his desire? Mele says Brett needs only the desire to try to solve the puzzle. But is this true?

Surely, if Brett is actually trying to solve the chess puzzle, he does desire to try to solve the puzzle. It would be very peculiar (if not impossible) for Brett to be engaged in the attempt to solve the puzzle, and for him to lack the desire to try to solve it. However, I maintain, given the account we are developing, that it would be equally peculiar, and downright impossible, for Brett to be engaged in the activity of trying to solve the puzzle, while being totally indifferent to his solving the puzzle (while lacking the desire to solve the puzzle). For the desire component of *M*1, which causes *B*1, and thereby makes *M*1's causing of *B*1 the attempt to solve the puzzle, is, on this account, the desire to solve the puzzle. Solving the puzzle is the intentional object or goal or purpose or reason for which *M*1 is causing *B*1, when an attempt to solve the puzzle is made.

Mele maintains that this is incorrect. He maintains that the desire component of *M*1 need only be the desire *to try to solve the puzzle*. Let's pursue this. Surely a desire to try is not the same as a desire to solve the puzzle. They have different satisfaction conditions. Thus far, Mele is on solid ground. However, if Brett desires to try to solve the puzzle, there must be something (trying to solve the puzzle) that Brett desires. On the account we are developing, this involves *M*1's causing *B*1 in the right way and for the right reason – in this case, with the right desire. But what is the right desire? Can the desire be to produce motions $B1$, alone? No. For that is the desire to go through the motions of trying, minus those motions being caused by the right mental state – minus their being caused by the right reason. That is the wrong intentional object for the desire in an attempt to solve the puzzle. To even be an attempt to solve the puzzle in the first place (that type of activity), let alone to desire to perform an attempt of this type, there must be a desire influencing $M1$. That desire must have solving the puzzle as a goal, as an intentional object. It must help initiate $M1$'s causing of $B1$, sustain $M1$'s causing of $B1$, and register success, were $M1$ to cause the completion of the entire set of bodily motions involved in actually pulling off the mate-in-two move in chess. That is, one (normally) should stop trying when what one is trying is accomplished. So the desire involved in $M1$, certainly has all of the earmarks of the desire to solve the chess puzzle. An attempt to solve the puzzle (that type of attempt) involves what certainly seems to be the desire to solve the puzzle. Now if Brett indeed wants to perform an attempt of that type (as Mele says he does), then, whether Brett knows it or not, what he wants to try to do is have a state like $M1$ cause movements like $B1$ in himself. For that is what is required of an attempt and an attempt to solve the puzzle is what he wants to perform. The intentional object of the desire to try to solve the puzzle is the desire that the relevant desire in $M1$ cause some of the relevant movements in the set that is $B1$ (the desire is that $M1 \rightarrow B1$). However, the relevant desire *in the attempt itself*, in $M1$, is the desire *to solve the puzzle.*[12]

Now if this is correct, the desire to try to solve the puzzle, has a different intentional object than the desire to solve the puzzle. Still, despite that, an attempt to solve the puzzle requires a desire to solve the puzzle. Mele's example exploits the fact that the desire to try to solve the puzzle is easier to satisfy than is the desire that actually exists in the attempt. For the desire to try is satisfied if $M1$ causes some of the events comprising the complex set $B1$. The desire within the attempt is satisfied only if the desire in $M1$ causes all of the necessary events comprising the successful completion of bodily motions involved in $B1$, in actually completing the movements involved *in solving the puzzle.*[13] The latter is much harder to satisfy. This is what Mele's example exploits. Despite this difference in intentional objects of the relevant desires, it is still the desire to solve the puzzle that is necessary for $M1$ to be the right conative state such that causing of elements in the set $B1$ will constitute the attempt to solve the puzzle. Otherwise Brett's desire may be enough to cause merely the attempt *to move the puzzle pieces around* ("merely going through the motions" in the hope that Belton will not notice the failure of earnest attempt and will give Brett the money anyway).

I submit, therefore, that Mele's arguments are unsuccessful. A trying to do A does require a desire to do A, not merely to try to do A. Our account has this implication, and I think there are good grounds for accepting our account. The account is coherent, consistent, elegant, and is systematically answering the issues with which we began. The test of any theory is how it does in the trenches. Mele does not base his arguments upon a theory of trying, but on intuition about his example of Brett. I hope to have shown that intuition is not, when tutored, on his side.

5. TRYING AND BELIEF

Let us now turn to Kirk Ludwig's (1992) claim that it is possible to try to do something that one believes to be impossible.[14] At first sight, this claim certainly seems to be correct. Who hasn't tried to do something that they thought very unlikely or nearly impossible? We might try to lift a heavy weight, climb a tall mountain, or finish a manuscript in a very short time. We might try any of these with very low expectations, so low in fact that we might think it is just about impossible. None of this seems to stand in the way of our ability to try. Therefore, it comes as no small surprise to me that I find myself with a theory of trying that is incompatible with the seemingly obvious truth that we can try to do what we believe is impossible.

This is incompatible with the account of trying we are developing for the following reason. As we have noted, one's intention *M*1 will have certain goals or ends as intentional objects of one's attempt. Call the desired ends or goals *G*. Why would *M*1 cause some set of bodily movements *B*1, unless one had an idea about how *B*1 might lead to goal *G*? *M*1's causing *B*1, with no conception of how or why *B*1 might lead to *G*, even though one wanted *G* to happen, would not be an attempt at doing *G*, but an exercise in futility. *M*1 might cause *B*1 out of despair, but hardly with the intent that *B*1 lead to *G*, and, consequently, even if *B*1 did surprisingly lead to *G*, since its doing so was unforeseen, it would not cause it for the right reason, and would not be teleological. Therefore, *M*1's causing *B*1 would not be an attempt to bring about *G*, by doing *B*1. At least, if I am not mistaken, this somewhat surprising result is what our account of trying implies.

In order to see things more clearly, let us walk through an example of the type that Ludwig gives. Ken parks his car in Bob's drive. The next day an angry Bob insists that Ken move the car right now. Ken remembers his car's battery having gone dead the night before. Fearing for his safety, Ken figures that if Bob sees him trying to start the car, even though Ken thinks there is zero chance that it will start, Bob will not harm Ken. Ken gets in the car, pumps the gas, smiles at Bob, turns the key. The car starts. (It was Ken's other car in Bob's other drive that had the dead battery.)

Ludwig maintains that Ken did not start the car accidentally, because he was trying to start it, he intended to start it, and he did start it. In fact, Ludwig maintains that Ken's starting of the car was intentional action, despite Ken's believing that his starting of the car was impossible on this occasion.

I believe that if we look more closely, we are lead to say that Ken did start the car accidentally because he was not trying to start the car at all, if Ken truly believed it was impossible to start it. To see this, we must not let the belief in the impossibility of the action wane. Let's borrow another example and then come back to the present one. Myles Brand (1984) and Terry Horgan (in conversation) both have presented the following example. Let Ken be trapped on a ledge. His only escape is to jump across a chasm. If he makes it, Ken will survive. If he doesn't make it, he falls to his death. If he doesn't jump, Ken dies on the ledge. The jump is further than Ken has ever jumped before and Ken thinks it is impossible to make it to the other side. But if it is life or death, can't Ken give it a try and leap? Now here, as in the car example of Ludwig's, clouding our assessment of this case is uncertainty about the firmness of Ken's belief that he cannot do the relevant thing. How firmly does he believe it to be impossible? Ken may believe that somehow, miraculously, he may be underestimating his abilities and he may surprise himself and make it to the other side. However, what if the ledge Ken is on is the Grand Canyon at its widest point? Ken knows this. Surely then Ken's belief that it is impossible to jump to the other side will not wax and wane. Now would a leap by Ken be an attempt to leap to safety? No! Unless he were demented, a leap by Ken would be an attempt at suicide, not at escape from the ledge.

Now in the car case something similar may be going on. It may seem to Ludwig or others, that Ken indeed is trying to start his car because his belief in the impossibility of its starting is not firm. For example, a car's battery may run down, but sometimes if one waits long enough it will recover just enough to start, if it is not run down too far. To eliminate this possibility, let's fix the example so that Ken will not lapse into giving up his belief that it is impossible to start the car. Let's add to the example that Ken recalls taking the dead battery from his car and locking the car hood afterwards. This should both solidify Ken's belief in the impossibility of the car's starting and help test Ludwig's thesis. Cars without batteries don't start.

Now what can we all agree that Ken both tries and does? Ken gets in the car ($B1$), pumps the gas ($B2$), and turns the key ($B3$). But what makes these things an attempt to start the car (with that goal G)? Ken's intention $M1$'s causing $B1-B3$ cannot constitute an attempt to start the car just because Ken wants or hopes it will start so that Bob will not harm him or call the police. Ken must also see a connection between doing these things ($B1-B3$) and the car's starting (G). It would seem that Ken's intention $M1$ must cause the bodily movements $B1-B3$ because he believes there is some possibility that $B1-B3$ will lead to G (or at least he does not believe it is this is impossible). I think we can draw this lesson from Ken's leap at the Grand Canyon at its widest point. If he sees no possible way his intention's ($M1$) causing his leaping ($B1$) can lead to his escape (G), then his leaping is not an attempt at escape. But then neither is Ken's intention's ($M1$) causing $B1-B3$ an attempt at starting the car (G). Indeed, I rather suspect that Ken would not even be intending to start his car nor intending to try to start his car, if he believe that action to be impossible.

The best explanation of what Ken is doing is that he is trying to appease Bob. That is what Ken intends and believes may be possible to do by getting in the car and going through the motions *as if* trying to start the car. But, knowing what Ken knows, going through those motions will not constitute a genuine attempt to start it. Rather it constitutes an attempt to "go through the motions" in hope of satisfying Bob or trying to demonstrate to Bob that the car would not start. Ken's actual intention $M2$ has a different intentional object than the intention to start the car $M1$. Thus, we can imagine Ken's surprise when the car actually starts!

Ludwig would reply that Ken was trying to start the car because his intention $M1$ was causing what it normally causes ($B1-B3$) when one tries to start a car. However, this is what one's intention normally causes *when one believes that it is possible for B1 – B3 to lead to car-starting (G)*. Since Ken does *not* believe this is possible, there is no reason to accept that Ken's intention $M1$'s causing $B1-B3$ constitute an attempt, given what Ken *now believes* (that there is no battery in the car).

Similarly, Ludwig suggests that what makes it plausible to say Ken tries to start his car is that "the action undertaken is conceived of as designed to bring about a certain end, although in the circumstances the agent believes that it cannot succeed" (Ludwig 1992, 267). This cannot be correct. For suppose Ken has a wild imagination and imagines that Gary (an engineer) might someday built a whistle-activated ignition system. Ken is absolutely sure, in his mind, that no one has yet invented the device. Ken does not know that Gary has invented it and installed it on Ken's wife's car. Now Ken wants to start his wife's car and "conceives of whistling as designed to bring about his wife's car's starting, although in the circumstances he believes that it cannot succeed" (believing the device not yet to exist). If Ken intends to start his wife's car now, whistles (before he turns the key in the ignition), and the car starts, his whistling does not constitute an attempt to start his wife's car even though it may cause the car's engine to turn or start. It is not an attempt because Ken does not conceive of a *link* between his whistling now and his starting his wife's car *in his circumstances*.

A better example, for Ludwig's purposes (but one which still fails) is the Able example. Able has lost the use of his right arm. Unbeknownst to Able, and while under anesthesia, the doctor has restored the use of Able's right arm. As the anesthetic wears off, but before telling Able what he has done, the doctor insists that Able try to move his right arm. Even though from bitter experience Able believes it is impossible for him to move is arm, cannot Able try to move his right arm?

This is a better example for Ludwig's purposes because in the earlier example there was something obvious that Ken was trying to do besides trying to start his car, viz. trying to appease Bob. In the Able example, there is nothing else that is obvious. Able either attempts to move his arm or not. Still the example fails to support Ludwig's thesis.

To see this, let us first dispense with one obvious way to view this example that supports the view that Able can try to move his arm. This is where Able *suspends disbelief* (engages in what from his perspective is self-deception). Under these circumstances, Able may clearly try to move his right arm, but, since he suspends disbelief, he no longer believes that moving his right arm is impossible. Therefore, instances of trying under self-deception do not support Ludwig's thesis. Notice that Able's intention to move his arm *M*1 would cause his arm's movement *B*1 (because the doctor's restoration to Able of use of his right arm was a success). Thus, *M*1's causing *B*1 would constitute an attempt (indeed, a successful attempt) to move his right arm, on our account as well. So Ludwig needs a case where the disbelief in the possibility of trying is not suspended.

So let Able steadfastly believe that it is impossible for him to move his right arm. Ludwig would insist that still Able can try to move his arm. However, if Able sees no possible connection between anything Able is doing and his right arm's moving, how can anything Able is doing be an attempt to move his arm? The lesson we learned from the example of Ken seems to be that it could not.

Still Ludwig would, I think, insist that Able could try to move his right arm. Now I think there is an interpretation of the Able case that explains why Ludwig (or anyone) may maintain that Able can try to move his right arm in this case, but I do not think it helps Ludwig.

What constitutes the attempt to move one's arm? Consistent with the theory of trying that we are developing, an attempt is constituted by an intention *M*1's causing a relevant effect *E*. In cases of mental trying *M*1 may cause some mental state *M*2. In cases of bodily trying, *M*1 may cause *B*1 with the goal of *B*1 bringing about some goal *G*. However, there is a further consideration in the case of bodily trying that is not to be overlooked. When a bodily trying takes place, the causation of a relevant bodily motion by an intention *M*1 has to take place by an appropriate set of neural signals traveling down the efferent pathways to the relevant portions of the body. In the case of non-paralyzed Able, when he successfully tries to move his right arm, *M*1 causes signals to travel to the muscles in the right arm and to contract, thereby causing the motions of his right arm (*B*1). However, when Able has lost the use of his right arm, Able's intention *M*1 may cause signals *to be sent* that never get to the muscles in the right arm, and therefore fail to cause motion of the right arm.

Normally, failure of Able's intention to cause motion of his right arm (by the normal means) does not mean that Able failed to try to move his arm, because Able may not know or believe that the signals will not get through. He may not know or believe that his attempt will fail. Normally, equipped with the desire to move his right arm and lacking the belief that it is impossible to move his right arm, Able's intention to move his right arm will cause events in his central nervous system, the causing of which constitutes his attempt to move his right arm. His intention *M*1 causes the neural signals to be sent *S*. In such a case of a failed attempt at bodily trying, *M*1's causing *S* may suffice for an attempt.

So far so good, but doesn't this support Ludwig's thesis? It does not. In Able's case, since losing the use of his right arm he has tried to move his right arm and failed so many times that he now believes that there is no connection between what he can do, and his right arm's movement. What can he do? He can cause in himself a certain kind of feeling that normally, when he is not paralyzed, accompanies his causing of his right arm to move. There is a kind of feedback that we will call "efferent copy" (Adams & Mele 1989, 1992) that comes from the brain's sending an efferent signal to the muscles to move. Able may not know the name of this feedback, but he is probably well acquainted with the way it feels when it happens (with "what it's like"). If, while still paralyzed, the doctor insists that Able try to move his right arm, Able knows he can produce in himself this feeling. And he knows that, when he is not paralyzed, this feeling is followed by his right arm's movement. But in this case, Able is quite sure that it is impossible that his producing in himself this feeling will result in his right arm's moving. Able's compliance with the doctor's request to "try to move your right arm", when Able believes it to be impossible for him to move it, may consist in his brain's sending a signal to his arm "to move" and the sending of efferent copy to the brain that the signal has been sent. Now if this is what *constitutes* Able's attempt, when he believes his arm to be paralyzed, that fails to make it an attempt to move his right arm. Rather, Able knows well that he can cause this (cause what feels like "this" – insert the way it feels here). If Able's attempt is so constituted (when he has lost use of his right arm), then, since *he has no doubt that he can do this*, he certainly can try to produce this feeling in himself, regardless of whether his right arm moves or not. That is, Able knows he can try to *do this* – where we insert the way it feels when he tries. However, given what Able now believes – *that there is no possible connection between his currently doing THIS and his right arm's moving* – his currently *doing THIS* hardly constitutes an attempt to move his right arm.

Now if one still thinks, with Ludwig, that this does constitute an attempt by Able to move his right arm, I suspect it is because one is again relaxing Able's belief in the impossibility of his moving his arm. So instead of being paralyzed, supposed that Able's arm has been severed. He can still *do THIS* – insert the feeling. But he now believes that it is impossible for *doing THIS* to lead to his arm's moving (suppose he tries to move it several times, for example, surprised to find that it is really severed). Once he is convinced of the impossibility of the connection, and with no beliefs in the supernatural or telekinesis and so on, surely it is false to maintain that Able still is trying to move his right arm. His *doing THIS* does not constitute such an attempt precisely because Able believes that it is impossible for it to lead to his right arm's moving. It does not constitute an attempt to move his right arm even though under normal circumstances, where his arm is routinely connected to his body, it would. In that case too, it would constitute the attempt only if the intention were causing the appropriate outcomes, while nested in the appropriate background of beliefs and desires.

To this point our theory of trying has looked at deviant causal chains, the role of desire in trying and in desiring to try, and the role of belief in trying. It may seem that many of these same considerations that apply to trying would apply to intending. At least, it seems this way to me. Indeed, on the account developed thus far it would seem that an intention to do an action *A* is involved in causing the relevant stages of the attempt to do *A*. However, this view has been challenged in an interesting way by Michael Bratman. Bratman's ideas have received much attention since he first raised concerns about the simple picture that I have suggested above. The way Bratman's challenge relates to the current view is that he claims there are rational constraints upon intending that do not apply to trying. I now turn to the consideration of Bratman's reasons for saying this.

6. INTENDING *VERSUS* TRYING

Is it possible rationally to *attempt*[15] to do things that it would be irrational for you to *intend* to do? Michael Bratman (1987) has argued that it is possible. Since the view that we are developing seems to imply that if Ken tries to do *A*, then Ken intends to do *A* (either explicitly or implicitly[16]) and that the intention to do *A* causes relevant stages that Ken believes may lead to *A*, we need to come to grips with Bratman's claims to the contrary.

Bratman arrives at his view by considering the planning component of intention. In particular, Bratman maintains the following: "It should be possible (other things equal) for me successfully to execute all my intentions in a world in which my beliefs are true" (Bratman 1987, 113). Bratman maintains that to intend to do *A* and intend to do *B*, when one knows one cannot do both, violates this constraint, making one criticizably irrational. With this constraint on what it is for one to be rational in forming intentions, Bratman goes on to construct a video-game example that has received much attention in the literature.

The example goes like this. Al is playing two video games simultaneously, game 1 and game 2. Each game has moving targets and Al shoots at each target with the controls of the respective game. With his left hand Al shoots at the target on game 1. With his right hand Al shoots at the target on game 2. Were Al to hit the target on game 1, he would do so intentionally, for he was trying to hit that target. Were Al to hit the target on game 2, he would do so intentionally, for he was trying to hit that target.

There is a distinctive feature of these games. They share information. If a player is about to hit the targets on both games at the same time, the games compute this fact (from the trajectories of the targets and the trajectories of the missiles fired) and both games are shut down. Therefore, it is impossible to hit both targets (target 1 and target 2). Now suppose that Al knows this about the games he is playing. So Al knows that it is impossible to hit both targets 1 and 2. Further, since Al knows he cannot hit both targets, he would be irrational to intend to hit both. If Al were intending to hit target 1 and he were intending to hit target 2, knowing that he cannot hit both, Al's intentions violate the rationality constraint above. Al would be criticizably irrational, since he would knows he cannot execute all of his intentions.

Still, Bratman maintains that if Al hits target 1, he does so intentionally. And, if Al hits target 2, he does so intentionally. What makes Al's hitting target 1, say, intentional, if he does not intend to hit target 1? Doesn't Al have at least to intend to *hit each* target (though not both), so that his intention to hit 1 explains why his hitting 1, when he does, is intentionally accomplished? Here is Bratman's reply:

> My response is to reject the contention that [Al] must intend to hit each target ... What [Al] need[s] to do is *try* to hit each target. But this does not mean that [Al] must *intend* to hit each target. Perhaps [Al] must intend *something* – to shoot at each target, for example...If [Al] nevertheless do[es] intend to hit each target, [Al is] criticizably irrational. (Bratman 1987, 117)

I take Bratman's position[17] to be that what makes Al's hitting target 1 intentional, if Al does hit that target, is that Al was trying to hit it. (Similarly, were Al to hit target 2, his hitting it would be intentional because Al was trying to hit it.) Thus, Bratman thinks Al can *try* without threat of irrationality) to do what he cannot *intend* (because of such threat). Al can try to hit each target, but he cannot intend to hit each target. It should also be clear, by now, that this is inconsistent with the theory of trying that we have been developing here. For on our account thus far, what make's Al's set of bodily movements ($B1$) the attempt to hit target 1 is that they are caused in the right way by his intention ($M1 =$ the intention to hit target 1). Something's got to go. In what follows, I will suggest that it is Bratman's view that requires modification, not mine.

Notice that in the quote Bratman tries a move that is reminiscent of a move made by Mele. Bratman suggests that Al doesn't need to *intend to hit the target*, he needs only to try. Does Bratman mean that Al needs only to *intend to try*?[18] Earlier, when discussing a similar move by Mele, I argued that an attempt to *A*, by its very nature, requires a desire to do *A*. Since then, I have maintained that it also requires the lack of a belief that doing *A* is impossible. Consistent with this I would maintain that an attempt to hit target 1 requires a desire to hit target 1 and the lack of a belief that it is impossible to hit target 1. Now if this is right, and I think it is, then for Al's bodily movements *B*1 to constitute his attempt to hit target 1, Al must desire to hit target 1 and believe that *B*1 may lead to his hitting target 1.[19] Then, given his beliefs and desires, his intention *M*1's causing *B*1 (movements involved in firing missiles at target 1) constitutes Al's attempt to hit target 1. What is the content of his intention *M*1? If Bratman were to say, with Mele, that it is the intention to try to hit target 1, then we must ask all over again, what intention exists in the attempt itself? To intend to try to make the attempt is to intend to initiate and sustain the complex causing of relevant bodily movements *B*1 by relevant intention *M*1. But what is the content of intention *M*1 itself? It can hardly be the intention to try. For that is the intention to have *M*1, whatever its content is, begin to cause *B*1. What is the content of the *M*1 that exists *within the attempt itself*? It, I maintain, is the intention to hit target 1. So Mele's move would not work here, I submit, for similar reasons to why it did not work earlier when we consider desire and desires to try. Thus, Bratman should not be suggesting that strategy in the quote above.

What else may he be suggesting? If he is simply saying that the attempt to hit target 1 itself, does not contain the intention to hit target 1, why does he think that? Does he give an argument or a theory of trying from which this follows as a consequence? No. He does not. He uses this example conjoined with a theory of intending and its role in practical reasoning. He does not, however, put together anything like a theory of trying. So my guess is that he is not suggesting these things as a result of a more involved theory. He may be suggesting it only as something that seems intuitively obvious or plausible. However, often in very good philosophy what seems intuitively obvious or plausible is jettisoned because it is inconsistent with a theory that has gained plausibility on grounds of coherence, comprehensiveness, elegance, and explanatory power. So Bratman's example must not be taken solely at face value, when it comes into conflict with a deeper theory.

What of Bratman's idea that the intentional object of Al's attempt to hit target 1, say, may not be to actually hit target 1, but only to shoot at it? Will that make Al's attempt one to hit the target, or only to shoot at it? Will that make Al's hitting target 1 intentional, if he does hit it? I think the answer to both questions is "no". Notice that Bratman seems to maintain that an attempt to hit target 1 requires an intention to do *something*. What Bratman is suggesting is that the intentional object may slide back and forth from the more distant goal to a more proximate goal. Instead of intending to hit the target, Al intends only to shoot at it. But recall that when discussing Ludwig's position, if we were confronted with someone who, say, were apparently straining to lift a heavy weight, we would want to know whether they were trying to lift the weight or just to pull mightily at it. Notice that the intentional object here slides too, from the more distant lifting of the weight to the more proximate lifting mightily at it. Now if one believed it were impossible to lift the weight, what is one trying to do, when tugging at the weight for all they're worth? Trying to lift it? Or trying to pull mightily at it? I suggest that one would be trying only the latter. If true, then in Bratman's example too, if we let the intentional object slide to a more proximal target (shooting at, but not hitting) target 1, then Al may not be trying to hit target 1 at all. He is trying only to shoot at it. Of course he realizes that he may hit it, but that does not entail that he is trying to hit it. We often engage in many attempts that we realize may have certain consequences that we are prepared to accept and for which we are prepared to accept responsibility. That does not mean that we are intending all of those consequences, as is well known (to which the literature on "double-effect" attests). If Al is trying only to shoot at target 1, not to hit it, he may have less determination, and may move his arm in different ways, and so on. I suppose Al could even attempt to shoot at, but miss, target 1.[20] And if Bratman suggests that Al is intending to shoot at, but not miss, target 1, then frankly I fail to see why Al is not intending to hit target 1 (not merely intending to shoot at it).

As I will now try to show, there are more good reasons to reject that one rationally can try to do what one rationally cannot intend. So in the video game I would maintain that either Al can try to hit each target and be rational, but then he can intend to hit each target and be rational, or that Al cannot intend to hit each and be rational, but then neither can he try and be rational.

Furthermore, I wish to point out that Bratman struggles with his own rationality constraint, when discussing "acting with an intention". He realizes that acting with an intention may be a kind of trying or endeavoring. So he claims that there are two senses of "acting with an intention" or "endeavoring". In one sense, it follows that if Al endeavors to A, then Al has an intention to A. In another sense, supposedly, this does not follow. Bratman needs this distinction because, as we shall see, he is aware that where endeavoring to A does imply an intention to A, there can be rational pressure placed on one's endeavoring just as there can be rational pressure placed upon one's intentions. My claim will be that Bratman does not adequately defend his claim that there are two kinds of endeavoring – one that escapes these rational pressures and one that does not. If I am right, then Bratman will be forced to abandon either the idea that Al cannot intend to hit each target in the video-game example (give up the rationality constraint on intention) or give up that Al can rationally try to hit each target (keep the rationality constraint, but give up the asymmetry of the application of the constraint to intention and to trying).

Let's begin with the following quote by Bratman (still discussing the video game example):

> Given that I endeavor to hit target 1, do I shoot *with the intention* of hitting it? There seems to be one sense of the expression "with the intention" according to which I *do* shoot with the intention of hitting target 1. This is the sense of acting with the intention of A-ing that is equivalent to endeavoring to A. Now, one lesson of the video-games example is that, in this endeavoring sense, I may act with the intention of A-ing and yet not intend to A. After all, I endeavor to hit target 1; yet, as we have seen there is good reason to deny that I intend to hit target 1 (Bratman 1987, 129).

Now it is well and good for Bratman to *say* this, but what good reason is there *to accept* that there are cases where one is endeavoring to *A* without intending to *A*? He cannot *use* the video-game example to support this claim. For it is only on the basis of the claim that one can endeavor (or try) to do what one does not intend that he can *use* the video-game example to argue that it is rational to try to do what it is not rational to intend to do. So to attempt to use the video-game example to support this view of endeavoring would be viciously circular.

Bratman does argue for a "strong" and a "weak" sense of "acting with an intention" (Bratman 1987, ch. 9). On the strong reading we get a type of acting with an intention to do *A* that Bratman calls endeavoring and this endeavoring implies that one does have an intention in action to do *A*. On his supposed weak reading, one is also endeavoring to do *A*, but Bratman says one need not be acting with an intention to do *A*. Bratman says, "...one may endeavor to *A* without strictly speaking intending to *A*" (Bratman 1987, 130). Presumably, this weak sense is the one Bratman needs in the video-game example, where Al is trying (i.e., endeavoring) to hit each target, but not intending to hit each target. However, when giving reasons for accepting these two readings of "acting with an intention", Bratman continually refers us back to what he has shown in the former chapter where he introduces the video-game example. So we are not offered a *new* reason for the distinction. So there are no non-question-begging reasons given to accept this dualistic theory of endeavoring.

At one point Bratman discusses an example of George Wilson's where Wilson maintains that a case of acting with an intention (opening curtains with an intention of opening them), may, in the act, not be subject to a consistency constraint (Bratman's rationality constraint). Here is what Bratman says:

> On Wilson's view...once I begin to endeavor to open [the curtains] I no longer have an intention to open them that is subject to such consistency demands. But I do not see why we should suppose that my endeavoring to open the curtains rules out an intention to open them beginning now, an intention subject to demands for strong consistency. And in the normal case it seems to me I will both endeavor and intend so to act. Of course, it is possible to endeavor to open them without intending to open them; that is the lesson of the video-game example. But that does not mean that endeavoring to open them precludes a present-directed intention so to act. (Bratman 1987, 132.)

Here our theory can agree with everything Bratman says except the conclusion he wants to draw from the video game example. But he still has not given us any compelling reason to accept that conclusion, nor any of the distinctions he wants to draw about there being two kinds of endeavoring.

At a later point, Bratman tries to mount support for his distinction between senses of "endeavoring" by saying that if we had this distinction we could make sense of another phenomenon, viz. that one might rationally intend to move a log though one believes one will fail. Bratman's point is that if I am trying to move the log and that means I intend to move it, then I am irrational because I also believe I will fail. If, however, there is a kind of endeavoring that does not imply that I intend to move the log, I'm off the hook of being irrational.

My reply to this should be clear, given our discussion of Ludwig's examples. As long as one does not believe it is impossible to move the log, one may intend to move it. But in the example, one believes that one will fail. Does that mean that one cannot intend to move the log? No. I don't think so. Now this requires that the belief constraint on what one can intend must be very low. In order to intend to do something or intend to try to do something, one need not have a very high estimate of success. Indeed, I would maintain that one needs only a belief in the possibility of success in order to tug on the log with the intention of moving it.[21] Still one tries to move the log, one does not believe that it is impossible to move the log, one desires to move it, one sees how tugging motions that one is engaged in may lead to the log's moving as an outcome, and one settles on undertaking those activities now. Frankly, I fail to see how putting a plan like this into action could fail to be a case where one intends to try to move the log, and where, within the attempt itself, one's intention is to move the log.[22] This is what our theory of trying implies and Bratman has not given us any good reasons to abandon this view.

Furthermore, Bratman sees that his rationality constraint does apply to some cases of endeavoring. Consider the following pasage.

> We can make a related point by using the notion of *rational agglomerativity*. Given the role of intentions in coordination, there is rational pressure for an agent to put his various intentions together into a larger intention. If I both intend to hit target 1 and intend to hit target 2, there will be rational pressure for me to intend to hit both targets. But the same is not, in general, true about endeavoring. I may both endeavor to hit target 1 and endeavor to hit target 2, and yet not be under rational pressure to endeavor to hit both targets. Indeed, in those cases in which I know that I cannot hit both targets I am under strong rational pressure not to endeavor (not to try) to hit them both (Bratman 1987, 134).

Notice the internal tension in this very quote. On the one hand, Al's endeavoring to hit each target *is a case where he knows he cannot hit both.* It is just the kind of case Bratman is addressing at the end of this quote. Bratman is pointing out that there can be rational pressure on Al's endeavoring to hit each target because *Al knows* that he cannot hit both targets. On the other hand, a bit earlier in the quote, Bratman says he may endeavor to hit both targets without being under rational pressure to endeavor to hit both? I don't think

Bratman can have it both ways. Either Al is not under rational pressure to endeavor to hit both targets or he is under this rational pressure. If he is not under it, then why cannot Al *intend* to hit each target without being under this rational pressure to intend to hit both? Our theory claims that if Al is endeavoring to hit each target, then Al does intend to hit each. So if it goes this way, Bratman should drop the consistency constraint in the video game example. Or, if there is rational pressure on Al not to intend to hit each target, then there should also be rational pressure on Al not to endeavor to hit each target. But then, while Bratman may maintain the rationality constraint on intending, he must apply it to endeavoring as well. Hence, there is no asymmetry in applying it to intending, but not to trying.

7. CONCLUSION

In this paper I have set out to develop and defend a theory of trying. The theory is a causal theory which says that a trying is a teleological causing of mental states (mental trying) or bodily motions (bodily trying) in the right way. We have discussed what makes something an attempt and what makes it the particular attempt it is – the attempt to do *A*, rather than *B*. We have, in passing, seen why all trying is intentional – because it is controlled activity guided by an intention to do *A*. Even if one fails to do *A*, if one's attempt begins, it is the intentional attempt to do *A* because it is guided by an intention to do *A*. Indirectly, we are also somewhat closer to seeing why minded creatures are those that try. It is because minded creatures will have the appropriate constellation of beliefs, desires, and intentions that are needed to launch and guide an attempt to do a specific action *A*. And, consequently, in so far as we praise and blame intentional action more severely than unintentional action, we have made progress on the front of seeing why moral praise or blame is so closely tied to trying.

Finally, we have made progress in both fleshing out the theory and applying it to several claims in the recent literature by Mele, Ludwig, and Bratman. In each case, we have seen good reason to reject their claims. Attempts to do *A* require the desire to do *A* within them as components of the attempt (contrary to the views of Mele). Attempts to do *A* require some beliefs about the possibility of one's activities in the attempt leading to the goal or intentional object of the attempt. At least attempts to do *A* require a lack of a belief in the impossibility of one's activities leading to one's goal or intentional object (contrary to the views of Ludwig). And finally, we have seen that the apparent asymmetry between rational constraints on intending and trying that is maintained by Bratman, cannot be sustained. Bratman has not adequately supported his claim that there is an asymmetry between what one can rationally intend and what one can rationally attempt. Therefore, something's got to give. Bratman will have either to reject his rationality constraint or reject his claimed asymmetry of that principle's application.

In closing, I cannot help point out that if I am right about Bratman, then his attack on the "Simple View" of the relation between intention and intentional action falls as well. It may well be true, despite Bratman's arguments to the contrary, that intentionally doing act *A* requires the intention to do *A* after all (Adams 1986; McCann 1986).

Central Michigan University

NOTES

[1] The 1-800-CALL-AT&T number does not always work from some non-AT&T phones. It is the other one that I sometimes have to try to remember. You know the one.

[2] E.J. Lowe (1996, 157 ff.) suggests that we can tell that trying is not a propositional attitude from two considerations: first, trying is always trying to do something not trying that such and such be the case, and second, that infants and animals can try but may lack the appropriate concepts of self and deed to have the relevant conception of self or deed needed for a propositional attitude. Colin McGinn (1982, 91) made the points before Lowe. These are NOT my reasons for denying that trying is a propositional attitude. It is clear that infants and animals move, but it is not clear that they try to do things, if they do not have reasons or purposes behind the movements. When they do have reasons or purposes, they do have conceptions of ends to be achieved (in the sense that something is determining that end rather than another end). Also, desires are more naturally desires to do things than desires that things be so and so (wishes are more wishes that such and such than desires). Yet we do not take this to prove that desires are not propositional attitudes. Indeed, we think they are. So I would submit that this evidence is weaker than the evidence I am providing for the conclusion that trying is not a propositional attitude. My evidence is that attempts require causings. Propositional attitudes do not, on any given occasion.

[3] For simplicity, I avoid adding that it could be one or more mental states causing one or more mental states or event or causing one or more bodily states or events. This should be understood.

[4] How do mental states represent goals or have intentional objects, you ask? I (Adams 1991) subscribe to a theory that is a composite of Fodor's (1990) representational theory of mind (RTM) conjoined with Dretske's (1988) theory of how representations come to have their content. A complete story is too long to tell here, but the details exist elsewhere (Adams & Aizawa 1994; Adams et al. 1993; Adams et al. 1992). Basically, a mental state has *O* as its intentional object if it has a structure "*O*" that means *O*. "*O*" means *O* because "*O*" has acquired the function to indicate states of type *O*. "*O*"'s causal role can then be explain in terms of its indicator function (or content).

[5] I do not believe that it is necessary to appeal to events of willing (Adams & Mele 1992), but I will not argue for that here. Let me just say that I think that what people call willing or volition is the actual causation of a mental state (mental trying) or bodily state (bodily trying) by a relevant complex of beliefs, desires, and intentions, with the content to "act now". I believe (and will argue elsewhere) that what people call willing is the actual signals being sent down the efferent causal pathways (and perhaps the afferent positive feedback from the signal's having been sent). In our discussion above, it would be *M*1's causing *M*2 or *M*1's causing *B*1 that people call willing or volition. But I see no reason to think that the will is a separate state of mind or cognitive functional state. For an account of a distinction between triggering causes and structuring causes, see Dretske (1988).

[6] Please note that when I say a representation of a goal is required, this should be conceived as a type of detector. The state is able to detect the presence or absence of the appropriate type of goal-state of affairs. The mental state obviously does not represent a future token state, say, of my document's being printed. For that state, being future, does not exist. However, the mental state might well be set to detect the state of my document's being (or not being) printed. This detecting ability of my mental state may figure in the causal attempt to bring it about that my document becomes printed.

[7] Some (Ginet 1990) would add that attempts have a phenomenal characteristic, an "actish feel". I am also quite skeptical about this. I believe that such phenomenal accompaniment of an attempt is neither a necessary nor a sufficient feature to make something an attempt. In this I agree with Mele (Adams & Mele 1992, and Mele 1992). McGinn (1982, 90) also seems to dissent (although compare his remarks about the role of one's 'body image' on p. 93).

[8] I agree with Mele (Adams & Mele 1989; Mele 1992, 202 ff.) that appeals to self-referential intentions and volitions (Harman 1976; Searle 1983; Ginet 1990) do not solve these problems of causal deviance in an account of intentional action. So I shall not take up that line here nor replay the objections to that line in constructing a theory of trying here. Because of the close relation between trying and intentional action, the same defects would re-occur.

[9] Brand says this for intentional action. Therefore, I shall presume he says the same for trying. I know that Mele accepts this (Adams & Mele 1992).

[10] I suppose it is also possible that I want to try to do something that requires my intentions causing my panic. Suppose I want to get my adrenaline up. The only way I know to do this is to get myself into a panic. To do this I must form the intention to actually do something (skydive right now, say) that I am confident will cause my adrenaline to flow. Did I try to increase my flow of adrenaline? I suppose I did, but it was hardly proximately caused. However, my increased adrenal output was somewhat under my control.

[11] I am prepared to argue that the content of the intention must be to *do A*. However, that is more than I need. I need only to consider the content of the relevant desires that contribute to, comprise, or influence the relevant intention. So I will look only at the desire component of the intention *M*1.

[12] When I say "in *M*1", I mean that either an intention is a complex of beliefs and desires and settling on some particular options now, in which case the desire will literally be a component of the intention, or the relevant desires, beliefs, and other states influence the intention. Either way, the relevant desire will be the desire to solve the puzzle – or so I claim. Remember that I also say "in the attempt" because, as a component theorist, the attempt is *M*1's causing *B*1. So *M*1 is a component of the attempt. And if desires are components of intentions then the desires are components of attempts, as well.

[13] I realize that set of movements *B*1 will be somewhat disjunctive or plastic, as we say. There may be many different ways to "skin a cat". So there may be many different precise trajectories that bodily movements can take and all of the different ones may lead to solving the chess puzzle. My point is only that to be successful a path of the movements in the set *B*1 must end with the temporal stage that constitutes getting the chess pieces into a solving position.

[14] Ludwig thinks it is also possible to succeed in doing (intentionally) what one believe to be impossible to do. I will only indirectly argue against this. If my views are correct, they indirectly imply that Ludwig is wrong about this (Adams 1994).

[15] Bratman's arguments are restricted to rational intending.

[16] Not everything that one intends need to race before the mind's eye at the time of action. As John Searle (1983) correctly points out, some actions like shifting one's gears in a manual transmission car are cases where no conscious intentions need form. However, unlike Searle, the consequence I draw is not that there are no intentions in these cases, but that they are implicit and presupposed and routinized or habituated, not that they do not exist. Since they are part of the permanent wiring of the brain, after a task such as learning to drive has been mastered, when

performing such tasks, it would be inefficient to require them to consciously form each time we do the routine tasks.

[17] I should note that Bratman's arguments are very detailed and he covers exquisite subtleties in his book that I am not going to stop to pursue here. He covers (and rejects, with good reason) such suggestions as that Al is intending to hit either target 1 or 2. Bratman covers many other interesting possibilities as well.

[18] Whether or not Bratman would say this, we find Al Mele saying it (Mele 1992, 1994), so it is a move one might make.

[19] Al would have a similar set of desires, beliefs, and intentions with respect to hitting target 2.

[20] My boyhood friends once engaged in a game of shooting at, but intending to miss, one another with pistols, in order to see what it is like to be shot at with live ammunition. Sadly one of them was shot. Fortunately, he was not killed. Although what they did was incredibly stupid, they were not trying to hit each other.

[21] Myles Brand (1984) also accepts that there may be a very low estimate of success when one intends to do an action.

[22] As is clear, this means I place a very weak belief component upon intending. I defend this elsewhere (Adams 1986).

REFERENCES

Adams, F. (1986), "Intention and Intentional Action: The Simple View," *Mind & Language* **1**, 281–301.

Adams, F. (1989), "Review of Michael Bratman's *Intentions, Plans, and Practical Reasons*," *Ethics* **100**, 1998–1999.

Adams, F. (1989), "Tertiary Waywardness Tamed," *Critica* **21**, 117–125.

Adams, F. (1991), "Causal Contents" in B. McLaughlin (ed.), *Dretske and His Critics*. Oxford, Basil Blackwell, pp. 131–156.

Adams, F. (1995a), "Trying: You've Got to Believe," *Journal of Philosophical Research*, 20, 549–61.

Adams, F. (1995b), "Trying, Desire, and Desiring to Try," *Canadian Journal of Philosophy* **24**, 613–626.

Adams, F. & K. Aizawa (1994), "Fodorian Semantics" in S. Stich & T. Warfield (eds.), *Mental Representations*. Oxford, Basil Blackwell, pp. 223–242.

Adams, F. et al. (1993), "Thoughts Without Objects," *Mind & Language* **8**, 90–104.

Adams, F. & A. Mele (1989), "The Role of Intention in Intentional Action," *Canadian Journal of Philosophy* **19**, 511–532.

Adams, F. & A. Mele (1992), "The Intention/Volition Debate," *Canadian Journal of Philosophy* **22**, 323–338.

Adams, F. et al. (1992), "The Semantics of Thoughts," *Pacific Philosophical Quarterly* **73**, 375–389.

Brand, M. (1984), *Intending And Acting*. Cambridge, MA., MIT Press.

Bratman, M. (1987), *Intentions, Plans, and Practical Reasons*. Cambridge, MA., Harvard University Press.

Cleveland, T. (1992), "Trying Without Willing," *Australasian Journal of Philosophy* **70**, 324–342.

Davidson, D. (1980), *Essays on Actions & Events*. Oxford, The Clarendon Press.

Dretske, F. (1988), *Explaining Behavior*. Cambridge, MA., MIT Press.

Fodor, J. (1990), *A Theory of Content and Other Essays*. Cambridge, MA., MIT Press.

Ginet, C. (1990), *On Action*. Cambridge, Cambridge University Press.

Green, O.H. (1994), "Toe Wiggling and Starting Cars: A Re-Examination of Trying," *Philosophia* **23**, 171–191.
Harman, G. (1976), "Practical Reasoning," *Review of Metaphysics* **79**, 431–463.
Hunter, J.F.M. (1987), "Trying," *The Philosophical Quarterly* **37**, 392–401.
Lowe, E.J. (1996), *Subjects of Experience*. Cambridge, Cambridge University Press.
Ludwig, K. (1992), "Impossible Doings," *Philosophical Studies* **65**, 257–281.
McCann, H.J. (1986), "Rationality and the Range of Intention," *Midwest Studies* **10**, 191–211.
McCann, H.J. (1994), "Paralysis and The Springs of Action," *Philosophia* **23**, 193–205.
McGinn, C. (1982), *The Character of Mind*. Oxford, Oxford University Press.
Mele, A. (1987), "Intentional Action and Wayward Causal Chains: The Problem of Tertiary Waywardness", *Philosophical Studies* **57**, 55–60.
Mele, A. (1990), "He Wants to Try," *Analysis* **50**, 251–253.
Mele, A. (1991), "He Wants to Try Again: A Rejoinder," *Analysis* **51**, 225–228.
Mele, A. (1992), *Springs of Action*. Oxford, Oxford University Press.
Mele, A. (1994), "Desiring to Try: Reply to Adams' 'Trying, Desire, and Desiring to Try'," *Canadian Journal of Philosophy* **24**, 627–636.
Searle, J. (1983), *Intentionality*. Cambridge, Cambridge University Press.
Thalberg, I. (1972), *Perception, Emotion, and Action*. Ithaca, NY., Cornell University Press.
Thomson, J. (1977), *Acts and Other Events*. Ithaca, NY., Cornell University Press.

INDEX OF NAMES

(Only proper names mentioned in the text are included.)

G. Holmström-Hintikka and R. Tuomela (eds.), Contemporary Action Theory. Vol. I, 315–316.

TABLE OF CONTENTS

MIX
Papier aus verantwortungsvollen Quellen
Paper from responsible sources
FSC® C105338
FSC
www.fsc.org

If you have any concerns about our products,
you can contact us on
ProductSafety@springernature.com

In case Publisher is established outside the EU,
the EU authorized representative is:
Springer Nature Customer Service Center GmbH
Europaplatz 3, 69115 Heidelberg, Germany

Printed by Libri Plureos GmbH
in Hamburg, Germany